API Design for C++

API Design for C++

Martin Reddy

AMSTERDAM • BOSTON • HEIDELBERG • LONDON
NEW YORK • OXFORD • PARIS • SAN DIEGO
SAN FRANCISCO • SINGAPORE • SYDNEY • TOKYO
Morgan Kaufmann Publishers is an imprint of Elsevier

ELSEVIER

Acquiring Editor: Todd Green
Editorial Assistant: Robyn Day
Project Manager: André Cuello
Designer: Eric DeCicco

Morgan Kaufmann is an imprint of Elsevier
30 Corporate Drive, Suite 400, Burlington, MA 01803, USA

Library of Congress Cataloging-in-Publication Data
Application submitted

British Library Cataloguing-in-Publication Data
A catalogue record for this book is available from the British Library.

ISBN: 978-0-12-385003-4

Printed and bound by CPI Group (UK) Ltd, Croydon, CR0 4YY

Transferred to digital print 2012

For information on all MK publications visit our website at www.mkp.com

Contents

Foreword

I should begin by confessing that I do not consider myself a world-class API designer or software engineer. I do, however, consider myself an expert researcher in the areas of computer graphics and geometric modeling. It was in this line of work that I first met Martin at Pixar Animation Studios.

As a graphics researcher I was accustomed to writing mathematically sophisticated papers. I was also formally trained as a computer scientist at a major university and had written my share of code. Armed with this background, when I was presented with the opportunity to lead a group of software engineers working on a new generation of animation software for Pixar, I figured that it couldn't be any more difficult than research. After all, research is, by definition, the creation of the unknown, whereas engineering is the implementation of well-understood subjects. I could not have been more wrong.

I came to realize that software engineering was, without a doubt, the most difficult challenge I had ever been presented with. After more years than I care to admit, I eventually gave up and went back to graphics research.

I can't tell you how much I would have benefitted from a book such as "API Design for C++." Many of the lessons we learned the hard way have been captured by Martin in this insightful, easy-to-use book. Martin approaches the subject not from the perspective of an academic software researcher (although he draws heavily from results and insights gained there), but from the perspective of an in-the-trenches software engineer and manager. He has experienced firsthand the importance of good software design and has emerged as an articulate voice of what "good" means. In this book he presents effective strategies for achieving that goal.

I particularly like that Martin is not focusing just on API design, but more broadly on software life cycles, allowing him to cover topics such as versioning, strategies for backward compatibility, and branching methodologies.

In short, this book should be of great value to those creating or managing software activities. It is a comprehensive collection of best practices that have proven themselves time and time again.

Tony DeRose
Senior Scientist and Research Group Lead, Pixar Animation Studios

Preface

Writing large applications in C++ is a complex and tricky business. However, designing reusable C++ interfaces that are robust, stable, easy to use, and durable is even more difficult. The best way to succeed in this endeavor is to adhere to the tenets of good Application Programming Interface (API) design.

An API presents a logical interface to a software component and hides the internal details required to implement that component. It offers a high-level abstraction for a module and promotes code reuse by allowing multiple applications to share the same functionality.

Modern software development has become highly dependent on APIs, from low-level application frameworks to data format APIs and graphical user interface (GUI) frameworks. In fact, common software engineering terms such as modular development, code reuse, componentization, dynamic link library or DLL, software frameworks, distributed computing, and service-oriented architecture all imply the need for strong API design skills.

Some popular C and C++ APIs that you may already be aware of include the Standard Template Library (STL), Boost, the Microsoft Windows API (Win32), Microsoft Foundation Classes (MFC), libtiff, libpng, zlib, libxml++, OpenGL, MySQL++, Nokia's Qt, wxWidgets, GTK+, KDE, Skype-Kit, POSIX pthreads, Intel's Threading Building Blocks, the Netscape Plugin API, and the Apache module API. In addition, many of Google's open-source projects are C++, as is much of the code on the sourceforge.net, bitbucket.org, and freshmeat.net Web sites.

APIs such as these are used in all facets of software development, from desktop applications, to mobile computing and embedded systems, to Web development. For example, the Mozilla Firefox Web browser is built on top of more than 80 dynamic libraries, each of which provides the implementation for one or more APIs.

Elegant and robust API design is therefore a critical aspect of contemporary software development. One important way in which this differs from standard application development is the far greater need for change management. As we all know, change is an inevitable factor in software development; new requirements, feature requests, and bug fixes cause software to evolve in ways that were never anticipated when it was first devised. However, changes to an API that's shared by hundreds of end-user applications can cause major upheaval and ultimately may cause clients to abandon an API. The primary goal of good API design is therefore to provide your clients with the functionality they need while also causing minimal impact to their code—ideally zero impact—when you release a new version.

WHY YOU SHOULD READ THIS BOOK

If you write C++ code that another engineer relies upon, you're an API designer and this book has been written for you.

Interfaces are the most important code that you write because a problem with your interface is far more costly to fix than a bug in your implementation. For instance, an interface change may require all of the applications based on your code to be updated, whereas an implementation-only change can be integrated transparently and effortlessly into client applications when they adopt the new

API version. Put in more economic terms, a poorly designed interface can seriously reduce the long-term survival of your code. Learning how to create high-quality interfaces is therefore an essential engineering skill, and the central focus of this book.

As Michi Henning noted, API design is more important today than it was 20 years ago. This is because many more APIs have been designed in recent years. These also provide richer and more complex functionality and are shared by more end-user applications (Henning, 2009). Despite this fact, no other books currently on the market concentrate on the topic of API design for C++.

It's worth noting that this book is not meant to be a general C++ programming guide—there are already many good examples of these on the market. I will certainly cover lots of object-oriented design material and present many handy C++ tips and tricks. However, I will focus on techniques for representing clean modular interfaces in C++. By corollary, I will not dive as deeply into the question of how to implement the code behind these interfaces, such as specific algorithm choices or best practices limited to the code within the curly braces of your function bodies.

However, this book will cover the full breadth of API development, from initial design through implementation, testing, documentation, release, versioning, maintenance, and deprecation. I will even cover specialized API topics such as creating scripting and plugin APIs. While many of these topics are also relevant to software development in general, the focus here will be on the particular implications for API design. For example, when discussing testing strategies I will concentrate on automated API testing techniques rather than attempting to include end-user application testing techniques such as GUI testing, system testing, or manual testing.

In terms of my own credentials to write this book, I have led the development of APIs for research code shared by several collaborating institutions, in-house animation system APIs that have been used to make Academy Award-winning movies, and open-source client/server APIs that have been used by millions of people worldwide. Throughout all of these disparate experiences, I have consistently witnessed the need for high-quality API design. This book therefore presents a practical distillation of the techniques and strategies of industrial-strength API design that have been drawn from a range of real-world experiences.

WHO IS THE TARGET AUDIENCE

While this book is not a beginner's guide to C++, I have made every effort to make the text easy to read and to explain all terminology and jargon clearly. The book should therefore be valuable to new programmers who have grasped the fundamentals of C++ and want to advance their design skills, as well as senior engineers and software architects who are seeking to gain new expertise to complement their existing talents.

There are three specific groups of readers that I have borne in mind while writing this book.

1. **Practicing software engineers and architects**. Junior and senior developers who are working on a specific API project and need pragmatic advice on how to produce the most elegant and enduring design.
2. **Technical managers**. Program and product managers who are responsible for producing an API product and who want to gain greater insight into the technical issues and development processes of API design.

3. **Students and educators**. Computer science and software engineering students who are learning how to program and are seeking a thorough resource on software design that is informed by practical experience on large-scale projects.

FOCUSING ON C++

While there are many generic API design methodologies that can be taught—skills that apply equally well to any programming language or environment—ultimately an API has to be expressed in a particular programming language. It is therefore important to understand the language-specific features that contribute to exemplary API design. This book is therefore focused on the issues of designing APIs for a single language (C++) rather than diluting the content to make it applicable for all languages. While readers who wish to develop APIs for other languages, such as Java or C#, may still gain much general insight from this text, the book is directly targeted at C++ engineers who must write and maintain APIs for other engineers to consume.

C++ is still one of the most widely used programming languages for large software projects and tends to be the most popular choice for performance-critical code. As a result, there are many diverse C and C++ APIs available for you to use in your own applications (some of which I listed earlier). I will therefore concentrate on aspects of producing good APIs in C++ and include copious source code examples to illustrate these concepts better. This means that I will deal with C++-specific topics such as templates, encapsulation, inheritance, namespaces, operators, const correctness, memory management, use of STL, the pimpl idiom, and so on.

Additionally, this book has been published during an exciting time in the evolution of C++. A new version of the C++ specification has been approved by ISO/IEC. Most C++ compilers currently aim to conform to the standard that was first published in 1998, known as C++98. A later revision of this standard was published in 2003 to correct several defects. Since that time, the standards committee has been working on a major new version of the specification. This version is now ratified and is referred to as C++11, because it was approved in 2011 (when this book was first printed, C++11 was not officially approved and was referred to as C++0x at that time).

Many of the major C++ compilers have already started to implement the new features of C++11. In terms of API design, several of these new language features can be used to produce more elegant and sturdy interfaces. As such, I have endeavored to highlight and explain those areas of C++11 throughout the book. This book should therefore remain a relevant resource for several years to come.

CONVENTIONS

While it is more traditional to employ the term "user" to mean a person who uses a software application, such as a user of Microsoft Word or Mozilla Firefox, in the context of API design I will apply the term to mean a software developer who is creating an application and is using an API to achieve this. In other words, I will generally be talking about API users and not application users. The term "client" will be used synonymously in this regard. Note that the term "client," in addition to referring to a human user of your API, can also refer impersonally to other pieces of software that must call functions in your API.

While there are many file format extensions used to identify C++ source and header files, such as .cpp, .cc, .cxx, .h, .hh, and .hpp, I will standardize on the use of .cpp and .h throughout this book. I will also use the terms module and component interchangeably to mean a single .cpp and .h file pair. These are notably not equivalent to a class because a component or module may contain multiple classes. I will use the term library to refer to a physical collection, or package, of components, that is, library > module/component > class.

The term method, while generally understood in the object-oriented programming community, is not strictly a C++ term; it originally evolved from the Smalltalk language. The equivalent C++ term is member function, although some engineers prefer the more specific definition of virtual member function. Because I am not particularly concerned with the subtleties of these terms in this book, I will use method and member function interchangeably. Similarly, although the term data member is the more correct C++ expression, I will treat the term member variable as a synonym.

In terms of typographical conventions, I will use a fixed-width font to typeset all source code examples, as well as any filenames or language keywords that may appear in the text. Also, I will prefer upper camel case for all class and function names in the examples that I present, that is, CamelCase instead of camelCase or snake_case, although obviously I will preserve the case for any external code that I reference, such as std::for_each(). I follow the convention of using an "m" prefix in front of data members, for example, mMemberVar, and "s" in front of static variables, for example, sStaticVar.

It should be pointed out that the source examples within the book are often only code snippets and are not meant to show fully functional samples. I will also often strip comments from the example code in the book. This is done for reasons of brevity and clarity. In particular, I will often omit any preprocessor guard statements around a header file. I will assume that the reader is aware that every C/C++ header should enclose all of its content within guard statements and that it's good practice to contain all of your API declarations within a consistent namespace (as covered in Chapters 3 and 6). In other words, it should be assumed that each header file that I present is implicitly surrounded by code, such as the following.

```
#ifndef MY_MODULE_H
#define MY_MODULE_H

// required #include files...

namespace apibook {

// API declarations ...

}

#endif
```

TIP

I will also highlight various API design tips and key concepts throughout the book. These callouts are provided to let you search quickly for a concept you wish to reread. If you are particularly pressed for time, you could simply scan the book for these tips and then read the surrounding text to gain greater insight for those topics that interest you the most.

BOOK WEB SITE

This book also has a supporting Web site, **http://APIBook.com/**. On this site you can find general information about the book, as well as supporting material, such as the complete set of source code examples contained within the text. Feel free to download and play with these samples yourself—they were designed to be as simple as possible, while still being useful and illustrative. I have used the cross-platform CMake build system to facilitate compiling and linking the examples so they should work on Windows, Mac OS X, and UNIX operating systems.

I will also publish any information about new revisions of this book and any errata on this Web site, as well as useful links to other related API resources on the Internet, such as interesting toolkits, articles, and utilities.

The book Web site also provides access to a utility that I wrote called API Diff. This program lets you compare two versions of an API and review differences to code or comments in a visual side-by-side format. You can also generate a report of everything that changed in a particular release so that your clients know exactly what to look out for. This utility is available for Windows, Mac OS X, and Linux.

Acknowledgments

This book has benefited greatly from the technical review and feedback of several of my esteemed colleagues. I am indebted to them for taking the time to read early versions of the manuscript and provide thoughtful suggestions for improvement. In particular, I thank Paul Strauss, Eric Gregory, Rycharde Hawkes, Nick Long, James Chalfant, Brett Levin, Marcus Marr, Jim Humelsine, and Geoff Levner. Thanks also to Javier Estrada, Ivan Komarov, Dan Smith, Alexandros Gezerlis, QiFo Lin, Çağdaş Çalık, and Markus Geimer who sent me feedback on earlier printings of the book.

My passion for good API design has been forged through my relationship with many great software engineers and managers. As a result of working at several different companies and institutions, I've been exposed to a range of design perspectives, software development philosophies, and problem-solving approaches. Throughout these varied experiences, I've had the privilege to meet and learn from some uniquely talented individuals. Some of these giants whose shoulders I have stood upon include:

- **SRI International**: Bob Bolles, Adam Cheyer, Elizabeth Churchill, David Colleen, Brian Davis, Michael Eriksen, Jay Feuquay, Marty A. Fischler, Aaron Heller, Lee Iverson, Jason Jenkins, Luc Julia, Yvan G. Leclerc, Pat Lincoln, Chris Marrin, Ray C. Perrault, and Brian Tierney.
- **Pixar Animation Studios**: Brad Andalman, David Baraff, Ian Buono, Gordon Cameron, Ed Catmull, Chris Colby, Bena Currin, Gareth Davis, Tony DeRose, Mike Ferris, Kurt Fleischer, Sebastian Grassia, Eric Gregory, Tara Hernandez, Paul Isaacs, Oren Jacob, Michael Kass, Chris King, Brett Levin, Tim Milliron, Alex Mohr, Cory Omand, Eben Osbty, Allan Poore, Chris Shoeneman, Patrick Schork, Paul Strauss, Kiril Vidimče, Adam Woodbury, David Yu, Dirk van Gelder, Brad West, and Andy Witkin.
- **The Bakery Animation Studio**: Sam Assadian, Sebastien Guichou, Arnauld Lamorlette, Thierry Lauthelier, Benoit Lepage, Geoff Levner, Nick Long, Erwan Maigret, and Barış Metin.
- **Linden Lab**: Nat Goodspeed, Andrew de Laix, Howard Look, Brad Kittenbrink, Brian McGroarty, Adam Moss, Mark Palange, Jim Purbrick, and Kent Quirk.

In particular, I acknowledge the great impact that Yvan G. Leclerc made on my life during my early years at SRI International. Yvan was my first manager and also a true friend. He taught me how to be a good manager of people, how to be a rigorous scientist and engineer, and, at the same time, how to enjoy life to its fullest. It is a great sorrow that incredible individuals such as Yvan are taken from us too soon.

Many thanks must also go to Morgan Kaufmann Publishers for all of their work reviewing, copy editing, typesetting, and publishing this book. This work would quite literally not exist without their backing and energy. In particular, I acknowledge the contribution of Todd Green, Robyn Day, André Cuello, and Melissa Revell.

Most importantly, I thank my wife, Genevieve M. Vidanes, for encouraging me to write this book and for putting up with me while I spent many late nights hunched over the keyboard. As this is my second book, she knew full well how much it would impact our personal life. Nonetheless, she supported me throughout the whole process, while also knowing exactly when to make me pause and take a break. Thank you Genevieve for your constant love and support.

Author Biography

Dr. Martin Reddy is CTO of ToyTalk Inc. and previously CEO of Code Reddy Inc. He holds a Ph.D. in computer science and has over 15 years of experience in the software industry. During this time, Dr. Reddy has produced more than 40 professional publications, four software patents, and coauthored the book *Level of Detail for 3D Graphics*. He is a member of the Association of Computing Machinery (ACM) and a Senior Member of the Institute of Electrical and Electronic Engineers (IEEE).

Dr. Reddy worked for 6 years at Pixar Animation Studios, where he was lead engineer for the studio's in-house animation system. This work involved the design and implementation of various high-performance APIs to support Academy Award-winning and nominated films, such as *Finding Nemo*, *The Incredibles*, *Cars*, *Ratatouille*, and *Wall-E*.

He then took on the role of engineering manager at The Bakery Animation Studio, where he led the development of the startup studio's animation software. This included the design and implementation of many key APIs as well as devising the overall animator workflow and user interface.

Earlier in his career, Dr. Reddy worked for 5 years at SRI International on distributed 3D terrain visualization technologies, which involved the development of several open source geospatial APIs. He cofounded a successful effort to create an ISO standard to represent 3D geospatial models on the Web and was elected as a director of the Web3D Consortium for 2 consecutive years.

Through his consulting company, Dr. Reddy has provided his technical expertise to various software companies, including Linden Lab and Planet 9 Studios. The former involved API design and infrastructure improvements for the open source product Second Life, an online 3D virtual world that has been used by over 20 million people around the world.

Introduction

1.1 WHAT ARE APPLICATION PROGRAMMING INTERFACES?

An Application Programming Interface (API) provides an abstraction for a problem and specifies how clients should interact with software components that implement a solution to that problem. The components themselves are typically distributed as a software library, allowing them to be used in multiple applications. In essence, APIs define reusable building blocks that allow modular pieces of functionality to be incorporated into end-user applications.

An API can be written for yourself, for other engineers in your organization, or for the development community at large. It can be as small as a single function or involve hundreds of classes, methods, free functions, data types, enumerations, and constants. Its implementation can be proprietary or open source. The important underlying concept is that an API is a well-defined interface that provides a specific service to other pieces of software.

A modern application is typically built on top of many APIs, where some of these can also depend on further APIs. This is illustrated in Figure 1.1, which shows an example application that depends directly on the API for three libraries (1–3), where two of those APIs depend on the API for a further two libraries (4 and 5). For instance, an image viewing application may use an API for loading GIF images, and that API may itself be built upon a lower-level API for compressing and decompressing data.

API development is ubiquitous in modern software development. Its purpose is to provide a logical interface to the functionality of a component while also hiding any implementation details. For example, our API for loading GIF images may simply provide a `LoadImage()` method that accepts a filename and returns a 2D array of pixels. All of the file format and data compression details are hidden behind this simple interface. This concept is also illustrated in Figure 1.1, where client code only accesses an API via its public interface, shown as the dark section at the top of each box.

1.1.1 Contracts and Contractors

As an analogy, consider the task of building your own home. If you were to build a house entirely on your own, you would need to possess a thorough understanding of architecture, plumbing, electronics, carpentry, masonry, and many other trades. You would also need to perform every task yourself and keep track of the minutest of details for every aspect of the project, such as whether you have enough wood for your floorboards or whether you have the right fasteners to fit the screws that you've bought. Finally, because you are the only person working on the project, you can only perform a single task at any point in time and hence the total time to complete the project could be very large.

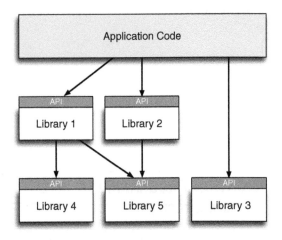

FIGURE 1.1

An application that calls routines from a hierarchy of APIs. Each box represents a software library where the dark section represents the public interface, or API, for that library, while the white section represents the hidden implementation behind that API.

An alternative strategy is to hire professional contractors to perform key tasks for you (Figure 1.2). You could hire an architect to design the plans for the house, a carpenter for all of your woodwork needs, a plumber to install the water pipes and sewage system for your house, and an electrician to set up the power systems. Taking this approach, you negotiate a contract with each of your contractors—telling them what work you want done and agreeing upon a price—they then perform that work for you. If you're lucky, maybe you even have a good friend who is a contractor and he offers you his services for free. With this strategy, you are freed from the need to know everything about all aspects of building a house and instead you can take a higher-level supervisory role to select the best contractors for your purpose and ensure that the work of each individual contractor is assembled together to produce the vision of your ideal home.

The analogy to APIs is probably obvious: the house that you're building equates to a software program that you want to write, and the contractors provide APIs that abstract each of the tasks you need to perform and hide the implementation details of the work involved. Your task then resolves to selecting the appropriate APIs for your application and integrating them into your software. The analogy of having skilled friends who provide contracting services for free is meant to represent the use of freely available open source libraries in contrast to commercial libraries that require a licensing fee to use in your software. The analogy could even be extended by having some of the contractors employing subcontractors, which corresponds to certain APIs depending on other APIs to perform their task.

The contractor analogy is a common one in object-oriented programming. Early practitioners in the field talked about an object defining a binding contract for the services or behavior that it provides. An object then implements those services when asked to by a client program, potentially by subcontracting some of the work out to other objects behind the scenes (Meyer, 1987; Snyder, 1986).

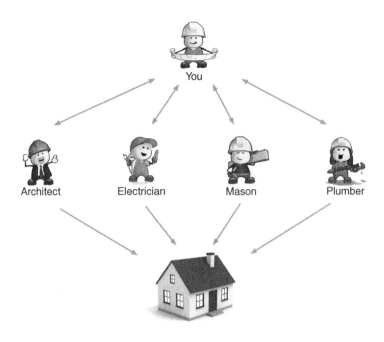

FIGURE 1.2

Using contractors to perform specialized tasks to build a house.

1.1.2 APIs in C++

Strictly speaking, an API is simply a description of how to interact with a component. That is, it provides an abstraction and a functional specification for a component. In fact, many software engineers prefer to expand the acronym API as Abstract Programming Interface instead of Application Programming Interface.

In C++, this is embodied as one or more header (.h) files plus supporting documentation files. An implementation for a given API is often represented as a library file that can be linked into end-user applications. This can be either a static library, such as a .lib file on Windows or .a on Mac OS X and Linux, or a dynamic library such as a .dll file on Windows, .dylib on Mac, or .so on Linux.

A C++ API will therefore generally include the following elements:

1. **Headers**: A collection of .h header files that define the interface and allow client code to be compiled against that interface. Open source APIs also include the source code (.cpp files) for the API implementation.
2. **Libraries**: One or more static or dynamic library files that provide an implementation for the API. Clients can link their code against these library files in order to add the functionality to their applications.
3. **Documentation**: Overview information that describes how to use the API, often including automatically generated documentation for all of the classes and functions in the API.

As an example of a well-known API, Microsoft's Windows API (often referred to as the Win32 API) is a collection of C functions, data types, and constants that enable programmers to write applications that run on the Windows platform. This includes functions for file handling, process and thread management, creating graphical user interfaces, talking to networks, and so on.

The Win32 API is an example of a plain C API rather than a C++ API. While you can use a C API directly from a C++ program, a good example of a specific C++ API is the Standard Template Library (STL). The STL contains a set of container classes, iterators for navigating over the elements in those containers, and various algorithms that act on those containers (Josuttis, 1999). For instance, the collection of algorithms includes high-level operations such as `std::search()`, `std::reverse()`, `std::sort()`, and `std::set_intersection()`. The STL therefore presents a logical interface to the task of manipulating collections of elements, without exposing any of the internal details for how each algorithm is implemented.

TIP

An API is a logical interface to a software component that hides the internal details required to implement it.

1.2 WHAT'S DIFFERENT ABOUT API DESIGN?

Interfaces are the most important code that a developer writes. That's because problems in an interface are far more costly to fix than problems in the associated implementation code. As a result, the process of developing shared APIs demands more attention than standard application or Graphical User Interface (GUI) development. Of course, both should involve best design practices; however, in the case of API development, these are absolutely critical to its success. Specifically, some of the key differentiating factors of API development include the following.

- An API is an interface designed for developers, in much the same way that a GUI is an interface designed for end users. In fact, it's been said that an API is a user interface for programmers (Arnold, 2005). As such, your API could be used by thousands of developers around the world, and it will undoubtedly be used in ways that you never intended (Tulach, 2008). You must anticipate this in your design. A well-designed API can be your organization's biggest asset. Conversely, a poor API can create a support nightmare and even turn your users toward your competitors (Bloch, 2005), just as a buggy or difficult-to-use GUI may force an end user to switch to a different application.
- Multiple applications can share the same API. Figure 1.1 showed that a single application can be composed of multiple APIs. However, any one of those APIs could also be reused in several other applications. This means that while problems in the code for any given application will only affect that one application, errors in an API can affect all of the applications that depend on that functionality.
- You must strive for backward compatibility whenever you change an API. If you make an incompatible change to your interface, your clients' code may fail to compile, or worse their code could compile but behave differently or crash intermittently. Imagine the confusion and chaos that would arise if the signature of the `printf()` function in the standard C library was

different for different compilers or platforms. The simple "Hello World" program may not look so simple any more:

```
#include <stdio.h>
#ifdef _WIN32
#include <windows.h>
#endif
#ifdef __cplusplus
#include <iostream>
#endif

int main(int argc, char *argv[])
{
#if defined(__STRICT_ANSI__)
    printf("Hello World\n");
#elif defined(_WIN32)
    PrintWithFormat("Hello World\n");
#elif defined(__PRINTF_DEPRECATED__)
    fprintf(stdout, "Hello World\n");
#elif defined(__PRINTF_VECTOR__)
    const char *lines[2] = {"Hello World", NULL};
    printf(lines);
#elif defined(__cplusplus)
    std::cout << "Hello World" << std::endl;
#else
#error No terminal output API found
#endif
    return 0;
}
```

This may seem like a contrived example, but it's actually not that extreme. Take a look at the standard header files that come with your compiler and you will find declarations that are just as convoluted and inscrutable, or perhaps worse.

- Due to the backward compatibility requirement, it's critical to have a change control process in place. During the normal development process, many developers may fix bugs or add new features to an API. Some of these developers may be junior engineers who do not fully understand all of the aspects of good API design. As a result, it's important to hold an API review before releasing a new version of the API. This involves one or more senior engineers checking that all changes to the interface are acceptable, have been made for a valid reason, and are implemented in the best way to maintain backward compatibility. Many open source APIs also enforce a change request process to gain approval for a change before it is added to the source code.
- APIs tend to live for a long time. There can be a large upfront cost to produce a good API because of the extra overhead of planning, design, versioning, and review that's necessary. However, if done well, the long-term cost can be substantially mitigated because you have the ability to make radical changes and improvements to your software without disrupting your clients. That is, your development velocity can be greater due to the increased flexibility that the API affords you.

- The need for good documentation is paramount when writing an API, particularly if you do not provide the source code for your implementation. Users can look at your header files to glean how to use it, but this does not define the behavior of the API, such as acceptable input values or error conditions. Well-written, consistent, and extensive documentation is therefore an imperative for any good API.
- The need for automated testing is similarly very high. Of course, you should always test your code, but when you're writing an API you may have hundreds of other developers, and thousands of their users, depending on the correctness of your code. If you are making major changes to the implementation of your API, you can be more confident that you will not break your clients' programs if you have a thorough suite of regression tests to verify that the desired API behavior has not changed.

Writing good APIs is difficult. While the necessary skills are founded on general software design principles, they also require additional knowledge and development processes to address the points just listed. However, the principles and techniques of API design are rarely taught to engineers. Normally, these skills are only gained through experience—by making mistakes and learning empirically what does and does not work (Henning, 2009). This book is an attempt to redress this situation, to distill the strategies of industrial-strength, future-proof API design that have been evolved through years of software engineering experience into a comprehensive, practical, and accessible format.

TIP

An API describes software used by other engineers to build their applications. As such, it must be well-designed, documented, regression tested, and stable between releases.

1.3 WHY SHOULD YOU USE APIs?

The question of why you should care about APIs in your own software projects can be interpreted in two different ways: (1) why should you design and write your own APIs or (2) why should you use APIs from other providers in your applications? Both of these perspectives are tackled in the following sections as I present the various benefits of using APIs in your projects.

1.3.1 More Robust Code

If you are writing a module to be used by other developers, either for fellow engineers within your organization or for external customers of your library, then it would be a wise investment to create an API for them to access your functionality. Doing so will offer you the following benefits.

- **Hides implementation**. By hiding the implementation details of your module, you gain the flexibility to change the implementation at a future date without causing upheaval for your users. Without doing so, you will either (i) restrict yourself in terms of the updates you can make to your code or (ii) force your users to rewrite their code in order to adopt new versions of your library. If you make it too onerous for your clients to update to new versions of your software, then it's highly likely that they will either not upgrade at all or look elsewhere for an API that will not be as much work for them to maintain. Good API design can therefore significantly affect the success of your business or project.

- **Increases longevity**. Over time, systems that expose their implementation details tend to devolve into spaghetti code where every part of the system depends on the internal details of other parts of the system. As a result, the system becomes fragile, rigid, immobile, and viscous (Martin, 2000). This often results in organizations having to spend significant effort and money to evolve the code toward a better design or simply rewrite it from scratch. By investing in good API design up front and paying the incremental cost to maintain a coherent design, your software can survive for longer and cost less to maintain in the long run. I'll delve much deeper into this point at the start of Chapter 4.
- **Promotes modularization**. An API is normally devised to address a specific task or use case. As such, APIs tend to define a modular grouping of functionality with a coherent focus. Developing an application on top of a collection of APIs promotes loosely coupled and modular architectures where the behavior of one module is not dependent on the internal details of another module.
- **Reduces code duplication**. Code duplication is one of the cardinal sins of software engineering and should be stamped out whenever possible. By keeping all of your code's logic behind a strict interface that all clients must use, you centralize the behavior in a single place. Doing so means that you have to update only one place to change the behavior of your API for all of your clients. This can help remove duplication of implementation code throughout your code base. In fact, many APIs are created after discovering duplicated code and deciding to consolidate it behind a single interface. This is a good thing.
- **Removes hardcoded assumptions**. Many programs may contain hardcoded values that are copied throughout the code, for example, using the filename `"myprogram.log"` whenever data are written to a log file. Instead, APIs can be used to provide access to this information without replicating these constant values across the code base. For example, a `GetLogFilename()` API call could be used to replace the hardcoded `"myprogram.log"` string.
- **Easier to change the implementation**. If you have hidden all of the implementation details of your module behind its public interface then you can change those implementation details without affecting any code that depends on the API. For example, you might decide to change a file parsing routine to use `std::string` containers instead of allocating, freeing, and reallocating your own `char *` buffers.
- **Easier to optimize**. Similarly, with your implementation details hidden successfully, you can optimize the performance of your API without requiring any changes to your clients' code. For example, you could add a caching solution to a method that performs some computationally intensive calculation. This is possible because all attempts to read and write your underlying data are performed via your API, so it becomes much easier to know when you must invalidate your cached result and recompute the new value.

1.3.2 Code Reuse

Code reuse is the use of existing software to build new software. It is one of the holy grails of modern software development. APIs provide a mechanism to enable code reuse.

In the early years of software development, it was common for a company to have to write all of the code for any application they produced. If the program needed to read GIF images or parse a text file, the company would have to write all that code in-house. Nowadays, with the proliferation of good commercial and open source libraries, it makes much more sense to simply reuse code that others have written. For example, there are various open source image reading APIs and XML parsing APIs that you can download and use in your application today. These libraries have been refined and debugged by many developers around the world and have been battle-tested in many other programs.

In essence, software development has become much more modular, with the use of distinct components that form the building blocks of an application and talk together via their published APIs. The benefit of this approach is that you don't need to understand every detail of every software component, in the same way that for the earlier house building analogy you can delegate many details to professional contractors. This can translate into faster development cycles, either because you can reuse existing code or decouple the schedule for various components. It also allows you to concentrate on your core business logic instead of having to spend time reinventing the wheel.

One of the difficulties in achieving code reuse, however, is that you often have to come up with a more general interface than you originally intended. That's because other clients may have additional expectations or requirements. Effective code reuse therefore follows from a deep understanding of the clients of your software and designing a system that integrates their collective interests with your own.

C++ APIs AND THE WEB

The trend toward applications that depend on third-party APIs is particularly popular in the field of cloud computing. Here, Web applications rely more and more on Web services (APIs) to provide core functionality. In the case of Web mashups, the application itself is sometimes simply a repackaging of multiple existing services to provide a new service, such as combining the Google Maps API with a local crimes statistics database to provide a map-based interface to the crime data.

In fact, it's worth taking a few moments to highlight the importance of C++ API design in Web development. A superficial analysis might conclude that server-side Web development is confined to scripting languages, such as PHP, Perl, or Python (the "P" in the popular LAMP acronym), or .NET languages based on Microsoft's ASP (Active Server Pages) technology. This may be true for small-scale Web development. However, it is noteworthy that many large-scale Web services use a C++ backend to deliver optimal performance.

In fact, Facebook developed a product called HipHop to convert their PHP code into C++ to improve the performance of their social networking site. C++ API design therefore does have a role to play in scalable Web service development. Additionally, if you develop your core APIs in C++, not only can they form a high-performance Web service, but your code can also be reused to deliver your product in other forms, such as desktop or mobile phone versions.

As an aside, one potential explanation for this shift in software development strategy is the result of the forces of globalization (Friedman, 2008; Wolf, 2004). In effect, the convergence of the Internet, standard network protocols, and Web technologies has created a leveling of the software playing field. This has enabled companies and individuals all over the world to create, contribute, and compete with large complex software projects. This form of globalization promotes an environment where companies and developers anywhere in the world can forge a livelihood out of developing software subsystems. Other organizations in different parts of the world can then build end-user applications by assembling and augmenting these building blocks to solve specific problems. In terms of our focus here, APIs provide the mechanism to enable this globalization and componentization of modern software development.

1.3.3 **Parallel Development**

Even if you're writing in-house software, your fellow engineers will very likely need to write code that uses your code. If you use good API design techniques, you can simplify their lives and, by extension, your own (because you won't have to answer as many questions about how your code works or how to use it). This becomes even more important if multiple developers are working in parallel on code that depends upon each other.

For example, let's say that you're working on a string encryption algorithm that another developer wants to use to write data out to a configuration file. One approach would be to have the other developer wait until you're finished with your work and then he can use it in his file writer module. However, a far more efficient use of time would be for the two of you to meet early on and agree upon an appropriate API. Then you can put that API in place with placeholder functionality that your colleague can start calling immediately, such as

```cpp
#include <string>

class StringEncryptor
{
public:
    /// set the key to use for the Encrypt() and Decrypt() calls
    void SetKey(const std::string &key);

    /// encrypt an input string based upon the current key
    std::string Encrypt(const std::string &str) const;

    /// decrypt a string using the current key - calling
    /// Decrypt() on a string returned by Encrypt() will
    /// return the original string for the same key.
    std::string Decrypt(const std::string &str) const;
};
```

You can then provide a simple implementation of these functions so that at least the module will compile and link. For example, the associated .cpp file might look like

```cpp
void StringEncryptor::SetKey(const std::string &key)
{
}

std::string StringEncryptor::Encrypt(const std::string &str)
{
    return str;
}

std::string StringEncryptor::Decrypt(const std::string &str)
{
    return str;
}
```

In this way, your colleague can use this API and proceed with his work without being held up by your progress. For the time being, your API will not actually encrypt any strings, but that's just a minor implementation detail! The important point is that you have a stable interface—a contract—that you both agree upon, and that it behaves appropriately, for example, `Decrypt(Encrypt ("Hello")) == "Hello"`. When you finish your work and update the `.cpp` file with the correct implementation, your colleague's code will simply work without any further changes required on his part.

In reality, it's likely that there will be interface issues that you didn't anticipate before you started writing the code and you will probably have to iterate on the API a few times to get it just right. However, for the most part, the two of you can work in parallel with minimal holdups.

This approach also encourages test-driven, or test-first, development. By stubbing out the API early on, you can write unit tests to validate the desired functionality and run these continuously to make sure that you haven't broken your contract with your colleague.

Scaling this process up to an organizational level, your project could have separate teams that may be remote from each other, even working to different schedules. By defining each team's dependencies up front and creating APIs to model these, each team can work independently and with minimal knowledge of how the other teams are implementing their work behind the API. This efficient use of resources, and the corresponding reduction in redundant communication, can correlate to a significant overall cost saving for an organization.

1.4 WHEN SHOULD YOU AVOID APIS?

Designing and implementing an API usually requires more work than writing normal application code. That's because the purpose of an API is to provide a robust and stable interface for other developers to use. As such, the level of quality, planning, documentation, testing, support, and maintenance is far higher for an API than for software that is to be used within a single application.

As a result, if you are writing an internal module that does not require other clients to communicate with it, then the extra overhead of creating and supporting a stable public interface for your module may not be worth the effort, although this is not a reason to write sloppy code. Spending the extra time to adhere to the principles of API design will not be wasted effort in the long run.

On the flip side of the coin, consider that you're a software developer who wants to use a third-party API in your application. The previous section discussed a number of reasons why you might want to reuse external APIs in your software. However, there may be cases where you wish to avoid using a particular API and pay the cost to implement the code yourself or look for an alternate solution. For example:

- **License restrictions**. An API may provide everything that you need functionality-wise, but the license restrictions may be prohibitive for your needs. For example, if you want to use an open source package that is distributed under the GNU General Public License (GPL), then you are required to release any derived works under the GPL also. This means that using this package in your program would require you to release the entire source code for your application, a constraint that may not be acceptable for a commercial application. Other licenses, such as the GNU Lesser General Public License (LGPL), are more permissive and tend to be more common for software libraries. Another licensing aspect is that the dollar cost for a commercial API may be too high for your project or the licensing terms may be too restrictive, such as requiring a license fee per developer or even per user.

- **Functionality mismatch**. An API may appear to solve a problem that you have, but may do it in a way that doesn't match the constraints or functional requirements of your application. For example, perhaps you're developing an image processing tool and you want to provide a Fourier transform capability. There are many implementations of the Fast Fourier Transform (FFT) available, but a large number of these are 1D algorithms, whereas you require a 2D FFT because you are dealing with 2D image data. Additionally, many 2D FFT algorithms only work on data sets with dimensions that are a power of 2 (e.g., 256 × 256 or 512 × 512 pixels). Furthermore, perhaps the API that you found doesn't work on the platforms that you must support or perhaps it doesn't match the performance criteria that you have specified for your application.
- **Lack of source code**. While there are many open source APIs, sometimes the best API for your case may be a closed source offering. That is, only the header files for the interface are made available to you, but the underlying C++ source files are not distributed with the library. This has several important implications. Among these is the fact that if you encounter a bug in the library, you are unable to inspect the source code to understand what might be going wrong. Reading the source can be a valuable technique for tracking down a bug and potentially discovering a workaround for the issue.

    Furthermore, without access to the source code for an API, you lose the ability to change the source in order to fix a bug. This means that the schedule for your software project could be affected adversely by unanticipated problems in a third-party API you're using and by time spent waiting for the owners of that API to address your bug reports and distribute a fixed patch.
- **Lack of documentation**. An API may appear to fulfill a need that you have in your application, but if the API has poor or non-existent documentation then you may decide to look elsewhere for a solution. Perhaps it is not obvious how to use the API, perhaps you cannot be sure how the API will behave under certain situations, or perhaps you simply don't trust the work of an engineer who hasn't taken the time to explain how his code should be used.

1.5 API EXAMPLES

APIs are everywhere. Even if you have only been programming for a short amount of time, chances are that you have written code to use an API or two and maybe you've also written one yourself.

1.5.1 Layers of APIs

An API can be any size, from a single function to a large collection of classes. It can also provide access to functionality at any architectural level, from low-level operating system calls all the way up to GUI toolkits. The following list presents various common APIs, many of which you've probably heard of already, to give you an appreciation for how prevalent API development is.

- **Operating System (OS) APIs**. Every OS must provide a set of standard APIs to allow programs to access OS-level services. For example, the POSIX API defines functions such as `fork()`, `getpid()`, and `kill()` for managing UNIX-style processes. Microsoft's Win32 API includes functions such as `CreateProcess()`, `GetCurrentProcess()`, and `TerminateProcess()` for managing Windows processes. These are stable low-level APIs that should never change, otherwise many programs could break!

- **Language APIs**. The C language provides a standard API, implemented as the libc library and supporting man pages, which includes familiar functions such as `printf()`, `scanf()`, and `fopen()`. The C++ language also offers the Standard Template Library (STL), which provides an API for various container classes (e.g., `std::string`, `std::vector`, `std::set`, and `std::map`), iterators (e.g., `std::vector<double>::iterator`), and generic algorithms (e.g., `std::sort()`, `std::for_each()`, and `std::set_union()`). For example, the following code snippet uses the STL API to iterate through all elements in a vector and print them out:

```
#include <vector>
#include <iostream>
void PrintVector(const std::vector<float> &vec)
{
    std::vector<float>::const_iterator it;
    for (it = vec.begin(); it != vec.end(); ++it)
    {
        std::cout << *it << std::endl;
    }
}
```

- **Image APIs**. Gone are the days when developers needed to write their own image reading and writing routines. There is now a wide range of open source packages out there for you to download and use in your own programs. For example, there's the popular libjpeg library that provides an implementation of a JPEG/JFIF decoder and encoder. There's the extensive libtiff library for reading and writing various flavors of TIFF files. And there's the libpng library for handling PNG format images. All of these libraries define APIs that let you write code to read and write the image formats without having to know anything about the underlying file formats themselves. For example, the follow code snippet uses the libtiff API to find the dimensions of a TIFF image.

```
TIFF *tif = TIFFOpen("image.tiff", "r");
if (tif)
{
    uint32 w, h;
    TIFFGetField(tif, TIFFTAG_IMAGEWIDTH, &w);
    TIFFGetField(tif, TIFFTAG_IMAGELENGTH, &h);
    printf("Image size = %d x %d pixels\n", w, h);
    TIFFClose(tif);
}
```

- **Three-Dimensional Graphics APIs**. The two classic real-time 3D graphics APIs are OpenGL and DirectX. These let you define 3D objects in terms of small primitives, such as triangles or polygons; specify the surface properties of those primitives, such as color, normal, and texture; and define the environment conditions, such as lights, fog, and clipping panes. Thanks to standard APIs such as these, game developers can write 3D games that will work on graphics cards old and new, from many different manufacturers. That's because each graphics card manufacturer distributes drivers that provide the implementation details behind the OpenGL or DirectX API. Before the widespread use of these APIs, a developer had to write a 3D application for a specific piece of graphics hardware, and this program would probably not work on another machine with different graphics hardware. These APIs also enable a host of higher-level scene graph APIs, such as OpenSceneGraph, OpenSG, and OGRE. The following code segment shows the classic example of rendering a triangle, with a different color for each vertex, using the OpenGL API:

```
glClear(GL_COLOR_BUFFER_BIT);
glBegin(GL_TRIANGLES);
    glColor3f(0.0, 0.0, 1.0); /* blue */
    glVertex2i(0, 0);
    glColor3f(0.0, 1.0, 0.0); /* green */
    glVertex2i(200, 200);
    glColor3f(1.0, 0.0, 0.0); /* red */
    glVertex2i(20, 200);
glEnd();
glFlush();
```

- **Graphical User Interface APIs**. Any application that wants to open its own window needs to use a GUI toolkit. This is an API that provides the ability to create windows, buttons, text fields, dialogs, icons, menus, and so on. The API will normally also provide an event model to allow the capturing of mouse and keyboard events. Some popular C/C++ GUI APIs include the wxWidgets library, Nokia's Qt API, GTK+, and X/Motif. It used to be the case that if a company wanted to release an application on more than one platform, such as Windows and Mac, they would have to rewrite the user interface code using a different GUI API for each platform or they would have to develop their own in-house cross-platform GUI toolkit. However, these days most modern GUI toolkits are available for multiple platforms—including Windows, Mac, and Linux—which makes it far easier to write cross-platform applications. As a sample of a modern cross-platform GUI API, the following complete program shows a bare minimum Qt program that pops up a window with a Hello World button:

```
#include <QApplication>
#include <QPushButton>

int main(int argc, char *argv[])
{
    QApplication app(argc, argv);
    QPushButton hello("Hello world!");
    hello.resize(100, 30);
    hello.show();
    return app.exec();
}
```

Of course, this list is just a brief cross section of all the possible APIs that are out there. You'll also find APIs to let you access data over networks, to parse and generate XML files, to help you write multi-threaded programs, or to solve complex mathematical problems. The point of the aforementioned list was simply to demonstrate the breadth and depth of APIs that have been developed to help you build your applications and to give you a flavor for what code based on these APIs looks like.

TIP

APIs are used everywhere in modern software development, from OS- and language-level APIs to image, audio, graphics, concurrency, network, XML, mathematics, Web browsing, or GUI APIs.

1.5.2 A Real-Life Example

The aforementioned list of API examples was purposefully arranged by architectural level to show the range of APIs that you might use when building an application. You will often use APIs from several architectural levels when building a large software product. For example, Figure 1.3 presents an example architecture diagram for the Second Life Viewer developed by Linden Lab. This is a large open source program that lets users interact with each other in an online 3D virtual world, with the ability to perform voice chat and text messaging between users. The diagram demonstrates the use and layering of APIs in a large C++ software project.

Of particular note is the layer of Internal APIs, by which I mean the set of modules that a company develops in-house for a particular product, or suite of products. While Figure 1.3 simply shows these as a single layer for the purpose of simplicity, the set of Internal APIs will form an additional stack of layers. From foundation-level routines that provide in-house string, dictionary, file I/O, threading routines, and so on to APIs that provide the core business logic of the application, all the way up to custom GUI APIs for managing the application's user interface.

Obviously, Figure 1.3 doesn't provide an exhaustive list of all the APIs used in this application. It simply shows a few examples of each architectural layer. However, Table 1.1 presents the complete set of third-party dependencies for the application to give you an idea of how many open source and commercial closed source dependencies a contemporary software project is built upon. When you factor in system and OS libraries as well, this list grows even further.

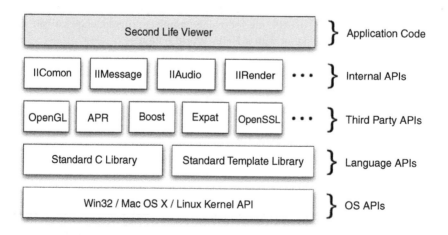

FIGURE 1.3

Architecture diagram for the Second Life Viewer.

Table 1.1 List of open- and closed-source APIs used by the Second Life Viewer

API	Description
APR	The Apache Portable Runtime
Boost	Set of portable C++ utility libraries
c-ares	Asyncronous DNS resolution library
cURL	Client URL request library
Expat	Stream-oriented XML Parser
FMOD	Commercial audio engine and MP3 stream decoder
FreeGLUT	Open source version of the OpenGL Utility Toolkit (GLUT)
FreeType	Font rasterization engine
glh_linear	C++ OpenGL helper library
jpeglib	JPEG decoder library
KDU	Commercial Kakadu (KDU) JPEG-2000 decoder library
libpng	PNG image library
llqtwebkit	Qt's WebKit embeddable Web browser
Ogg Vorbis	Compressed audio format library
OpenGL	3D graphics rendering engine
openjpeg	Open-source JPEG-2000 library, alternative to KDU
OpenSSL	Secure Sockets Layer (SSL) library
Quicktime	Library for playing video clips
Vivox	Commercial voice chat library
xmlrpc-epi	XML-RPC protocol library
zlib	Lossless data compression library

APIs AND SDKs

The term Software Development Kit (SDK) is closely related to the term API. Essentially, an SDK is a platform-specific package that you install on your computer in order to build applications against one or more APIs.

At a minimum, an SDK will include the header (.h) files for you to compile your program against and the library (.dylib, .so, .dll) files that provide the API implementations for you to link your application against. However, an SDK may include other resources to help you use the APIs, such as documentation, example source code, and supporting tools.

As an example, Apple publishes various iPhone APIs that let you write applications that run on iPhone, iPod Touch, and iPad devices. Examples include the UIKit user interface API, the WebKit API to embed Web browser functionality in your applications, and the Core Audio API for audio services.

Apple also provides the iPhone SDK, which is a downloadable installer that contains the frameworks (headers and libraries) that implement the various iPhone APIs. These are the files that you compile and link against to give your programs access to the underlying functionality of the APIs. The iPhone SDK also includes API documentation, sample code, various templates for Apple's Integrated Development Environment (IDE) called XCode, and the iPhone Simulator that lets you run iPhone apps on your desktop computer.

1.6 FILE FORMATS AND NETWORK PROTOCOLS

There are several other forms of communication "contracts" commonly used in computer applications. One of the most familiar is the file format. This is a way to save in-memory data to a file on disk using a well-known layout of those data. For example, the JPEG File Interchange Format (JFIF) is an image file format for exchanging JPEG-encoded imagery, commonly given the .jpg or .jpeg file extension. The format of a JFIF file header is shown in Table 1.2.

Given the format for a data file, such as the JFIF/JPEG format given in Table 1.2, any program can read and write image files in that format. This allows the easy interchange of image data between different users and the proliferation of image viewers and tools that can operate on those images.

Similarly, client/server applications, peer-to-peer applications, and middleware services work by sending data back and forward using an established protocol, usually over a network socket. For example, the Subversion version control system uses a client/server architecture where the master repository is stored on the server and individual clients synchronize their local clients with the server (Rooney, 2005). In order to make this work, the client and the server must agree upon the format of those data transmitted across the network. This is known as the client/server protocol or line protocol. If the client sends a data stream that does not conform to this protocol, then the server will not be able to understand the message. It is therefore critical that the specification of the client/server protocol is well defined and that both the client and the server conform to the specification.

Both of these cases are conceptually similar to an API in that they define a standard interface, or specification, for information to be exchanged. Also, any changes to the specification must consider the impact on existing clients. Despite this similarity, file formats and line protocols are not actually APIs because they are not programming interfaces for code that you link into your application. However, a good rule of thumb is that whenever you have a file format or a client/server protocol, you should also have an associated API to manage changes to that specification.

Table 1.2 JFIF file format header specification

Field	Byte size	Description
APP0 marker	2	Always 0xFFE0
Length	2	Length of segment excluding APP0 marker
Identifier	5	Always 0x4A46494600 ("JFIF\0")
Version	2	0x0102
Density units	1	Units for pixel density fields, 0 = no units
X density	2	Integer horizontal pixel density
Y density	2	Integer vertical pixel density
Thumbnail width (w)	1	Horizontal size of embedded thumbnail
Thumbnail height (h)	1	Vertical size of embedded thumbnail
Thumbnail data	$3 \times w \times h$	Uncompressed 24-bit RGB raster data

> **TIP**
>
> Whenever you create a file format or client/server protocol, you should also create an API for it. This allows details of the specification, and any future changes to it, to be centralized and hidden.

For example, if you specify a file format for your application's data, you should also write an API to allow reading and writing files in that format. For one, this is simply good practice so that knowledge of the file format is not distributed throughout your application. More importantly, having an API allows you to easily change the file format in the future without having to rewrite any code outside of the API implementation. Finally, if you do end up with multiple different versions of a file format, then your API can abstract that complexity away so that it can read and write data in any version of the format or it can know if the format is written with a newer version of the API and take appropriate steps. In essence, the actual format of data on the disk becomes a hidden implementation detail that your application does not need to be concerned with.

This advice applies just as well to client/server applications, where the definition of a common protocol, and a common API to manage that protocol, can allow the client and server teams to work relatively independently of each other. For instance, you may begin using UDP as the transport layer for part of your system but later decide to switch to TCP (as indeed happened with the Second Life code base). If all network access had already been abstracted behind an appropriate API, then such a major implementation change would have little to no disruptive impact on the rest of the system.

1.7 ABOUT THIS BOOK

Now that I have covered the basics of what an API is and the pros and cons of API development, I'll dive into details such as how to design good APIs, how to implement them efficiently in C++, and how to version them without breaking backward compatibility. The progression of chapters in this book roughly follows the standard evolution of an API, from initial design through implementation, versioning, documentation, and testing.

Chapter 2: *Qualities*

I begin the main text with a chapter that answers the following question: what is a good API? This will cover a wide gamut of qualities that you should be aware of when designing your APIs, such as information hiding, minimal completeness, and loose coupling. As I do throughout the book, I illustrate these concepts with many C++ source code examples to show how they relate to your own projects.

Chapter 3: *Patterns*

The next couple of chapters tackle the question of how you design a good API. Accordingly, Chapter 3 looks at some specific design patterns and idioms that are particularly helpful in API design. These include the pimpl idiom, Singleton, Factory Method, Proxy, Adapter, Façade, and Observer.

Chapter 4: *Design*

Continuing the topic of how to design a good API, Chapter 4 discusses functional requirement gathering and use case modeling to drive the design of a clean and usable interface, as well as some techniques of object-oriented analysis and object-oriented design. This chapter also includes a discussion on many of the problems that a large software project faces. These observations are taken from real-world experiences and provide insight into the issues that arise when doing large-scale API development.

Chapter 5: *Styles*

The next few chapters focus on creating high-quality APIs with C++. This is a deep and complex topic and is, of course, the specific focus of this book. I therefore begin by describing various styles of C and C++ APIs that you could adopt in your projects, such as flat C APIs, object-oriented APIs, template-based APIs, and data-driven APIs.

Chapter 6: C++ Usage

Next I discuss various C++ language features that can impact good API design. This includes numerous important issues such as good constructor and operator style, namespaces, pointer versus reference parameters, the use of friends, and how to export symbols in a dynamic library.

Chapter 7: *Performance*

In this chapter I analyze performance issues in APIs and show you how to build high-performing APIs in C++. This involves the use of const references, forward declarations, data member clustering, and inlining. I also present various tools that can help you assess the performance of your code.

Chapter 8: *Versioning*

With the foundations of API design in hand, I start to expand into more complex aspects, starting with API versioning and how to maintain backward compatibility. This is one of the most important—and difficult—aspects of robust API design. Here I will define the various terms backward, forward, functional, source, and binary compatibility and describe how to evolve an API with minimal impact to your clients.

Chapter 9: *Documentation*

Next I dedicate a chapter to the topic of API documentation. Because an API is ill-defined without proper supporting documentation, I present good techniques for commenting and documenting your API, with specific examples using the excellent Doxygen tool.

Chapter 10: *Testing*

The use of extensive testing lets you evolve an API with the confidence that you are not breaking your clients' programs. Here I present various types of automated testing, including unit, integration, and performance tests, and present examples of good testing methodologies for you to use in your own projects. This covers topics such as test-driven development, stub and mock objects, testing private code, and contract programming.

Chapter 11: *Scripting*

I follow this with a couple of more specialized topics, beginning with API scripting. This is an optional subject that is not applicable to all APIs. However, you may decide to provide scripting access to your API so that power users of your application can write scripts to perform custom actions. I therefore talk about how to create script bindings for a C++ API so that it can be called from languages such as Python and Ruby.

Chapter 12: *Extensibility*

Another advanced topic is that of user extensibility: creating an API that allows programmers to write custom C++ plugins that extend the basic functionality you ship with the API. This can be a critical mechanism to promote adoption of your API and to help it survive for the long term. Additionally, I cover how to create extensible interfaces using inheritance and templates.

Appendix A: *Libraries*

The book concludes with an appendix on how to create static and dynamic libraries. You must be able to create libraries in order for your code to be used by others. There are also interface design issues to consider when creating dynamic libraries, such as the set of symbols that you export publicly. I therefore discuss differences between static and shared libraries and demonstrate how you can make your compiler produce these libraries to allow the reuse of your code in other applications.

Qualities

2

This chapter aims to answer the following question: What are the basic qualities of a good API? Most developers would agree that a good API should be elegantly designed but still highly usable. It should be a joy to use but also fade into the background (Henning, 2009). These are fine qualitative statements, but what are the specific design aspects that enable these? Obviously every API is different; however, there are certain qualities that promote high-quality API design and should be adhered to whenever possible, as well as many that make for poor designs that should be avoided.

There are no absolutes in API design: you cannot apply a fixed set of rules to every situation. However, while there may be individual cases where you decide that it is best for your project to deviate from certain advice in this chapter, you should do so only after reasoned and considered judgment. The guidance here should form the bedrock of your API design decisions.

This chapter concentrates on generic, language-neutral qualities of an API, such as information hiding, consistency, and loose coupling. It provides a C++ context for each of these concepts, but overall the advice in this chapter should be useful to you whether you are working on a C++, Java, C#, or Python project. Later chapters deal with C++-specific issues, such as const correctness, namespaces, and constructor usage.

Many of the topics of this chapter also provide a jumping off point into deeper treatments later in the book. For example, while I mention use of the Pimpl idiom as a solution for hiding internal details in C++, I dedicate more space to this important topic in the following chapter on design patterns.

2.1 MODEL THE PROBLEM DOMAIN

An API is written to solve a particular problem or perform a specific task. So, first and foremost, the API should provide a coherent solution for that problem and should be formulated in such a way that models the actual domain of the problem. For example, it should provide a good abstraction of the problem area and should model the key objects of that domain. Doing so can make the API easier for your users to use and understand because it will correlate more closely with their preexisting knowledge and experience.

2.1.1 Provide a Good Abstraction

An API should provide a logical abstraction for the problem that it solves. That is, it should be formulated in terms of high-level concepts that make sense in the chosen problem domain rather than exposing low-level implementation issues. You should be able to give your API documentation to a non-programmer and that person should be able to understand the concepts of the interface and how it is meant to work.

Furthermore, it should be apparent to the non-technical reader that the group of operations provided by the API makes sense and belongs together as a unit. Each class should have a central purpose, which should be reflected in the name of the class and its methods. In fact, it's good practice to have another person review your API early on to make sure that it presents a logical interface to fresh eyes.

Because coming up with a good abstraction is not a simple task, I dedicate most of Chapter 4 to this complex topic. However, it should be noted that there is no single correct abstraction for any given problem. Most APIs could be modeled in several different ways, each of which may provide a good abstraction and a useful interface. The key point is that there is some consistent and logical underpinning to your API.

For example, let's consider an API for a simple address book program. Conceptually, an address book is a container for the details of multiple people. It seems logical then that our API should provide an AddressBook object that contains a collection of Person objects, where a Person object describes the name and address of a single contact. Furthermore, you want to be able to perform operations such as adding a person to the address book or removing them. These are operations that update the state of the address book and so logically should be part of the AddressBook object. This initial design can then be represented visually using Unified Modeling Language (UML) as shown in Figure 2.1.

For those not familiar with UML, Figure 2.1 shows an AddressBook object that contains a one-to-many composition of Person objects as well as two operations: AddPerson() and DeletePerson(). The Person object contains a set of public attributes to describe a single person's name and address. I will refine this design in a moment, but for the moment it serves as an initial logical abstraction of the problem domain.

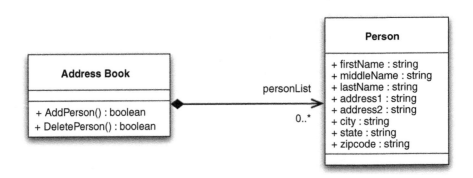

FIGURE 2.1

High-level UML abstraction of an address book API.

UML CLASS DIAGRAMS

The UML specification defines a collection of visual notations to model object-oriented software systems (Booch et al., 2005). This book often uses the UML class diagram to depict class designs, as in Figure 2.1. In these diagrams, a single class is represented with a box that is segmented into three parts:

1. The upper section contains the class name.
2. The middle section lists attributes of the class.
3. The lower section enumerates methods of the class.

Each of the entries in the middle and lower sections of the class box can be prefixed with a symbol to indicate the access level, or visibility, for that attribute or method. These symbols include:

+ indicates a public class member
− indicates a private class member
# indicates a protected class member

Relationships between classes are illustrated with various styles of connecting lines and arrowheads. Some of the common relationships possible in a UML class diagram are:

Association: A simple dependency between two classes where neither owns the other, shown as a solid line. Association can be directional, indicated with an open arrowhead such as ">".
Aggregation: A "has-a," or whole/part, relationship where neither class owns the other, shown as a line with a hollow diamond.
Composition: A "has-a" relationship where the lifetime of the part is managed by the whole. This is represented as a line with a filled diamond.
Generalization: A subclass relationship between classes, shown as a line with a hollow triangle arrowhead.

Each side of a relationship can also be annotated to define its multiplicity. This lets you specify whether the relationship is one to one, one to many, or many to many. Some common multiplicities include:

0..1 = Zero or one instances
1 = Exactly one instance
0..* = Zero or more instances
1..* = One or more instances

2.1.2 Model the Key Objects

An API should also model the key objects for the problem domain. This process is often called object-oriented design or object modeling because it aims to describe the hierarchy of objects in the specific problem domain. The goal of object modeling is to identify the collection of major objects, the operations that they provide, and how they relate to each other.

Once again, there is no single correct object model for a given problem domain. Instead, the task of creating an object model should be driven by the specific requirements for the API. Different demands on an API may require a different object model to best represent those demands. For example, continuing our address book example, let's assume that we've received the following requirements for our API.

1. Each person may have multiple addresses.
2. Each person may have multiple telephone numbers.
3. Telephone numbers can be validated and formatted.

4. An address book may contain multiple people with the same name.
5. An existing address book entry can be modified.

These requirements will have a large impact on the object model for the API. Our original design in Figure 2.1 only supports a single address per person. In order to support more than one address, you could add extra fields to the Person object (e.g., HomeAddress1, WorkAddress1), but this would be a brittle and inelegant solution. Instead, you could introduce an object to represent an address, for example, Address, and allow a Person object to contain multiple of these.

The same is true of telephone numbers: you should factor these into their own object, for example, TelephoneNumber, and allow the Person object to hold multiple of these. Another reason to create an independent TelephoneNumber object is that we need to support operations such as IsValid(), to validate a number, and GetFormattedNumber(), to return a nicely formatted version of the number. These are operations that naturally operate on a telephone number, not a person, which suggests that telephone numbers should be represented by their own first-class objects.

The requirement that multiple People objects may hold the same name essentially means that a person's name cannot be used to uniquely identify an instance of the Person object. You therefore need some way to uniquely identify a Person instance, for example, so that you can locate and update an existing entry in the address book. One way to satisfy this requirement would simply be to generate a universally unique identifier (UUID) for each person. Putting all of this together, you might conclude that the key objects for our address book API are as follows:

- **Address Book**: Contains zero or more Person objects, with operations such as AddPerson(), DeletePerson(), and UpdatePerson().
- **Person**: Fully describes the details for a single person, including zero or more addresses and telephone numbers. Each person is differentiated by a UUID.
- **Address**: Describes a single address, including a type field such as "Home" or "Work."
- **Telephone Number**: Describes a single address, including a type field such as "Home" or "Cell." Also supports operations such as IsValid() and GetFormattedNumber().

This updated object model can be represented as a UML diagram, as shown in Figure 2.2.

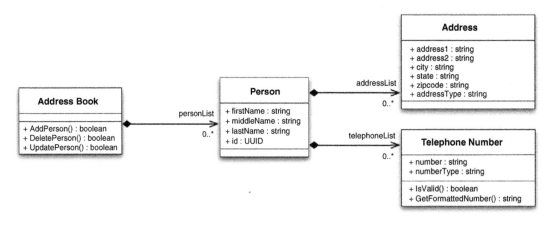

FIGURE 2.2

UML diagram of key objects in our address book API.

It's important to note that the object model for an API may need to change over time. As new requirements are received or new functionality is added, the optimal breakdown of classes and methods to meet those needs may change. It is therefore always wise to reevaluate your object model in the light of new requirements to assess whether your object model would benefit from a redesign too. For example, you may anticipate the need for international addresses and decide to create a more general Address object to handle this capability. However, don't go over the top and try to create an object model that is more general than you need. Make sure you read the upcoming section on being minimally complete too!

2.2 HIDE IMPLEMENTATION DETAILS

The primary reason for creating an API is to hide any implementation details so that these can be changed at a later date without affecting any existing clients. Therefore, the most important quality of an API is that it actually achieves this purpose. That is, any internal details—those parts that are most likely to change—must be kept secret from the client of the API. David L. Parnas referred to this concept as information hiding (Parnas, 1972).

There are two main categories of techniques relating to this goal: physical and logical hiding. Physical hiding means that the private source code is simply not made available to users. Logical hiding entails the use of language features to limit access to certain elements of the API.

2.2.1 Physical Hiding: Declaration versus Definition

In C and C++, the words declaration and definition are precise terms with very specific meanings. A declaration simply introduces a name, and its type, to the compiler without allocating any memory for it. In contrast, a definition provides details of a type's structure or allocates memory in the case of variables. (The term function prototype, as used by C programmers, is equivalent to the term function declaration.) For example, the following are all declarations:

```
extern int i;
class MyClass;
void MyFunc(int value);
```

In contrast, the following are all definitions:

```
int i = 0;

class MyClass
{
public:
    float x, y, z;
};

void MyFunc(int value)
{
    printf("In MyFunc(%d).", value);
}
```

TIP

A declaration introduces the name and type of a symbol to the compiler. A definition provides the full details for that symbol, be it a function body or a region of memory.

In terms of classes and methods, the following code introduces a class definition with a single method declaration:

```
class MyClass
{
public:
    void MyMethod();
};
```

The implementation (body) of a method is provided in its definition:

```
void MyClass::MyMethod()
{
    printf("In MyMethod() of MyClass.\n");
}
```

Generally speaking, you provide declarations in your .h files and associated definitions in your .cpp files. However, it's also possible to provide a definition for a method at the point where you declare it in a .h file, for example,

```
class MyClass
{
public:
    void MyMethod()
    {
        printf("In MyMethod() of MyClass.\n");
    }
};
```

This technique implicitly requests the compiler to inline the MyMethod() member function at all points where it is called. In terms of API design, this is therefore a bad practice because it exposes the code for how the method has been implemented and directly inlines the code into your clients' programs. You should therefore strive to limit your API headers to only provide declarations. Later chapters discuss exceptions to this rule to support templates and conscious acts of inlining.

TIP

Physical hiding means storing internal details in a separate file (.cpp) from the public interface (.h).

Note that I will sometimes inline function implementations like this in the code examples of this book. However, this is done solely for the purposes of clarity and simplicity and should be avoided for any real-world APIs that you develop.

2.2.2 Logical Hiding: Encapsulation

The object-oriented concept of encapsulation provides a mechanism for limiting access to members of an object. In C++ this is implemented using the following access control keywords for classes and structs (classes and structs are functionally equivalent, differing only in their default access level). These access levels are illustrated in Figure 2.3.

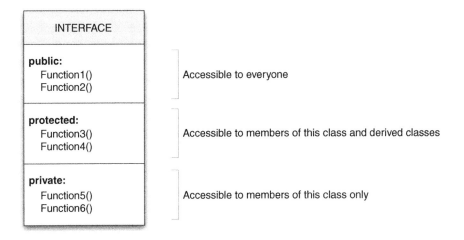

FIGURE 2.3

The three access levels for C++ classes.

- **Public**: Members are accessible outside of the class/struct. This is the default access level for structs.
- **Protected**: Members are accessible within the specific class and any derived classes only.
- **Private**: Members are accessible only within the specific class they are defined within. This is the default access level for classes.

ENCAPSULATION IN OTHER LANGUAGES

While C++ provides the public, protected, and private access controls for your class members, other object-oriented languages provide different levels of granularity. For example, in the Smalltalk language, all instance variables are private and all methods are public, whereas the Java language provides public, private, protected, and package-private levels of visibility.

Package-private in Java means that a member can be accessed only by classes within the same package. This is the default visibility in Java. Package-private is a great way to allow other classes in a JAR file to access internal members without exposing them globally to your clients. For example, it's particularly useful for unit tests that need to verify the behavior of private methods.

C++ does not have the concept of package-private visibility. Instead, it uses the more permissive notion of friendship to allow named classes and functions to access protected and private members of a class. Friendship can be used to enhance encapsulation, but it can also overexpose internal details to your clients if used carelessly.

Most likely, your users will not care about respecting your public API boundary. If you give them hooks into your internal workings that let them achieve what they want, they will use them to get their job done. While this may appear to be good for them, because they were able to find a solution to their immediate problem, it may make it more difficult for you to change those implementation details in the future and so stifle your ability to improve and optimize your product.

TIP

Encapsulation is the process of separating the public interface of an API from its underlying implementation.

As an example of the length some users will go to, the multiplayer first-person shooter game Counter-Strike has been a popular target for exploitation hacks since it appeared in around 2000. One of the most well known of these is the "wallhack." This is essentially a modified OpenGL driver that renders walls partially or fully transparent. This gives players the clear advantage that they can literally see through walls. While you may not be creating a game or targeting gamers as your clients, the moral is that users will do whatever they can to get what they want. If some users modify OpenGL graphics drivers to give them an advantage in a game, there are presumably others who will use your API's exposed internal details so that they can deliver the functionality that their boss has asked for.

To illustrate this with a more directly applicable example, Roland Faber reports some of the difficulties that occurred at Siemens when one group decided to rely upon the internal details of an API from another group in the same company (Faber, 2010):

> A team outside of Europe had to provide a remote control for a user interface implemented in Germany. Because the automation interface was incomplete, they decided to use internal interfaces instead without notifying the architects. The system integration suffered from unexpected problems due to uncoordinated interface changes, and costly refactoring was unavoidable.

The following sections therefore discuss how to use the access control features of your programming language to provide the maximum level of information hiding for your APIs. The later chapter on C++ usage also points out some cases where certain C++ language features can affect encapsulation, such as friends and external linkage.

TIP

Logical hiding means using the C++ language features of protected and private to restrict access to internal details.

2.2.3 Hide Member Variables

The term encapsulation is also often used to describe the bundling of data with the methods that operate on those data. This is implemented in C++ by having classes that can contain both variables and methods. However, in terms of good API design, you should never make member variables public. If data members form part of the logical interface of the API, then you should instead provide getter and/or setter methods that provide indirect access to the member variables. For example, you should avoid writing

```
class Vector3
{
public:
    double x, y, z;
};
```

Instead, you should prefer

```
class Vector3
{
public:
    double GetX() const;
    double GetY() const;
    double GetZ() const;
    void SetX(double val);
    void SetY(double val);
    void SetZ(double val);

private:
    double mX, mY, mZ;
};
```

The latter syntax is obviously more verbose and involves more typing on your part as the programmer, but the extra few minutes spent doing this could save you hours, or even days, further down the line should you decide to change the interface. Some of the additional benefits of using getter/setter routines, rather than exposing member variables directly, include the following.

- **Validation**. You can perform validation on the values to ensure that the internal state of the class is always valid and consistent. For example, if you have a method that lets clients set a new RGB color, you could check that each of the supplied red, green, and blue values are within the valid range, for example, 0 to 255 or 0.0 to 1.0.
- **Lazy evaluation**. Calculating the value of a variable may incur a significant cost, which you would prefer to avoid until necessary. By using a getter method to access the underlying data value, you can defer the costly calculation until the value is actually requested.
- **Caching**. A classic optimization technique is to store the value of a frequently requested calculation and then directly return that value for future requests. For example, a machine's total memory size can be found on Linux by parsing the /proc/meminfo file. Instead of performing a file read for every request to find the total memory size, it would be better to cache the result after the first read and then simply return that cached value for future requests.
- **Extra computation**. If necessary, you can perform additional operations whenever the client tries to access a variable. For example, perhaps you always want to write the current state of a UserPreferences object to a configuration file on disk whenever the user changes the value of a preference setting.
- **Notifications**. Other modules may wish to know when a value has changed in your class. For example, if you are implementing a data model for a progress bar, the user interface code will want to know when the progress value has been updated so that it can update the GUI. You might therefore wish to issue a change notification as part of a setter method.
- **Debugging**. You may want to add debugging or logging statements so that you can track when variables are accessed or changed by clients or you may wish to add assert statements to enforce assumptions.
- **Synchronization**. You may release the first version of your API and then later find that you need to make it thread safe. The standard way to do this is to add mutex locking whenever a value is accessed. This would only be possible if you have wrapped access to the data values in getter/setter methods.

- **Finer access control**. If you make a member variable public, then clients can read and write that value as they wish. However, by using getter/setter methods, you can provide a finer level of read/write control. For example, you can make the value be read-only by not providing a setter method.
- **Maintaining invariant relationships**. Some internal data values may depend on each other. For example, in a car animation system you may calculate the velocity and acceleration of the car based on the time it takes to travel between key frames. You can calculate velocity based on the change in position over time, and acceleration based on the change in velocity over time. However, if a client can access your internal state for this calculation, they could change the acceleration value so that it does not correlate to the car's velocity, thus producing unexpected results.

Furthermore, if the member variables are not actually part of the logical interface—that is, they represent internal details that are not relevant to the public interface—then they should simply be hidden from the interface. For example, consider the following definition for a stack of integers:

```
Class IntegerStack
{
public:
    static const int MAX_SIZE = 100;
    void Push(int val);
    int Pop();
    bool IsEmpty() const;
    int mStack[MAX_SIZE];
    int mCurSize;
};
```

Clearly this is a really bad API because it exposes the way that the stack has been (poorly) implemented as a fixed array of integers and it exposes the internal state of the stack via the mCurSize variable. If at some future date you decided to improve the implementation of this class, for example, by using a std::vector or std::list rather than a fixed-size statically allocated array, then you may find this difficult to do. That's because you have exposed the existence of the mStack and mCurSize variables and so client code could be relying on the ability to access these variables directly. By changing your implementation you could break your clients' code.

Instead, these member variables should be hidden from the start so that client code cannot access them:

```
Class IntegerStack
{
public:
    void Push(int val);
    int Pop();
    bool IsEmpty() const;

private:
    static const int MAX_SIZE = 100;
    int mStack[MAX_SIZE];
    int mCurSize;
};
```

I have stated that member variables should never be public, but can they be declared as protected? If you make a variable protected, then it can be accessed directly by any clients that subclass your class, and then exactly the same arguments apply as for the public case. As such, you should never make your member variables protected either. As Alan Snyder states, inheritance severely compromises the benefits of encapsulation in object-oriented programming languages (Snyder, 1986).

TIP

Data members of a class should always be declared private, never public or protected.

The only semiplausible argument for exposing member variables is for performance reasons. Executing a C++ function call incurs the overhead of pushing the method's parameters and return address onto the call stack, as well as reserving space for any local variables in the routine. Then when the method completes, the call stack has to be unwound again. The cost to perform these actions may be noticeable for performance-critical regions of code, such as within a tight loop performing operations on a large number of objects. Code that directly accesses a public member variable may be two to three times faster than code that has to go through getter/setter methods.

However, even in these cases, you should never expose member variables. First of all, the overhead of a method call will very likely be insignificant for practically all of your API calls. Even if you are writing performance-critical APIs, the careful use of inlining, combined with a modern optimizing compiler, will normally completely eradicate the method call overhead, giving you all the performance benefits of directly exposing member variables. If you're still concerned, try timing your API with inlined getter/setters and then with public member variables. The accompanying source code for this book includes a sample program to do just this. See http://APIBook.com/ to download this code and try it out yourself. I'll also discuss this issue further in the chapter on performance.

2.2.4 Hide Implementation Methods

In addition to hiding all member variables, you should also hide all methods that do not need to be public. This is the principle of information hiding: segregating the stable interface for a class from the internal design decisions used to implement it. Early studies of several large programs found that those using information hiding techniques were four times easier to modify than programs that did not (Korson and Vaishnavi, 1986). While your own mileage may vary, it should be clear that hiding the internal details of your API will make for more maintainable and evolvable software.

The key point to remember is that a class should define what to do, not how it is done. For example, let's consider a class that lets you download a file from a remote http server:

```
#include <string>
#include <cstddef>
#include <sys/socket.h>
#include <unistd.h>

class URLDownloader
{
public:
    URLDownloader();
```

```
    bool DownloadToFile(const std::string &url,
                        const std::string &localFile);
    bool SocketConnect(const std::string &host, int port);
    void SocketDisconnect();
    bool IsSocketConnected() const;
    int GetSocket() const;
    bool SocketWrite(const char *buffer, size_t bytes);
    size_t SocketRead(char *buffer, size_t bytes);
    bool WriteBufferToFile(char *buffer,
                           const std::string &filename);

private:
    int mSocketID;
    struct sockaddr_in mServAddr;
    bool mIsConnected;
};
```

All of the member variables have been correctly declared as private, which is a good start. However, several implementation-specific methods have been exposed, such as routines to open and read data from a socket and a routine to write the resulting in-memory buffer to a file on disk. The client doesn't need to know any of this. All the client wants to do is specify a URL and then magically have a file created on disk with the contents of that remote location.

There is also a particularly egregious method in there: GetSocket(). This is a public method that returns access to a private member variable. By calling this method, a client can get the underlying socket handle and could directly manipulate that socket without the knowledge of the URLDownloader class. What is particularly disturbing is that GetSocket() is declared as a const method, meaning that it does not modify the state of the class. While this is strictly true, the client could then use the returned integer socket handle to modify the state of the class. The same kind of leaking of internal state can happen if you return a non-const pointer or reference to one of your private member variables (Meyers, 2005). Doing so gives your clients a handle on your internal data members and therefore lets them modify the state of your objects without going through your API.

TIP
_____

Never return non-const pointers or references to private data members. This breaks encapsulation.

Obviously a better design for our URLDownloader class would be to make every method private, except for the constructor and the DownloadToFile() method. Everything else is implementation detail. You are then free to change the implementation without affecting any clients of the class.

There is still something very unsatisfying about this situation though. I have hidden the implementation details from the compiler's point of view, but a person can still look at the header file and see all of the internal details for your class. In fact, this is very likely because you must distribute the header file to allow clients to compile their code against your API. Also, you must #include all header files needed for the private members of your class, even though they are not dependencies of the public interface. For example, the URLDownloader header needs to #include all of the platform-specific socket headers.

This is an unfortunate limitation of the C++ language: all public, protected, and private members of a class must appear in the declaration for that class. Ideally, the header for our class would look like

```
#include <string>

class URLDownloader
{
public:
    URLDownloader();
    bool DownloadToFile(const std::string &url,
                        const std::string &localFile);
};
```

Then all of the private members could be declared somewhere else, such as in the `.cpp` file. However, this is not possible with C++ (the reason is so that the size of all objects can be known at compile time). Nevertheless, there are still ways to hide private members from your public header files (Headington, 1995). One popular technique is called the Pimpl idiom. This involves isolating all of a class's private data members inside of a separate implementation class or struct in the `.cpp` file. The `.h` file then only needs to contain an opaque pointer to this implementation class. I'll discuss this extremely valuable technique in more detail in the patterns chapter, coming up next.

I strongly urge that you adopt the Pimpl idiom in your APIs so that all implementation details can be completely hidden from your public header files. However, if you decide against this direction, you should at least attempt to remove private methods from the header when they are not necessary by moving them to the `.cpp` file and converting them to static functions (Lakos, 1996). This can be done when the private method only accesses public members of the class or if it accesses no members of the class at all (such as a routine that accepts a filename string and returns the extension for that filename). Many engineers feel that just because a class uses a private method that it must be included in the class declaration. However, this simply exposes more implementation details than necessary.

TIP

Prefer declaring private functionality as static functions within the .cpp file rather than exposing them in public headers as private methods. (Using the Pimpl idiom is even better though.)

2.2.5 Hide Implementation Classes

In addition to hiding the internal methods and variables for your classes, you should also endeavor to hide any actual classes that are purely implementation detail. Most programmers are used to hiding methods and variables, although many forget to also consider that not all classes are public. Indeed, some classes are only needed for your implementation and should not be revealed as part of the public interface of your API.

For example, consider a simple `Fireworks` class: an interface that lets you specify the location of a fireworks animation on the screen and lets you control the color, speed, and number of fire particles. Clearly the API will need to keep track of each particle of the firework effect so that it can update each particle's position per frame. This implies that a `FireParticle` class should be introduced to contain the state for a single fire particle. However, clients of the API never need to access this class; it's purely required for the API's implementation. This class could therefore be made private, by nesting it in the `Fireworks` class within a private section.

```
#include <vector>

class Fireworks
{
public:
    Fireworks();

    void SetOrigin(double x, double y);
    void SetColor(float r, float g, float b);
    void SetGravity(float g);
    void SetSpeed(float s);
    void SetNumberOfParticles(int num);

    void Start();
    void Stop();
    void NextFrame(float dt);

private:
    class FireParticle
    {
    public:
        double mX, mY;
        double mVelocityX, mVelocityY;
        double mAccelerationX, mAccelerationY;
        double mLifeTime;
    };

    double mOriginX, mOriginY;
    float mRed, mGreen, mBlue;
    float mGravity;
    float mSpeed;
    bool mIsActive;
    std::vector<FireParticle *> mParticles;
};
```

Note that I do not use getter/setter methods for the FireParticle class. You could certainly do so if you wanted to, but it's not strictly necessary because the class is not accessible from the public interface. Some engineers also prefer to use a struct instead of a class in cases such as these, to reflect that the structure is a Plain Old Data (POD) type.

Again, you could also attempt to hide the contents of the FireParticle class from even appearing in the header file so that it is even hidden from casual inspection of the header file. I will discuss how to do this in the next chapter.

2.3 MINIMALLY COMPLETE

A good API should be minimally complete. That is, it should be as small as possible, but no smaller.

It is perhaps obvious that an API should be complete: that it provides clients with all the functionality they need, although it may be less obvious what that functionality actually is. To answer this question you should perform requirements gathering and use case modeling early on so that you understand what the API is expected to do. You can then assert that it actually delivers on those expectations. I will talk more about requirements and use cases in the chapter on design.

Less obvious is the apparent contradiction for an API to be minimal. However, this is one of the most important qualities that you can plan for, and one that has a massive impact on the long-term maintenance and evolution of your API. In a very real sense, the decisions that you make today will constrain what you can do tomorrow. It also has a large impact on the ease of use of the API because a compact interface is one that can easily fit inside the head of your users (Blanchette, 2008). I will therefore dedicate the following sections to discuss various techniques to keep your API minimal, and why this is a good thing.

TIP

Remember Occam's razor: "pluralitas non-est ponenda sine necessitate" (plurality should not be posited without necessity).

2.3.1 Don't Overpromise

Every public element in your API is a promise—a promise that you will support that functionality for the lifetime of the API. You can break that promise, but doing so may frustrate your clients and cause them to rewrite their code. Even worse, they may decide to abandon your API because they have grown weary of continually having to fix up their code because you can't keep your API stable or they may simply not be able to use your API anymore because you have removed functionality that supported their unique use case.

The key point is that once you release an API and have clients using it, adding new functionality is easy, but removing functionality is really difficult. The best advice then is: when in doubt, leave it out (Bloch, 2008; Tulach, 2008).

This advice can be counter to the best intentions of the API designer. As an engineer, you want to provide a flexible and general solution to the problem you are solving. There is a temptation to add extra levels of abstraction or generality to an API because you think it might be useful in the future. You should resist this temptation for the following reasons.

1. The day may never come when you need the extra generality.
2. If that day does come, you may have more knowledge about the use of your API and a different solution may present itself from the one you envisioned originally.
3. If you do need to add the extra functionality, it will be easier to add it to a simple API than a complex one.

As a result, you should try to keep your APIs as simple as you can: minimize the number of classes you expose and the number of public members in those classes. As a bonus, this will also make your API easier to understand, easier for your users to keep a mental model of the API in their heads, and easier for you to debug.

TIP

When in doubt, leave it out! Minimize the number of public classes and functions in your API.

2.3.2 Add Virtual Functions Judiciously

One subtle way that you can expose more functionality than you intended is through inheritance, that is, by making certain member functions virtual. Doing so allows your clients to subclass your class and reimplement any virtual methods. While this can be very powerful, you should be aware of the potential pitfalls.

- You can implement seemingly innocuous changes to your base classes that have a detrimental impact on your clients. This can happen because you evolve the base class in isolation, without knowing all the ways that your clients have built upon your virtual API. This is often referred to as the "fragile base class problem" (Blanchette, 2008).
- Your clients may use your API in ways that you never intended or imagined. This can result in the call graph for your API executing code that you do not control and that may produce unexpected behavior. As an extreme example, there is nothing to stop a client calling `delete this` in an overridden method. This may even be a valid thing to want to do, but if you did not design your implementation to allow this, then your code will very likely crash.
- Clients may extend your API in incorrect or error-prone ways. For example, you may have a thread-safe API but, depending on your design, a client could override a virtual function and provide an implementation without performing the appropriate mutex locking operations, opening up the potential for difficult-to-debug race conditions.
- Overridden functions may break the internal integrity of your class. For example, the default implementation of a virtual method may call other methods in the same class to update its internal state. If an overridden method does not perform these same calls, then the object could be left in an inconsistent state and behave unexpectedly or crash.

In addition to these API-level behavioral concerns, there are standard concerns that you should be aware of when using virtual functions in C++:

- Virtual function calls must be resolved at run time by performing a vtable lookup, whereas non-virtual function calls can be resolved at compile time. This can make virtual function calls slower than non-virtual calls. In reality, this overhead may be negligible, particularly if your function does non-trivial work or if it is not called frequently.
- The use of virtual functions increases the size of an object, typically by the size of a pointer to the vtable. This may be an issue if you wish to create a small object that requires a very large number of instances. Again, in practice this will likely be insignificant when compared to the amount of memory consumed by your various member variables.
- Adding, reordering, or removing a virtual function will break binary compatibility. This is because a virtual function call is typically represented as an integer offset into the vtable for the class. Therefore, changing its order or causing the order of any other virtual functions to change means that existing code will need to be recompiled to ensure that it still calls the right functions.
- Virtual functions cannot always be inlined. You may reasonably think that it does not make sense to declare a virtual as inline at all because virtual functions are resolved at run time, whereas inlining is a compile-time optimization. However, there are certain constrained situations where a compiler can inline a virtual function. All the same, these are far fewer than the cases where a non-virtual function can be inlined. (Remember that the `inline` keyword in C++ is merely a hint to the compiler.)

- Overloading is tricky with virtual functions. A symbol declared in a derived class will hide all symbols with the same name in the base class. Therefore, a set of overloaded virtual functions in a base class will be hidden by a single overriding function in a subclass. There are ways to get around this (Dewhurst, 2002), but it's better to simply avoid overloading virtual functions.

Ultimately, you should only allow overriding if you explicitly intend for this to be possible. A class with no virtual functions tends to be more robust and requires less maintenance than one with virtual functions. As a general rule of thumb, if your API does not call a particular method internally, then that method probably should not be virtual. You should also only allow subclassing in situations where it makes sense: where the potential subclasses form an "is-a" relationship with the base class.

In fact, Herb Sutter states that you should prefer to make virtual functions private and only consider making them protected if derived classes need to invoke the virtual function's base implementation (Sutter, 2001). As a result, Sutter suggests that interfaces should be non-virtual and they should use the Template Method design pattern where appropriate. This is often referred to as the Non-Virtual Interface idiom (NVI).

If you still decide that you want to allow subclassing, make sure that you design your API to allow it safely. Remember the following rules:

1. Always declare your destructor to be virtual if there are any virtual functions in your class. This is so that subclasses can free any extra resources that they may have allocated.
2. Always document how methods of your class call each other. If a client wants to provide an alternative implementation for a virtual function, they will need to know which other methods need to be called within their implementation in order to preserve the internal integrity of the object.
3. Never call virtual functions from your constructor or destructor. These calls will never be directed to a subclass (Meyers, 2005). This does not affect the appearance of your API, but it's a good rule to know all the same.

TIP

Avoid declaring functions as overridable (virtual) until you have a valid and compelling need to do so.

2.3.3 Convenience APIs

Keeping an API as small as possible can be a difficult task. There is a natural tension between reducing the number of functions in your API while also making the API easy to use for a range of clients. This is an issue that most API designers face: whether to keep the API pure and focused or whether to allow convenience wrappers. (By the term convenience wrappers, I mean utility routines that encapsulate multiple API calls to provide simpler higher-level operations.)

On the one hand, there is the argument that an API should only provide one way to perform one task. This ensures that the API is minimal, singularly focused, consistent, and easy to understand. It also reduces the complexity of the implementation, with all of the associated benefits of greater stability and easier debugging and maintenance. Grady Booch refers to this as primitiveness, that is, the quality that a method needs access to the internal details of a class in order to be implemented efficiently, as opposed to non-primitive methods that can be entirely built on top of primitive ones, without access to any internal state (Booch et al., 2007).

On the other hand, there is also the argument that an API should make simple things easy to do. Clients should not be required to write lots of code to perform basic tasks. Doing so can give rise to blocks of boilerplate code that get copied and pasted to other parts of the source code; whenever blocks of code are copied there is the potential for code divergence and bugs. Also, you may wish to target your API to a range of clients, from those who want lots of control and flexibility to those who just want to perform a single task as simply as possible.

Both of these goals are useful and desirable. Fortunately, they do not need to be mutually exclusive. There are several ways you can provide higher-level convenience wrappers for your core API's functionality without diluting its primary purpose. The important point is that you do not mix your convenience API in the same classes as your core API. Instead, you can produce supplementary classes that wrap certain public functionality of your core API. These convenience classes should be fully isolated from your core API, for example, in different source files or even completely separate libraries. This has the additional benefit of ensuring that your convenience API depends only on the public interface of your core API, not on any internal methods or classes. Let's look at a real-world example of this.

The OpenGL API provides platform-independent routines for writing 2D and 3D applications. It operates on the level of simple primitives—such as points, lines, and polygons—that are transformed, lit, and rasterized into a frame buffer. The OpenGL API is extremely powerful, but it is also aimed at a very low level. For example, creating a sphere in OpenGL would involve modeling it explicitly as a surface of small flat polygons, as demonstrated in the following code snippet.

```
for (int i = 0; i <= stacks; ++i)
{
    GLfloat stack0 = ((i - 1.0) / stacks - 0.5) * M_PI;
    GLfloat stack1 = ((GLfloat) i / stacks - 0.5) * M_PI;
    GLfloat z0 = sin(stack0);
    GLfloat z1 = sin(stack1);
    GLfloat r0 = cos(stack0);
    GLfloat r1 = cos(stack1);

    glBegin(GL_QUAD_STRIP);
    for (int j = 0; j <= slices; ++j)
    {
        GLfloat slice = (j - 1.0) * 2 * M_PI / slices;
        GLfloat x = cos(slice);
        GLfloat y = sin(slice);
        glNormal3f(x * r0, y * r0, z0);
        glVertex3f(x * r0, y * r0, z0);
        glNormal3f(x * r1, y * r1, z1);
        glVertex3f(x * r1, y * r1, z1);
    }
    glEnd();
}
```

However, most OpenGL implementations also include the OpenGL Utility Library, or GLU. This is an API built on top of the OpenGL API that provides higher-level functions, such as mip-map generation, coordinate conversions, quadric surfaces, polygon tessellation, and simple camera positioning. These functions are defined in a completely separate library to the OpenGL library, and the functions all begin with the `glu` prefix to differentiate them from the core OpenGL API. For example, the following code snippet shows how easy it is to create a sphere using GLU.

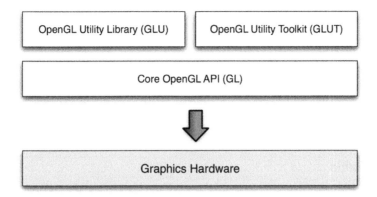

FIGURE 2.4

An example of a core API (OpenGL) separated from convenience APIs layered on top of it (GLU and GLUT).

```
GLUquadric *qobj = gluNewQuadric();
gluSphere(qobj, radius, slices, stacks);
gluDeleteQuadric(qobj);
```

This is a great example of how to maintain the minimal design and focus of a core API while also providing additional convenience routines that make it easier to use that API. In fact, other APIs built on top of OpenGL provide further utility classes, such as Mark Kilgard's OpenGL Utility Toolkit (GLUT). This API offers routines to create various solid and wireframe geometric primitives (including the Utah teapot), as well as simple window management functions and event processing. Figure 2.4 shows the relationship among GL, GLU, and GLUT.

Ken Arnold refers to this concept as progressive disclosure, meaning that your API should present the basic functionality via an easy-to-use interface while reserving advanced functionality for a separate layer (Arnold, 2005). He notes that this concept is often seen in GUI designs in the form of an Advanced or Export button that discloses further complexity. In this way, you can still provide a powerful API while ensuring that the expert use cases don't obfuscate the basic workflows.

TIP

Add convenience APIs as separate modules or libraries that sit on top of your minimal core API.

2.4 EASY TO USE

A well-designed API should make simple tasks easy and obvious. For example, it should be possible for a client to look at the method signatures of your API and be able to glean how to use it, without any additional documentation. This API quality follows closely from the quality of minimalism: if your API is simple, it should be easy to understand. Similarly, it should follow the rule of least surprise. This is done by employing existing models and patterns so that the user can focus on the task at hand rather than being distracted by the novelty or involution of your interface (Raymond, 2003).

Of course, this is not an excuse for you to ignore the need for good supporting documentation. In fact, it should make the task of writing documentation much easier. As we all know, a good example can go a long way. Providing sample code can greatly aid the ease of use of your API. Good developers should be able to read example code written using your API and understand how to apply it to their own tasks.

The following sections discuss various aspects and techniques to make your API easier to understand and ultimately easier to use. Before I do so though, it should be noted that an API may provide additional complex functionality for expert users that is not so easy to use. However, this should not be done at the expense of keeping the simple case easy.

2.4.1 Discoverable

A discoverable API is one where users are able to work out how to use the API on their own, without any accompanying explanation or documentation. To illustrate this with a counterexample from the field of UI design, the Start button in Windows XP does not provide a very discoverable interface for locating the option to shut down the computer. Likewise, the Restart option is accessed rather unintuitively by clicking on the Turn Off Computer button.

Discoverability does not necessarily lead to ease of use. For example, it's possible for an API to be easy for a first-time user to learn but cumbersome for an expert user to use on a regular basis. However, in general, discoverability should help you produce a more usable interface.

There are a number of ways in which you can promote discoverability when you design your APIs. Devising an intuitive and logical object model is one important way, as is choosing good names for your classes and functions. Indeed, coming up with clear, descriptive, and appropriate names can be one of the most difficult tasks in API design. I present specific recommendations for class and function names in Chapter 4 when I discuss API design techniques. Avoiding the use of abbreviations can also play a factor in discoverability (Blanchette, 2008) so that users don't have to remember if your API uses `GetCurrentValue()`, `GetCurrValue()`, `GetCurValue()`, or `GetCurVal()`.

2.4.2 Difficult to Misuse

A good API, in addition to being easy to use, should also be difficult to misuse. Scott Meyers suggests that this is the most important general interface design guideline (Meyers, 2004). Some of the most common ways to misuse an API include passing the wrong arguments to a method or passing illegal values to a method. These can happen when you have multiple arguments of the same type and the user forgets the correct order of the arguments or where you use an `int` to represent a small range of values instead of a more constrained `enum` type (Bloch, 2008). For example, consider the following method signature:

```
std::string FindString(const std::string &text,
                       bool search_forward,
                       bool case_sensitive);
```

It would be easy for users to forget whether the first `bool` argument is the search direction or the case sensitivity flag. Passing the flags in the wrong order would result in unexpected behavior and probably cause the user to waste a few minutes debugging the problem, until they realized that they had transposed the `bool` arguments. However, you could design the method so that the compiler catches this kind of error for them by introducing a new `enum` type for each option. For example,

```
enum SearchDirection {
    FORWARD,
    BACKWARD
};
enum CaseSensitivity {
    CASE_SENSITIVE,
    CASE_INSENSITIVE
};
std::string FindString(const std::string &text,
                       SearchDirection direction,
                       CaseSensitivity case_sensitivity);
```

Not only does this mean that users cannot mix up the order of the two flags, because it would generate a compilation error, but also the code they have to write is now more self-descriptive. Compare

```
result = FindString(text, true, false);
```

with

```
result = FindString(text, FORWARD, CASE_INSENSITIVE);
```

TIP

Prefer enums to booleans to improve code readability.

For more complex cases where an enum is insufficient, you could even introduce new classes to ensure that each argument has a unique type. For example, Scott Meyers illustrates this approach with use of a Date class that is constructed by specifying three integers (Meyers, 2004, 2005):

```
class Date
{
public:
    Date(int year, int month, int day);
    ...
};
```

Meyers notes that in this design clients could pass the year, month, and day values in the wrong order, and they could also specify illegal values, such as a month of 13. To get around these problems, he suggests the introduction of specific classes to represent a year, month, and day value, such as

```
class Year
{
public:
    explicit Year(int y) : mYear(y) {}
    int GetYear() const { return mYear; }

private:
    int mYear;
};
```

```
class Month
{
public:
    explicit Month(int m) : mMonth(m) {}
    int GetMonth() const { return mMonth; }
    static Month Jan() { return Month(1); }
    static Month Feb() { return Month(2); }
    static Month Mar() { return Month(3); }
    static Month Apr() { return Month(4); }
    static Month May() { return Month(5); }
    static Month Jun() { return Month(6); }
    static Month Jul() { return Month(7); }
    static Month Aug() { return Month(8); }
    static Month Sep() { return Month(9); }
    static Month Oct() { return Month(10); }
    static Month Nov() { return Month(11); }
    static Month Dec() { return Month(12); }

private:
    int mMonth;
};

class Day
{
public:
    explicit Day(int d) : mDay(d) {}
    int GetDay() const { return mDay; }

private:
    int mDay;
};
```

Now, the constructor for the `Date` class can be expressed in terms of these new `Year`, `Month`, and `Day` classes:

```
class Date
{
public:
    Date(const Year &y, const Month &m, const Day &d);
    ...
};
```

Using this design, clients can create a new `Date` object with the following unambiguous and easy-to-understand syntax. Also, any attempts to specify the values in a different order will result in a compile-time error.

```
Date birthday(Year(1976), Month::Jul(), Day(7));
```

TIP

Avoid functions with multiple parameters of the same type.

2.4.3 **Consistent**

A good API should apply a consistent design approach so that its conventions are easy to remember, and therefore easy to adopt (Blanchette, 2008). This applies to all aspects of API design, such as naming conventions, parameter order, the use of standard patterns, memory model semantics, the use of exceptions, error handling, and so on.

In terms of the first of these, consistent naming conventions imply reuse of the same words for the same concepts across the API. For example, if you have decided to use the verb pairs Begin and End, you should not mingle the terms Start and Finish. As another example, the Qt3 API mixes the use of abbreviations in several of its method names, such as prevValue() and previousSibling(). This is another example of why the use of abbreviations should be avoided at all costs.

The use of consistent method signatures is an equally critical design quality. If you have several methods that accept similar argument lists, you should endeavor to keep a consistent number and order for those arguments. To give a counterexample, I refer you to the following functions from the standard C library:

```
void bcopy(const void *s1, void *s2, size_t n);
char *strncpy(char *restrict s1, const char *restrict s2, size_t n);
```

Both of these functions involve copying n bytes of data from one area of memory to another. However, the bcopy() function copies data from s1 into s2, whereas strncpy() copies from s2 into s1. This can give rise to subtle memory errors if a developer were to decide to switch usage between the two functions without a close reading of the respective man pages. To be sure, there is a clue to the conflicting specifications in the function signatures: note the use of the const pointer in each case. However, this could be missed easily and won't be caught by a compiler if the source pointer is not declared to be const.

Note also the inconsistent use of the words "copy" and "cpy."

Let's take another example from the standard C library. The familiar malloc() function is used to allocate a contiguous block of memory, and the calloc() function performs the same operation with the addition that it initializes the reserved memory with zero bytes. However, despite their similar purpose, they have different function signatures:

```
void *calloc(size_t count, size_t size);
void *malloc(size_t size);
```

The malloc() function accepts a size in terms of bytes, whereas calloc() allocates (count * size) bytes. In addition to being inconsistent, this violates the principle of least surprise. As a further example, the read() and write() standard C functions accept a file descriptor as their first parameter, whereas the fgets() and fputs() functions require the file descriptor to be specified last (Henning, 2009).

TIP

Use consistent function naming and parameter ordering.

These examples have been focused on a function or method level, but of course consistency is important at a class level, too. Classes that have similar roles should offer a similar interface.

The STL is a great example of this. The std::vector, std::set, std::map, and even std::string classes all offer a size() method to return the number of elements in the container. Because they also all support the use of iterators, once you know how to iterate through a std::set you can apply the same knowledge to a std::map. This makes it easier to memorize the programming patterns of the API.

You get this kind of consistency for free through polymorphism: by placing the shared functionality into a common base class. However, often it doesn't make sense for all your classes to inherit from a common base class, and you shouldn't introduce a base class purely for this purpose, as it increases the complexity and class count for your interface. Indeed, it's noteworthy that the STL container classes do not inherit from a common base class. Instead, you should explicitly design for this by manually identifying the common concepts across your classes and using the same conventions to represent these concepts in each class. This is often referred to as static polymorphism.

You can also make use of C++ templates to help you define and apply this kind of consistency. For example, you could create a template for a 2D coordinate class and specialize it for integers, floats, and doubles. In this way you are assured that each type of coordinate offers exactly the same interface. The following code sample offers a simple example of this:

```cpp
template <typename T>
class Coord2D
{
public:
    Coord2D(T x, T y) : mX(x), mY(y) {};

    T GetX() const { return mX; }
    T GetY() const { return mY; }

    void SetX(T x) { mX = x; }
    void SetY(T y) { mY = y; }

    void Add(T dx, T dy) { mX += dx; mY += dy; }
    void Multiply(T dx, T dy) { mX *= dx; mY *= dy; }

private:
    T mX;
    T mY;
};
```

With this template definition, you can create variables of type Coord2D<int>, Coord2D<float>, and Coord2D<double> and all of these will have exactly the same interface.

A further aspect of consistency is the use of familiar patterns and standard platform idioms. When you buy a new car, you don't have to relearn how to drive. The concept of using brake and accelerator pedals, a steering wheel, and a gear stick (be it manual or automatic) is universal the world over. If you can drive one car, it's very likely that you can drive a similar one, even though the two cars may be different makes, models, or have the steering wheel on different sides.

Likewise, the easiest APIs to use are those that require minimal new learning for your users. For example, most C++ developers are familiar with the STL and its use of container classes and itera- tors. Therefore, if you decide to write an API with a similar purpose, it would be advantageous to mimic the patterns of the STL because other developers will then find the use of your API to be familiar and easy to adopt.

2.4.4 Orthogonal

In mathematics, two vectors are said to be orthogonal if they are perpendicular (at 90 degrees) to each other, that is, their inner product is zero. This makes them linearly independent, meaning that no set of scalars can be applied to the first vector to produce the second vector. To take a geographic analogy, the perpendicular directions east and north are independent of each other: no amount of walking east will take you north. Said in slightly more computer lingo, changes to your east coor- dinate have no effect on your north coordinate.

In terms of API design, orthogonality means that methods do not have side effects. Calling a method that sets a particular property should change only that property and not additionally change other publicly accessible properties. As a result, making a change to the implementation of one part of the API should have no effect on other parts of the API (Raymond, 2003). Striving for orthogonality produces APIs with behaviors that are more predictable and comprehensible. Further- more, code that does not create side effects, or relies on the side effects of other code, is much easier to develop, test, debug, and change because its effects are more localized and bounded (Hunt and Thomas, 1999).

TIP

An orthogonal API means that functions do not have side effects.

Let's look at a specific example. Perhaps you have stayed in a motel where the controls of the shower are very unintuitive. You want to be able to set the power and the temperature of the water, but instead you have a single control that seems to affect both properties in a complex and non- obvious way. This could be modeled using the following API:

```
class CheapMotelShower
{
public:
    float GetTemperature() const; // units = Fahrenheit
    float GetPower() const; // units = percent, 0..100
    void SetPower(float p);

private:
    float mTemperature;
    float mPower;
};
```

Just to illustrate this further, let's consider the following implementation for the public methods of this class.

```
float CheapMotelShower::GetTemperature() const
{
    return mTemperature;
}

float CheapMotelShower::GetPower() const
{
    return mPower;
}

void CheapMotelShower::SetPower(float p)
{
    if (p < 0) p = 0;
    if (p > 100) p = 100;
    mPower = p;
    mTemperature = 42.0f + sin(p/38.0f) * 45.0f;
}
```

In this case you can see that setting the power of the water flow also affects the temperature of the water via a non-linear relationship. As a result, it's not possible to achieve certain combinations of temperature and power, and naturally the preferred combination of hot water and full power is unattainable. Also, if you were to change the implementation of the `SetPower()` method, it would have the side effect of affecting the result of the `GetTemperature()` method. In a more complex system, this interdependence may be something that we as programmers forget about, or are simply unaware of, and so a simple change to one area of code may have a profound impact on the behavior of other parts of the system.

Instead, let's consider an ideal, orthogonal, interface for a shower, where the controls for temperature and power are independent:

```
class IdealShower
{
public:
    float GetTemperature() const; // units = Fahrenheit
    float GetPower() const; // units = percent, 0..100
    void SetTemperature(float t);
    void SetPower(float p);

private:
    float mTemperature;
    float mPower;
};

float IdealShower::GetTemperature() const
{
```

```
    return mTemperature;
}

float IdealShower::GetPower() const
{
    return mPower;
}

void IdealShower::SetTemperature(float t)
{
    if (t < 42) t = 42;
    if (t > 85) t = 85;
    mTemperature = t;
}

void IdealShower::SetPower(float p)
{
    if (p < 0) p = 0;
    if (p > 100) p = 100;
    mPower = p;
}
```

Two important factors to remember for designing orthogonal APIs are as follow.

1. **Reduce redundancy**. Ensure that the same information is not represented in more than one way. There should be a single authoritative source for each piece of knowledge.
2. **Increase independence**. Ensure that there is no overlapping of meaning in the concepts that are exposed. Any overlapping concepts should be decomposed into their basal components.

Another popular interpretation of orthogonal design is that different operations can all be applied to each available data type. This is a definition that is commonly used in the fields of programming language and CPU design. In the latter case, an orthogonal instruction set is one in which instructions can use any CPU register in any addressing mode, as opposed to a non-orthogonal design where certain instructions could only use certain registers. Again, in terms of API design, the STL provides an excellent example of this. It offers a collection of generic algorithms and iterators that can be used on any container. For example, the STL `std::count` algorithm can be applied to any of the `std::vector`, `std::set`, or `std::map` containers. Hence the choice of algorithm is not dependent on the container class being used.

2.4.5 **Robust Resource Allocation**

One of the trickiest aspects of programming in C++ is memory management. This is particularly so for developers who are used to managed languages such as Java or C#, where objects are freed automatically by a garbage collector. In contrast, most C++ bugs arise from some kind of misuse of pointers or references, such as

- **Null dereferencing**: trying to use `->` or `*` operators on a NULL pointer.
- **Double freeing**: calling `delete` or `free()` on a block of memory twice.

- **Accessing invalid memory**: trying to use `->` or `*` operators on a pointer that has not been allocated yet or that has been freed already.
- **Mixing allocators**: using `delete` to free memory that was allocated with `malloc()` or using `free()` to return memory allocated with `new`.
- **Incorrect array deallocation**: using the `delete` operator instead of `delete []` to free an array.
- **Memory leaks**: not freeing a block of memory when you are finished with it.

These problems arise because it's not possible to tell whether a plain C++ pointer is referencing valid memory or if it is pointing to unallocated or freed memory. It is therefore reliant upon the programmer to track this state and ensure that the pointer is never dereferenced incorrectly. However, as we know, programmers are fallible. Nevertheless these particular kinds of problems can be avoided through the use of managed (or smart) pointers, such as the following:

1. **Shared pointers**. These are reference-counted pointers where the reference count can be incremented by one when a piece of code wants to hold onto the pointer and decremented by one when it is finished using the pointer. When the reference count reaches zero, the object pointed to by the pointer is automatically freed. This kind of pointer can help avoid the problems of accessing freed memory by ensuring that the pointer remains valid for the period that you wish to use it.
2. **Weak pointers**. A weak pointer contains a pointer to an object, normally a shared pointer, but does not contribute to the reference count for that object. If you have a shared pointer and a weak pointer referencing the same object, and the shared pointer is destroyed, the weak pointer immediately becomes NULL. In this way, weak pointers can detect whether the object being pointed to has expired: if the reference count for the object it is pointing to is zero. This helps avoid the dangling pointer problem where you can have a pointer that is referencing freed memory.
3. **Scoped pointers**. These pointers support ownership of single objects and automatically deallocate their objects when the pointer goes out of scope. They are sometimes also called auto pointers. Scoped pointers are defined as owning a single object and as such cannot be copied.

These smart pointers are not part of the original C++98 specification. However, they are included in the new C++11 standard as `std::shared_ptr`, `std::weak_ptr`, and `std::unique_ptr`, respectively. They were also included in Technical Report 1 (TR1), which was a precursor to the official C++11 specification. Some older compilers may therefore still provide the TR1 implementations in the `std::tr1` namespace. The Boost libraries also provide an implementation of these smart pointers, including `boost::shared_ptr`, `boost::weak_ptr`, and `boost::scoped_ptr`, respectively.

Use of these smart pointers can make your API much easier to use and less prone to the kind of memory errors listed previously. For instance, use of `std::shared_ptr` can alleviate the need for users to free a dynamically created object explicitly. Instead, the object will automatically be deleted when it is no longer referenced. For example, consider an API that allows you to create instances of an object via a factory method called `CreateInstance()`:

```
#include <memory>

typedef std::shared_ptr<class MyObject> MyObjectPtr;

class MyObject
{
public:
```

```
    static MyObjectPtr CreateInstance();
    ~MyObject();

private:
    MyObject(); // must use factory method to create instance
};
```

Where the implementation of the factory method looks like

```
MyObjectPtr MyObject::CreateInstance()
{
    return MyObjectPtr(new MyObject());
}
```

Given this API, a client could create instances of MyObject as follows:

```
int main(int argc, char *argv[])
{
    MyObjectPtr ptr(MyObject::CreateInstance());
    ptr = MyObject::CreateInstance();
    return 0;
}
```

In this example, two instances of MyObject are created, and both of these instances are destroyed by the end of the program: the first instance is destroyed on the assignment operator and the second instance is destroyed when ptr goes out of scope. If instead the CreateInstance() method simply returned a MyObject * type, then the destructor would never get called in this example. The use of smart pointers can therefore make memory management simpler, and hence make your API easier for clients to use.

In general, if you have a function that returns a pointer that your clients should delete or if you expect the client to need the pointer for longer than the life of your object, then you should return it using a smart pointer, such as a std::shared_ptr. However, if ownership of the pointer will be retained by your API, then you can return a standard pointer. For example,

```
// ownership of MyObject* is transferred to the caller
std::shared_ptr<MyObject> GetObject() const;

// ownership of MyObject* is retained by the API
MyObject* GetObject() const;
```

TIP

Return a dynamically allocated object using a smart pointer if the client is responsible for deallocating it.

It's worth noting that these kinds of memory management issues are simply a specific case of the more general category of resource management. For instance, similar types of problems can be encountered with the manipulation of mutex locks or file handles. The concepts of smart pointers can be generalized to the task of resource management with the following observation: resource allocation is object construction and resource deallocation is object destruction. This is often referred to with the acronym RAII, which stands for Resource Acquisition Is Initialization.

As an example, examine the following code that illustrates a classic synchronization bug:

```
void SetName(const std::string &name)
{
    mMutex.lock();

    if (name.empty()) {
        return;
    }
    mName = name;

    mMutex.unlock();
}
```

Obviously, this code will fail to unlock the mutex if an empty string is passed into the method. As a result, the program will deadlock on the next attempt to call the method because the mutex will still be locked. However, you could create a class called ScopedMutex, whose constructor locks the mutex and whose destructor unlocks it again. With such a class, you could rewrite the aforementioned method as follows:

```
void SetName(const std::string &name)
{
    ScopedMutex locker(mMutex);

    if (name.empty())
        return;

    mName = name;
}
```

Now you can be assured that the lock will be released whenever the method returns because the mutex will be unlocked whenever the ScopedMutex variable goes out of scope. As a result, you do not need to meticulously check every return statement to ensure that they've explicitly freed the lock. As a bonus, the code is also much more readable.

The take-home point in terms of API design is that if your API provides access to the allocation and deallocation of some resource, then you should consider providing a class to manage this, where resource allocation happens in the constructor and deallocation happens in the destructor (and perhaps additionally through a public Release() method so that clients have more control over when the resource is freed).

TIP

Think of resource allocation and deallocation as object construction and destruction.

2.4.6 **Platform Independent**

A well-designed C++ API should always avoid platform-specific #if/#ifdef lines in its public headers. If your API presents a high-level and logical model for your problem domain, as it should, there are very few cases where the API should be different for different platforms. About the only cases where this may be appropriate are when you are writing an API to interface with a platform-specific resource, such as a routine that draws in a window and requires the appropriate window handle to be passed in for the native operating system. Barring these kinds of situations, you should never write public header files with platform-specific #ifdef lines.

For example, let's take the case of an API that encapsulates the functionality offered by a mobile phone. Some mobile phones offer built-in GPS devices that can deliver the geographic location of the phone, but not all devices offer this capability. However, you should never expose this situation directly through your API, such as in the following example:

```
class MobilePhone
{
public:
    bool StartCall(const std::string &number);
    bool EndCall();
#if defined TARGET_OS_IPHONE
    bool GetGPSLocation(double *lat, double *lon);
#endif
};
```

This poor design creates a different API on different platforms. Doing so forces the clients of your API to introduce the same platform specificity into their own applications. For example, in the aforementioned case, your clients would have to guard any calls to GetGPSLocation() with precisely the same #if conditional statement, otherwise their code may fail to compile with an undefined symbol error on other platforms.

Furthermore, if in a later version of the API you also add support for another device class, say Windows Mobile, then you would have to update the #if line in your public header to include _WIN32_WCE. Then, your clients would have to find all instances in their code where they have embedded the TARGET_OS_IPHONE define and extend it to also include _WIN32_WCE. This is because you have unwittingly exposed the implementation details of your API.

Instead, you should hide the fact that the function only works on certain platforms and provide a method to determine whether the implementation offers the desired capabilities on the current platform. For example,

```
class MobilePhone
{
public:
    bool StartCall(const std::string &number);
    bool EndCall();
    bool HasGPS() const;
    bool GetGPSLocation(double &lat, double &lon);
};
```

Now your API is consistent over all platforms and does not expose the details of which platforms support GPS coordinates. The client can now write code to check whether the current device supports a GPS device, by calling `HasGPS()`, and if so they can call the `GetGPSLocation()` method to return the actual coordinate. The implementation of the `HasGPS()` method might look something like

```
bool MobilePhone::HasGPS() const
{
#if defined TARGET_OS_IPHONE
    return true;
#else
    return false;
#endif
}
```

This is far superior to the original design because the platform-specific `#if` statement is now hidden in the `.cpp` file instead of being exposed in the header file.

TIP

Never put platform-specific #if or #ifdef statements into your public APIs. It exposes implementation details and makes your API appear different on different platforms.

2.5 LOOSELY COUPLED

In 1974, Wayne Stevens, Glenford Myers, and Larry Constantine published their seminal paper on structured software design. This paper introduced the two interrelated concepts of coupling and cohesion (Stevens et al., 1974), which I define as

- **Coupling.** A measure of the strength of interconnection between software components, that is, the degree to which each component depends on other components in the system.
- **Cohesion.** A measure of how coherent or strongly related the various functions of a single software component are.

Good software designs tend to correlate with low (or loose) coupling and high cohesion, that is, a design that minimizes the functional relatedness and connectedness between different components. Achieving this goal allows components to be used, understood, and maintained independently of each other.

TIP

Good APIs exhibit loose coupling and high cohesion.

Steve McConnell presents a particularly effective analogy for loose coupling. Model railroad cars use simple hook or knuckle couplers to connect cars together. These allow easy linking of train cars—normally by just pushing two cars together—with a single point of connection. This is therefore an example of a loosely coupled system. Imagine how much more difficult it would be to connect the cars if you had to employ several types of connections, perhaps involving screws and wires, or if only certain cars could interface with certain other kinds of cars (McConnell, 2004).

One way to think of coupling is that given two components, A and B, how much code in B must change if A changes. Various measures can be used to evaluate the degree of coupling between components.

- **Size**. Relates to the number of connections between components, including the number of classes, methods, arguments per method, etc. For example, a method with fewer parameters is more loosely coupled to components that call it.
- **Visibility**. Refers to the prominence of the connection between components. For example, changing a global variable in order to affect the state of another component indirectly is a poor level of visibility.
- **Intimacy**. Refers to the directness of the connection between components. If A is coupled to B and B is coupled to C, then A is indirectly coupled to C. Another example is that inheriting from a class is a tighter coupling than including that class as a member variable (composition) because inheritance also provides access to all protected members of the class.
- **Flexibility**. Relates to the ease of changing the connections between components. For example, if the signature of a method in A needs to change so that B can call it, how easy is it to change that method and all dependent code.

One particularly abhorrent form of tight coupling that should always be avoided is having two components that depend on each other directly or indirectly, that is, a dependency cycle or circular dependency. This makes it difficult or impossible to reuse a component without also including all of its circularly dependent components. This form of tight coupling is discussed further in Chapter 4.

The following sections present various techniques to reduce coupling between classes and methods within your API (inter-API coupling).

However, there is also the interesting question of how your API design decisions affect the cohesion and coupling of your clients' applications (intra-API coupling). Because your API is designed to solve a specific problem, that unity of purpose should translate well into your API being a component with high cohesion in your clients' program. However, in terms of coupling, the larger your API is—the more classes, methods, and arguments you expose—the more ways in which your API can be accessed and coupled to your clients application. As such, the quality of being minimally complete can also contribute toward loose coupling. There is also the issue of how much coupling with other components you have designed into your API. For example, the libpng library depends on the libz library. This coupling is exposed at compile time via a reference to the `zlib.h` header in `png.h` and also at link time. This requires clients of libpng to be aware of the libz dependency and ensure that they also build and link against this additional library.

2.5.1 Coupling by Name Only

If class A only needs to know the name of class B, that is, it does not need to know the size of class B or call any methods in the class, then class A does not need to depend on the full declaration of B.

In these cases, you can use a forward declaration for class B, rather than including the entire interface, and so reduce the coupling between the two classes (Lakos, 1996). For example,

```
class MyObject; // only need to know the name of MyObject

class MyObjectHolder
{
public:
    MyObjectHolder();

    void SetObject(MyObject *obj);
    MyObject *GetObject() const;

private:
    MyObject *mObj;
};
```

In this case, if the associated .cpp file simply stores and returns the MyObject pointer, and restricts any interaction with it to pointer comparisons, then it does not need to #include "MyObject.h" either. In that case, the MyObjectHolder class can be decoupled from the physical implementation of MyObject.

TIP
_____

Use a forward declaration for a class unless you actually need to #include its full definition.

2.5.2 **Reducing Class Coupling**

Scott Meyers recommends that whenever you have a choice, you should prefer declaring a function as a non-member non-friend function rather than as a member function (Meyers, 2000). Doing so improves encapsulation and also reduces the degree of coupling of those functions to the class. For example, consider the following class snippet that provides a PrintName() member function to output the value of a member variable to stdout. The function uses a public getter method, GetName(), to retrieve the current value of the member variable.

```
// myobject.h
class MyObject
{
public:
    void PrintName() const;
    std::string GetName() const;
    ...

protected:
    ...
```

```
private:
    std::string mName;
    ...
};
```

Following Meyers' advice, you should prefer the following representation:

```
// myobject.h
class MyObject
{
public:
    std::string GetName() const;
    ...

protected:
    ...

private:
    std::string mName;
    ...
};
```

```
void PrintName(const MyObject &obj);
```

This latter form reduces coupling because the free function `PrintName()` can only access the public methods of `MyObject` (and only the const public methods in this particular case). Whereas in the form where `PrintName()` is a member function, it can also access all of the private and protected member functions and data members of `MyObject`, as well as any protected members of any base classes if it had any. Preferring the non-member non-friend form therefore means that the function is not coupled to the internal details of the class. It is therefore far less likely to break when the internal details of `MyObject` are changed (Tulach, 2008).

This technique also contributes to more minimally complete interfaces, where a class contains only the minimal functionality required to implement it, while functionality that is built on top of its public interface is declared outside of the class (as in the example of convenience APIs discussed earlier). It's worth noting that this happens a lot in the STL, where algorithms such as `std::for_each()` and `std::unique()` are declared outside of each container class.

To better convey the conceptual relatedness of `MyObject` and `PrintName()`, you could declare both of these within a single namespace. Alternatively, you could declare `PrintName()` within its own namespace, such as `MyObjectHelper`, or even as a static function within a new helper class called `MyObjectHelper`. As already covered in the section on convenience APIs, this helper namespace can, and should, be contained in a separate module. For example,

```
// myobjecthelper.h
namespace MyObjectHelper
{
    void PrintName(const MyObject &obj);
};
```

TIP

Prefer using non-member non-friend functions instead of member functions to reduce coupling.

2.5.3 **Intentional Redundancy**

Normally, good software engineering practice aims to remove redundancy: to ensure that each significant piece of knowledge or behavior is implemented once and only once (Pierce, 2002). However, reuse of code implies coupling, and sometimes it's worth the cost to add a small degree of duplication in order to sever an egregious coupling relationship (Parnas, 1979). This intentional duplication may take the form of code or data redundancy.

As an example of code redundancy, consider two large components that are dependent on each other. However, when you investigate the dependency more deeply it turns out that it resolves to one component relying on a trivial piece of functionality in the other, such as a function to calculate minimum or maximum. Standard practice would be to find a lower-level home for this functionality so that both components may depend on that smaller piece of functionality instead of on each other. However, sometimes this kind of refactoring doesn't make sense, for example, if the functionality is simply not generic enough to be demoted to a lower level in the system. Therefore, in certain cases, it may make sense to actually duplicate the code in order to avoid the coupling (Lakos, 1996).

In terms of adding data redundancy, consider the following API for a text chat system that logs each message sent by a user:

```cpp
#include "ChatUser.h"
#include <string>
#include <vector>

class TextChatLog
{
public:
    bool AddMessage(const ChatUser &user, const std::string &msg);
    int GetCount() const;
    std::string GetMessage(int index);

private:
    struct ChatEvent
    {
        ChatUser mUser;
        std::string mMessage;
        size_t mTimestamp;
    };

    std::vector<ChatEvent> mChatEvents;
};
```

This design accepts individual text chat events, taking an object that describes a user and the message that they typed. This information is augmented with the current timestamp and added to an internal list.

The GetCount() method can then be used to find how many text chat events have occurred, and the GetMessage() method will return a formatted version of a given chat event, such as

    Joe Blow [09:46]: What's up?

However, the TextChatLog class is clearly coupled with the ChatUser class, which may be a very heavy class that pulls in many other dependencies. You may therefore decide to investigate this situation and find that TextChatLog only ever uses the name of the user, that is, it keeps the ChatUser object around but only ever calls the ChatUser::GetName() method. One solution to remove the coupling between the two classes would therefore be to simply pass the name of the user into the TextChatLog class, as in the following refactored version:

```
#include <string>
#include <vector>

class TextChatLog
{
public:
    bool AddMessage(const std::string &user, const std::string &msg);
    int GetCount() const;
    std::string GetMessage(int index);

private:
    struct ChatEvent
    {
        std::string mUserName;
        std::string mMessage;
        size_t mTimestamp;
    };

    std::vector<ChatEvent> mChatEvents;
};
```

This creates a redundant version of the user's name (it is now stored in the TextChatLog as well as the ChatUser classes), but it breaks the dependency between the two classes. It may also have the additional benefit of reducing the memory overhead of TextChatLog, if sizeof(std::string) < sizeof(ChatUser).

Nonetheless, even though this is an intentional duplication, it is still duplication and should be undertaken with great care, consideration, and excellent comments. For example, if the chat system was updated to allow users to change their names, and it was decided that when this happens all previous messages from that user should update to show their new name, then you may have to revert back to the original tightly coupled version (or risk more coupling by requiring ChatUser to inform TextChatLog whenever a name change occurs).

TIP
___

Data redundancy can sometimes be justified to reduce coupling between classes.

2.5.4 **Manager Classes**

A manager class is one that owns and coordinates several lower-level classes. This can be used to break the dependency of one or more classes upon a collection of low-level classes. For example, consider a structured drawing program that lets you create 2D objects, select objects, and move them around a canvas. The program supports several kinds of input devices to let users select and move objects, such as a mouse, tablet, and joystick. A naive design would require both select and move operations to know about each kind of input device, as shown in Figure 2.5.

Alternatively, you could introduce a manager class to coordinate access to each of the specific input device classes. In this way, the `SelectObject` and `MoveObject` classes only need to depend on this single manager class, and then only the manager class needs to depend on the individual input device classes. This may also require creating some form of abstraction for the underlying classes. For example, note that `MouseInput`, `TabletInput`, and `JoystickInput` each have a slightly different interface. Our manager class could therefore put in place a generic input device interface that abstracts away the specifics of a particular device. The improved, more loosely coupled, design is shown in Figure 2.6.

Note that this design also scales well too. This is because more input devices can be added to the system without introducing any further dependencies for `SelectObject` or `MoveObject`. Also, if you decided to add additional manipulation objects, such as `RotateObject` and `ScaleObject`, they only need a single dependency on `InputManager` instead of each introducing further coupling to the underlying device classes.

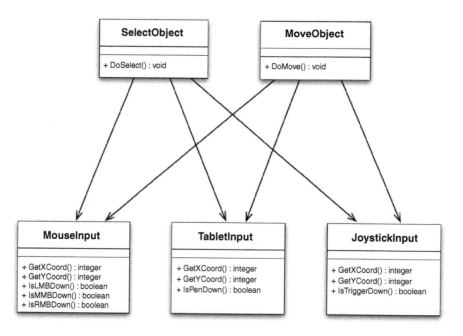

FIGURE 2.5

Multiple high-level classes each coupled to several low-level classes.

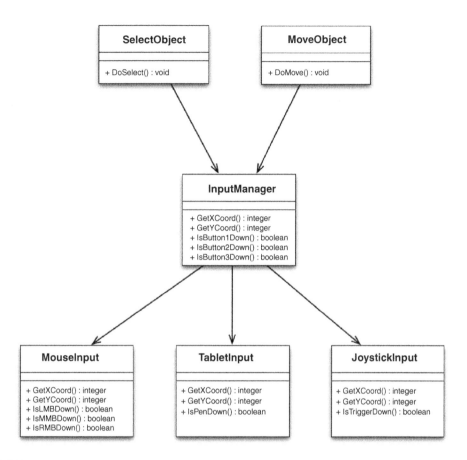

FIGURE 2.6

Using a manager class to reduce coupling to lower-level classes.

TIP

Manager classes can reduce coupling by encapsulating several lower-level classes.

2.5.5 Callbacks, Observers, and Notifications

The final technique that I'll present to reduce coupling within an API relates to the problem of notifying other classes when some event occurs.

Imagine an online 3D multiplayer game that allows multiple users to play against each other. Internally, each player may be represented with a unique identifier, or UUID, such as e5b43bba-fbf2-4f91-ac71-4f2a12d04847. However, users want to see the names of other players, not inscrutable UUID strings. The system therefore implements a player name cache, NameCache, to store the correspondence between the UUID and the human-readable name.

Now, let's say the class that manages the pregame lobby, PreGameLobby, wants to display the name of each player. The set of operations may proceed as follows.

1. The PreGameLobby class calls NameCache::RequestName()
2. The NameCache sends a request to the game server for the name of the player with this UUID
3. The NameCache receives the player name information from the server
4. The NameCache calls PreGameLobby::SetPlayerName()

However, in this case, PreGameLobby depends on NameCache to call the RequestName() method, and NameCache depends on PreGameLobby to call the SetPlayerName() method. This is an overly brittle and tightly coupled design. Consider what would happen if the in-game system also needed to know a player's name in order to display it above the user. Would you then extend NameCache to also call the InGame::SetPlayerName() method, further tightening the coupling?

A better solution would be to have the PreGameLobby and InGame classes register interest in updates from the NameCache. Then the NameCache can notify any interested parties without having a direct dependency on those modules. There are several ways that this can be done, such as callbacks, observers, and notifications. I will go into the details of each of these in a moment, but first here are a number of general issues to be aware of when using any of these schemes.

- **Reentrancy.** When writing an API that calls out to unknown user code, you have to consider that this code may call back into your API. In fact, the client may not even realize that this is happening. For example, if you are processing a queue of objects and you issue a callback as you process each individual object, it is possible that the callback will attempt to modify the state of the queue by adding or removing objects. At a minimum, your API should guard against this behavior with a coding error. However, a more elegant solution would be to allow this reentrant behavior and implement your code such that it maintains a consistent state.
- **Lifetime management.** Clients should have a clean way to disconnect from your API, that is, to declare that they are no longer interested in receiving updates. This is particularly important when the client object is deleted because further attempts to send messages to it could cause a crash. Similarly, your API may wish to guard against duplicate registrations to avoid calling the same client code multiple times for the same event.
- **Event ordering.** The sequence of callbacks or notifications should be clear to the user of your API. For example, the Cocoa API does a good job of making it clear whether a notification is sent before or after an event by using names such as willChange and didChange. However, the Qt toolkit is less specific about this: a changed signal is sometimes sent before the object in question is actually updated.

These points highlight the general issue that you should always make it clear to your clients what they can and cannot do—what assumptions they can and cannot make about your API—within their callback code. This can be done through your API documentation or can be enforced more explicitly by giving the callback a limited interface that only exposes a safe subset of all potential operations.

Callbacks

In C/C++, a callback is a pointer to a function within module A that is passed to module B so that B can invoke the function in A at an appropriate time. Module B knows nothing about module A and has no include or link dependencies upon A. This makes callbacks particularly useful to allow low-level code to execute high-level code that it cannot have a link dependency on. As such, callbacks are a popular technique to break cyclic dependencies in large projects.

It is also sometimes useful to supply a "closure" with the callback function. This is a piece of data that module A passes to B, and which module B includes in the function callback to A. This is a way for module A to pass through some state that will be important to receive in the callback function. The following header file shows how you can define a simple callback API in C++:

```cpp
#include <string>

class ModuleB
{
public:
    typedef void (*CallbackType)(const std::string &name, void *data);
    void SetCallback(CallbackType cb, void *data);
    ...

private:
    CallbackType mCallback;
    void *mClosure;
};
```

This class could then invoke the callback function, if one has been set, with code like the following:

```cpp
if (mCallback)
{
    (*mCallback)("Hello World", mClosure);
}
```

Of course, a more sophisticated example would support adding multiple callbacks to ModuleB, perhaps storing them in a std::vector, and then invoke each registered callback in turn.

One complication with using callbacks in object-oriented C++ programs is that it is non-trivial to use a non-static (instance) method as a callback. This is because the "this" pointer of the object also needs to be passed. The accompanying source code for this book shows one example of achieving this by creating a static wrapper method for the instance method callback and passing the "this" pointer through as an extra callback argument.

The Boost library also provides a far more elegant solution to this problem with the boost::bind functionality. This is implemented using functors (functions with state) that can be realized in C++ as a class with private member variables to hold the state and an overloaded operator() to execute the function.

Observers

Callbacks present a solution that work well in plain C programs, although, as just noted, their usage can be convoluted in object-oriented C++ programs without using something like boost::bind. Instead, a more object-oriented solution is to use the concept of observers.

This is a software design pattern where an object maintains a list of its dependent objects (observers) and notifies them by calling one of their methods. This is a very important pattern for minimizing coupling in API design. In fact, I have dedicated an entire section to it in the patterns chapter. As such, I will defer detailed treatment of observers until that point.

Notifications

Callbacks and observers tend to be created for a particular task, and the mechanism to use them is normally defined within the objects that need to perform the actual callback. An alternative solution is to build a centralized mechanism to send notifications, or events, between unconnected parts of the system. The sender does not need to know about the receiver beforehand, which lets us reduce coupling between the sender and the receiver. There are several kinds of notification schemes, but one particularly popular one is signals and slots.

The signals and slots concept was introduced by the Qt library as a generic way to allow any event, such as a button click or a timer event, to be sent to any interested method to act upon. However, there are now several alternative implementations of signals and slots available for use in plain C++ code, including Boost's `boost::signals` and `boost::signals2` library.

Signals can be thought of simply as callbacks with multiple targets (slots). All of the slots for a signal are called when that signal is invoked, or "emitted." To give a concrete example, the following code snippet uses `boost::signal` to create a signal that takes no arguments. You then connect a simple object to the signal. Finally, you emit the signal, which causes `MySlot::operator()` to be called, resulting in a message being printed to stdout.

```
class MySlot
{
public:
    void operator()() const
    {
        std::cout << "MySlot called!" << std::endl;
    }
};

// Create an instance of our MySlot class
MySlot slot;

// Create a signal with no arguments and a void return value
boost::signal<void ()> signal;

// Connect our slot to this signal
signal.connect(slot);

// Emit the signal and thereby call all of the slots
signal();
```

In practical use, a low-level class could therefore create and own a signal. It then allows any unconnected classes to add themselves as slots to this signal. Then the low-level class can emit its signal at any appropriate time and all of the connected slots will be called.

2.6 STABLE, DOCUMENTED, AND TESTED

A well-designed API should be stable and future proof. In this context, stable does not necessarily mean that the API never changes, but rather that the interface should be versioned and should not change incompatibly from one version to the next. Related to this, the term future proof means that an API should be designed to be extensible so that it can be evolved elegantly rather than changed chaotically.

A good API should also be well documented so that users have clear information about the capabilities, behavior, best practices, and error conditions for the API. Finally, there should be extensive automated tests written for the implementation of the API so that new changes can be made with the confidence that existing use cases have not been broken.

These topics have been condensed into a single section at the end of the chapter not because they are of minor concern or importance, quite the opposite in fact. These issues are so fundamentally important to the development of high-quality, robust, and easy-to-use APIs that I have dedicated entire chapters to each topic.

I've included this placeholder section here because I feel that a chapter on API qualities should at least reference these important topics. However, for specific details, I refer you to the separate chapters on versioning, extensibility, documentation, and testing for complete coverage of each respective topic.

Patterns

3

The previous chapter discussed the qualities that differentiate a good API from a bad API. The next couple of chapters focus on the techniques and principles of building high-quality APIs. This particular chapter covers a few useful design patterns and idioms that relate to C++ API design.

A design pattern is a general solution to a common software design problem. The term was made popular by the book *Design Patterns: Elements of Reusable Object-Oriented Software*, also known as the Gang of Four book (Gamma et al., 1994). That book introduced the following list of generic design patterns, organized into three main categories:

Creational Patterns	
Abstract Factory	Encapsulates a group of related factories.
Builder	Separates a complex object's construction from its representation.
Factory Method	Lets a class defer instantiation to subclasses.
Prototype	Specifies a prototypical instance of a class that can be cloned to produce new objects.
Singleton	Ensures a class has only one instance.
Structural Patterns	
Adapter	Converts the interface of one class into another interface.
Bridge	Decouples an abstraction from its implementation so that both can be changed independently.
Composite	Composes objects into tree structures to represent part–whole hierarchies.
Decorator	Adds additional behavior to an existing object in a dynamic fashion.
Façade	Provides a unified higher-level interface to a set of interfaces in a subsystem.
Flyweight	Uses sharing to support large numbers of fine-grained objects efficiently.
Proxy	Provides a surrogate or placeholder for another object to control access to it.
Behavioral Patterns	
Chain of Responsibility	Gives more than one receiver object a chance to handle a request from a sender object.
Command	Encapsulates a request or operation as an object, with support for undoable operations.
Interpreter	Specifies how to represent and evaluate sentences in a language.
Iterator	Provides a way to access the elements of an aggregate object sequentially.
Mediator	Defines an object that encapsulates how a set of objects interact.

Memento	Captures an object's internal state so that it can be restored to the same state later.
Observer	Allows a one-to-many notification of state changes between objects.
State	Allows an object to appear to change its type when its internal state changes.
Strategy	Defines a family of algorithms, encapsulates each one, and makes them interchangeable at run time.
Template Method	Defines the skeleton of an algorithm in an operation, deferring some steps to subclasses.
Visitor	Represents an operation to be performed on the elements of an object structure.

Since initial publication of the design pattern book in 1994, several more design patterns have been added to this list, including an entire new categorization of concurrency design patterns. The original authors have also recently suggested an improved categorization of core, creational, periphery, and other (Gamma et al., 2009).

However, it is not the intent of this API book to provide coverage of all these design patterns. There are plenty of other books on the market that focus solely on that topic. Instead, I will concentrate on those design patterns that are of particular importance to the design of high-quality APIs and discuss their practical implementation in C++. I will also cover C++ idioms that may not be considered true generic design patterns, but which are nevertheless important techniques for C++ API design. Specifically, I will go into details for the following techniques:

- **Pimpl idiom**. This technique lets you completely hide internal details from your public header files. Essentially, it lets you move private member data and functions to the `.cpp` file. It is therefore an indispensable tool for creating well-insulated APIs.
- **Singleton and Factory Method**. These are two very common creational design patterns that are good to understand deeply. Singleton is useful when you want to enforce that only one instance of an object is ever created. It has some rather tricky implementation aspects in C++ that I will cover, including initialization and multithreading issues. The Factory Method pattern provides a generalized way to create instances of an object and can be a great way to hide implementation details for derived classes.
- **Proxy, Adapter, and Façade**. These structural patterns describe various solutions for wrapping an API on top of an existing incompatible or legacy interface. This is often the entire goal of writing an API: to improve the interface of some poorly designed ball of code. Proxy and Adapter patterns provide a one-to-one mapping of new classes to preexisting classes, whereas the Façade provides a simplified interface to a larger collection of classes.
- **Observer**. This behavioral pattern can be used to reduce direct dependencies between classes. It allows conceptually unrelated classes to communicate by allowing one class (the observer) to register for notifications from another class (the subject). As such, this pattern is an important aspect of designing loosely coupled APIs.

In addition to these patterns and idioms, I will also discuss the Visitor behavioral pattern in Chapter 12 at the end of the book. The Visitor pattern gives clients a way to provide their own algorithms to operate on data structures in your API. It is most useful when designing a point of extensibility for your clients, which is why I have deferred it until the extensibility chapter.

3.1 **PIMPL IDIOM**

The term pimpl was first introduced by Jeff Sumner as shorthand for "pointer to implementation" (Sutter, 1999). This technique can be used as a way to avoid exposing private details in your header files (see Figure 3.1). It is therefore an important mechanism to help you maintain a strong separation between your API's interface and implementation (Sutter and Alexandrescu, 2004). While pimpl is not strictly a design pattern (it's a workaround to C++ specific limitations), it is an idiom that can be considered a special case of the Bridge design pattern.

If you change one programming habit after reading this book, I hope you'll choose to pimpl more API code.

TIP

Use the pimpl idiom to keep implementation details out of your public header files.

3.1.1 **Using Pimpl**

Pimpl relies on the fact that it's possible to define a data member of a C++ class that is a pointer to a forward declared type. That is, where the type has only been introduced by name and has not yet been fully defined, thus allowing you to hide the definition of that type within the .cpp file. This is often called an opaque pointer because the user cannot see the details for the object being pointed to. In essence, pimpl is a way to employ both logical and physical hiding of your private data members and functions.

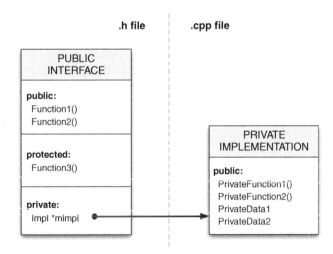

FIGURE 3.1

The pimpl idiom, where a public class has a private pointer to a hidden implementation class.

Let's take a look at an example to illustrate this. Consider the following API for an "auto timer": a named object that prints out how long it was alive when it is destroyed.

```
// autotimer.h
#ifdef _WIN32
#include <windows.h>
#else
#include <sys/time.h>
#endif
#include <string>

class AutoTimer
{
public:
    /// Create a new timer object with a human-readable name
    explicit AutoTimer(const std::string &name);
    /// On destruction, the timer reports how long it was alive
    ~AutoTimer();

private:
    // Return how long the object has been alive
    double GetElapsed() const;

    std::string mName;
#ifdef _WIN32
    DWORD mStartTime;
#else
    struct timeval mStartTime;
#endif
};
```

This API violates a number of the important qualities presented in the previous chapter. For example, it includes platform-specific defines and it makes the underlying implementation details of how the timer is stored on different platforms visible to anyone looking at the header file. To be fair, the API does a good job of only exposing the necessary methods as public (i.e., the constructor and destructor) and marking the remaining methods and data members as private. However, C++ requires you to declare these private members in the public header file, which is why you have to include the platform-specific #if directives.

What you really want to do is to hide all of the private members in the .cpp file. Then you wouldn't need to include any of those bothersome platform specifics. The pimpl idiom lets you do this by placing all of the private members into a class (or struct) that is forward declared in the header but defined in the .cpp file. For example, you could recast the aforementioned header as follows using pimpl:

```
// autotimer.h
#include <string>

class AutoTimer
{
```

```
public:
    explicit AutoTimer(const std::string &name);
    ~AutoTimer();

private:
    class Impl;
    Impl *mImpl;
};
```

Now the API is much cleaner! There are no platform-specific preprocessor directives, and the reader cannot see any of the class's private members by looking at the header file.

The implication, however, is that our AutoTimer constructor must now allocate an object of type AutoTimer::Impl and then destroy it in its destructor. Also, all private members must be accessed via the mImpl pointer. However, for most practical cases, the benefit of presenting a clean implementation-free API far outweighs this cost.

To be complete, let's take a look at what the underlying implementation looks like in order to work with this pimpled class. The resulting .cpp file looks a little bit messy due to the platform-specific #ifdef lines, but the important thing is that this messiness is completely contained in the .cpp file now.

```
// autotimer.cpp
#include "autotimer.h"
#include <iostream>
#if _WIN32
#include <windows.h>
#else
#include <sys/time.h>
#endif

class AutoTimer::Impl
{
public:
    double GetElapsed() const
    {
#ifdef _WIN32
    return (GetTickCount() - mStartTime) / 1e3;
#else
    struct timeval end_time;
    gettimeofday(&end_time, NULL);
    double t1 = mStartTime.tv_usec / 1e6 + mStartTime.tv_sec;
    double t2 = end_time.tv_usec / 1e6 + end_time.tv_sec;
    return t2 - t1;
#endif
    }

    std::string mName;
#ifdef _WIN32
```

```
   DWORD mStartTime;
#else
   struct timeval mStartTime;
#endif
};

AutoTimer::AutoTimer(const std::string &name) :
   mImpl(new AutoTimer::Impl())
{
   mImpl->mName = name;
#ifdef _WIN32
   mImpl->mStartTime = GetTickCount();
#else
   gettimeofday(&mImpl->mStartTime, NULL);
#endif
}

AutoTimer::~AutoTimer()
{
   std::cout << mImpl->mName << ": took " << mImpl->GetElapsed()
      << " secs" << std::endl;
   delete mImpl;
   mImpl = NULL;
}
```

Here you see the definition of the `AutoTimer::Impl` class, containing all of the private methods and variables that were originally exposed in the header. Note also that the `AutoTimer` constructor allocates a new `AutoTimer::Impl` object and initializes its members while the destructor deallocates this object.

In the aforementioned design, I declared the `Impl` class as a private nested class within the `AutoTimer` class. Declaring it as a nested class avoids polluting the global namespace with this implementation-specific symbol, and declaring it as private means that it does not pollute the public API of your class. However, declaring it to be private imposes the limitation that only the methods of `AutoTimer` can access members of the `Impl`. Other classes or free functions in the `.cpp` file will not be able to access `Impl`. As an alternative, if this poses too much of a limitation, you could instead declare the `Impl` class to be a public nested class, as in the following example:

```
// autotimer.h
class AutoTimer
{
public:
   explicit AutoTimer(const std::string &name);
   ~AutoTimer();

   // allow access from other classes/functions in autotimer.cpp
   class Impl;
```

```
private:
    Impl *mImpl;
};
```

TIP

When using the pimpl idiom use a private nested implementation class. Only use a public nested Impl class (or a public non-nested class) if other classes or free functions in the .cpp must access Impl members.

Another design question worth considering is how much logic to locate in the `Impl` class. Some options include:

1. Only private member variables
2. Private member variables and methods
3. All methods of the public class, such that the public methods are simply thin wrappers on top of equivalent methods in the `Impl` class.

Each of these options may be appropriate under different circumstances. However, in general, I recommend option 2: putting all private member variables and private methods in the `Impl` class. This lets you maintain the encapsulation of data and methods that act on those data and lets you avoid declaring private methods in the public header file. Note that I adopted this design approach in the example given earlier by putting the `GetElapsed()` method inside of the `Impl` class. Herb Sutter notes a couple of caveats with this approach (Sutter, 1999):

1. You can't hide private virtual methods in the implementation class. These must appear in the public class so that any derived classes are able to override them.
2. You may need to add a pointer in the implementation class back to the public class so that the `Impl` class can call public methods. Although you could also pass the public class into the implementation class methods that need it.

3.1.2 **Copy Semantics**

A C++ compiler will create a copy constructor and assignment operator for your class if you don't explicitly define them. However, these compiler-generated constructors will only perform a shallow copy of your object. This is bad for pimpled classes because it means that if a client copies your object then both objects will point to the same implementation object, `Impl`. However, both objects will attempt to delete this same `Impl` object in their destructors, which will most likely lead to a crash. Two options for dealing with this are as follows.

1. **Make your class uncopyable.** If you don't intend for your users to create copies of an object, then you can declare the object to be non-copyable. You can do this by explicitly declaring a copy constructor and assignment operator. You don't have to provide implementations for these; just the declarations are sufficient to prevent the compiler from generating its own default versions. Declaring these as private is also a good idea so that attempts to copy an object will generate a compile error rather than a link error. Alternatively, if you are using the Boost libraries,

then you could also simply inherit from `boost::noncopyable`. Also, the new C++11 specification lets you disable these default functions completely (see Chapter 6 for details).

2. **Explicitly define the copy semantics**. If you do want your users to be able to copy your pimpled objects, then you should declare and define your own copy constructor and assignment operator. These can then perform a deep copy of your object, that is, create a copy of the `Impl` object instead of just copying the pointer. I will cover how to write your own constructors and operators in the C++ usage chapter later in this book.

The following code provides an updated version of our `AutoTimer` API where I have made the object be non-copyable by declaring a private copy constructor and assignment operator. The associated `.cpp` file doesn't need to change.

```
#include <string>

class AutoTimer
{
public:
    explicit AutoTimer(const std::string &name);
    ~AutoTimer();

private:
    // Make this object be non-copyable
    AutoTimer(const AutoTimer &);
    const AutoTimer &operator =(const AutoTimer &);

    class Impl;
    Impl *mImpl;
};
```

3.1.3 Pimpl and Smart Pointers

One of the inconvenient and error-prone aspects of pimpl is the need to allocate and deallocate the implementation object. Every now and then you may forget to delete the object in your destructor or you may introduce bugs by accessing the `Impl` object before you've allocated it or after you've destroyed it. As a convention, you should therefore ensure that the very first thing your constructor does is to allocate the `Impl` object (preferably via its initialization list), and the very last thing your destructor does is to delete it.

Alternatively, you could rely upon smart pointers to make this a little easier. That is, you could use a shared pointer or a scoped pointer to hold the implementation object pointer. Because a scoped pointer is non-copyable by definition, using this type of smart pointer for objects that you don't want your users to copy would also allow you to avoid having to declare a private copy constructor and assignment operator. In this case, our API can simply appear as:

```
#include <memory>
#include <string>

class AutoTimer
{
```

```
public:
    explicit AutoTimer(const std::string &name);
    ~AutoTimer();

private:
    class Impl;
    std::unique_ptr<Impl> mImpl;
};
```

Alternatively, you could use a std::shared_ptr, which would allow the object to be copied without incurring the double delete issues identified earlier. Using a shared pointer would of course mean that any copy would point to the same Impl object in memory. If you need the copied object to have a copy of the Impl object, then you will still need to write your own copy constructor and assignment operators (or use a copy-on-write pointer, as described in the performance chapter).

TIP

Think about the copy semantics of your pimpl classes and consider using a smart pointer to manage initialization and destruction of the implementation pointer.

Using either a shared or a scoped pointer means that the Impl object will be freed automatically when the AutoTimer object is destroyed: you no longer need to delete it explicitly in the destructor. So the destructor of our autotimer.cpp file can now be reduced to simply:

```
AutoTimer::~AutoTimer()
{
    std::cout << mImpl->mName << ": took " << mImpl->GetElapsed()
              << " secs" << std::endl;
}
```

3.1.4 Advantages of Pimpl

There are many advantages to employing the pimpl idiom in your classes. These include the following.

- **Information hiding**. Private members are now completely hidden from your public interface. This allows you to keep your implementation details hidden (and proprietary in the case of closed-source APIs). It also means that your public header files are cleaner and more clearly express the true public interface. As a result, they can be read and digested more easily by your users. One further benefit of information hiding is that your users cannot use dirty tactics as easily to gain access to your private members, such as doing the following, which is actually permissible in most C++ compilers (Lakos, 1996), although officially it's illegal in C++98 (Sec 17.4.3.1.1/2):

```
#define private public  // make private members be public!
#include "yourapi.h"    // can now access your private members
#undef private           // revert to default private semantics
```

- **Reduced coupling**. As shown in the `AutoTimer` example earlier, without pimpl, your public header files must include header files for all of your private member variables. In our example, this meant having to include `windows.h` or `sys/time.h`. This increases the compile-time coupling of your API on other parts of the system. Using pimpl, you can move those dependencies into the `.cpp` file and remove those elements of coupling.
- **Faster compiles**. Another implication of moving implementation-specific includes to the `.cpp` file is that the include hierarchy of your API is reduced. This can have a very direct effect on compile times (Lakos, 1996). I will detail the benefits of minimizing include dependencies in the performance chapter.
- **Greater binary compatibility**. The size of a pimpled object never changes because your object is always the size of a single pointer. Any changes you make to private member variables (recall that member variables should always be private) will only affect the size of the implementation class that is hidden inside of the `.cpp` file. This makes it possible to make major implementation changes without changing the binary representation of your object.
- **Lazy Allocation**. The `mImpl` class can be constructed on demand. This may be useful if the class allocates a limited or costly resource such as a network connection.

3.1.5 Disadvantages of Pimpl

The primary disadvantage of the pimpl idiom is that you must now allocate and free an additional implementation object for every object that is created. This increases the size of your object by the size of a pointer and may introduce a performance hit for the extra level of pointer indirection required to access all member variables, as well as the cost for additional calls to `new` and `delete`. If you are concerned with the memory allocator performance, then you may consider using the "Fast Pimpl" idiom (Sutter, 1999) where you overload the `new` and `delete` operators for your `Impl` class to use a more efficient small-memory fixed-size allocator.

There is also the extra developer inconvenience to prefix all private member accesses with something like `mImpl->`. This can make the implementation code harder to read and debug due to the additional layer of indirection. This becomes even more complicated when the `Impl` class has a pointer back to the public class. You must also remember to define a copy constructor or disable copying of the class. However, these inconveniences are not exposed to users of your API and are therefore not a concern from the point of view of your API's design. They are a burden that you the developer must shoulder in order that all of your users receive a cleaner and more efficient API. To quote a certain science officer and his captain: "The needs of the many outweigh the needs of the few. Or the one."

One final issue to be aware of is that the compiler will no longer catch changes to member variables within const methods. This is because member variables now live in a separate object. Your compiler will only check that you don't change the value of the `mImpl` pointer in a const method, but not whether you change any members pointed to by `mImpl`. In effect, every member function of a pimpled class could be defined as const (except of course the constructor or destructor). This is demonstrated by the following const method that legally changes a variable in the `Impl` object:

```
void PimpledObject::ConstMethod() const
{
    mImpl->mName = "string changed by a const method";
}
```

3.1.6 **Opaque Pointers in C**

While I have focused on C++ so far, you can create opaque pointers in plain C too. The concept is the same: you create a pointer to a struct that is only defined in a .c file. The following header file demonstrates what this might look like in C:

```
/* autotimer.h */
/* declare an opaque pointer to an AutoTimer structure */
typedef struct AutoTimer *AutoTimerPtr;

/* functions to create and destroy the AutoTimer structure */
AutoTimerPtr AutoTimerCreate();
void AutoTimerDestroy(AutoTimerPtr ptr);
```

The associated .c file may then look as follows:

```
#include "autotimer.h"
#include <stdio.h>
#include <string.h>
#include <stdlib.h>

#if _WIN32
#include <windows.h>
#else
#include <sys/time.h>
#endif

struct AutoTimer
{
    char *mName;
#if _WIN32
    DWORD mStartTime;
#else
    struct timeval mStartTime;
#endif
} AutoTimer;

AutoTimerPtr AutoTimerCreate(const char *name)
{
    AutoTimerPtr ptr = malloc(sizeof(AutoTimer));
    if (ptr)
    {
        ptr->mName = strdup(name);
#if _WIN32
        ptr->mStartTime = GetTickCount();
#else
        gettimeofday(&ptr->mStartTime, NULL);
#endif
    }
    return ptr;
}
```

```
static double GetElapsed(AutoTimerPtr ptr)
{
#if _WIN32
    return (GetTickCount() - ptr->mStartTime) / 1e3;
#else
    struct timeval end_time;
    gettimeofday(&end_time, NULL);
    double t1 = ptr->mStartTime.tv_usec / 1e6 +
            ptr->mStartTime.tv_sec;
    double t2 = end_time.tv_usec / 1e6 + end_time.tv_sec;
    return t2 - t1;
#endif
}

void AutoTimerDestroy(AutoTimerPtr ptr)
{
    if (ptr)
    {
        printf("%s: took %f secs\n", ptr->mName, GetElapsed(ptr));
        free(ptr);
    }
}
```

3.2 SINGLETON

The Singleton design pattern (Gamma et al., 1994) is used to ensure that a class only ever has one instance. The pattern also provides a global point of access to that single instance (Figure 3.2). You can think of a singleton as a more elegant global variable. However, it offers several advantages over the use of global variables because it

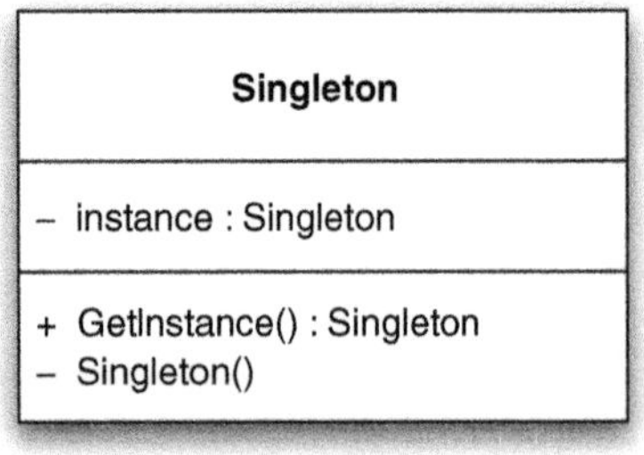

Singleton
− instance : Singleton
+ GetInstance() : Singleton − Singleton()

FIGURE 3.2

UML diagram of the Singleton design pattern.

1. Enforces that only one instance of the class can be created.
2. Provides control over the allocation and destruction of the object.
3. Allows support for thread-safe access to the object's global state.
4. Avoids polluting the global namespace.

The Singleton pattern is useful for modeling resources that are inherently singular in nature. For example, a class to access the system clock, the global clipboard, or the keyboard. It's also useful for creating manager classes that provide a single point of access to multiple resources, such as a thread manager or an event manager. However, the singleton is still essentially a way to add global variables to your system, albeit in a more manageable fashion. It can therefore introduce global state and dependencies into your API that are difficult to refactor later, as well as making it difficult to write unit tests that exercise isolated parts of your code.

I have decided to cover the concept of singletons here partly because they offer a useful and common API design technique. However, another reason is that because they are fairly intricate to implement robustly in C++, it's worth discussing some of the implementation details. Also, because many programmers have a tendency to overuse the Singleton pattern, I wanted to highlight some of the disadvantages of singletons as well as provide alternative techniques.

TIP

A Singleton is a more elegant way to maintain global state, but you should always question whether you need global state.

3.2.1 Implementing Singletons in C++

The Singleton pattern involves creating a class with a static method that returns the same instance of the class every time it is called. This static method is often called `GetInstance()`, or similar. There are several C++ language features to consider when designing a singleton class.

- You don't want clients to be able to create new instances. This can be done by declaring the default constructor to be private, thus preventing the compiler from automatically creating it as public.
- You want the singleton to be non-copyable, to enforce that a second instance cannot be created. As seen earlier, this can be done by declaring a private copy constructor and a private assignment operator.
- You want to prevent clients from being able to delete the singleton instance. This can be done by declaring the destructor to be private. (Note, however, that some compilers, such as Borland 5.5 and Visual Studio 6, produce an error incorrectly if you try to declare a destructor as private.)
- The `GetInstance()` method could return either a pointer or a reference to the singleton class. However, if you return a pointer, clients could potentially delete the object. You should therefore prefer returning a reference.

The general form of a singleton in C++ can therefore be given as follows (Alexandrescu, 2001):

```
class Singleton
{
public:
    static Singleton &GetInstance();
```

```
private:
   Singleton();
   ~Singleton();
   Singleton(const Singleton &);
   const Singleton &operator =(const Singleton &);
};
```

Then user code can request a reference to the singleton instance as follows:

```
Singleton &obj = Singleton::GetInstance();
```

Note that declaring the constructor and destructor to be private also means that clients cannot create subclasses of the singleton. However, if you wish to allow this, you can of course simply declare them to be protected instead.

TIP

Declare the constructor, destructor, copy constructor, and assignment operator to be private (or protected) to enforce the Singleton property.

In terms of implementation, one of the areas to be very careful about is how the singleton instance is allocated. The important C++ initialization issue to be cognizant of is explained by Scott Meyers as follows:

> *The relative order of initialization of non-local static objects in different translation units is undefined (Meyers, 2005).*

This means that it would be dangerous to initialize our singleton using a non-local static variable. A non-local object is one that is declared outside of a function. Static objects include global objects and objects declared as static inside of a class, function, or a file scope. As a result, one way to initialize our singleton would be to create a static variable inside a method of our class, as follows:

```
Singleton &Singleton::GetInstance()
{
   static Singleton instance;
   return instance;
}
```

One nice property of this approach is that the instance will only be allocated when the GetInstance() method is first called. This means that if the singleton is never requested, the object is never allocated. However, on the down side, this approach is not thread safe. Also, Andrei Alexandrescu notes that this technique relies on the standard last-in-first-out deallocation behavior of static variables, which can result in singletons being deallocated before they should in situations where singletons call other singletons in their destructors. As an example of this problem, consider two singletons: Clipboard and LogFile. When Clipboard is instantiated, it also instantiates LogFile to output some diagnostic information. At program exit, LogFile is destroyed first because it was created last and then Clipboard is destroyed. However, the Clipboard destructor tries to call LogFile to log the fact that it is being destroyed, but LogFile has already been freed. This will most likely result in a crash on program exit.

In his *Modern C++ Design* book, Alexandrescu presents several solutions to this destruction order problem, including resurrecting the singleton if it is needed after it has been destroyed, increasing the longevity of a singleton so that it can outlive other singletons, and simply not deallocating the singleton (i.e., relying on the operating system to free all allocated memory and close any file handles). If you find yourself needing to implement one of these solutions, I refer you to this book for details (Alexandrescu, 2001).

3.2.2 Making Singletons Thread Safe

The implementation of GetInstance() presented earlier is not thread safe because there is a race condition in the initialization of the Singleton static. If two threads happen to call this method at the same time, then the instance could be constructed twice or it could be used by one thread before it has been fully initialized by the other thread. This race condition is more evident if you look at the code that the compiler will generate for this method. Here's an example of what the GetInstance() method might get expanded to by a compiler:

```
Singleton &Singleton::GetInstance()
{
    // Example code that a compiler might generate...
    extern void __DestructSingleton();
    static char __buffer[sizeof(Singleton)];
    static bool __initialized = false;
    if (! __initialized)
    {
        new(__buffer) Singleton();    // placement new syntax
        atexit(__DestructSingleton); // destroy instance on exit
        __initialized = true;
    }
    return *reinterpret_cast<Singleton *>(__buffer);
}

void __DestructSingleton()
{
    // call destructor for static __buffer Singleton object
}
```

As with most solutions to non-thread-safe code, you can make this method thread safe by adding a mutex lock around the code that exhibits the race condition:

```
static Mutex sMutex;

Singleton &Singleton::GetInstance()
{
    ScopedLock lock(&sMutex);    // unlocks mutex on function exit
```

```
    static Singleton instance;
    return instance;
}
```

The potential problem with this solution is that it may be expensive because the lock will be acquired every time the method is called. It should be noted that this may not actually be a performance issue for your API. Always measure performance in real-world uses before deciding to optimize. For example, if this method is not called frequently by your clients, then this solution should be perfectly acceptable. As a workaround for clients who report performance problems, you could suggest that they call this method once (or once per thread) and cache the result in their own code. However, if the performance of this method really is an issue for you, then you're going to have to get a bit more complicated.

A commonly proposed solution to optimize this kind of over aggressive locking behavior is to use the Double Checked Locking Pattern (DCLP), which looks like:

```
static Mutex sMutex;

Singleton &Singleton::GetInstance()
{
    static Singleton *instance = NULL;

    if (! instance)      // check #1
    {
        ScopedLock lock(&sMutex);

        if (! instance) // check #2
        {
            instance = new Singleton();
        }
    }

    return *instance;
}
```

However, the DCLP is not guaranteed to work on all compilers and under all processor memory models. For example, a shared-memory symmetric multiprocessor normally commits writes to memory in bursts, which may cause the writes for different threads to be reordered. Using the volatile keyword is often seen as a solution to this problem because it synchronizes read and write operations to the volatile data. However, even this approach can be flawed in a multithreaded environment (Meyers and Alexandrescu, 2004). You may be able to use platform-specific memory barriers to get around these problems or, if you're only using POSIX threads, you could use pthread_once(), but at this point it's probably worth stepping back a bit and recognizing that perhaps you simply shouldn't try to optimize the GetInstance() method as formulated earlier. The various compiler and platform idiosyncrasies mean that your API may work fine for some clients, but will fail in complex and difficult-to-debug ways for other clients. Ultimately these difficulties are a product of trying to enforce thread safety in a language that has no inherent awareness or support for concurrency.

If the performance of a thread-safe GetInstance() is critical to you, then you might consider avoiding the lazy instantiation model presented earlier and instead initialize your singleton on startup, for example, either before main() is called or via a mutex-locked API initialization call.

One benefit common to both of these options is that you don't have to change the implementation of your Singleton class to support multithreading.

1. **Static initialization**. Static initializers get called before main(), where you can normally assume that the program is still single threaded. As a result, you could create your singleton instance as part of a static initializer and avoid the need for any mutex locking. Of course, you need to make sure that your constructor doesn't depend on non-local static variables in other .cpp files. However, bearing this caveat in mind, you could add the following static initialization call to the singleton.cpp file to ensure that the instance is created before main() is called.

```
static Singleton &foo = Singleton::GetInstance();
```

2. **Explicit API initialization**. You could consider adding an initialization routine for your library if you don't already have one. In this case, you could remove the mutex locks from the GetInstance() method and instead instantiate the singleton as part of this library initialization routine, placing the mutex locks at this point.

```
static Mutex sMutex;

void APIInitialize()
{
    ScopedLock lock(&sMutex);

    Singleton::GetInstance();
}
```

This has the benefit that you can specify the order of initialization of all your singletons, in case you have a singleton dependency issue (hopefully you don't). While it is somewhat ugly to require users to explicitly initialize your library, recall that this is only necessary if you need to provide a thread-safe API.

TIP

Creating a thread-safe Singleton in C++ is hard. Consider initializing it with a static constructor or an API initialization function.

3.2.3 Singleton versus Dependency Injection

Dependency injection is a technique where an object is passed into a class (injected) instead of having the class create and store the object itself. Martin Fowler coined the term in 2004 as a more specific form of the Inversion of Control concept. As a simple example, consider the following class that depends on a database object:

```
class MyClass
{
    MyClass() :
        mDatabase(new Database("mydb", "localhost", "user", "pass"))
    {}
```

```
private:
   Database *mDatabase;
};
```

The problem with this approach is that if the `Database` constructor is changed or if someone changes the password for the account called "user" in the live database, then you will have to change `MyClass` to fix the problem. Also, from an efficiency point of view, every instance of `MyClass` will create a new `Database` instance. As an alternative, you can use dependency injection to pass a preconfigured `Database` object into `MyClass`, as follows:

```
class MyClass
{
   MyClass(Database *db) :
      mDatabase(db)
   {}

private:
   Database *mDatabase;
};
```

In this way, `MyClass` no longer has to know how to create a `Database` instance. Instead, it gets passed an already constructed and configured `Database` object for it to use. This example demonstrates constructor injection, that is, passing the dependent object via the constructor, but you could just as easily pass in dependencies via a setter member function or you could even define a reusable interface to inject certain types of objects and then inherit from that interface in your classes.

Of course, the `Database` object needs to be created somewhere. This is typically the job of a dependency container. For example, a dependency container would be responsible for creating instances of the `MyClass` class and passing it an appropriate `Database` instance. In other words, a dependency container can be thought of as a generic factory class. The only real difference between the two is that a dependency container will maintain state, such as the single `Database` instance in our case.

TIP

Dependency injection makes it easier to test code that uses Singletons.

Dependency injection can therefore be viewed as a way to avoid the proliferation of singletons by encouraging interfaces that accept the single instance as an input rather than requesting it internally via a `GetInstance()` method. This also makes for more testable interfaces because the dependencies of an object can be substituted with stub or mock versions for the purposes of unit testing (this is discussed further in the testing chapter).

3.2.4 Singleton versus Monostate

Most problems associated with the Singleton pattern derive from the fact that it is designed to hold and control access to global state. However, if you don't need to control when the state is initialized or don't need to store state in the singleton object itself, then other techniques can be used, such as the Monostate design pattern.

The Monostate pattern allows multiple instances of a class to be created where all of those instances use the same static data. For instance, here's a simple case of the Monostate pattern:

```
// monostate.h
class Monostate
{
public:
    int GetTheAnswer() const { return sAnswer; }

private:
    static int sAnswer;
};

// monostate.cpp
int Monostate::sAnswer = 42;
```

In this example, you can create multiple instances of the `Monostate` class, but all calls to the `GetTheAnswer()` method will return the same result because all instances share the same static variable `sAnswer`. You could also hide the declaration of the static variable from the header completely by just declaring it as a file-scope static variable in `monostate.cpp` instead of a private class static variable. Because static members do not contribute to the per instance size of a class, doing this will have no physical impact on the API, other than to hide implementation details from the header.

Some benefits of the Monostate pattern are that it

- Allows multiple instances to be created.
- Offers transparent usage because no special `GetInstance()` method is needed.
- Exhibits well-defined creation and destruction semantics using static variables.

As Robert C. Martin notes, Singleton enforces the structure of singularity by only allowing one instance to be created, whereas Monostate enforces the behavior of singularity by sharing the same data for all instances (Martin, 2002).

TIP

Consider using Monostate instead of Singleton if you don't need lazy initialization of global data or if you want the singular nature of the class to be transparent.

As a further real-world example, the Second Life source code uses the Monostate pattern for its `LLWeb` class. This example uses a version of Monostate where all member functions are declared static.

```
class LLWeb
{
public:
    static void InitClass();

    /// Load the given url in the user's preferred web browser
```

```
static void LoadURL(const std::string& url);

/// Load the given url in the Second Life internal web browser
static void LoadURLInternal(const std::string &url);

/// Load the given url in the operating system's web browser
static void LoadURLExternal(const std::string& url);

/// Returns escaped url (eg, " " to "%20")
static std::string EscapeURL(const std::string& url);
};
```

In this case, LLWeb is simply a manager class that provides a single access point to the functionality for opening Web pages. The actual Web browser functionality itself is implemented in other classes. The LLWeb class does not hold any state itself, although of course internally any of the static methods could access static variables.

One of the drawbacks with this static method version of Monostate is that you cannot subclass any of the static methods because static member functions cannot be virtual. Also, because you no longer instantiate the class, you cannot write a constructor or destructor to perform any initialization or cleanup. This is necessary in this case because LLWeb accesses dynamically allocated global state instead of relying on static variables that are initialized by the compiler. The creator of LLWeb got around this limitation by introducing an initClass() static method that requires a client program to initialize the class explicitly. A better design may have been to hide this call within the .cpp file and invoke it lazily from each of the public static methods. However, in that case, the same thread safety concerns raised earlier would be applicable.

3.2.5 Singleton versus Session State

In a recent retrospective interview, authors of the original design patterns book stated that the only pattern they would consider removing from the original list is Singleton. This is because it is essentially a way to store global data and tends to be an indicator of poor design (Gamma et al., 2009).

Therefore, as a final note on the topic of singletons, I urge you to really think about whether a singleton is the correct pattern for your needs. It's often easy to think that you will only ever need a single instance of a given class. However, requirements change and code evolves, and in the future you may find that you need to support multiple instances of the class.

For example, consider that you are writing a simple text editor. You use a singleton to hold the current text style (e.g., bold, italics, underlined) because the user can only ever have one style active at one time. However, this restriction is only valid because of the initial assumption that the program can edit only one document at a time. In a later version of the program, you are asked to add support for multiple documents, each with their own current text style. Now you have to refactor your code to remove the singleton. Ultimately, singletons should only be used to model objects that are truly singular in their nature. For example, because there is only one system clipboard, it may still be reasonable to model the clipboard for the text editor as a singleton.

Often it's useful to think about introducing a "session" or "execution context" object into your system early on. This is a single instance that holds all of the state for your code rather than representing that state with multiple singletons. For example, in the text editor example, you might introduce a `Document` object. This will have accessors for things such as the current text style, but those objects do not have to be enforced as singletons. They are just plain classes that can be accessed from the `Document` class as `document->GetTextStyle()`. You can start off with a single `Document` instance, accessible by a call such as `Document::GetCurrent()` for instance. You might even implement `Document` as a singleton to begin with. However, if you later need to add support for multiple contexts (i.e., multiple documents), then your code is in a much healthier state to support this because you only have one singleton to refactor instead of dozens. J.B. Rainsberger refers to this as a Toolbox Singleton, where the application becomes the singleton, not the individual classes (Rainsberger, 2001).

TIP

There are several alternatives to the Singleton pattern, including dependency injection, the Monostate pattern, and use of a session context.

3.3 FACTORY METHODS

A Factory Method is a creational design pattern that allows you to create objects without having to specify the specific C++ type of the object to create. In essence, a factory method is a generalization of a constructor. Constructors in C++ have several limitations, such as the following.

1. **No return result**. You cannot return a result from a constructor. This means that you cannot signal an error during the initialization of an object by returning a NULL pointer, for instance (although you can signal an error by throwing an exception within a constructor).
2. **Constrained naming**. A constructor is easily distinguished because it is constrained to have the same name as the class that it lives in. However, this also limits its flexibility. For example, you cannot have two constructors that both take a single integer argument.
3. **Statically bound creation**. When constructing an object, you must specify the name of a concrete class that is known at compile time, for example, you might write: `Foo *f = new Foo()`, where `Foo` is a specific type that must be known by the compiler. There is no concept of dynamic binding at run time for constructors in C++.
4. **No virtual constructors**. You cannot declare a virtual constructor in C++. As just noted, you must specify the exact type of the object to be constructed at compile time. The compiler therefore allocates the memory for that specific type and then calls the default constructor for any base classes (unless you explicitly specify a non-default constructor in the initialization list). It then calls the constructor for the specific type itself. This is also why you cannot call virtual methods from the constructor and expect them to call the derived override (because the derived class hasn't been initialized yet).

In contrast, factory methods circumvent all of these limitations. At a basic level, a factory method is simply a normal method call that can return an instance of a class. However, they are often used in combination with inheritance, where a derived class can override the factory method and return an instance of that derived class. It's also very common and useful to implement factories using abstract base classes (ABC) (DeLoura, 2001). I will focus on the abstract base class case here, so let's recap what these kinds of classes are before I dive further into using factory methods.

3.3.1 Abstract Base Classes

An ABC is a class that contains one or more pure virtual member functions. Such a class is not concrete and cannot be instantiated using the new operator. Instead, it is used as a base class where derived classes provide the implementations of the pure virtual methods. For example,

```
// renderer.h
#include <string>

class IRenderer
{
public:
    virtual ~IRenderer() {}
    virtual bool LoadScene(const std::string &filename) = 0;
    virtual void SetViewportSize(int w, int h) = 0;
    virtual void SetCameraPosition(double x, double y, double z) = 0;
    virtual void SetLookAt(double x, double y, double z) = 0;
    virtual void Render() = 0;
};
```

This defines an abstract base class to describe an extremely simple 3D graphics renderer. The "= 0" suffix on the methods declares them as pure virtual methods, meaning that they must be overridden in a derived class for that class to be concrete. Note that it is not strictly true to say that pure virtual methods provide no implementation. You can actually provide a default implementation for pure virtual methods in your .cpp file. For example, you could provide an implementation for SetViewportSize() in renderer.cpp and then a derived class would be able to call IRenderer::SetViewportSize(), although it would still have to explicitly override the method as well.

An abstract base class is therefore useful to describe abstract units of behaviors that can be shared by multiple classes; it specifies a contract that all concrete derived classes must conform to. In Java, this is referred to as an interface (with the constraint that Java interfaces can only have public methods, static variables, and they cannot define constructors). I have named the aforementioned IRenderer class with an "I" prefix to indicate that it's an interface class.

Of course, you can also provide methods with implementations in the abstract base class: not all of the methods have to be pure virtual. In this regard, abstract base classes can be used to simulate mixins, which can be thought of loosely as interfaces with implemented methods.

As with any class that has one or more virtual methods, you should always declare the destructor of an abstract base class to be virtual. The following code illustrates why this is important.

```
class IRenderer
{
    // no virtual destructor declared
    virtual void Render() = 0;
};
```

```
class RayTracer : public IRenderer
{
   RayTracer();
   ~RayTracer();
   void Render(); // provide implementation for ABC method
};

int main(int, char **)
{
   IRenderer *r = new RayTracer();
   // delete calls IRenderer::~IRenderer, not RayTracer::~RayTracer
   delete r;
}
```

3.3.2 **Simple Factory Example**

Now that I have reviewed what an abstract base class is, let's use it to provide a simple factory method. I'll continue with the `renderer.h` example given earlier and start by declaring the factory for objects of type `IRenderer`.

```
// rendererfactory.h
#include "renderer.h"
#include <string>

class RendererFactory
{
public:
   IRenderer *CreateRenderer(const std::string &type);
};
```

That's all there is to declaring a factory method: it's just a normal method that can return an instance of an object. Note that this method cannot return an instance of the specific type `IRenderer` because that's an abstract base class and cannot be instantiated. However, it can return instances of derived classes. Also, you can use the string argument to `CreateRenderer()` to specify which derived type you want to create.

Let's assume that you have implemented three concrete classes derived from `IRenderer`: Open-GLRenderer, `DirectXRenderer`, and `MesaRenderer`. Let's further specify that you don't want users of your API to have any knowledge of the existence of these types: they must be completely hidden behind the API. Based on these conditions, you can provide an implementation of the factory method as follows:

```
// rendererfactory.cpp
#include "rendererfactory.h"
#include "openglrenderer.h"
#include "directxrenderer.h"
```

```
#include "mesarenderer.h"

IRenderer *RendererFactory::CreateRenderer(const std::string &type)
{
    if (type == "opengl")
        return new OpenGLRenderer();

    if (type == "directx")
        return new DirectXRenderer();

    if (type == "mesa")
        return new MesaRenderer();

    return NULL;
}
```

This factory method can therefore return any of the three derived classes of IRenderer, depending on the type string that the client passes in. This lets users decide which derived class to create at run time, not compile time as a normal constructor requires you to do. This is an enormous advantage because it means that you can create different classes based on user input or on the contents of a configuration file that is read at run time.

Also, note that the header files for the various concrete derived classes are only included in the factory's .cpp file. They do not appear in the rendererfactory.h public header. In effect, these are private header files and do not need to be distributed with your API. As such, users can never see the private details of your different renderers, and they can't even see the specific types used to implement these different renderers. Users only ever specify a renderer via a string variable (or an enum, if you prefer).

TIP

Use Factory Methods to provide more powerful class construction semantics and to hide subclass details.

This example demonstrates a perfectly acceptable factory method. However, one potential drawback is that it contains hardcoded knowledge of the available derived classes. If you add a new renderer to the system, you have to edit rendererfactory.cpp. This is not terribly burdensome, and most importantly it will not affect your public API. However, it does mean that you cannot add support for new derived classes at run time. More specifically, it means that your users cannot add new renderers to the system. These concerns are addressed by presenting an extensible object factory.

3.3.3 Extensible Factory Example

To decouple the concrete derived classes from the factory method and to allow new derived classes to be added at run time, you can update the factory class to maintain a map that associates type names to object creation callbacks (Alexandrescu, 2001). You can then allow new derived classes to be registered and unregistered using a couple of new method calls. The ability to register new classes at run time allows this form of the Factory Method pattern to be used to create extensible plugin interfaces for your API, as detailed in Chapter 12.

One further issue to note is that the factory object must now hold state. As such, it would be best to enforce that only one factory object is ever created. This is the reason why most factory objects are also singletons. In the interests of simplicity, however, I will use static methods and variables in our example here. Putting all of these points together, here's what our new object factory might look like:

```cpp
// rendererfactory.h
#include "renderer.h"
#include <string>
#include <map>

class RendererFactory
{
public:
    typedef IRenderer *(*CreateCallback)();
    static void RegisterRenderer(const std::string &type, CreateCallback cb);
    static void UnregisterRenderer(const std::string &type);
    static IRenderer *CreateRenderer(const std::string &type);

private:
    typedef std::map<std::string, CreateCallback> CallbackMap;
    static CallbackMap mRenderers;
};
```

For completeness, the associated `.cpp` file might look like:

```cpp
#include "rendererfactory.h"

// instantiate the static variable in RendererFactory
RendererFactory::CallbackMap RendererFactory::mRenderers;

void RendererFactory::RegisterRenderer(const std::string &type, CreateCallback cb)
{
    mRenderers[type] = cb;
}

void RendererFactory::UnregisterRenderer(const std::string &type)
{
    mRenderers.erase(type);
}

IRenderer *RendererFactory::CreateRenderer(const std::string &type)
```

```
{
    CallbackMap::iterator it = mRenderers.find(type);
    if (it != mRenderers.end())
    {
        // call the creation callback to construct this derived type
        return (it->second)();
    }
    return NULL;
}
```

A user of your API can now register (and unregister) new renderers in your system. The compiler will ensure that the user's new renderer conforms to your IRenderer abstract interface, that is, it provides an implementation for all of the pure virtual methods in IRenderer. To illustrate this, the following code shows how a user could define their own renderer, register it with the object factory, and then ask the factory to create an instance of it.

```
class UserRenderer : public IRenderer
{
public:
    ~UserRenderer() {}
    bool LoadScene(const std::string &filename) { return true; }
    void SetViewportSize(int w, int h) {}
    void SetCameraPosition(double x, double y, double z) {}
    void SetLookAt(double x, double y, double z) {}
    void Render() { std::cout << "User Render" << std::endl; }
    static IRenderer *Create() { return new UserRenderer(); }
};

int main(int, char **)
{
    // register a new renderer
    RendererFactory::RegisterRenderer("user", UserRenderer::Create);

    // create an instance of our new renderer
    IRenderer *r = RendererFactory::CreateRenderer("user");
    r->Render();
    delete r;

    return 0;
}
```

One point worth noting here is that I added a Create() function to the UserRenderer class. This is because the register method of the factory needs to take a callback that returns an object. This callback doesn't have to be part of the IRenderer class (it could be a free function, for example). However, adding it to the IRenderer class is a good idea to keep all of the related functionality in the same place. In fact, you could even enforce this convention by adding the Create() call as another pure virtual method on the IRenderer abstract base class.

Finally, I note that in the extensible factory example given here, a renderer callback has to be visible to the `RegisterRenderer()` function at run time. However, this doesn't mean that you have to expose the built-in renderers of your API. These can still be hidden either by registering them within your API initialization routine or by using a hybrid of the simple factory and the extensible factory, whereby the factory method first checks the type string against a few built-in names. If none of those match, it then checks for any names that have been registered by the user. This hybrid approach has the potentially desirable behavior that users cannot override your built-in classes.

3.4 API WRAPPING PATTERNS

Writing a wrapper interface that sits on top of another set of classes is a relatively common API design task. For example, perhaps you are working with a large legacy code base and rather than rearchitecting all of that code you decide to design a new cleaner API that hides the underlying legacy code (Feathers, 2004). Or perhaps you have written a C++ API and need to expose a plain C interface for certain clients. Or perhaps you have a third-party library dependency that you want your clients to be able to access but you don't want to expose that library directly to them.

The downside of creating a wrapper API is the potential performance hit that you may experienced due to the extra level of indirection and the overhead of any extra state that needs to be stored at the wrapper level. However, this is often worth the cost in order to expose a higher-quality or more focused API, such as in the cases just mentioned.

Several structural design patterns deal with the task of wrapping one interface on top of another. I will describe three of these patterns in the following sections. These are, in increasing deviation between the wrapper layer and the original interface: Proxy, Adapter, and Façade.

3.4.1 The Proxy Pattern

The Proxy design pattern (Figure 3.3) provides a one-to-one forwarding interface to another class: calling `FunctionA()` in the proxy class will cause it to call `FunctionA()` in the original class. That is, the proxy class and the original class have the same interface. This can be thought of as a single-component wrapper, to use the terminology of Lakos (1996), that is, a single class in the proxy API maps to a single class in the original API.

This pattern is often implemented by making the proxy class store a copy of, or more likely a pointer to, the original class. Then the methods of the proxy class simply redirect to the method with

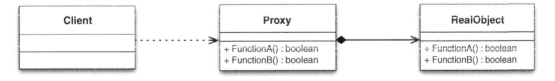

FIGURE 3.3

UML diagram of the Proxy design pattern.

the same name in the original object. A downside of this technique is the need to reexpose functions in the original object, a process that essentially equates to code duplication. This approach therefore requires diligence to maintain the integrity of the proxy interface when making changes to the original object. The following code provides a simple example of this technique. Note that I declare the copy constructor and assignment operator as private member functions to prevent clients from copying the object. You could of course allow copying by providing explicit implementations of these functions. I will cover how to do this in the later chapter on C++ usage.

```cpp
class Proxy
{
public:
    Proxy() : mOrig(new Original())
    {}
    ~Proxy()
    {
        delete mOrig;
    }

    bool DoSomething(int value)
    {
        return mOrig->DoSomething(value);
    }

private:
    Proxy(const Proxy &);
    const Proxy &operator =(const Proxy &);

    Original *mOrig;
};
```

An alternative solution is to augment this approach by using an abstract interface that is shared by both the proxy and original APIs. This is done to try and better keep the two APIs synchronized, although it requires you to be able to modify the original API. The following code demonstrates this approach:

```cpp
class IOriginal
{
public:
    virtual bool DoSomething(int value) = 0;
};

class Original : public IOriginal
{
public:
    bool DoSomething(int value);
};

class Proxy : public IOriginal
```

```
{
public:
    Proxy() : mOrig(new Original())
    {}
    ~Proxy()
    {
        delete mOrig;
    }

    bool DoSomething(int value)
    {
        return mOrig->DoSomething(value);
    }

private:
    Proxy(const Proxy &);
    const Proxy &operator =(const Proxy &);

    Original *mOrig;
};
```

TIP

A Proxy provides an interface that forwards function calls to another interface of the same form.

A Proxy pattern is useful to modify the behavior of the Original class while still preserving its interface. This is particularly useful if the Original class is in a third-party library and hence not easily modifiable directly. Some use cases for the proxy pattern include the following.

1. **Implement lazy instantiation of the** Original **object.** In this case, the Original object is not actually instantiated until a method call is invoked. This can be useful if instantiating the Original object is a heavyweight operation that you wish to defer until absolutely necessary.
2. **Implement access control to the** Original **object.** For example, you may wish to insert a permissions layer between the Proxy and the Original objects to ensure that users can only call certain methods on the Original object if they have the appropriate permission.
3. **Support debug or "dry run" modes.** This lets you insert debugging statements into the Proxy methods to log all calls to the Original object or you can stop the forwarding to certain Original methods with a flag to let you call the Proxy in a dry run mode; for example, to turn off writing the object's state to disk.
4. **Make the** Original **class be thread safe.** This can be done by adding mutex locking to the relevant methods that are not thread safe. While this may not be the most efficient way to make the underlying class thread safe, it is a useful stop gap if you cannot modify Original.
5. **Support resource sharing.** You could have multiple Proxy objects share the same underlying Original class. For example, this could be used to implement reference counting or copy-on-write semantics. This case is actually another design pattern, called the Flyweight pattern, where multiple objects share the same underlying data to minimize memory footprint.

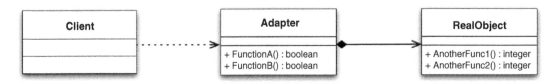

FIGURE 3.4

UML diagram of the Adapter design pattern.

6. **Protect against future changes in the** `Original` **class.** In this case, you anticipate that a dependent library will change in the future so you create a proxy wrapper around that API that directly mimics the current behavior. When the library changes in the future, you can preserve the old interface via your proxy object and simply change its underlying implementation to use the new library methods. At which point, you will no longer have a proxy object, but an adapter, which is a nice segue to our next pattern.

3.4.2 The Adapter Pattern

The Adapter design pattern (Figure 3.4) translates the interface for one class into a compatible but different interface. This is therefore similar to the Proxy pattern in that it's a single-component wrapper. However, the interface for the adapter class and the original class may be different.

This pattern is useful to be able to expose a different interface for an existing API to allow it to work with other code. As in the case for the proxy pattern, the two interfaces in question could come from different libraries. For example, consider a geometry package that lets you define a series of primitive shapes. The parameters for certain methods may be in a different order from those that you use in your API, or they may be specified in a different coordinate system, or using a different convention such as (center, size) versus (bottom-left, top-right), or the method names may not follow your API's naming convention. You could therefore use an adapter class to convert this interface into a compatible form for your API. For example,

```
class RectangleAdapter
{
public:
    RectangleAdapter() :
        mRect(new Rectangle())
    {}
    ~RectangleAdapter()
    {
        delete mRect;
    }

    void Set(float x1, float y1, float x2, float y2)
    {
        float w = x2 - x1;
        float h = y2 - y1;
```

```
        float cx = w / 2.0f + x1;
        float cy = h / 2.0f + y1;
        mRect->setDimensions(cx, cy, w, h);
    }

private:
    RectangleAdapter(const RectangleAdapter &);
    const RectangleAdapter &operator =(const RectangleAdapter &);

    Rectangle *mRect;
};
```

In this example, the RectangleAdapter uses a different method name and calling conventions to set the dimensions of the rectangle than the underlying Rectangle class. The functionality is the same in both cases. You're just exposing a different interface to allow you to work with the class more easily.

TIP

An Adapter translates one interface into a compatible but different interface.

It should be noted that adapters can be implemented using composition (as in the aforementioned example) or inheritance. These two flavors are often referred to as object adapters or class adapters, respectively. In the inheritance case, RectangleAdapter would derive from the Rectangle base class. This could be done using public inheritance if you wanted to also expose the interface of Rectangle in your adapter API, although it is more likely that you would use private inheritance so that only your new interface is made public.

Some benefits of the adapter pattern for API design include the following.

1. **Enforce consistency across your API**. As discussed in the previous chapter, consistency is an important quality of good APIs. Using an adapter pattern, you can collate multiple disparate classes that all have different interface styles and provide a consistent interface to all of these. The result is that your API is more uniform and therefore easier to use.
2. **Wrap a dependent library of your API**. For example, your API may provide the ability to load a PNG image. You want to use the libpng library to implement this functionality, but you don't want to expose the libpng calls directly to the users of your API. This could be because you want to present a consistent and uniform API or because you want to protect against potential future API changes in libpng.
3. **Transform data types**. For example, consider that you have an API, MapPlot, that lets you plot geographic coordinates on a 2D map. MapPlot only accepts latitude and longitude pairs (using the WGS84 datum), specified as two double parameters. However, your API has a GeoCoordinate type that can represent coordinates in several coordinate systems, such as Universal Transverse Mercator or Lambert Conformal Conic. You could write an adapter that accepts your GeoCoordinate object as a parameter, converts this to geodetic coordinates (latitude, longitude), if necessary, and passes the two doubles to the MapPlot API.

4. **Expose a different calling convention for your API**. For example, perhaps you have written a plain C API and you want to provide an object-oriented version of it for C++ users. You could create adapter classes that wrap the C calls into C++ classes. It's open to debate whether this can be strictly considered an adapter pattern, as design patterns are concerned primarily with object-oriented systems, but if you allow some flexibility in your interpretation of the term then you'll see that the concept is the same. The following code gives an example of a C++ adapter for a plain C API. (I'll discuss differences between C and C++ APIs in more detail in the next chapter on styles.)

```cpp
class CppAdapter
{
public:
   CppAdapter()
   {
      mHandle = create_object();
   }
   ~CppAdapter()
   {
      destroy_object(mHandle);
      mHandle = NULL;
   }

   void DoSomething(int value)
   {
      object_do_something(mHandle, value);
   }

private:
   CppAdapter(const CppAdapter &);
   const CppAdapter &operator =(const CppAdapter &);

   CHandle *mHandle;
};
```

3.4.3 The Façade Pattern

The Façade design pattern (Figure 3.5) presents a simplified interface for a larger collection of classes. In effect, it defines a higher-level interface that makes the underlying subsystem easier to use. To use Lakos' categorization, the Façade pattern is an example of a multicomponent wrapper (Lakos, 1996). Façade is therefore different from Adapter because Façade simplifies a class structure, whereas Adapter maintains the same class structure.

As your API grows, so can the complexity of using that interface. The Façade pattern is a way to structure your API into subsystems to reduce this complexity and in turn make the API easier to use for the majority of your clients. A façade might provide an improved interface while still allowing access to the underlying subsystems. This is the same as the concept of convenience APIs described in the previous chapter, where additional classes are added to provide aggregated functionality that

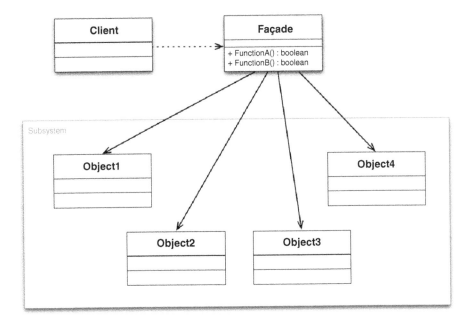

FIGURE 3.5

UML diagram of the Façade design pattern.

make simple tasks easy. Alternatively, a façade might completely decouple the underlying subsystems from the public interface so that these are no longer accessible. This is often called an "encapsulating façade."

> **TIP**
>
> A Façade provides a simplified interface to a collection of other classes. In an encapsulating façade, the underlying classes are not accessible.

Let's take a look at an example to illustrate this pattern. Let's assume that you are on holiday and have checked into a hotel. You decide that you want to have dinner and then go to watch a show. To do so, you'll have to call a restaurant to make a dinner reservation, call the theater to book seats, and perhaps also arrange a taxi to pick you up from your hotel. You could express this in C++ as three separate objects that you have to interact with.

```
class Taxi
{
public:
    bool BookTaxi(int npeople, time_t pickup_time);
};
```

```
class Restaurant
{
public:
    bool ReserveTable(int npeople, time_t arrival_time);
};

class Theater
{
public:
    time_t GetShowTime();
    bool ReserveSeats(int npeople, int tier);
};
```

However, let's assume that you're staying in a high-end hotel that has a helpful concierge who can assist you with all of this. In fact, the concierge will be able to find out the time of the show and then, using his local knowledge of the city, work out an appropriate time for your dinner and the best time to order your taxi. Translating this into terms of our C++ design, you now only have to interact with a single object with a far simpler interface.

```
class ConciergeFacade
{
public:
    enum ERestaurant {
        RESTAURANT_YES,
        RESTAURANT_NO
    };
    enum ETaxi {
        TAXI_YES,
        TAXI_NO
    };

    time_t BookShow(int npeople, ERestaurant addRestaurant, ETaxi addTaxi);
};
```

There are various useful applications of the Façade pattern in terms of API design.

1. **Hide legacy code**. Often you have to deal with old, decayed, legacy systems that are brittle to work with and no longer offer a coherent object model. In these cases, it can be easier to create a new set of well-designed APIs that sit on top of the old code. Then all new code can use these new APIs. Once all existing clients have been updated to the new APIs, the legacy code can be completely hidden behind the new façade (making it an encapsulating façade).

2. **Create convenience APIs**. As discussed in the previous chapter, there is often a tension between providing general, flexible routines that provide more power versus simple easy-to-use routines that make the common use cases easy. A façade is a way to address this tension by allowing both to coexist. In essence, a convenience API is a façade. I used the example earlier of the OpenGL library, which provides low-level base routines, and the GLU library, which provides higher-level and easier-to-use routines built on top of the GL library.

3. **Support reduced- or alternate-functionality APIs**. By abstracting away the access to the underlying subsystems, it becomes possible to replace certain subsystems without affecting your client's code. This could be used to swap in stub subsystems to support demonstration or test versions of your API. It could also allow swapping in different functionality, such as using a different 3D rendering engine for a game or using a different image reading library. As a real-world example, the Second Life viewer can be built against the proprietary KDU JPEG-2000 decoder library. However, the open source version of the viewer is built against the slower OpenJPEG library.

3.5 OBSERVER PATTERN

It's very common for objects to call methods in other objects. After all, achieving any non-trivial task normally requires several objects collaborating together. However, in order to do this, an object A must know about the existence and interface of an object B in order to call methods on it. The simplest approach to doing this is for A.cpp to include B.h and then to call methods on that class directly. However, this introduces a compile-time dependency between A and B, forcing the classes to become tightly coupled. As a result, the generality of class A is reduced because it cannot be reused by another system without also pulling in class B. Furthermore, if class A also calls classes C and D, then changes to class A could affect all three of these tightly coupled classes. Additionally, this compile-time coupling means that users cannot dynamically add new dependencies to the system at run time.

TIP

An Observer lets you decouple components and avoid cyclic dependencies.

I will illustrate these problems, and show how the observer pattern helps, with reference to the popular Model–View–Controller (MVC) architecture.

3.5.1 Model–View–Controller

The MVC architectural pattern requires the isolation of business logic (the Model) from the user interface (the View), with the Controller receiving user input and coordinating the other two. MVC separation supports the modularization of an application's functionality and offers a number of benefits.

1. Segregation of Model and View components makes it possible to implement several user interfaces that reuse the common business logic core.
2. Duplication of low-level Model code is eliminated across multiple UI implementations.
3. Decoupling of Model and View code results in an improved ability to write unit tests for the core business logic code.
4. Modularity of components allows core logic developers and GUI developers to work simultaneously without affecting the other.

The MVC model was first described in 1987 by Steve Burbeck and Trygve Reenskaug at Xerox PARC and remains a popular architectural pattern in applications and toolkits today. For example, modern UI toolkits such as Nokia's Qt, Apple's Cocoa, Java Swing, and Microsoft's Foundation Class library were all inspired by MVC. Taking the example of a single checkbox button, the current on/off state of the button is stored in the Model, the View draws the current state of the button on the screen, and the Controller updates the Model state and View display when the user clicks on the button.

TIP

The MVC architectural pattern promotes the separation of core business logic, or the Model, from the user interface, or View. It also isolates the Controller logic that affects changes in the Model and updates the View.

The implication of MVC separation on code dependency means that View code can call Model code (to discover the latest state and update the UI), but the opposite is not true: Model code should have no compile-time knowledge of View code (because it ties the Model to a single View). Figure 3.6 illustrates this dependency graph.

In a simple application, the Controller can effect changes to the Model based on user input and also communicate those changes to the View so that the UI can be updated. However, in real-world applications the View will normally also need to update to reflect additional changes to the underlying Model. This is necessary because changing one aspect of the Model may cause it to update other dependent Model states. This requires Model code to inform the View layer when state changes happen. However, as already stated, the Model code cannot statically bind and call the View code. This is where observers come in.

The Observer pattern is a specific instance of the Publish/Subscribe, or pub/sub, paradigm. These techniques define a one-to-many dependency between objects such that a publisher object can notify all subscribed objects of any state changes without depending on them directly. The observer pattern

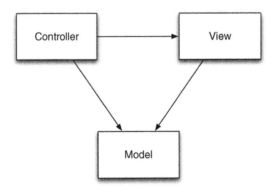

FIGURE 3.6

An overview of dependencies in the MVC model. Both the Controller and the View depend on the Model, but Model code has no dependency on Controller code or View code.

is therefore an important technique in terms of API design because it can help you reduce coupling and increase code reuse.

3.5.2 **Implementing the Observer Pattern**

The typical way to implement the observer pattern is to introduce two concepts: the subject and the observer (also referred to as the publisher and subscriber). One or more observers register interest in the subject, and then the subject notifies all registered observers of any state changes. This is illustrated in Figure 3.7.

This can be implemented using base classes to specify the abstract interface for both of these cases, as follows:

```
#include <map>
#include <vector>

class IObserver
{
public:
    virtual ~IObserver() {}
    virtual void Update(int message) = 0;
```

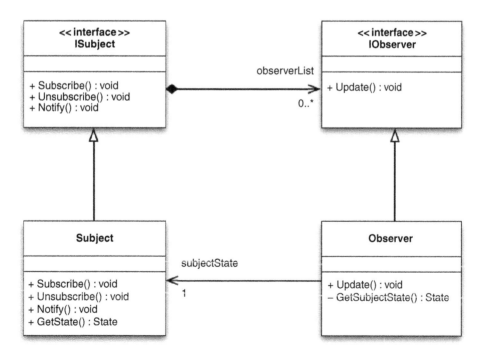

FIGURE 3.7

UML representation of the Observer pattern.

```
};

class ISubject
{
public:
    ISubject();
    virtual ~ISubject();
    virtual void Subscribe(int message, IObserver *observer);
    virtual void Unsubscribe(int message, IObserver *observer);
    virtual void Notify(int message);

private:
    typedef std::vector<IObserver *> ObserverList;
    typedef std::map<int, ObserverList> ObserverMap;
    ObserverMap mObservers;
};
```

In this design, I've added support for the subject to be able to register and emit notifications for multiple different message types. This allows observers to subscribe to only the specific messages they are interested in. For example, a subject that represents a stack of elements might wish to send out separate notifications when elements are added to or removed from that stack. Using the aforementioned interfaces, you can define a minimal concrete subject class as follows:

```
#include "observer.h"

class MySubject : public ISubject
{
public:
    enum Messages { ADD, REMOVE };
};
```

Finally, you can create observer objects by simply inheriting from the IObserver abstract base class and implementing the Update() method. The following code demonstrates putting all of these concepts together:

```
#include "subject.h"
#include <iostream>

class MyObserver : public IObserver
{
public:
    explicit MyObserver(const std::string &str) :
        mName(str)
    {}

    void Update(int message)
    {
        std::cout << mName << " Received message ";
        std::cout << message << std::endl;
```

```
      }

   private:
      std::string mName;
   };

   int main(int, char **)
   {
      MyObserver observer1("observer1");
      MyObserver observer2("observer2");
      MyObserver observer3("observer3");
      MySubject subject;

      subject.Subscribe(MySubject::ADD, &observer1);
      subject.Subscribe(MySubject::ADD, &observer2);
      subject.Subscribe(MySubject::REMOVE, &observer2);
      subject.Subscribe(MySubject::REMOVE, &observer3);

      subject.Notify(MySubject::ADD);
      subject.Notify(MySubject::REMOVE);

      return 0;
   }
```

This example demonstrates creating three separate observer classes and subscribes them for different combinations of the two messages defined by the MySubject class. Finally, the calls to subject.Notify() cause the subject to traverse its list of observers that have been subscribed for the given message and calls the Update() method for each of them. The important point to note is that the MySubject class has no compile-time dependency on the MyObserver class. The relationship between the two classes is dynamically created at run time by Subscribe().

Of course, there may be a small performance cost for this flexibility—the cost of iterating through a list of observers before making the (virtual) function call. However, this cost is generally insignificant when compared to the benefits of reduced coupling and increased code reuse. Also, as I covered in the previous chapter, you must take care to unsubscribe any observers before you destroy them otherwise the next notification could cause a crash.

3.5.3 **Push versus Pull Observers**

There are many different ways to implement the Observer pattern, with the example I just presented being only one such method. However, I will note two major categories of observers: push-based and pull-based. This categorization determines whether all the information is pushed to an observer via arguments to the Update() method or whether the Update() method is simply used to send a notification about the occurrence of an event; if the observer wishes to discover more details, then they must query the subject object directly. As an example, a notification that the user has pressed the Return key in a text entry widget may pass the actual text that the user typed as a parameter of the Update() method (push) or it may rely on the observer calling a GetText() method on the subject to discover this information if it needs it (pull).

Figure 3.7 illustrates a pull observer pattern because the Update() method has no arguments and the observer can query the subject for its current state. This approach allows you to use the same simple IObserver for all observers in the system. By comparison, a push-based solution would require you to define different abstract interfaces for each Update() method that requires a unique signature. A push-based solution is useful for sending small commonly used pieces of data along with a notification, such as the checkbox on/off state for a checkbox state change. However, it may be inefficient for larger pieces of data, such as sending the entire text every time a user presses a key in a text box widget.

Design

4

The preceding chapters laid the groundwork and developed the background to let you start designing your own APIs. I have analyzed the various qualities that contribute to good API design and looked at standard design patterns that apply to the design of maintainable APIs.

This chapter puts all of this information together and covers the specifics of high-quality API design, from overall architecture planning down to class design and individual function calls. However, good design is worth little if the API doesn't give your users the features they need. I will therefore also talk about defining functional requirements to specify what an API should do. I'll also specifically cover the creation of use cases and user stories as a way to describe the behavior of the API from the user's point of view. These different analysis techniques can be used individually or together, but they should always precede any attempt to design the API: you can't design what you don't understand.

Figure 4.1 shows the basic workflow for designing an API. This starts with an analysis of the problem, from which you can design a solution and then implement that design. This is a continual and iterative process: new requirements should trigger a reassessment of the design, as should changes from other sources such as major bug fixes. This chapter focuses on the first two stages of this process: analysis and design. The following chapters deal with the remaining implementation issues such as C++ usage, documentation, and testing.

Before I jump into these design topics, however, I will spend a little bit of time looking at why good design is so important. This opening section is drawn from experience working on large code bases that have persisted for many years and have had dozens or hundreds of engineers working on them. Lessons learned from witnessing code bases evolve, or devolve, over many years offer compelling motivation to design it well from the start and—just as importantly—to maintain high standards from then on. The consequences of not doing so can be very costly. To mix metaphors: good API design is a journey, not a first step.

4.1 A CASE FOR GOOD DESIGN

This chapter focuses on the techniques that result in elegant API design. However, it's likely that you've worked on projects with code that does not live up to these grand ideals. You've probably worked with legacy systems that have weak cohesion, expose internal details, have no tests, are poorly documented, and exhibit non-orthogonal behavior. Despite this, some of these systems were probably well designed when they were originally conceived. However, over time, the software has decayed, becoming difficult to extend and requiring constant maintenance.

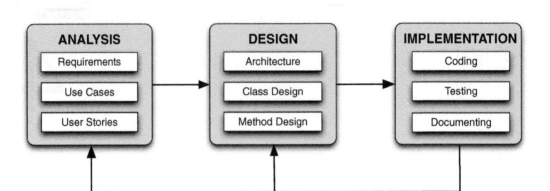

FIGURE 4.1

Stages of API development from analysis to design to implementation.

4.1.1 Accruing Technical Debt

All large successful companies grew from meager beginnings. A classic example of this is Hewlett-Packard, which began with two electrical engineers in a Palo Alto garage in 1939 and eventually grew to become the first technology company in the world to post revenues exceeding $100 billion. The qualities that make a successful startup company are very different from those needed to maintain a multibillion dollar publicly traded corporation. Companies often go through several large organizational changes as they grow, and the same thing is true of their software practices.

A small software startup needs to get its product out as soon as possible to avoid being beaten to market by a competitor or running out of capital. The pressure on a software engineer in this environment is to produce a lot of software, and quickly. Under these conditions, the extra effort required to design and implement long-term APIs is often seen as an unaffordable luxury. This is a fair decision when the options are between getting to market quickly or your company perishing. I once spoke with a software architect for a small startup who forbade the writing of any comments, documentation, or tests because he felt that it would slow the development down too much.

However, if a piece of software becomes successful, then the pressure turns toward providing a stable, easy-to-use, and well-documented product. New requirements start appearing that necessitate the software being extended in ways it was never meant to support. All of this must be built upon the core of a product that was not designed to last for the long term. The result, in the words of Ward Cunningham, is the accrual of technical debt (Cunningham, 1992):

> *Shipping first time code is like going into debt. A little debt speeds development so long as it is paid back promptly with a rewrite. [...] The danger occurs when the debt is not repaid. Every minute spent on not-quite-right code counts as interest on that debt. Entire engineering organizations can be brought to a stand-still under the debt load of an unconsolidated implementation.*

Steve McConnell expands on this definition to note that there are two types of debt: unintentional and intentional. The former is when software designed with the best of intentions turns out to be error prone, when a junior engineer writes low-quality code, or when your company buys another company whose software turns out to be a mess. The latter is when a conscious strategic decision is made to cut corners due to time, cost, or resource constraints, with the intention that the "right" solution will be put in place after the deadline.

The problem, of course, is that there is always another important deadline, so it's perceived that there's never enough time to go back and do the right fix. As a result, the technical debt gradually accrues: short-term glue code between systems lives on and becomes more deeply embedded, last-minute hacks remain in the code and turn into features that clients depend upon, coding conventions and documentation are ignored, and ultimately the original clean design degrades and becomes obfuscated. Robert C. Martin defined four warning signs that a code base is reaching this point (Martin, 2000). Here is a slightly modified version of those indicators.

- **Fragility**. Software becomes fragile when it has unexpected side effects or when implementation details are exposed to the point that apparently unconnected parts of the system depend on the internals of other parts of the system. The result is that changes to one part of the system can cause unexpected failures in seemingly unrelated parts of the code. Engineers are therefore afraid to touch the code and it becomes a burden to maintain.
- **Rigidity**. A rigid piece of software is one that is resistant to change. In effect, the design becomes brittle to the point that even simple changes cannot be implemented without great effort, normally requiring extensive, time-consuming, and risky refactoring. The result is a viscous code base where efforts to make new changes are slowed significantly.
- **Immobility**. A good engineer will spot cases where code can be reused to improve the maintainability and stability of the software. Immobile code is software that is immune to these efforts, making it difficult to be reused elsewhere. For example, the implementation may be too entangled with its surrounding code or it may be hardcoded with domain-specific knowledge.
- **Non-transferability**. If only a single engineer in your organization can work on certain parts of the code then it can be described as non-transferable. Often the owner will be the developer who originally wrote the code or the last unfortunate person who attempted to clean it up. For many large code bases, it's not possible for every engineer to understand every part of the code deeply, so having areas that engineers cannot easily dive into and work with effectively is a bad situation for your project.

The result of these problems is that dependencies between components grow, causing conceptually unrelated parts of the code to rely upon each other's internal implementation details. Over time, this culminates in most program state and logic becoming global or duplicated (see Figure 4.2). This is often called spaghetti code or the big ball of mud (Foote and Yoder, 1997).

4.1.2 Paying Back the Debt

Ultimately, a company will reach the point where they have accrued so much technical debt that they spend more time maintaining and containing their legacy code base than adding new features for their customers. This often results in a "next-generation" project to fix the problems with the old system. For example, when I met the software architect mentioned a few paragraphs back, the company had since grown and become successful, and his team was busily rewriting all of the code that he had originally designed.

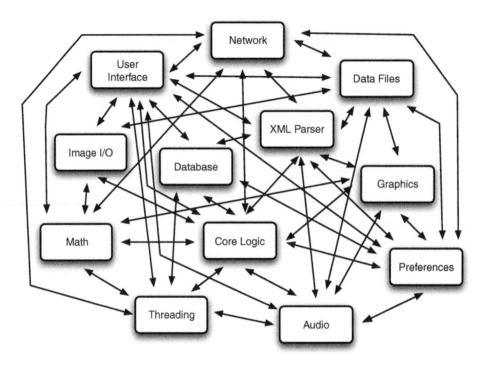

FIGURE 4.2

A decayed tightly coupled system that has devolved into a big ball of mud.

In terms of strategy, there are two extremes for such a next-generation project to consider:

1. **Evolution**: Design a system that incorporates all of the new requirements and then iteratively refactor the existing system until it reaches that point.
2. **Revolution**: Throw away the old code and then design and implement a completely new system from scratch.

Both of these options have their pros and cons, and both are difficult. I've heard the problem described as having to change the engine in a car, but the car is traveling at 100 mph, and you can't stop the car.

In the evolution case, you always have a functional system that can be released. However, you still have to work within the framework of the legacy design, which may no longer be the best way to express the problem. New requirements may have fundamentally changed the optimal workflow for key use cases. A good way to go about the evolution approach is to hide old ugly code behind new well-designed APIs (e.g., by using the wrapper patterns presented in Chapter 3, such as Façade), incrementally update all clients to go through these cleaner APIs, and put the code under automated testing (Feathers, 2004; Fowler et al., 1999).

In the revolution case, you are freed from the shackles of old technology and can design a new tool with all the knowledge you've learned from the old one (although as a pragmatic step, you may still harvest a few key classes from the old system to preserve critical behavior). You can also put new processes in place, such as requiring extensive unit test coverage for all new code, and use the opportunity to switch tools, such as adopting a new bug tracking system or source control management system. However, this option requires a lot more time and effort (i.e., money) to get to the point of a usable system, and in the meantime you either stop all development on the old tool or continue delivering new features in the old system, which keeps raising the bar for the new system to reach in order to be successful. You must also be mindful of the second-system syndrome, where the new system fails because it is overengineered and overambitious in its goal (Brooks, 1995).

In both of these cases, the need for a next-generation project introduces team dynamic issues and planning complexities. For example, do you keep a single team focused on both new and old systems? This is desirable from a personnel point of view. However, short-term tactical needs tend to trump long-term strategic development so it may be hard to sustain the next-generation project in the face of critical bug fixes and maintenance for the old one. Alternatively, if you split the development team in two, then this can create a morale problem, where developers working on the old system feel that they've been classed as second-rate developers and left behind to support a code base with no future.

Furthermore, the need for a technical restart can often instigate a business and company reorganization as well. This causes team structures and relationships to be reassessed and reshaped. It can also materially affect people's livelihoods, particularly when companies decide to downsize as part of refocusing the business. And all of this happens because of poor API design? Well, perhaps that's being a little dramatic. Reorganizations are a natural process in the growth of a company and can happen for many reasons: a structure that works for a startup with 10 people doesn't work for a successful business of 10,000. However, the failure of software to react to the needs of the business is certainly one way that reorganizations can be triggered. For instance, in June 2010, Linden Lab laid off 30% of its workforce and underwent a company-wide reorganization, primarily because the software couldn't be evolved fast enough to meet the company's revenue targets.

4.1.3 Design for the Long Term

Investing in a large next-generation effort to replace a decayed code base can cost a company millions of dollars. For example, just to pay the salary for a team of 20 developers, testers, writers, and managers for 1 year at an average salary of $100,000 would cost $2,000,000. However, the adoption of good design principles can help avoid this drastic course of action. Let's start by enumerating some of the reasons why this scenario can arise.

1. A company simply doesn't create a good software design in the first place because of a belief that it will cost valuable time and money early on.
2. The engineers on the project are ignorant of good design techniques or believe that they don't apply to their project.
3. The code was never intended to last very long, for example, it was written hastily for a demo or it was meant to be throw-away prototype code.
4. The development process for the software project doesn't make technical debt visible so knowledge of all the parts of the system that need to be fixed gets lost or forgotten over time. (Agile processes such as Scrum attempt to keep debt visible through the use of a product backlog.)

5. The system was well designed at first, but its design gradually degraded over time due to unregulated growth. For example, letting poor changes be added to the code even if they compromised the design of the system. In the words of Fred Brooks, the system loses its conceptual integrity (Brooks, 1995).

6. Changing requirements often necessitate the design to evolve too, but the company continually postpones this refactoring work, either intentionally or unintentionally, in preference to short-term fixes, hacks, and glue code.

7. Bugs are allowed to exist for long periods of time. This is often caused by a drive to continually add new functionality without a focus on the overall quality of the end product.

8. The code has no tests so regressions creep into the system as engineers modify functionality and parts of the code base ultimately turn into scary wastelands where engineers fear to make changes.

Let's tackle a few of these problems. First, the perception that good design slows you down too much. Truthfully, it may actually be the least expensive overall decision to write haphazardly structured software that gets you to market quicker and then to rewrite the code completely once you have a hold on the market. Also, certain aspects of writing good software can indeed appear to be more time-consuming, such as writing the extra code to pimpl your classes or writing automated tests to verify the behavior of your APIs. However, good design doesn't take as long as you might think, and it always pays off in the long run. Keeping a strong separation between interface and implementation pays dividends in the maintainability of your code, even in the short term, and writing automated tests gives you the confidence to change functionality rapidly without breaking existing behavior. It's noteworthy that Michael Feathers defines legacy code as code without tests, making the point that legacy doesn't have to mean old; you could be writing legacy code today (Feathers, 2004).

The beauty of APIs is that the underlying implementation can be as quick and dirty or as complete and elegant as you need. Good API design is about putting in place a stable logical interface to solve a problem. However, the code behind that API can be simple and inefficient at first. Then you can add more implementation complexity later, without breaking that logical design. Related to this, APIs let you isolate problems to specific components. By managing the dependencies between components you can limit the extent of problems. Conversely, in spaghetti code, where each component depends on the internals of other components, behavior becomes non-orthogonal and bugs in one component can affect other components in non-obvious ways. The important message is therefore to take the time to put a good high-level design in place first—to focus on the dependencies and relationships between components. That is the primary focus of this chapter.

Another aspect of the problem is that if you don't continue to keep a high bar for your code quality then the original design decays gradually as the code evolves. Cutting corners to meet a deadline is okay, as long as you go back and do it right afterward. Remember to keep paying back your technical debt. Code has a tendency to live much longer than you think it will. It's good to remember this fact when you weaken an API because you may have to support the consequences for a long time to come. It's therefore important to realize the impact of new requirements on the design of the API and to refactor your code to maintain a consistent and up-to-date design. It's equally important to enforce change control over your API so that it doesn't evolve in an unsupervised or chaotic fashion. I will discuss ways to achieve these goals in Chapter 8 when I talk about API versioning.

4.2 GATHERING FUNCTIONAL REQUIREMENTS

The first step in producing a good design for a piece of software is to understand what it actually needs to do. It's amazing how much development time is wasted by engineers building the wrong thing. It's also quite eye opening to see how often two engineers can hear the same informal description of a piece of work and come away with two completely different ideas about what it involves. This is not necessarily a bad thing: it's good to have minds that work differently to provide alternative perspectives and solutions. The problem is that the work was not specified in enough detail such that everyone involved could form a shared understanding and work toward the same goal. This is where requirements come in. There are several different types of requirements in the software industry, including the following.

- **Business requirements**: describe the value of the software in business terms, that is, how it advances the needs of the organization.
- **Functional requirements**: describe the behavior of the software, that is, what the software is supposed to accomplish.
- **Non-functional requirements**: describe the quality standards that the software must achieve, that is, how well the software works for users.

I will concentrate primarily on functional and non-functional requirements in the following sections. However, it is still extremely important to ensure that the functionality of your software aligns with the strategic goals of your business, as otherwise you run the risk of harming the long-term success of your API.

4.2.1 What Are Functional Requirements?

Functional requirements are simply a way to understand what to build so that you don't waste time and money building the wrong thing. It also gives you the necessary up front information to devise an elegant design that implements these requirements. In our diagram of the phases of software development (Figure 4.1), functional requirements sit squarely in the analysis phase.

In terms of API development, functional requirements define the intended functionality for the API. These should be developed in collaboration with the clients of the API so that they represent the voice and needs of the user (Wiegers, 2003). Explicitly capturing requirements also lets you agree upon the scope of functionality with the intended users. Of course, the users of an API are also developers, but that doesn't mean that you should assume that you know what they want just because you are a developer too. At times it may be necessary to second-guess or research requirements yourself. Nevertheless, you should still identify target users of your API, experts in the domain of your API, and drive the functional requirements from their input. For example, you can hold interviews, meetings, or use questionnaires to ask users:

- What tasks they expect to achieve with the API?
- What an optimal workflow would be from their perspective?
- What are all the potential inputs, including their types and valid ranges?
- What are all the expected outputs, including type, format, and ranges?
- What file formats or protocols must be supported?
- What (if any) mental models do they have for the problem domain?
- What domain terminology do they use?

If you are revising or refactoring an existing API, you can also ask developers to comment on the code that they currently must write to use the API. This can help identify cumbersome workflows and unused parts of an API. You can also ask them how they would prefer to use the API in an ideal world (Stylos, 2008).

TIP

Functional requirements specify how your API should behave.

Functional requirements can also be supported by non-functional requirements. These are requirements that judge the operational constraints of an API rather than how it actually behaves. These qualities can be just as critical to a user as the functionality provided by the API. Examples of non-functional requirements include aspects such as:

- **Performance**. Are there constraints on the speed of certain operations?
- **Platform compatibility**. Which platforms must the code run on?
- **Security**. Are there data security, access, or privacy concerns?
- **Scalability**. Can the system handle real-world data inputs?
- **Flexibility**. Will the system need to be extended after release?
- **Usability**. Can the user easily understand, learn, and use the API?
- **Concurrency**. Does the system need to utilize multiple processors?
- **Cost**. How much will the software cost?

4.2.2 Example Functional Requirements

Functional requirements are normally managed in a requirements document where each requirement is given a unique identifier and a description. A rationale for the requirement may also be provided to explain why it is necessary. It's typical to present the requirements as a concise list of bullet points and to organize the document into different themed sections so that requirements relating to the same part of the system can be colocated.

Good functional requirements should be simple, easy to read, unambiguous, verifiable, and free of jargon. It's important that they do not over-specify the technical implementation: functional requirements should document what an API should do and not how it does it.

To illustrate these points, here's an example list of functional requirements for a user interacting with an Automated Teller Machine (ATM).

REQ 1.1. The system shall prevent further interaction if it's out of cash or is unable to communicate with the financial institution.

REQ 1.2. The system shall validate that the inserted card is valid for financial transactions on this ATM.

REQ 1.3. The system shall validate that the PIN number entered by the user is correct.

REQ 1.4. The system shall dispense the requested amount of money, if it is available, and debit the user's account by the same amount.

REQ 1.5. The system shall notify the user if the transaction could not be completed. In that case, no money shall be taken from the user's account.

4.2.3 **Maintaining the Requirements**

There is no such thing as stable requirements; you should always expect them to change over time. This happens for a variety of reasons, but the most common reason is that users (and you) will have a clearer idea of how the system should function as you start building it. You should therefore make sure that you version and date your requirements so that you can refer to a specific version of the document and you know how old it is.

On average, 25% of a project's functional requirements will change during development, accounting for 70–85% of the code that needs to be reworked (McConnell, 2004). While it's good to stay in sync with the evolving needs of your clients, you should also make sure that everyone understands the cost of changing requirements. Adding new requirements will cause the project to take longer to deliver. It may also require significant changes to the design, causing a lot of code to be rewritten.

In particular, you should be wary of falling into the trap of requirement creep. Any major changes to the functional requirements should trigger a revision of the schedule and costing for the project. In general, any new additions to the requirements should be evaluated against the incremental business value that they deliver. Assessing a new requirement from this pragmatic viewpoint should help weigh the benefit of the change against the cost of implementing it.

4.3 **CREATING USE CASES**

A use case describes the behavior of an API based on interactions of a user or another piece of software (Jacobson, 1992). Use cases are essentially a form of functional requirement that specifically captures who does what with an API and for what purpose rather than simply providing a list of features, behaviors, or implementation notes. Focusing on use cases helps you design an API from the perspective of the client.

It's not uncommon to produce a functional requirement document as well as a set of use cases. For example, use cases can be used to describe an API from the user's point of view, whereas functional requirements can be used to describe a list of features or the details of an algorithm. However, concentrating on just one of these techniques can often be sufficient, too. In which case, I recommend creating use cases because these resonate most closely with the way a user wants to interact with a system. When using both methods, you can either derive functional requirements from the use cases or vice versa, although it's more typical to work with your users to produce use cases first and then derive a list of functional requirements from these use cases.

TIP

Use cases describe the requirements for your API from the perspective of the user.

Ken Arnold uses the analogy of driving a car to illustrate the importance of designing an interface based on its usage rather than its implementation details. He notes that you are more likely to come up with a good experience for drivers by asking the question "How does the user control the car?" instead of "How can the user adjust the rate of fuel pumped into each of the pistons?" (Arnold, 2005).

4.3.1 Developing Use Cases

Every use case describes a goal that an "actor" is trying to achieve. An actor is an entity external to the system that initiates interactions, such as a human user, a device, or another piece of software. Each actor may play different roles when interacting with the system. For example, a single actor for a database may take on the role of administrator, developer, or database user. A good way to approach the process of creating use cases is therefore (1) identify all of the actors of the system and the roles that each plays, (2) identify all of the goals that each role needs to accomplish, and (3) create use cases for each goal.

Each use case should be written in plain English using the vocabulary of the problem domain. It should be named to describe the outcome of value to the actor. Each step of the use case should start with the role followed by an active verb. For example, continuing our ATM example, the following steps describe how to validate a user's PIN number.

Step 1. User inserts ATM card.
Step 2. System validates that ATM card is valid for use with the ATM machine.
Step 3. System prompts the user to enter PIN number.
Step 4. User enters PIN number.
Step 5. System checks that the PIN number is correct.

4.3.2 Use Case Templates

A good use case represents a goal-oriented narrative description of a single unit of behavior. It includes a distinct sequence of steps that describes the workflow to achieve the goal of the use case. It can also provide clear pre- and postconditions to specify the state of the system before and after the use case, that is, to explicitly state the dependencies between use cases, as well as the trigger event that causes a use case to be initiated.

Use cases can be recorded with different degrees of formality and verbosity. For example, they can be as simple as a few sentences or they can be as formal as structured, cross-referenced specifications that conform to a particular template. They can even be described visually, such as with the UML Use Case Diagram (Cockburn, 2000).

TIP

Use cases can be simple lists of short goal-oriented descriptions or can be more formal structured specifications that follow a prescribed template.

In the more formal instance, there are many different template formats and styles for representing use cases textually. These templates tend to be very project specific and can be as short or extensive as appropriate for that project. Don't get hung up on the details of your template: it's more important to communicate the requirements clearly than to conform to a rigid notation (Alexander, 2003). Nonetheless, a few common elements of a use case template include the following.

Name: A unique identifier for the use case, often in verb–noun format such as Withdraw Cash or Buy Stamps.
Version: A number to differentiate different versions of the use case.
Description: A brief overview that summarizes the use case in one or two sentences.
Goal: A description of what the user wants to accomplish.

Actors: The actor roles that want to achieve the goal.

Stakeholder: The individual or organization that has a vested interest in the outcome of the use case, for example, an ATM User or the Bank.

Basic Course: A sequence of steps that describe the typical course of events. This should avoid conditional logic where possible.

Extensions: A list of conditions that cause alternative steps to be taken. This describes what to do if the goal fails, for example, an invalid PIN number was entered.

Trigger: The event that causes the use case to be initiated.

Precondition: A list of conditions required for the trigger to execute successfully.

Postcondition: Describes the state of the system after the successful execution of the use case.

Notes: Additional information that doesn't fit well into any other category.

4.3.3 Writing Good Use Cases

Writing use cases should be an intuitive process. They are written in plain easy-to-read language to capture the user's perspective on how the API should be used. However, even supposedly intuitive tasks can benefit from general guidelines and words of advice.

- **Use domain terminology**. Use cases should be described in terms that are natural to the clients of an API. The terms that are used should be familiar to users and should come from the domain being targeted. In effect, users should be able to read use cases and understand the scenarios easily without them appearing too contrived.
- **Don't over-specify use cases**. Use cases should describe the black-box functionality of a system, that is, you should avoid specifying implementation details. You should also avoid including too much detail in your use cases. Alistair Cockburn uses the example of inserting coins into a candy machine. Instead of trying to specify different combinations of inserting the correct quantity, such as "person inserts three quarters, or 15 nickels or a quarter followed by 10 nickels," you just need to write "person inserts money."
- **Use cases don't define all requirements**. Use cases do not encompass all possible forms of requirements gathering. For example, they do not represent system design, lists of features, algorithm specifics, or any other parts of the system that are not user oriented. Use cases concentrate on behavioral requirements for how the user should interact with the API. You may still wish to compile functional and non-functional requirements in addition to use cases.
- **Use cases don't define a design**. While you can often create a high-level preliminary design from your use cases, you should not fall into the trap of believing that use cases directly define the best design. The fact that they don't define all requirements is one reason. For example, they don't define performance, security, or network aspects of the API, which can affect the particular design greatly. Also, use cases are written from the perspective of users. You may therefore need to reinterpret their feedback in light of conflicting or imprecise goals rather than treating them too literally (Meyer, 1997).
- **Don't specify design in use cases**. It is generally accepted that you should avoid describing user interfaces in use cases because UI is a design, not a requirement, and because UI designs are more changeable (Cockburn, 2000). While this axiom is not directly applicable to UI-less API design, it can be extrapolated to our circumstances by stating that you should keep API design specifics out of your use cases. Users may try to propose a particular solution for you to implement, but better solutions to the problem may exist. API design should therefore follow from your

use case analysis. In other words, use cases define how a user wants to achieve a goal regardless of the actual design.

- **Use cases can direct testing**. Use cases are not test plans in themselves because they don't specify specific input and output values. However, they do specify the key workflows that your users expect to be able to achieve. As such, they are a great source to direct automated testing efforts for your API. Writing a suite of tests that verify these key workflows will give you the confidence that you have reached the needs of your users, and that you don't break this functionality as you evolve the API in the future.
- **Expect to iterate**. Don't be too concerned about getting all of your use cases perfect the first time. Use case analysis is a process of discovery; it helps you learn more about the system you want to build. You should therefore look upon it as an iterative process where you can refine existing use cases as you expand your knowledge of the entire system (Alexander, 2003). However, it is well known that errors in requirements can impact a project significantly, causing major redesign and reimplementation efforts. This is why the first piece of advice I gave was to avoid making your use cases too detailed.
- **Don't insist on complete coverage**. For the same reasons that use cases do not encompass all forms of requirements, you should not expect your use cases to express all aspects of your API. However, you also don't need them to cover everything. Some parts of the system may already be well understood or do not need a user-directed perspective. There's also the logistical concern that because you will not have unlimited time and resources to compile exhaustive use cases, you should focus the effort on the most important user-oriented goals and workflows (Alexander, 2003).

Putting all of this information together, I will complete our ATM example by presenting a sample use case for entering a PIN number and use our template described earlier to format the use case.

Name: Enter PIN
Version: 1.0.
Description: User enters PIN number to validate her Bank account information.
Goal: System validates User's PIN number.
Stakeholders:
1. User wants to use ATM services
2. Bank wants to validate the User's account.

Basic Course:
1. System validates that ATM card is valid for use with the ATM machine.
2. System prompts the user to enter PIN number.
3. User enters PIN number.
4. System checks that the PIN number is correct.

Extensions:
a. System failure to recognize ATM card:
    a-1. System displays error message and aborts operation.
b. User enters invalid PIN:
    b-1. System displays error message and lets User retry.

Trigger: User inserts card into ATM.
Postcondition: User's PIN number is validated for financial transactions.

4.3.4 **Requirements and Agile Development**

Agile development is a general term for software development methods that align with the principles of the Agile Manifesto. Examples include Extreme Programming (XP), Scrum, and Dynamic Systems Development Method (DSDM). The Agile Manifesto (http://agilemanifesto.org/) was written in February 2001 by 17 contributors who wanted to find more lightweight and nimble alternatives to the traditional development processes of the time. It states that the following qualities should be valued when developing software:

- Individuals and interactions over processes and tools.
- Working software over comprehensive documentation.
- Customer collaboration over contract negotiation.
- Responding to change over following a plan.

Agile methodologies therefore deemphasize document-centric processes, instead preferring to iterate on working code. However, this does not mean that they are without any form of requirements. What it means is that the requirements are lightweight and easily changed. Maintaining a large, wordy, formal requirements document would not be considered agile. However, the general concept of use cases is very much a part of agile processes, such as Scrum and XP, which emphasize the creation of user stories.

A user story is a high-level requirement that contains just enough information for a developer to provide a reasonable estimate of the effort required to implement it. It is conceptually very similar to a use case, except that the goal is to keep them very short, normally just a single sentence. As a result, the brief informal use case is more similar to a user story than the formal template-driven or UML use case. Another important distinction is that user stories are not all completed up front. Many user stories will be added incrementally as the working code evolves. That is, you start writing code for your design early to avoid throwing away specifications that become invalid after you try to implement them.

TIP

User stories are a way to capture minimal requirements from users within an agile development process.

Another important aspect of user stories is that they are written by project stakeholders, not developers, that is, the customers, vendors, business owners, or support personnel interested in the product being developed. Keeping the user story short allows stakeholders to write them in a few minutes. Mike Cohn suggests the use of a simple format to describe user stories (Cohn, 2004):

As a [role] I want [something] so that [benefit].

For instance, referring back to our ATM example, here's an example of five different user stories for interacting with a cash machine:

- As a customer I want to withdraw cash so that I can buy things.
- As a customer I want to transfer money from my savings account to my checking account so I can write checks.
- As a customer I want to deposit money into my account so I can increase my account balance.

* As a bank business owner I want the customer's identity to be verified securely so that the ATM can protect against fraudulent activities.
* As an ATM operator I want to restock the ATM with money so the ATM will have cash for customers to withdraw.

Given a set of well-written user stories, engineers can estimate the scale of the development effort involved, usually in terms of an abstract quantity such as story points, and work on implementing these stories. Stakeholders will also often provide an indication of the priority of a user story to help prioritize the order of work from the backlog of all stories. Stakeholders then assess the state of the software at regular intervals, such as during a sprint review, and can provide further user stories to focus the next iteration of development. In other words, this implies active user involvement and favors an iterative development style over the creation of large up-front requirements documents.

Cohn also presents an easy-to-remember acronym to help you create good user stories. The acronym is INVEST, where each letter stands for a quality of a well-written user story (Cohn, 2004):

Independent
Negotiable
Valuable
Estimable
Small
Testable

In addition, all of the advice offered earlier for writing good use cases applies equally well to user stories. For example, because agile processes such as Scrum and XP do not tell you how to design your API, you must not forget that once you have built up your backlog of user stories, you still have to go through a separate design process to work out how best to implement those stories. This is the topic that I will concentrate on for the remainder of this chapter.

4.4 ELEMENTS OF API DESIGN

At last, we can talk about design! The secret to producing a good API design lies in coming up with an appropriate abstraction for the problem domain and then devising appropriate object and class hierarchies to represent that abstraction.

An abstraction is just a simplified description of something that can be understood without any knowledge of how it will be implemented programmatically. It tends to emphasize the important characteristics and responsibilities of that thing while ignoring details that are not important to understanding its basic nature. Furthermore, you often find that complex problems exhibit hierarchies, or layers, of abstractions (Henning, 2009).

For example, you could describe how a car works at a very high level with six basic components: a fuel system, engine, transmission, driveshaft, axle, and wheels. The fuel system provides the energy to turn the engine, which causes the transmission to rotate, while the driveshaft connects the transmission to the axle, allowing the power to reach the wheels and ultimately cause the vehicle to move forward. This is one level of abstraction that is useful to understand the most general principles of how a car achieves forward motion. However, you could also offer another level of abstraction that provides more detail for one or more of these components. For example, an internal combustion engine could be described with several interconnected components, including a piston, crankshaft, camshaft, distributor, flywheel, and timing belt. Furthermore, an engine can be categorized as one of several different types, such as an internal combustion engine, an electric engine, a gas/electric hybrid, or a hydrogen fuel cell.

Similarly, most designs for complex software systems exhibit structure at multiple levels of detail, and those hierarchies can also be viewed in different ways. Grady Booch suggests that there are two important hierarchical views of any complex system (Booch et al., 2007):

1. **Object Hierarchy**: Describes how different objects cooperate in the system. This represents a structural grouping based on a "part of" relationship between objects (e.g., a piston is part of an engine, which is part of a car).
2. **Class Hierarchy**: Describes the common structure and behavior shared between related objects. It deals with the generalization and specialization of object properties. This can be thought of as an "is a" hierarchy between objects (e.g., a hybrid engine is a type of car engine).

Both of these views are equally important when producing the design for a software system. Figure 4.3 attempts to illustrate these two concepts, showing a hierarchy of related objects and a hierarchy of classes that inherit behavior and properties.

Related to this, it is generally agreed that the design phase of software construction consists of two major activities (Bourque et al., 2004):

1. **Architecture design**: Describes the top-level structure and organization of a piece of software.
2. **Detailed design**: Describes individual components of the design to a sufficient level that they can be implemented.

Therefore, as a general approach, I suggest defining an object hierarchy to delineate the top-level conceptual structure (or architecture) of your system and then refine this with class hierarchies that specify concrete C++ classes for your clients to use. The latter process of defining the classes of your API also involves thinking about the individual functions and arguments that they provide. The rest of this chapter will therefore focus on each of these topics in turn:

1. Architecture design.
2. Class design.
3. Function design.

TIP

API design involves developing a top-level architecture and a detailed class hierarchy.

4.5 ARCHITECTURE DESIGN

Software architecture describes the coarse structure of an entire system: the collection of top-level objects in the API and their relationships to each other. By developing an architecture, you gain an understanding of the different components of the system in the abstract, as well as how they communicate and cooperate with each other.

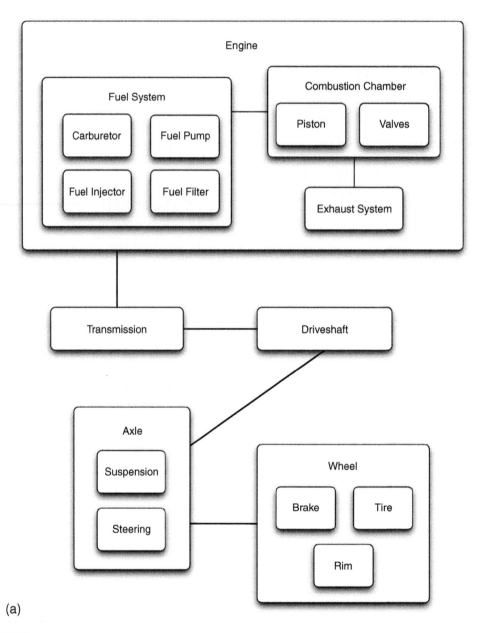

(a)

FIGURE 4.3

A car design shown as (a) a "part of" object hierarchy and

(Continued)

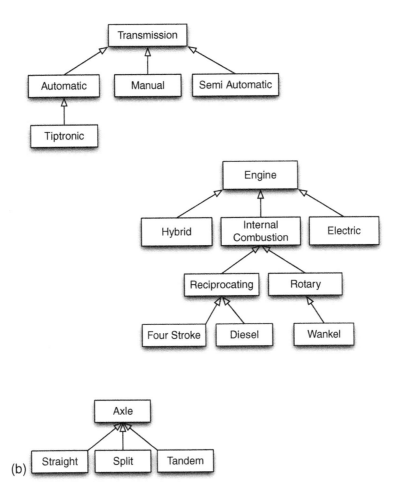

FIGURE 4.3—cont'd

(b) an "is a" class hierarchy. Arrows point from more specific to more general classes.

It's important to spend time thinking about the top-level architecture for your API because problems in your architecture can have a far-reaching and extensive impact on your system. Consequently, this section details the process of producing an architecture for your API and provides insight into how you can decompose a problem domain into an appropriate collection of abstract objects.

4.5.1 Developing an Architecture

There's no right or wrong architecture for any given problem. If you give the same set of requirements to two different architects then you'll undoubtedly end up with two different solutions. The important aspect is to produce a well-thought-out purposeful design that delivers a framework to implement the system and resolves trade-offs between the various conflicting requirements and constraints (Bass et al., 2003). At a high level, the process of creating an architecture for an API resolves to four basic steps.

1. Analyze the functional requirements that affect the architecture.
2. Identify and account for the constraints on the architecture.
3. Invent the primary objects in the system and their relationships.
4. Communicate and document the architecture.

The first of these steps is fed by the earlier requirements gathering stage (refer back to Figure 4.1), be it based on a formal functional requirements document, a set of goal-oriented use cases, or a collection of informal user stories. The second step involves capturing and accounting for all of the factors that place a constraint on the architecture you design. The third step involves defining the high-level object model for the system: key objects and how they relate to each other. Finally, the architecture should be communicated to the engineers who must implement it. Figure 4.4 illustrates each of these steps.

It's important to stress that the aforementioned sequence of steps is not a recipe that you perform only once and magically arrive at the perfect architecture. As stated already, software design is an iterative process. You will rarely get each step right the first time. However, the first release of your API is critical because changes after that point will incur higher cost. It's therefore important to try

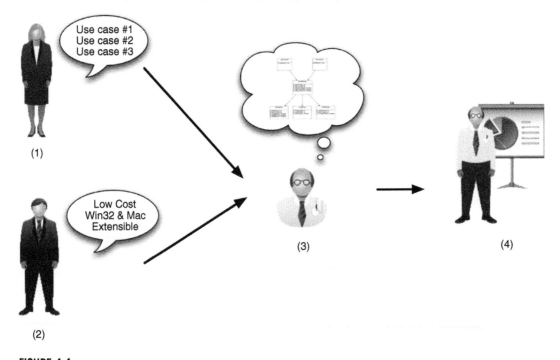

FIGURE 4.4

Steps to develop an API architecture: (1) gather user requirements, (2) identify constraints, (3) invent key objects, and (4) communicate design.

out your design early on and improve it incrementally before releasing it to clients who will then start to build upon it in their own programs.

4.5.2 Architecture Constraints

APIs aren't designed in a vacuum. There will always be factors that influence and constrain the architecture. Before the design process can proceed in earnest you must therefore identify and accommodate for these factors. Christine Hofmeister and her coauthors refer to this phase as global analysis (Hofmeister et al., 2009). The term global in this respect connotes that the factors impact the system holistically and that as a group they are often interdependent and contradictory. These factors fall into three basic categories.

1. Organizational factors, such as
   a. Budget
   b. Schedule
   c. Team size and expertise
   d. Software development process
   e. Build versus buy decision on subsystems
   f. Management focus (e.g., date versus feature versus quality).
2. Environmental factors, such as
   a. Hardware (e.g., set-top box or mobile device)
   b. Platform (e.g., Windows, Mac, and Linux)
   c. Software constraints (e.g., use of other APIs)
   d. Client/server constraints (e.g., building a Web service)
   e. Protocol constraints (e.g., POP vs IMAP for a mail client)
   f. File format constraints (e.g., must support GIF and JPEG images)
   g. Database dependencies (e.g., must connect to a remote database)
   h. Expose versus wrap decision on subsystems
   i. Development tools.
3. Operational factors, such as
   a. Performance
   b. Memory utilization
   c. Reliability
   d. Availability
   e. Concurrency
   f. Customizability
   g. Extensibility
   h. Scriptability
   i. Security
   j. Internationalization
   k. Network bandwidth

It's the job of the software architect to prioritize these factors, combined with the user constraints contained within the functional requirements, and to find the best compromises that produce a flexible and efficient design. Designing an API carefully for its intended audience can only serve to improve its usability and success. However, there's no such thing as a perfect design; it's all about trade-offs for the given set of organizational, environmental, and operational constraints. For example, if you are forced to deliver results under an aggressive schedule then you may have to focus on a simpler design that leverages third-party APIs as much as possible and restricts the number of supported platforms.

```
TIP

Architecture design is constrained by a multitude of unique organizational, environmental, and operational
factors.
```

Some constraints can be negotiated. For example, if one of the client's requirements places undue complexity on the system, the client may be willing to accept an alternative solution that costs less money or can be delivered sooner.

In addition to identifying the factors that will impact your initial architecture, you should also assess which of these are susceptible to change during development. For example, the first version of the software may not be very extensible, but you know that you will eventually want to move to a plugin model that lets users add their own functionality. Another common example is internationalization. You may not care about supporting more than one language at first, but later on this may become a new requirement, and one that can have a deep impact on the code. Your design should therefore anticipate the constraints that you reasonably expect to change in the future. You may be able to come up with a design that can support change or, if that's not feasible, you may need to think about contingency plans. This is often referred to as "design for change" (Parnas, 1979).

```
TIP

Always design for change. Change is inevitable.
```

It's also worth thinking about how you can isolate your design from changes in any APIs that your project will depend upon. If your use of another API is completely internal, then there's no problem. However, if you need to expose the concepts of a dependent API in your own public interface, then you should consider whether it's possible to limit the degree to which it is made visible. In some cases this simply may not be practical. For example, if you use `boost::shared_ptr` to return smart pointers from your API, then your clients will also need to depend on the Boost headers. However, in other cases you may be able to provide wrappers for the dependent API so that you do not force your clients to depend directly on that API. For example, the KDE API is built on top of the Qt library. However, KDE uses a thin wrapper over the Qt API so that users are not directly dependent on the Qt API. As a specific example, KDE offers classes such as `KApplication`, `KObject`, and `KPushButton` instead of exposing Qt's `QApplication`, `QObject`, and `QPushButton` classes directly. Wrapping dependent APIs in this way gives you an extra layer of indirection to protect against changes in a dependent API and to work around bugs or platform-specific limitations.

4.5.3 Identifying Major Abstractions

Once you have analyzed the requirements and constraints of the system, you are ready to start building a high-level object model. Essentially, this means identifying major abstractions in the problem

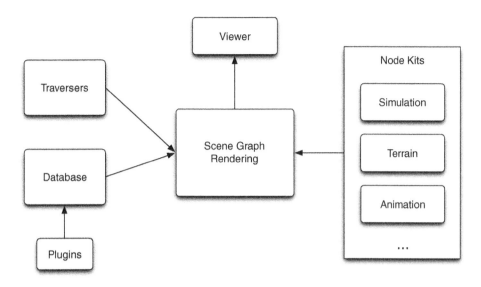

FIGURE 4.5

Example top-level architecture for the OpenSceneGraph API.

domain and decomposing these into a hierarchy of interconnected objects. Figure 4.5 presents an example of this process. It shows a top-level architecture for the OpenSceneGraph API, an open source 3D graphics toolkit for visual simulation applications (http://www.openscenegraph.org/).

By basing the architecture on actual concepts in the problem domain, your design should remain general and robust to future changes in requirements. Recall that I listed this as the first API quality in Chapter 2: a good API should model the problem domain. However, decomposing a problem into a set of good abstractions is not an easy task. For well-understood problems, such as writing a compiler or a Web server, you can take advantage of the collective knowledge that has been distilled and published by many other designers over time. However, for new problems that have had little or no previous research applied to them, the task of inventing a good classification can be far from obvious.

This is not a problem that is unique to computer science. Classification of the biology of our planet into a logical taxonomy has been an area of debate ever since the days of Aristotle. In the 18th century, Carolus Linnaeus proposed a two-kingdom model for life, composed of vegetables and animals. This was later refined to include microscopic life forms in the 19th century. Modern advances in electron microscopy have increased the number of kingdoms to five or six. However, research in the 21st century has contested the traditional view of kingdoms and proposed an alternative "supergroup" model. Additionally, the topic of deciding which characteristics should be used to create classifications has received much debate. Aristotle classified animals according to their method of reproduction, the binomial system groups organisms by their morphology (similar structure or appearance), while Darwinian-inspired taxonomies favor classification by common descent (whether organisms have a common ancestor).

4.5.4 **Inventing Key Objects**

Despite the difficulty of classifying the major abstractions in a system, I can still offer some advice on how to tackle the problem. Accordingly, here are a number of techniques that you can draw upon to decompose a system into a set of key objects and identify their relationship to each other (Booch et al., 2007).

- **Natural Language**. Using the analogy to natural language, it has been observed that (in general) nouns tend to represent objects, verbs represent functions, and adjectives and possessive nouns represent attributes (Bourque et al., 2004). I can illustrate this by returning to our address book API from Chapter 2. Real-world concepts of an address book and a person are both nouns and make sense to represent key objects in the API, whereas actions such as adding a person to the address book or adding a telephone number for a person are verbs and should be represented as function calls on the objects that they modify. However, a person's name is a possessive noun and makes more sense to be an attribute of the `Person` object rather than a high-level object in its own right.
- **Properties**. This technique involves grouping objects that have similar properties or qualities. This can be done using discrete categories that each object is unambiguously either a member of or not, such as red objects versus blue objects, or can involve a probabilistic grouping of objects that depends on how closely each object matches some fuzzy criterion or concept, such as whether a film is categorized as an action or romance story.
- **Behaviors**. This method groups objects by the dynamic behaviors that they share. This involves determining the set of behaviors in the system and assigning these behaviors to different parts of the system. You can then derive the set of objects by identifying the initiators and participants of these behaviors.
- **Prototypes**. In this approach, you attempt to discover more general prototypes for the objects that were initially identified. For example, a beanbag, bar stool, and recliner are all types of chairs, despite having very different forms and appearance. However, you can classify each of them based on the degree to which they exhibit affordances of a prototypical chair.
- **Domains (Shlaer–Mellor)**. The Shlaer–Mellor method first partitions a system horizontally to create generic "domains" and then partitions these vertically by applying a separate analysis to each domain (Shlaer and Mellor, 1988). One of the benefits of this divide-and-conquer approach is that domains tend to form reusable concepts that can be applied to other design problems. For instance, using our earlier ATM example, a domain could be one of the following:
  - **Tangible domains**, such as an ATM machine or a bank note.
  - **Role domains**, such as an ATM user or a bank owner.
  - **Event domains**, such as a financial transaction.
  - **Security domains**, such as authentication and encryption.
  - **Interaction domains**, such as PIN entry or a cash withdrawal.
  - **Logging domains**, for the system to log information.
- **Domains (Neighbors)**. James Neighbors coined the term domain analysis as the technique of uncovering classes and objects shared by all applications in the problem domain (Neighbors, 1980). This is done by analyzing related systems in the problem domain to discover areas of commonality and distinctiveness, such as identifying the common elements in all bug tracking systems or general features of all genealogy programs.

- **Domains (Evans).** A related issue to Neighbors' domain analysis is the term domain-driven design. This was introduced by Eric Evans and seeks to produce designs for complex systems using an evolving model of the core business concepts (Evans, 2003).

TIP

Identifying the key objects for an API is difficult. Try looking at the problem from different perspectives and keep iterating and refining your model.

Most of these techniques work best when you have a well-organized and structured set of use cases to work from. For example, use cases are normally constructed as sentences where a thing performs some action, often to or on another thing. You can therefore use these as input for a simple natural language analysis by taking the steps of each use case and identifying the subject or object nouns and use these to develop an initial candidate list of objects.

Each of the aforementioned techniques can also involve different degrees of formal methods. For example, natural language analysis it not a very rigorous technique and is often discouraged by proponents of formal design methodologies. That's because natural language is intrinsically ambiguous and may express important concepts of the problem domain imprecisely or neglect significant architectural features. You should therefore be wary of naively translating all nouns in your use cases to key objects. At best, you should treat the result of this analysis as an initial candidate list from which to apply further careful analysis and refinement (Alexander, 2003). This refinement can involve identifying any gaps in the model, considering whether there are more general concepts that can be extracted from the list, and attempting to classify similar concepts.

In contrast, there are several formal techniques for producing a software design, including textual and graphical notations. One particularly widespread technique is the Universal Modeling Language (UML) (Booch et al., 2005). Using a set of graphical diagrams, UML can be used to specify and maintain a software design visually. For instance, UML 2.3 includes 14 distinct types of diagrams to represent the various structural and behavioral aspects of a design (see Figure 4.6). As a specific example, UML sequence diagrams portray the sequence of function calls between objects. These can be used during the analysis phase to represent use cases graphically. Then, during the design phase, the architect can use these formal diagrams to explore object interactions within the system and flesh out the top-level object model.

Formal design notations can also be used to generate actual code. This ranges from the simple translation of class diagrams into their direct source code equivalents to the more comprehensive notion of an "executable architecture." The latter is a sufficiently detailed description of an architecture that can be translated into executable software and run on a target platform. For example, the Shlaer–Mellor notation was eventually evolved into a profile of UML called Executable UML (Mellor and Balcer, 2002), which itself became a cornerstone of Model Driven Architecture. The basic principle behind this approach is that a model compiler takes several executable UML models, each of which defines a different crosscutting concern or domain, and combines these to produce high-level executable code. Proponents of executable architectures note the two-language problem that this entails: having a modeling language (e.g., UML) that gets translated into a separate programming language (e.g., C++, C#, or Java). Many of these proponents therefore posit the need for a single language that can bridge both of these concerns.

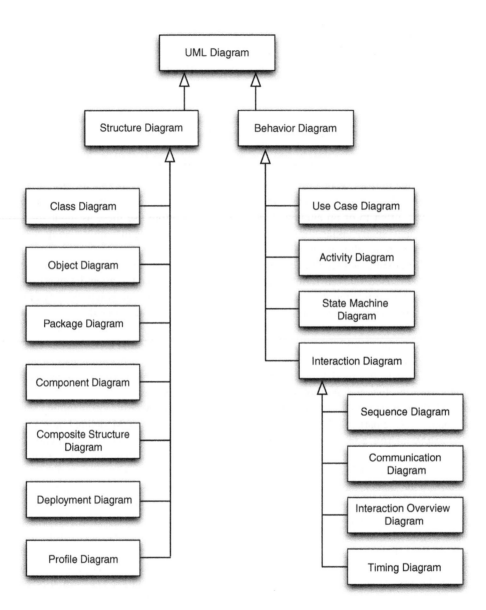

FIGURE 4.6

The 14 diagram types of UML 2.3.

4.5.5 **Architectural Patterns**

Chapter 2 covered various design patterns that can be used to solve recurring problems in software design, such as Singleton, Factory Method, and Observer. These tend to provide solutions that can be implemented at the component level. However, a class of software patterns called architectural patterns describe larger scale structures and organizations for entire systems. As such, some of these solutions may be useful to you when you are building an API that maps well to a particular architectural pattern. The following list classifies a number of the more popular architectural patterns (Bourque et al., 2004).

-   **Structural patterns**: Layers, Pipes and Filters, and Blackboard
-   **Interactive systems**: Model–View–Controller (MVC), Model–View–Presenter, and Presentation–Abstraction–Control
-   **Distributed systems**: Client/Server, Three Tier, Peer to Peer, and Broker
-   **Adaptable systems**: Micro-kernel and Reflection

Many of these architectural patterns present elegant designs to avoid dependency problems between different parts of your system, such as the MVC pattern discussed in detail in Chapter 2. At this point, it's worth noting that another important view of a system's architecture is the physical view of library files and their dependencies. I presented an example of this view back in Figure 1.3, where I showed the layers of APIs that make up a complex end-user application. Even within a single API you will likely have different layers of physical architecture, such as those that follow and are illustrated in Figure 4.7.

1. API-neutral low-level routines, such as string manipulation routines, math functions, or your threading model.
2. Core business logic that implements the primary function of your API.

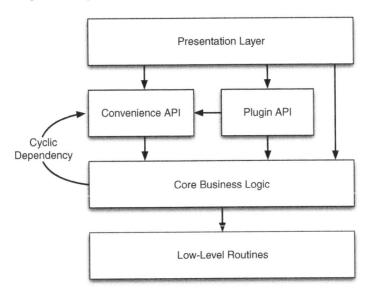

FIGURE 4.7

Example architectural layers of an API showing a cyclic, or circular, dependency between two components.

3. Plugin or Scripting APIs to allow users to extend the base functionality of the API.
4. Convenience APIs built on top of the core API functionality.
5. A presentation layer to provide a visual display of your API results.

In this case, it's important to impose a strict dependency hierarchy on the different architectural layers of your system, as otherwise you will end up with cyclic dependencies between layers (see Figure 4.7). The same is true for individual components within those layers. The general observation is that lower-level components should not depend on higher-level components of your architecture. For example, your core business logic cannot depend on your convenience API as this would introduce a cycle between the two (assuming that your convenience API also calls down into the core business logic). Referring back to the MVC architectural pattern, you will note that View depends on Model, but not vice versa. David L. Parnas referred to this concept as loop-free hierarchies (Parnas, 1979).

MENVSHARED

During my early years at Pixar, we got into a situation where we had a large number of cyclic dependencies between the core suite of animation libraries. These dependencies crept slowly into the system as we worked to meet many tight production deadlines.

In order to allow the system to continue to compile, we resorted to linking all of this interdependent code into a single huge shared library, called libmenvshared.so (pronounced men-vee-shared). This meant that any changes to one of the libraries in this shared library would require the entire shared library to be rebuilt, a process that could take at least 5–10 minutes.

As you can imagine, this became a significant bottleneck to the development team's velocity. In fact, the massive size of the menvshared library even caused linker crashes when we tried porting our code to another platform.

Thankfully, a brave few engineers were eventually able to tackle this problem and over many weeks we gradually teased apart the dependencies to finally get rid of menvshared.

Cyclic dependencies are bad for many reasons. For example, they mean that you cannot test each component independently and you cannot reuse one component without also pulling in the other. Basically, it's necessary to understand both components in order to understand either one (Lakos, 1996). This can also impact the speed of your development if you are forced to merge several components into one big über component, as described in the accompanying side bar. Chapters 1 and 2 presented various techniques to decouple dependencies, such as callbacks, observers, and notification systems. Fundamentally, an API should be an acyclic hierarchy of logically related components.

TIP

Avoid cyclic dependencies between components of your API.

4.5.6 Communicating the Architecture

Once an architecture has been developed, it can be documented in various ways. This can range from simple drawings or wiki pages to various formal methods that provide modeling notations for architectures, such as UML or the set of Architecture Description Languages (Medvidovic and Taylor, 2000).

Whichever approach you adopt, documenting the architecture is an important factor in communicating the design to engineers. Doing so gives them more information to implement the system according to your vision and also ensures that future changes continue to preserve the intent and integrity of the architecture. This is particularly important if the development team is large or distributed geographically.

One of the elements you should include in your architecture documentation is a rationale for the overall design. That is, which alternative designs and trade-offs were considered and why the final structure was judged to be superior. This design rationale can be very important for the long-term maintenance of the design and to save future designers from revisiting the same dead ends that you did. In fact, Martin Robillard notes that users of an API often find it difficult to learn and use an API if they don't understand its high-level architecture and design intents (Robillard, 2009).

TIP

Describe the high-level architecture and design rationale for your API in the accompanying user documentation.

Communication also allows for peer review of the design and for feedback and improvements to be received before the API is released. In fact, implementing design reviews early in the process to facilitate communication among architects, developers, and clients will help you produce a more comprehensive and durable design. If the API architect also writes some of the code then this can be an excellent way to communicate design principles through practical hands-on contribution.

Even though modern agile development methods deemphasize document heavy processes, because the design documents are frequently out of date, there is still a place for providing as much documentation about the system architecture as necessary, but no more. Augmenting any documentation with direct communication can be even more productive. This allows for a dialogue between the designer and the implementer and can avoid misunderstandings that can happen when reading specifications. Ultimately, it's the job of the architect to be a passionate communicator, to be available to answer engineer questions, and to ensure that the most efficient channels are used to keep architectural communication constantly stimulated (Faber, 2010).

PITCH YOUR STORY

While working in the R&D department at Pixar, our task as software engineers and managers was to produce powerful yet easy-to-use programs for highly creative artists. We therefore endeavored to communicate our software plans and designs using analogies and terminology familiar to filmmakers.

For example, our design team was referred to as our "Story" department, a reference to the department in a film studio responsible for the initial planning and structuring of a movie. Our software schedules and system designs were then presented to our production users on standard storyboards. These are physical wood boards with a regular grid of 4- × 6-inch hand-drawn index cards pinned to them. These boards were presented to artists in a "story pitch" format, to use filmmaking terminology, thus allowing us to present our material in a meeting style and structure that was familiar to our users. Finally, we also produced several "story reels," which were digital movies where hand-drawn examples of the proposed applications were animated and narrated to show end-user workflows.

This specific approach worked well in our case to communicate our software plans with talented but non-technical in-house users. Of course, this format will not be appropriate for all other software projects. However, the central tenet is that you should think deeply about how you can communicate your designs in the most natural and intuitive manner for your users.

4.6 CLASS DESIGN

With a high-level architecture in place, you can start refining the design to describe specific C++ classes and their relationship to other classes. This is the detailed design, in contrast to the top-level architecture design. It involves identifying actual classes that clients will use, how these classes relate to each other, and their major functions and attributes. For sufficiently large systems, this can also involve describing how classes are organized into subsystems.

Designing every single class in your API would be overkill for anything but the most trivial system. Instead, you should focus on the major classes that define the most important functionality. A good rule of thumb is the so-called "80/20 rule," that is, you should concentrate on 20% of the classes that define 80% of your system's behavior (McConnell, 2004).

TIP

Focus on designing 20% of the classes that define 80% of your API's functionality.

4.6.1 Object-Oriented Concepts

Before I talk more about the details of object-oriented design, let's take a moment to review some of the major object-oriented principles and their representation in C++. It is likely that you're already very familiar with these concepts, but let's summarize them here briefly in the interests of completeness and to ensure that we're on the same page.

- **Class**: A class is the abstract description, or specification, of an object. It defines the data members and member functions of the object.
- **Object**: An object is an entity that has state, behavior, and identity (Booch et al., 2007). It is an instance of a concrete class created at run time using the new operator or on the stack. A concrete class is one that can be instantiated, for example, it has no undefined pure virtual member functions.
- **Encapsulation**: This concept describes the compartmentalization of data and methods as a single object with access control specifications such as public, protected, and private to support hiding of implementation details.
- **Inheritance**: This allows for objects to inherit attributes and behaviors from a parent class and to introduce their own additional data members and methods. A class defined in this way is said to be a derived (or sub) class of the parent (or base) class. A subclass can override any base class method, although normally you only want to do this when that base class method is declared to be virtual. A pure virtual method (indicated by appending it's declaration with "= 0") is one where a subclass must provide an implementation of the method in order for it to be concrete (i.e., to allow instances of it to be created). C++ supports multiple inheritance, meaning that a subclass can inherit from more than one base class. Public inheritance is generally referred to as an "is-a" relationship between two objects, whereas private inheritance represents a "was-a" relationship (Lakos, 1996).
- **Composition**: This is an alternative technique to inheritance where one or more simple objects are combined to create more complex ones. This is done by declaring the simpler objects as member variables inside of the more complex object. The "has-a" relationship is used to describe the case where a class holds an instance of another type. The "holds-a" relationship describes a class holding a pointer or reference to the other type.

- **Polymorphism**: This is the ability of one type to appear as, and to be used like, another type. This allows objects of different types to be used interchangeably as long as they conform to the same interface. This is possible because the C++ compiler can delay checking the type of an object until run time, a technique known as late or dynamic binding. The use of templates in C++ can also be used to provide static (compile-time) polymorphism.

4.6.2 **Class Design Options**

When considering the creation of a class, there are many factors to be considered. As Scott Meyers notes, creating a new class involves defining a new type. You should therefore treat class design as type design and approach the task with the same thoughtfulness and attention that the designers of C++ put into the built-in types of the language (Meyers, 2005).

Here is a list of a few major questions that you should ask yourself when you embark upon designing a new class. This is not meant to be an exhaustive list, but it should provide a good starting point and help you define the major constraints on your design.

- **Use of inheritance**. Is it appropriate to add the class to an existing inheritance hierarchy? Should you use public or private inheritance? Should you support multiple inheritance? This affects which member functions should be virtual.
- **Use of composition**. Is it more appropriate to hold a related object as a data member rather than inheriting from it directly?
- **Use of abstract interfaces**. Is the class meant to be an abstract base class, where subclasses must override various pure virtual member functions?
- **Use of standard design patterns**. Can you employ a known design pattern to the class design? Doing so lets you benefit from well-thought-out and refined design methodologies and makes your design easier to use by other engineers.
- **Initialization and destruction model**. Will clients use `new` and `delete` or will you use a factory method? Will you override `new` and `delete` for your class to customize the memory allocation behavior? Will you use smart pointers?
- **Defining a copy constructor and assignment operator**. If the class allocates any resource such as memory, you should define both of these (as well as a destructor of course). This will impact how your objects will be copied and passed by value. (You can also declare these functions as private to prevent copying.)
- **Use of templates**. Does your class define a family of types rather than a single type? If so, then you may consider the use of templates to generalize your design.
- **Use of const and explicit**. Define arguments, return results, and methods as `const` wherever you can. Use the `explicit` keyword to avoid unexpected type conversions for single-parameter constructors.
- **Defining operators**. Define any operators that you need for your class, such as +, *=, [], ==, or <<.
- **Defining type coercions**. Consider whether you want your class to be automatically coercible to different types and declare the appropriate conversion operators.
- **Use of friends**. Friends breach the encapsulation of your class and are generally an indication of bad design. Use them as a last resort.
- **Non-functional constraints**. Issues such as performance and memory usage can place constraints on the design of your classes.

4.6.3 **Using Inheritance**

By far the biggest design decision that you will face when designing your classes is when and how to use inheritance, For example, should you use public inheritance, private inheritance, or composition to associate related classes in your API? Because inheritance is such an important topic, and one that is often misused or overused, I will focus on this part of class design over the next few sections. Let's begin with some general design recommendations.

- **Design for inheritance or prohibit it**. The most important decision you can make is to decide whether a class should support subclasses. If it should, then you must think deeply about which methods should be declared as virtual and document their behavior. If the class should not support inheritance, a good way to convey this is to declare a non-virtual destructor. See also the section called Prohibiting Subclassing in Chapter 12.
- **Only use inheritance where appropriate**. Deciding whether a class should inherit from another class is a difficult design task. In fact, this is perhaps the most difficult part of software design. I will present some guidance on this topic in the next section when I talk about the Liskov Substitution Principle (LSP).
- **Avoid deep inheritance trees**. Deep inheritance hierarchies increase complexity and invariably result in designs that are difficult to understand and software that is more prone to failure. The absolute limit of hierarchy depth is obviously subjective, but any more than two or three levels is already getting too complex (McConnell, 2004).
- **Use pure virtual member functions to force subclasses to provide an implementation**. A virtual member function can be used to define an interface that includes an optional implementation, whereas a pure virtual member function is used to define only an interface, with no implementation (although it is actually possible to provide a fallback implementation for a pure virtual method). Of course, a non-virtual method is used to provide behavior that cannot be changed by subclasses.
- **Don't add new pure virtual functions to an existing interface**. You should certainly design appropriate abstract interfaces with pure virtual member functions. However, be aware that after you release this interface to users, if you then add a new pure virtual method to the interface then you will break all of your clients' code. That's because clients' classes that inherit from the abstract interface will not be concrete until an implementation for the new pure virtual function is defined.
- **Don't overdesign**. In Chapter 2, I stated that a good API should be minimally complete. In other words, you should resist the temptation to add extra levels of abstraction that are currently unnecessary. For example, if you have a base class that is inherited by only a single class in your entire API, this is an indication that you have overdesigned the solution for the current needs of the system.

> **TIP**
>
> Avoid deep inheritance hierarchies.

Another important consideration is whether to utilize multiple inheritance, that is, designing classes that inherit from more than one base class. Bjarne Stroustrup argued for the addition of multiple inheritance to C++ using the example of a TemporarySecretary class, where this inherits from both a Secretary and a Temporary class (Alexandrescu, 2001). However, opinion is divided in the C++ community on whether multiple inheritance is a good thing. On the one hand, it offers the flexibilty to define composite relationships, such as the `TemporarySecretary` example. On the other hand, this can come at the cost of subtle semantics and ambiguities, such as the need to use virtual inheritance to deal with the "diamond problem" (where a class inherits ambiguously from two or more base classes that themselves inherit from a single common base class).

Most languages that allow inheriting from only a single base class still support inheriting from multiple, more constrained, types. For example, Java lets you inherit from multiple interface classes, and Ruby lets you inherit from multiple mixins. These are classes that let you inherit an interface (and implementation in the case of a mixin); however, they cannot be instantiated on their own.

Multiple inheritance can be a powerful tool if used correctly (see the STL iostreams classes for a good example). However, in the interest of robust and easy-to-use interfaces, I generally concur with Steve McConnell who recommends that you should avoid the use of multiple inheritance, except to use abstract interfaces or mixin classes (McConnell, 2004).

TIP

Avoid multiple inheritance, except for interfaces and mixin classes.

As a point of interest, the new C++11 specification includes a number of improvements relating to inheritance. One of particular note is the ability to specify explicitly your intent to override or hide a virtual method from a base class. This is done using the `[[override]]` and `[[hiding]]` attributes, respectively. This new functionality will be extremely helpful in avoiding mistakes such as misspelling the name of a virtual method in a derived class.

4.6.4 Liskov Substitution Principle

This principle, introduced by Barbara Liskov in 1987, provides guidance on whether a class should be designed as a subclass of another class (Liskov, 1987). The LSP states that if S is a subclass of T, then objects of type T can be replaced by objects of type S without any change in behavior.

At first glance, this may seem to be a simple restatement of the "is-a" inheritance relationship, where a class S may be considered a subtype of T if S is a more specific kind of T. However, the LSP is a more restrictive definition than "is-a."

Let's demonstrate this with the classic example of an ellipse shape type:

```
class Ellipse
{
public:
    Ellipse();
    Ellipse(float major, float minor);

    void SetMajorRadius(float major);
    void SetMinorRadius(float minor);
    float GetMajorRadius() const;
    float GetMinorRadius() const;

private:
    float mMajor;
    float mMinor;
};
```

You then decide to add support for a circle class. From a mathematical perspective, a circle is a more specific form of an ellipse, where the two axes are constrained to be equal. It is therefore tempting to declare a `Circle` class to be a subclass of `Ellipse`. For example,

```
class Circle : public Ellipse
{
public:
    Circle();
    explicit Circle(float r);

    void SetRadius(float r);
    float GetRadius() const;
};
```

The implementation of `SetRadius()` can then set major and minor radii of the underlying ellipse to the same value to enforce the properties of a circle.

```
void Circle::SetRadius(float r)
{
    SetMajorRadius(r);
    SetMinorRadius(r);
}

float Circle::GetRadius() const
{
    return GetMajorRadius();
}
```

However, this poses a number of problems. The most obvious is that `Circle` will also inherit and expose the `SetMajorRadius()` and `SetMinorRadius()` methods of `Ellipse`. These could be used to break the self-consistency of our circle by letting users change one radius without also changing the other. You could deal with this by overriding the `SetMajorRadius()` and `SetMinorRadius()` methods so that each sets both major and minor radii. However, this also poses several issues. First, you must go back and declare `Ellipse::SetMajorRadius()` and `Ellipse::SetMinorRadius()` to be virtual so that you can override them in the `Circle` class. This in itself should alert you that you're doing something wrong. Second, you have now created a non-orthogonal API: changing one property has the side effect of changing another property. Third, you have broken the Liskov Substitution Principle because you cannot replace uses of `Ellipse` with `Circle` without breaking behavior, as the following code demonstrates:

```
void TestEllipse(Ellipse &e)
{
    e.SetMajorRadius(10.0);
    e.SetMinorRadius(20.0);
    assert(e.GetMajorRadius() == 10.0 && e.GetMinorRadius() == 20.0);
}
...
Ellipse e;
Circle c;
TestEllipse(e);
TestEllipse(c);    // fails!
```

The problem resolves to the fact that you have changed the behavior of functions inherited from the base class.

So if you shouldn't use public inheritance to model a circle as a kind of ellipse, how should you represent it? There are two main ways that you can correctly build your `Circle` class upon the functionality of the `Ellipse` class: private inheritance and composition.

TIP

The LSP states that it should always be possible to substitute a base class for a derived class without any change in behavior.

Private Inheritance

Private inheritance lets you inherit the functionality, but not the public interface, of another class. In essence, all public members of the base class become private members of the derived class. I refer to this as a "was-a" relationship in contrast to the "is-a" relationship of public inheritance. For example, you can redefine your `Circle` class to inherit privately from `Ellipse` as follows.

```
class Circle : private Ellipse
{
public:
   Circle();
   explicit Circle(float r);

   void SetRadius(float r);
   float GetRadius() const;
};
```

In this case, `Circle` does not expose any of the member functions of `Ellipse`, that is, there is no public `Circle::SetMajorRadius()` method. This solution therefore does not suffer from the same problems as the public inheritance approach discussed earlier. In fact, objects of type `Circle` cannot be passed to code that accepts an `Ellipse` because the `Ellipse` base type is not publicly accessible.

Note that if you do want to expose a public or protected method of `Ellipse` in `Circle` then you can do this as follows.

```
class Circle : private Ellipse
{
public:
   Circle();
   explicit Circle(float r);

   // expose public methods of Ellipse
   using Ellipse::GetMajorRadius;
   using Ellipse::GetMinorRadius;

   void SetRadius(float r);
   float GetRadius() const;
};
```

Composition

Private inheritance is a quick way to fix an interface that violates the LSP if it already uses public inheritance. However, the preferred solution is to use composition. This simply means that instead of class S inheriting from T, S declares T as a private data member ("has-a") or S declares a pointer or reference to T as a member variable ("holds-a"). For example,

```
class Circle
{
public:
    Circle();
    explicit Circle(float r);

    void SetRadius(float r);
    float GetRadius() const;

private:
    Ellipse mEllipse;
};
```

Then the definition of the SetRadius() and GetRadius() methods might look like

```
void Circle::SetRadius(float r)
{
    mEllipse.SetMajorRadius(r);
    mEllipse.SetMinorRadius(r);
}

float Circle::GetRadius() const
{
    return mEllipse.GetMajorRadius();
}
```

In this case, the interface for Ellipse is not exposed in the interface for Circle. However, Circle still builds upon the functionality of Ellipse by creating a private instance of Ellipse. Composition therefore provides the functional equivalent of private inheritance. However, there is wide agreement by object-oriented design experts that you should prefer composition over inheritance (Sutter and Alexandrescu, 2004).

TIP

Prefer composition to inheritance.

The main reason for this preference is that inheritance produces a more tightly coupled design. When a class inherits from another type—be it public, protected, or private inheritance—the subclass gains access to all public and protected members of the base class, whereas with composition, the class is only coupled to the public members of the other class. Furthermore, if you only hold a pointer to the other object, then your interface can use a forward declaration of the class rather than #include its full definition. This results in greater compile-time insulation and improves the time it takes to compile your code. Finally, you should not force an inheritance relationship when it is not appropriate. The preceding discussion told us that a circle should not be treated as an ellipse for purposes of type inheritance. Note that there may still be a good case for a general Shape type that all shapes, including Circle and Ellipse, inherit from. However, a Circle should not inherit from Ellipse because it actually exhibits different behavior.

4.6.5 The Open/Closed Principle

Bertrand Meyer introduced the Open/Closed Principle (OCP) to state the goal that a class should be open for extension but closed for modification (Meyer, 1997). Essentially this means that the behavior of a class can be modified without changing its source code. This is a particularly relevant principle for API design because it focuses on the creation of stable interfaces that can last for the long term.

The principal idea behind the OCP is that once a class has been completed and released to users, it should only be modified to fix bugs. However, new features or changed functionality should be implemented by creating a new class. This is often achieved by extending the original class, either through inheritance or composition, although, as covered later in this book, you can also provide a plugin system to allow users of your API to extend its basic functionality.

As an example of the OCP used to practical effect, the simple factory method presented in Chapter 3 is not closed to modification or open for extensibility. That's because adding new types to the system requires changing the factory method implementation. As a reminder, here's the code for that simple renderer factory method.

```
IRenderer *RendererFactory::CreateRenderer(const std::string &type)
{
    if (type == "opengl")
        return new OpenGLRenderer();

    if (type == "directx")
        return new DirectXRenderer();

    if (type == "mesa")
        return new MesaRenderer();

    return NULL;
}
```

In contrast, the extensible renderer factory that was presented later in Chapter 3 allows for the system to be extended without modifying the factory method. This is done by allowing clients to register new types with the system at run time. This second implementation therefore demonstrates the Open/Closed Principle: the original code does not need to be changed in order to extend its functionality.

However, when adhered to strictly, the OCP can be difficult to achieve in real-world software projects and even contradicts some of the principles of good API design that have been advanced here. The constraint to never change the source code of a class after it is released is often impractical in large-scale complex systems, and the stipulation that any changes in behavior should trigger the creation of new classes can cause the original clean and minimal design to be diluted and fractured. In these cases, the OCP may be considered more of a guiding heuristic rather than a hard-and-fast rule. Also, while a good API should be as extensible as possible, there is tension between the OCP and the specific advice in this book that you should declare member functions to be virtual in a judicious and restrained manner.

Nevertheless, if I restate the OCP to mean that the interface of a class should be closed to change rather than considering the precise implementation behind that interface to be immutable, then you have a principle that aligns reasonably well with the focus of this book. That is, maintenance of a stable interface gives you the flexibility to change the underlying implementation without unduly affecting your client's code. Furthermore, the use of extensive regression testing can allow you to make internal code changes without impacting existing behavior that your users rely upon. Also, use of an appropriate plugin architecture (see Chapter 12) can provide your clients with a versatile point of extensibility.

TIP

Your API should be closed to incompatible changes in its interface, but open to extensibility of its functionality.

4.6.6 The Law of Demeter

The Law of Demeter (LoD), also known as the Principle of Least Knowledge, is a guideline for producing loosely coupled designs. The rule was proposed by Ian Holland based on experiences developing the Demeter Project at Northeastern University in the late 1980s (Lieberherr and Holland, 1989). It states that each component should have only limited knowledge about other components, and even then only closely related components. This can be expressed more concisely as only talk to your immediate friends.

When applied to object-oriented design, the LoD means that a function can:

- Call other functions in the same class.
- Call functions on data members of the same class.
- Call functions on any parameters that it accepts.
- Call functions on any local objects that it creates.
- Call functions on a global object (but you should never have globals).

By corollary, you should never call a function on an object that you obtained via another function call. For example, you should avoid chaining function calls such as

```
void MyClass::MyFunction()
{
    mObjectA.GetObjectB().DoAction();
}
```

One way to avoid this practice involves refactoring object A so that it provides direct access to the functionality in object B, thus allowing you to do the following:

```
void MyClass::MyFunction()
{
    mObjectA.DoAction();
}
```

Alternatively, you could refactor the calling code so that it has an actual object B to invoke the required function directly. This can be done either by storing an instance or reference to object B in `MyClass` or by passing object B into the function that needs it, for example,

```
void MyClass::MyFunction(const ObjectB &objectB)
{
    objectB.DoAction();
}
```

The downside of this technique is that you introduce lots of thin wrapper methods into your classes, increase the parameter count of your functions, or increase the size of your objects. However, the benefit is that you end up with more loosely coupled classes where the dependencies on other objects are made explicit. This makes the code much easier to refactor or evolve in the future. In fact, the latter solution of explicitly passing an object into a function has clear parallels with the modern practice of dependency injection (discussed in Chapter 3). Also, another application of the LoD involves creating a single method in object A that aggregates calls to multiple methods of object B, which resonates well with the Façade design pattern.

TIP

The Law of Demeter (LoD) states that you should only call functions in your own class or on immediately related objects.

4.6.7 Class Naming

While I have been largely concerned with the details of object-oriented design in these latest sections, once you have developed an appropriate collection of classes, an equally critical task is the development of expressive and consistent names for these classes. Accordingly, here are some guidelines for naming your classes.

- Simple class names should be powerful, descriptive, and self-explanatory. Moreover, they should make sense in the problem domain being modeled and should be named after the thing they are modeling, for example, Customer, Bookmark, or Document. As already noted, class names tend to form the nouns of your system: the principal objects of your design.
- Joshua Bloch states that good names drive good designs. Therefore, a class should do one thing and do it well, and a class name should instantly convey its purpose (Bloch, 2008). If a class is difficult to name, that's usually a sign that your design is lacking. Kent Beck offers the example that he originally used the generic compound name DrawingObject for an object in a graphical drawing system, but later refined this to the more expressive term Figure by referring to the field of typography (Beck, 2007).
- Sometimes it is necessary to use a compound name to convey greater specificity and precision, such as TextStyle, SelectionManager, or LevelEditor. However, if you are using any more than two or three words then this can indicate that your design is too confusing or complex.
- Interfaces (abstract base classes) tend to represent adjectives in your object model. They can therefore be named in this way, for example, Renderable, Clonable, or Observable. Alternatively, it's common to prefix interface classes with the uppercase letter "I," for example, IRenderer and IObserver.
- Avoid cryptic abbreviations. Good class names should be obvious and consistent. Don't force your users to try and remember which names you've abbreviated and which you have not. I will revisit this point later when I discuss function naming.

- You should include some form of namespace for your top-level symbols, such as classes and free functions, so that your names do not clash with those in other APIs that your clients may be using. This can be done either via the C++ `namespace` keyword or through the use of a short prefix. For example, all OpenGL function calls start with "gl" and all Qt classes begin with "Q."

4.7 FUNCTION DESIGN

The lowest granularity of API design is how you represent individual function calls. While this may seem like an obvious exercise and not worth covering in much detail, there are actually many function-level issues that affect good API design. After all, function calls are the most commonly used part of an API: they are how your clients access the API's behavior.

4.7.1 Function Design Options

There are many interface options you can control when designing a function call (Lakos, 1996). First of all, for free functions you should consider the following alternatives:

- Static versus non-static function.
- Pass arguments by value, reference, or pointer.
- Pass arguments as const or non-const.
- Use of optional arguments with default values.
- Return result by value, reference, or pointer.
- Return result as const or non-const.
- Operator or non-operator function.
- Use of exception specifications.

For member functions, you should consider all of these free function options as well as the following:

- Virtual versus non-virtual member function.
- Pure virtual versus non-pure virtual member function.
- Const versus non-const member function.
- Public, protected, or private member function.
- Use of the explicit keyword for non-default constructors.

In addition to these options that control the logical interface of a function, there are a couple of organizational attributes that you can specify for a function, such as

- Friend function versus non-friend function.
- Inline function versus non-inline function.

The proper application of these options can make a large impact on the quality of your API. For example, you should declare member functions as const wherever possible to advertise that they do not modify the object (see Chapter 6 on C++ usage for more details). Passing objects as const references can reduce the amount of memory copying that your API causes (see Chapter 7 on performance). Use of the `explicit` keyword can avoid unexpected side effects for non-default constructors (see Chapter 6). Also, inlining your functions can sometimes offer a performance advantage at the cost of exposing implementation details and breaking binary compatibility (see Chapters 7 and 8).

4.7.2 **Function Naming**

Function names tend to form the verbs of your system, describing actions to be performed or values to be returned. Here are some guidelines for naming your free and member functions.

- Functions used to set or return some value should fully describe that quantity using standard prefixes such as Get and Set. For example, a function that returns the zoom factor for a Web view might be called `GetZoomFactor()` or, less expressively, just `ZoomFactor()`.
- Functions that answer yes or no queries should use an appropriate prefix to indicate this behavior, such as Is, Are, or Has, and should return a bool result, for example, `IsEnabled()`, `ArePerpendicular()`, or `HasChildren()`. As an alternative, the STL tends to drop the initial verb, as can be seen in functions such as `empty()` instead of `IsEmpty()`. However, while terser, this naming style is ambiguous because it could also be interpreted as an operation that empties the container (unless you're astute enough to notice the const method decorator). The STL scheme therefore fails the qualities of discoverability and difficulty to misuse.
- Functions used to perform some action should be named with a strong verb, for example, `Enable()`, `Print()`, or `Save()`. If you are naming a free function, rather than a method of a class, then you should include the name of the object that the action will be applied to, for example, `FileOpen()`, `FormatString()`, `MakeVector3d()`.
- Use positive concepts to name your functions rather than framing them in the negative. For example, use the name `IsConnected()` instead of `IsUnconnected()`. This can help to avoid user confusion when faced with double negatives like `!IsUnconnected()`.
- Function names should describe everything that the routine does. For example, if a routine in an image processing library performs a sharpening filter on an image and saves it to disk, the method should be called something like `SharpenAndSaveImage()` instead of just `SharpenImage()`. If this makes your function names too long, then this may indicate that they are performing too many tasks and should be split up (McConnell, 2004).
- You should avoid abbreviations. Names should be self-explanatory and memorable, but the use of abbreviations can introduce confusing or obscure terminology. For example, the user has to remember if you are using `GetCurrentValue()`, `GetCurrValue()`, `GetCurValue()`, or `GetCurVal()`. Some software projects specify an explicit list of accepted abbreviations that must be conformed to, but in general it's simply easier for your users if they don't have to remember lists such as these.
- Functions should not begin with an underscore character (_). The C++ standard states that global symbols starting with an underscore are reserved for internal compiler use. The same is true for all symbols that begin with two underscores followed by a capital letter. While you can find legal combinations of leading underscore names that navigate these rules, it is generally best simply to avoid this practice in your function names (some developers use this convention to indicate a private member).
- Functions that form natural pairs should use the correct complementary terminology. For example, `OpenWindow()` should be paired with `CloseWindow()`, not `DismissWindow()`. The use of precise opposite terms makes it clearer to the user that one function performs the opposite function of another function (McConnell, 2004). The following list provides some common complementary terms.

Add/Remove	Begin/End	Create/Destroy
Enable/Disable	Insert/Delete	Lock/Unlock
Next/Previous	Open/Close	Push/Pop
Send/Receive	Show/Hide	Source/Target

4.7.3 Function Parameters

Use of good parameter names can also have a big impact on the discoverability of your API. For example, compare these two signatures for the standard C function `strstr()`, which searches for the first occurrence of a substring within another string:

```
char *strstr(const char *s1, const char *s2);
```

and

```
char *strstr(const char *haystack, const char *needle);
```

I think you'll agree that the second signature gives a much better indication of how to use the function simply through the use of descriptive parameter names.

Another factor is to make sure that you use the right data type for your parameters. For example, when you have methods that perform linear algebra calculations, you should prefer using double-precision floats to avoid loss of precision errors that are inherent in single-precision operations. Similarly, you should never use a floating-point data type to represent monetary values because of the potential for rounding errors (Beck, 2002).

There is also a balance to be sought in terms of the number of parameters that you specify for each function. Too many parameters can make the call more difficult to understand and to maintain. It can also imply greater coupling and may suggest that it is time to refactor the function. Therefore, wherever possible you should try to minimize the number of parameters to your public functions. In this regard, we have the often-cited research from the field of cognitive science, which states that the number of items we can hold in our short-term working memory is seven plus or minus two (Miller, 1956). This may suggest that you should not exceed around five to seven parameters, as otherwise the user will find it difficult to remember all of the options. Indeed, Joshua Bloch suggests that five or more parameters are too many (Bloch, 2008).

TIP

Avoid long parameter lists.

For functions that accept many optional parameters, you may consider passing the arguments using a Plain Old Data (POD) struct or map instead. For example,

```
struct OpenWindowParams
{
    OpenWindowParams();
    int mX;
    int mY;
```

```
    int mWidth:
    int mHeight:
    int mFlags:
    std::string mClassName:
    std::string mWindowName:
};
void OpenWindow(const OpenWindowParams &params):
```

This technique is also a good way to deal with argument lists that may change over the life of the API. A newer version of the API can simply add new fields to the end of the structure without changing the signature of the `OpenWindow()` function. You can also add a version field (set by the constructor) to allow binary compatible changes to the structure: the `OpenWindow()` function can then check the version field to determine what information is included in the structure. Other options include using a field that records the size of the structure in bytes or simply using a different structure.

REDUCING PARAMETER LISTS

All the way back in the 1980s, the Commodore Amiga platform provided an extensive set of stable and well-designed APIs to build applications that run under AmigaOS. The original routine to open a new screen on the Amiga takes a single argument: a structure containing all the necessary information to specify that screen.

```
struct Screen *OpenScreen(struct NewScreen *newscr):
```

The `NewScreen` structure looks like

```
struct NewScreen
{
    WORD LeftEdge, TopEdge, Width, Height, Depth:
    UBYTE DetailPen, BlockPen:
    UWORD ViewModes, Type:
    struct TextAttr *Font:
    UBYTE *DefaultTitle:
    struct Gadget *Gadgets:
    struct BitMap *CustomBitMap:
};
```

In Version 36 of the AmigaOS APIs, new functionality was added to this function. This was done by introducing the notion of tag lists, essentially an arbitrarily long list of keyword/value pairs. To support this new extensible scheme, a V36-only function was added to allow the explicit specification of these tag lists:

```
struct Screen *OpenScreenTagList(struct NewScreen *newscr,
                                 struct TagItem *taglist):
```

However, to maintain backwards compatibility, it was also possible to pass a new `ExtNewScreen` structure to the `OpenScreen()` function.

```
struct Screen *OpenScreen(struct ExtNewScreen *newscr):
```

This extended structure looks like

```
struct ExtNewScreen
{
    WORD LeftEdge, TopEdge, Width, Height, Depth:
    UBYTE DetailPen, BlockPen:
    UWORD ViewModes, Type:
```

```
    struct TextAttr *Font;
    UBYTE *DefaultTitle;
    struct Gadget *Gadgets;
    struct BitMap *CustomBitMap;
    struct TagItem *Extension;
};
```

When passing this new structure to OpenScreen() you had to set the NS_EXTENDED bit of the Type field to indicate that the structure included an Extension field at the end. In this way, you could pass either the old or the new form to newer versions of AmigaOS, but older versions of amiga.lib would safely ignore new data.

Note that this is a plain C API, which cannot support function overloading, so the two versions of the OpenScreen() function were not specified in the same version of the API. Newer versions of the API would specify the ExtNewScreen signature, although code that tried to pass an older NewScreen structure would still compile fine under a C compiler (perhaps with a warning). In C++, this type mismatch would cause a compile error, but in that case you could simply provide two overloaded versions of OpenScreen().

Taking this one step further, you can hide all of the public member variables and only allow the values to be accessed via getter/setter functions. The Qt API refers to this as a property-based API. For example,

```
QTimer timer;
timer.setInterval(1000);
timer.setSingleShot(true);
timer.start();
```

This lets you reduce the number of parameters required for functions; in this case, the start() function requires no parameters at all. The use of functions to set parameter values also offers the following benefits:

- Values can be specified in any order because function calls are order independent.
- The purpose of each value is more evident because you must use a named function to set the value, for example, setInterval().
- Optional parameters are supported by simply not calling the appropriate function.
- The constructor can define reasonable default values for all settings.
- Adding new parameters is backward compatible because no existing functions need to change signature. Only new functions are added.

Taking this even further, we could make each of the setter methods return a reference to its object instance (return *this;) so that you can chain a number of these methods together. This is called the Named Parameter Idiom (NPI). It offers the same benefits that I just enumerated while also letting your clients write less code. For instance, you could rewrite the QTimer example using the NPI as follows:

```
QTimer timer = QTimer().setInterval(1000).setSingleShot(true).start();
```

4.7.4 Error Handling

A large amount of the code that application developers write is purely there to handle error conditions. The actual amount of error handling code that is written will depend greatly on the particular application. However, it has been estimated that up to 90% of an application's code is related to handling exceptional or error conditions (McConnell, 2004). This is therefore an important area of API design that will be used frequently by your clients. In fact, it is included in Ken Pugh's *Three Laws of Interfaces* (Pugh, 2006):

1. An interface's implementation shall do what its methods say it does.
2. An interface's implementation shall do no harm.
3. If an interface's implementation is unable to perform its responsibilities, it shall notify its caller.

Accordingly, the three main ways of dealing with error conditions in your API are

1. Returning error codes.
2. Throwing exceptions.
3. Aborting the program.

The last of these is an extreme course of action that should be avoided at all costs—and indeed it violates the third of Pugh's three laws—although there are far too many examples of libraries out there that call abort() or exit(). As for the first two cases, different engineers have different proclivities toward each of these techniques. I will not take a side on the exceptions versus error code debate here, but rather I'll attempt to present impartially the arguments and drawbacks for each option. Whichever technique you select for your API, the most important issues are that you use a consistent error reporting scheme and that it is well documented.

TIP

Use a consistent and well-documented error handling mechanism.

The error codes approach involves returning a numeric code to indicate the success or failure of a function. Normally this error code is returned as the direct result of a function. For example, many Win32 functions return errors using the HRESULT data type. This is a single 32-bit value that encodes the severity of the failure, the subsystem responsible for the error, and an actual error code. The C standard library also provides examples of non-orthogonal error reporting design, such as the functions read(), waitpid(), and ioctl() that set the value of the errno global variable as a side effect. OpenGL provides a similar error reporting mechanism via an error checking function called glGetError().

The use of error codes produces client code that looks like

```
if (obj1.Function() == ERROR)
{
    HandleError();
}
if (obj2.Function() == ERROR)
{
    HandleError();
}
if (obj3.Function() == ERROR)
{
    HandleError();
}
```

As an alternative, you can use C++'s exception capabilities to signal a failure in your implementation code. This is done by throwing an object for your clients to catch in their code. For example, several of the Boost libraries throw exceptions to communicate error conditions to the client, such as the `boost::iostreams` and `boost::program_options` libraries. The use of exceptions in your API results in client code such as

```
try
{
    obj1.Function();
    obj2.Function();
    obj3.Function();
}
catch (const std::exception &e)
{
    HandleError();
}
```

The error codes technique provides a simple, explicit, and robust way to report errors for individual function calls. It's also the only option if you're developing an API that must be accessible from plain C programs. The main dilemma comes when you wish to return a result as well as an error code. The typical way to deal with this is to return the error code as the function result and use an out parameter to fill in the result value. For example,

```
int FindName(std::string *name);
...
std::string name;
if (FindName(&name) == OKAY)
{
    std::cout << "Name: " << name << std::endl;
}
```

Dynamic scripting languages such as Python handle this more elegantly by making it easy to return multiple values as a tuple. This is still an option with C++, however. For example, you could use `boost::tuple` to return multiple results from your function (or the C++11 version, `std::tuple`), as the following example demonstrates:

```
boost::tuple<int, std::string> FindName();
...
boost::tuple<int, std::string> result = FindName();
if (result.get<0>() == OKAY)
{
    std::cout << "Name: " << result.get<1>() << std::endl;
}
```

By comparison, exceptions let your clients separate their error handling code from the normal flow of control, making for more readable code. They offer the benefit of being able to catch one or more errors in a sequence of several function calls, without having to check every single return code, and they let you handle an error higher up in the call stack instead of at the exact point of failure. An exception can also carry more information than a simple error code. For example, standard

C++ exceptions include a human-readable description of the failure, accessible via a `what()` method. Also, most debuggers provide a way to break if an exception is thrown, making it easier to debug problems. Finally, exceptions are the only way to report failures in a constructor.

However, this flexibility does come with a cost. Handling an exception can be an expensive operation due to the run-time stack unwinding behavior. Also, an uncaught exception can cause your clients' programs to abort, resulting in data loss and frustration for their end users. Writing exception safe code is difficult and can lead to resource leaks if not done correctly. Typically the use of exceptions is an all-or-nothing proposition, meaning that if any part of an application uses exceptions then the entire application must be prepared to handle exceptions correctly. This means that the use of exceptions in your API also requires your clients to write exception safe code. It's noteworthy that Google forbids the use of exceptions in their C++ coding conventions because most of their existing code is not tolerant of exceptions.

If you do opt to use exceptions to signal unexpected situations in your code, here are some best practices to observe.

- Derive your own exceptions from `std::exception` and override the `what()` method to describe the failure.
- Consider using RAII techniques to maintain exception safety, that is, to ensure that resources get cleaned up correctly when an exception is thrown.
- Make sure that you document all of the exceptions that can be thrown by a function in its comments.
- You might be tempted to use exception specifications to document the exceptions that a function may throw. However, be aware that these constraints will be enforced by the compiler at run time, if at all, and that they can impact optimizations, such as the ability to inline a function. As a result, most C++ engineers steer clear of exception specifications such as the following:

```
void MyFunction1() throw();     // throws no exceptions
void MyFunction2() throw(A, B); // throws either A or B
```

- Create exceptions for the set of logical errors that can be encountered, not a unique exception for every individual physical error that you raise.
- If you handle exceptions in your own code, then you should catch the exception by reference (as in the aforementioned example) to avoid calling the copy constructor for the thrown object. Also, try to avoid the `catch(...)` syntax because some compilers also throw an exception when a programming error arises, such as an `assert()` or segmentation fault.
- If you have an exception that multiply inherits from more than one base exception class, you should use virtual inheritance to avoid ambiguities and subtle errors in your client's code where they attempt to catch your exceptions.

TIP

Derive your own exceptions from `std::exception`.

In terms of error reporting best practices, your API should fail as fast as possible once an error occurs and it should clean up any intermediate state, such as releasing resources that were allocated immediately before the error. However, you should also try to avoid returning an exceptional value, such as NULL, where it is not necessary. Doing so causes your clients to write more code to check for these cases. For example, if you have a function that returns a list of items, consider returning an empty list instead of NULL in exceptional cases. This requires your clients to write less code and reduces the chance that your clients will dereference a NULL pointer.

Also, any error code or exception description should represent the actual failure. Invent a new error code or exception if existing ones do not describe the error accurately. You will infuriate your users if they waste time trying to debug the wrong problem because your error reporting was inaccurate or plain wrong. You should also give them as much information as possible to track down the error. For example, if a file cannot be opened, then include the filename in the error description and the cause of the failure, for example, lack of permissions, file not found, or out of disk space.

TIP

Fail quickly and cleanly with accurate and thorough diagnostic details.

Styles

5

Previous chapters dealt with the issues of what qualities contribute to a high-quality API and how to go about designing a good API that exhibits those qualities. While I have illustrated these concepts with specific C++ examples, the abstract process of designing an API is language independent. However, in the next few chapters I will start to turn to more C++-specific aspects of producing an API.

This chapter covers the topic of API style. Style in this context means how you decide to represent the capabilities of your API. That is, your API may provide access to internal state and routines to perform required functionality, but what is the form of invoking these actions? The answer to this question may seem obvious: you create classes to represent each key object in your API and provide methods on those classes. However, there are other styles that you could adopt, and the object-oriented style may not be the best fit all the time. This chapter presents four very different API styles.

1. **Flat C APIs**: These are APIs that can be compiled by a C compiler. They simply involve a set of free functions along with any supporting data structures and constants. As this style of interface contains no objects or inheritance, it's often called flat.
2. **Object-Oriented C++ APIs**: As a C++ programmer, this is likely the style that you're most familiar with. It involves the use of objects with associated data and methods and the application of concepts such as inheritance, encapsulation, and polymorphism.
3. **Template-Based APIs**: C++ also supports generic programming and metaprogramming via its template functionality. This allows functions and data structures to be written in terms of generic types that can be specialized later by instantiating them with concrete types.
4. **Data-Driven APIs**: This type of interface involves sending named commands to a handler, with arguments that are packaged within a flexible data structure, rather than invoking specific methods or free functions.

I will now describe each of these API styles in turn and discuss situations where one particular style may be favored over another. Throughout the chapter I will use examples from the FMOD API to illustrate three of the aforementioned styles. FMOD is a commercial library for creating and playing back interactive audio that is used by many games companies, such as Activision, Blizzard, Ubisoft, and Microsoft. It provides a flat C API, a C++ API, and a Data-Driven API to access its core audio functionality. As such it provides an instructive comparison for most of the API styles covered in this chapter.

5.1 FLAT C APIs

The term flat API is meant to convey the fact that the C language does not support the notion of encapsulated objects and inheritance hierarchies. Hence, an API that uses pure C syntax must be represented with a more restricted set of language features, such as typedefs, structs, and function calls that exist in the global namespace. Due to the lack of the namespace keyword in C, APIs using this style must make sure to use a common prefix for all public functions and data structures to avoid name collisions with other C libraries.

Of course, you can still use internal linkage (Lakos, 1996) to hide symbol names in your implementation, such as declaring them static at the file scope level of your .c files. In this way you can be assured that any such functions will not be exported externally and hence will not collide with the same symbol name in another library. (This applies equally to C++ programs as well, of course. Although in C++ the use of anonymous namespaces is a preferred way to achieve the same result. I'll cover how to do this in the next chapter.)

There are many examples of popular C APIs that are in use today, including the following.

- **The Standard C Library**. If you're writing a C program, then you must be familiar with the standard C library. This comprises a collection of include files (such as stdio.h, stdlib.h, and string.h) and library routines for I/O, string handling, memory management, mathematical operations, and so on, such as printf(), malloc(), floor(), and strcpy(). Most C, and many C++, programs are built using this library.
- **The Windows API**. Often referred to as the Win32 API, this is the core set of interfaces used to develop applications for the Microsoft Windows range of operating systems. It includes a group of APIs across various categories, such as base services, the graphics device interface (GDI), the common dialog box library, and network services. Another library, called Microsoft Foundation Class (MFC), provides a C++ wrapper to the Windows API.
- **The Linux Kernel API**. The entire Linux kernel is written in plain C. This includes the Linux Kernel API, which provides a stable interface for low-level software such as device drivers to access operating system functionality. The API includes driver functions, data types, basic C library functions, memory management operations, thread and process functions, and network functions, among many others.
- **GNOME GLib**. This is a general-purpose open source utility library containing many useful low-level routines for writing applications. This includes string utilities, file access, data structures such as trees, hashes, and lists, and a main loop abstraction. This library provides the foundation for the GNOME desktop environment and was originally part of the GIMP Toolkit (GTK+).
- **The Netscape Portable Runtime (NSPR)**. The NPSR library provides a cross-platform API for low-level functionality, such as threads, file I/O, network access, interval timing, memory management, and shared library linking. It is used as the core of the various Mozilla applications, including the Firefox Web browser and Thunderbird e-mail client.
- **Image Libraries**. Most of the open source image libraries that help you add support for various image file formats to your applications are written entirely in C. For example, the libtiff, libpng, libungif, and jpeg libraries are all plain C APIs.

5.1.1 **ANSI C Features**

If you are used to writing C++ APIs, there will be many language features that you will have to do without when writing a plain C API. For example, C does not support classes, references, templates, the STL, default arguments, access levels (public, private, protected), or a bool type. Instead, C APIs are generally composed of only the following:

1. Built-in types such as `int`, `float`, `double`, `char`, and arrays and pointers to these.
2. Custom types created via the `typedef` and `enum` keywords.
3. Custom structures declared with the `struct` or `union` keywords.
4. Global free functions.
5. Preprocessor directives such as `#define`.

In fact, the complete set of C language keywords is quite short. The entire list is presented here as a reference.

- **auto**: defines a local variable as having a local lifetime.
- **break**: passes control out of a while, do, for, or switch statement.
- **case**: defines a specific branch point within a switch statement.
- **char**: the character data type.
- **const**: declares a variable value or pointer parameter to be unmodifiable.
- **continue**: passes control to the beginning of a while, do, or for statement.
- **default**: defines the fallback branch point for a switch statement.
- **do**: begins a do-while loop.
- **double**: the double-precision floating-point data type.
- **else**: declares the statements to perform if an if statement resolves to false.
- **enum**: defines a set of constants of type int.
- **extern**: introduces the name of an identifier that is defined elsewhere.
- **float**: the single-precision floating-point data type.
- **for**: defines a for loop.
- **goto**: transfers control to a labeled line of code.
- **if**: provides conditional execution of a sequence of statements.
- **int**: the integer data type.
- **long**: extends the size of certain built-in data types.
- **register**: instructs the compiler to store a variable in a CPU register.
- **return**: exits a function with an optional return value.
- **short**: reduces the size of certain built-in data types.
- **signed**: declares a data type to be able to handle negative values.
- **sizeof**: returns the size of a type or expression.
- **static**: preserves the value of a variable even after its scope ends.
- **struct**: allows multiple variables to be grouped into a single type.
- **switch**: causes control to branch to one of a list of possible statements.
- **typedef**: creates a new type in terms of existing types.
- **union**: groups multiple variables that share the same memory location.
- **unsigned**: declares a data type to only handle positive values.

- **void**: the empty data type.
- **volatile**: indicates that a variable can be changed by an external process.
- **while**: defines a loop that exits when the condition evaluates to false.

While C is not strictly a subset of C++, well-written ANSI C programs will tend to be legal C++ programs too. In general, a C++ compiler will impose greater type checking than a C compiler. When you are writing a plain C API, it is often a worthwhile task to try to compile your code with a C++ compiler and then fix any additional warnings or errors that are raised.

STRONGER TYPE CHECKING SAVES BRAIN CELLS

I recall one occasion early in my career when my manager at SRI International, Yvan Leclerc, had a crashing bug in a C program. He spent the best part of a day trying to track the problem down and eventually the two of us stepped through his code together, line by line.

After much scratching of heads, we finally noticed that he was using the `calloc()` function, but was only passing a single argument to it. As you may recall from Chapter 2, the `malloc()` function takes one parameter, whereas the `calloc()` function takes two parameters.

He had switched from using `malloc()` to `calloc()` in order to return an initialized block of memory but had forgotten to change the parameters to the function call. As a result, the returned block of memory was not the size he expected it to be. This is not an error in C (although these days most C compilers will at least give you a warning), but it is a compile error in C++. Using a C++ compiler to compile that C code would have turned up the problem immediately.

TIP

Try compiling your C API with a C++ compiler for greater type checking and to ensure that a C++ program can use your API.

5.1.2 Benefits of an ANSI C API

One of the main reasons to write an API in C is if it must integrate with an existing project that is written entirely in C. Situations like these are becoming rarer as more projects are being written from the ground up in C++, but occasions may arise when your clients place this restriction on your API. Examples include any of the existing large C APIs listed earlier. For instance, if you are working on a Linux Kernel API, then you will need to write this interface in C.

Another reason to prefer the creation of a plain C API is binary compatibility. If you are required to maintain binary compatibility between releases of your API library, this is much easier to achieve with a plain C API than a C++ one. I will discuss the details of this in the chapter on versioning, but suffice to say for now that seemingly minor changes to a C++ API can impact the binary representation for the resulting object and library files, thus breaking the ability for clients to simply drop in a replacement shared library and have it work without recompiling their code.

Of course, there's nothing to stop you from producing an API that works under both C and C++. In fact, you may even decide that you wish to create a C++ API, to take advantage of the additional object-oriented features of C++, but also create a plain C wrapping of this interface for use within C-only projects, or to expose a simple and low surface area version of your API for which binary compatibility is easier to enforce. The FMOD API is one such example of this, as it provides both a C++ and a C API.

5.1.3 **Writing an API in ANSI C**

The C language does not provide support for classes, so you cannot encapsulate data in objects along with the methods that act upon those data. Instead you declare structs (or unions) that contain data and then pass those as parameters to functions that operate on those data. For example, consider the following C++ class definition:

```
class Stack
{
public:
    void Push(int val);
    int Pop();
    bool IsEmpty() const;

private:
    int *mStack;
    int mCurSize;
};
```

This might look as follows in terms of a flat C API:

```
struct Stack
{
    int *mStack;
    int mCurSize;
};

void StackPush(struct Stack *stack, int val);
int StackPop(struct Stack *stack);
bool StackIsEmpty(const struct Stack *stack);
```

Note that each C function associated with the stack must accept the Stack data structure as a parameter, often as the first parameter. Also note that the name of the function should normally include some indication of the data that it operates on, as the name is not scoped within a class declaration as in C++. In this case I chose to prefix each function with the word "Stack" to make it clear that the functions operate on the Stack data structure. This example can be further improved by using an opaque pointer to hide the private data, such as

```
typedef struct Stack *StackPtr;

void StackPush(StackPtr stack, int val);
int StackPop(StackPtr stack);
bool StackIsEmpty(const StackPtr stack);
```

Additionally, C does not support the notion of constructors and destructors. Therefore, any structs must be explicitly initialized and destroyed by the client. This is normally done by adding specific API calls to create and destroy a data structure:

```
StackPtr StackCreate();
void StackDestroy(StackPtr stack);
```

Now that I've compared what a C and C++ API might look like for the same task, let's take a look at the code that the client must write in order to use each API style. First, here's an example of using the C++ API:

```
Stack *stack = new Stack();
if (stack)
{
    stack->Push(10);
    stack->Push(3);
    while (! stack->IsEmpty())
    {
        stack->Pop();
    }
    delete stack;
}
```

whereas the same operations performed with the C API might look like

```
StackPtr stack = StackCreate();
if (stack)
{
    StackPush(stack, 10);
    StackPush(stack, 3);
    while (! StackIsEmpty(stack))
    {
        StackPop(stack);
    }
    StackDestroy(stack);
}
```

5.1.4 Calling C Functions from C++

C++ compilers can also compile C code, and even though you're writing a C API, you may want to allow C++ clients to use your API too. This is a relatively easy task and one that I suggest you undertake as a matter of course when releasing a C API.

The first step is to make sure that your code actually compiles under a C++ compiler. As already noted earlier, because the C standard is more relaxed, a C compiler will let you get away with more sloppy code than a C++ compiler will.

As part of this process, you will of course want to make sure that you don't use any C++-reserved keywords in your code. For example, the following code is legal C, but will produce an error with a C++ compiler because class is a reserved word in C++:

```
enum class {FIRST, BUSINESS, ECONOMY};
```

Finally, C functions have different linkage to C++ functions; that is, the same function is represented differently in object files produced by a C and C++ compiler. One reason for this is that C++ supports function overloading: declaring methods with the same name but different parameters or return values. As a result, C++ function names are "mangled" to encode additional information in the symbol name such as the number and type of each parameter. Because of this linkage difference, you cannot compile C++ code that uses a function, say DoAction(), and then link this against a library produced by a C compiler that defines the DoAction() function.

To get around this problem, you must wrap your C API in an extern "C" construct, which tells the C++ compiler that the contained functions should use C-style linkage. A C compiler will not be able to parse this statement so it's best to conditionally compile it for C++ compilers only. The following code snippet illustrates this best practice:

```
#ifdef __cplusplus
extern "C" {
#endif

// your C API declarations

#ifdef __cplusplus
}
#endif
```

TIP

Use an extern "C" scope in your C API headers so that C++ programs can compile and link against your API correctly.

5.1.5 Case Study: FMOD C API

The following source code presents a small program using the FMOD C API to play a single sound sample. This is provided to give you a real-world example of using a flat C API. Note the use of function naming conventions in order to create multiple layers of namespace, where all functions begin with FMOD_, all system-level calls begin with FMOD_System_, and so on. Note, in the interest of readability, this example performs limited error checking. Obviously any real program would check that each function call completed without error.

```
#include "fmod.h"

int main(int argc, char *argv[])
{
    FMOD_SYSTEM *system;
    FMOD_SOUND *sound;
    FMOD_CHANNEL *channel = 0;
    unsigned int version;

    // Initialize FMOD
    FMOD_System_Create(&system);

    FMOD_System_GetVersion(system, &version);
    if (version < FMOD_VERSION)
    {
        printf("Error! FMOD version %08x required\n", FMOD_VERSION);
        exit(0);
    }
```

```
    FMOD_System_Init(system, 32, FMOD_INIT_NORMAL, NULL);

    // Load and play a sound sample
    FMOD_System_CreateSound(system, "sound.wav", FMOD_SOFTWARE, 0, &sound);
    FMOD_System_PlaySound(system, FMOD_CHANNEL_FREE, sound, 0, &channel);

    // Main loop
    while (!UserPressedEscKey())
    {
        FMOD_System_Update(system);
        NanoSleep(10);
    }

    // Shut down
    FMOD_Sound_Release(sound);
    FMOD_System_Close(system);
    FMOD_System_Release(system);
    return 0;
}
```

5.2 OBJECT-ORIENTED C++ APIs

When you consider writing an API in C++, you probably think in terms of object-oriented design. Object-Oriented Programming (OOP) is a style of programming where data and the functions that operate on those data are packaged together as an object. The origins of object-oriented programming date back to the 1960s with the development of the Simula and Smalltalk languages, although it didn't take off as a dominant programming model until the 1990s, with the introduction of languages such as C++ and Java.

As I have already covered many of the key techniques of OOP in previous chapters, I will not spend too much time on this API style. In particular, I refer you back to the Class Design section of the previous chapter, where I defined various OOP terms such as class, object, inheritance, composition, encapsulation, and polymorphism.

It should be noted that features such as method and operator overloading, default parameters, templates, exceptions, and namespaces are strictly not object-oriented concepts, although they are new features that were included in the C++ language and are not a part of the original C language. C++ supports several programming models other than OOP, such as procedural programming (as seen in the previous section), generic programming (which I will cover next), and even functional programming.

5.2.1 Advantages of Object-Oriented APIs

The primary benefit of using an object-oriented API is the ability to use classes and inheritance, that is, the ability to model software in terms of interconnected data rather than collections of procedures. This can provide both conceptual and technical advantages.

In terms of conceptual advantages, often the physical items and processes that you try to model in code can be described in terms of objects. For example, an address book is a physical item that we are all familiar with, and it contains descriptions for several people, which again is a conceptual unit that anyone can relate to easily. The core task of object-oriented programming is therefore to identify the key objects in a given problem space and to determine how they relate to each other. Many engineers believe that this is a more logical way to approach software design than thinking in terms of the set of all actions that must be performed (Booch et al., 2007).

As for the technical advantages, using objects provides a way to encapsulate all data and methods for a single conceptual unit in one place. It essentially creates a unique namespace for all related methods and variables. For example, the methods of our C++ `Stack` example earlier all exist within the `Stack` namespace, such as `Stack::Push()` or `Stack::Pop()`. Objects also provide the notion of public, protected, and private access, which is a critical concept for API design.

TIP

Object-oriented APIs let you model software in terms of objects instead of actions. They also offer the advantages of inheritance and encapsulation.

5.2.2 Disadvantages of Object-Oriented APIs

However, there can be downsides to using object-oriented concepts. Many of these result from abuses of the power of object-oriented techniques. The first is that adding inheritance to your object model can introduce a degree of complexity and subtlety that not all engineers may fully understand. For example, knowing that base class destructors must normally be marked as virtual to ensure that the correct destructor is always called, or knowing that an overridden method in a subclass will hide all overloaded methods with the same name in the base class.

Furthermore, deep inheritance hierarchies can make it challenging to figure out the complete interface offered by an object just by looking at header files because the interface may be distributed across multiple headers (of course, good documentation tools such as Doxygen can help abate this particular concern). Also, some engineers may abuse, or incorrectly use, the concepts of OOP, such as using inheritance in cases where it doesn't make sense (where the objects don't form an "is-a" relationship). This can cause strained and unclear designs that are difficult to work with.

Finally, creating a binary-compatible API using object-oriented C++ concepts is an extremely difficult task. If binary compatibility is your goal, you may wish to choose one of the other API styles described in this chapter, such as a flat C API or a data-driven API.

5.2.3 Case Study: FMOD C++ API

The following source code presents the same program described in the earlier section, except that this example uses the FMOD C++ API instead of the C API. Note that namespacing is now achieved using the C++ namespace feature so that all classes and functions exist within the FMOD namespace. Also note that the include file for the API has the same base name as the C API, except that it uses a `.hpp` extension to indicate that it is a C++ header. Once again, error checking has been largely omitted in order to make the code more legible.

```cpp
#include "fmod.hpp"

int main(int argc, char *argv[])
{
    FMOD::System *system;
    FMOD::Sound *sound;
    FMOD::Channel *channel = 0;
    unsigned int version;

    // Initialize FMOD
    FMOD::System_Create(&system);

    system->getVersion(&version);
    if (version < FMOD_VERSION)
    {
        printf("Error! FMOD version %08x required\n", FMOD_VERSION);
        exit(0);
    }

    system->init(32, FMOD_INIT_NORMAL, NULL);

    // Load and play a sound sample
    system->createSound("sound.wav", FMOD_SOFTWARE, 0, &sound);
    system->playSound(FMOD_CHANNEL_FREE, sound, 0, &channel);

    // Main loop
    while (! UserPressedEscKey())
    {
        system->update();
        NanoSleep(10);
    }

    // Shut down
    sound->release();
    system->close();
    system->release();
    return 0;
}
```

5.3 TEMPLATE-BASED APIs

Templates are a feature of C++ that allow you to write functions or classes in terms of generic yet-to-be-specified types. You can then specialize these templates by instantiating them with specific types. As a result, programming with templates is often called generic programming.

Templates are an extremely powerful and flexible tool. They can be used to write programs that generate code or that execute code at compile time (a technique known as metaprogramming). This can be used to achieve impressive results, such as unrolling loops, precomputing certain values in a mathematical series, generating lookup tables at compile time, and expanding recursive functions that recurse a predetermined number of times. As such, templates can be used to perform work at compile time and thus improve run-time performance.

However, it is not the focus of this book to provide a treatment of these aspects of template programming. There are many great books out there that already do this (Alexandrescu, 2001; Vandevoorde and Josuttis, 2002). Instead, our focus will be on the use of templates for API design. In this regard, there are several examples of well-designed template-based APIs that you can look to for reference and inspiration.

- **The Standard Template Library (STL).** All the STL container classes that you're familiar with, such as std::set, std::map, and std::vector, are class templates, which is the reason why they can be used to hold data of different types.
- **Boost.** These libraries provide a suite of powerful and useful features, many of which have been included in the new C++11 standard. Most of the Boost classes use templates, such as boost::shared_ptr, boost::function, and boost::static_pointer_cast.
- **Loki.** This is a library of class templates written by Andrei Alexandrescu to support his book on modern C++ design. It provides implementations of various design patterns, such as Visitor, Singleton, and Abstract Factory. This elegant code provides an exemplar of good template-based API design.

Even though templates in C++ are often used in combination with object-oriented techniques, it's worth noting that the two are completely orthogonal concepts. Templates can be used equally well with free functions and with structs and unions (although of course, as you already know, structs are functionally equivalent to classes in C++, except for their default access level).

5.3.1 An Example Template-Based API

Continuing our stack example, let's take a look at how you would create a generic stack declaration using templates and then instantiate it for integers. You can define the template-based stack class, in terms of a generic type T, as follows:

```
#include <vector>

template <typename T>
class Stack
{
public:
    void Push(T val);
    T Pop();
    bool IsEmpty() const;

private:
    std::vector<T> mStack;
};
```

Note that I have omitted the method definitions to keep the example clear. I will present some best practices for providing template definitions in the later chapter on C++ usage. It's also worth noting that there's nothing special about the name T. It's common to use the name T for your generic type, but you could equally well call it MyGenericType if you prefer.

With this declaration for a generic stack, you can then instantiate the template for the type `int` by creating an object of type `Stack<int>`. This will cause the compiler to generate code for this specific type instance. You could also define a simple typedef to make it more convenient to access this instance of the template, for example,

```
typedef Stack<int> IntStack;
```

Then this `IntStack` type can be used just as if you had written the class explicitly. For example,

```
IntStack *stack = new IntStack();
if (stack)
{
    stack->Push(10);
    stack->Push(3);
    while (! stack->IsEmpty())
    {
        stack->Pop();
    }
    delete stack;
}
```

5.3.2 Templates versus Macros

An alternative to the templates approach would be to use the C preprocessor to define a block of text that you can stamp into the header multiple times, such as

```
#include <vector>

#define DECLARE_STACK(Prefix, T) \
class Prefix##Stack \
{ \
public: \
    void Push(T val); \
    T Pop(); \
    bool IsEmpty() const; \
\
private: \
    std::vector<T> mStack; \
};

DECLARE_STACK(Int, int);
```

Aside from the ugliness of this code (e.g., having to end each line with a backslash and use preprocessor concatenation), the preprocessor has no notion of type checking or scoping. It is simply a text-copying mechanism. This means that because the declaration of the macro is not actually compiled, any errors in your macro will be reported on the single line where it is expanded, not where it is declared. Similarly, you cannot step into your methods with a debugger because the whole code block is expanded in a single line of your source file. In contrast, templates provide a type-safe way to generate code at compile time. And you will be able to debug into the actual lines of your class template.

In summary, unless you're writing a plain C API and therefore don't have access to templates, you should avoid using the preprocessor to simulate templates.

5.3.3 **Advantages of Template-Based APIs**

The obvious power of templates is that they let you create (instantiate) many different classes from a single root declaration. In the stack example given earlier, you could add support for string-based and floating-point stack classes simply by adding the following declarations:

```
typedef Stack<std::string> StringStack;
typedef Stack<double> DoubleStack;
```

As such, templates can help remove duplication because you don't need to copy, paste, and tweak the implementation code. Without templates, you would have to create (and maintain) a lot of very similar looking code to support IntStack, StringStack, and DoubleStack classes.

Another important property of templates is that they can provide static (compile-time) polymorphism, as opposed to the use of inheritance, which provides dynamic (run-time) polymorphism. One element of this is the fact that templates allow the creation of different classes that all exhibit the same interface. For example, every instance of our stack class—be it IntStack, DoubleStack, or String-Stack—is guaranteed to provide exactly the same set of methods. You can also use templates to create functions that accept any of these types, without the run-time cost of using virtual methods. This is achieved by generating different type-specific versions of the function at compile time. The following template function demonstrates this ability: it can be used to pop the top-most element from any of our stack types. In this example, two different versions of the function are generated at compile time:

```
template<typename T>
void PopAnyStack(T *stack)
{
    if (! stack->IsEmpty())
    {
        stack->Pop();
    }
}
...
IntStack int_stack;
StringStack string_stack;

int_stack.Push(10);
string_stack.Push("Hello Static Polymorphism!");

PopAnyStack(&string_stack);
PopAnyStack(&int_stack);
```

A further benefit of templates is that you can specialize certain methods of a class for a specific type instance. For instance, our generic stack template is defined as Stack<T>, but you could provide customized function implementations for certain types, such as for Stack<int>. This is very handy for optimizing the class for certain types or for adding customizations for certain types that behave uniquely. This can be done by providing a method definition with the following syntax:

```
template <>
void Stack<int>::Push(int val)
{
    // integer specific push implementation
}
```

5.3.4 Disadvantages of Template-Based APIs

In terms of disadvantages of using templates, the most critical one for API design is that the definition of your class templates will normally have to appear in your public headers. This is because the compiler must have access to the entire definition of your template code in order to specialize it. This obviously exposes your internal details, which you know is a major sin of API development. It also means that the compiler will recompile the inlined code each time the file is included, causing the generated code to be added to the object file for every module that uses the API. The result can be slower compilation times and code bloat. However, it should be noted that there are situations where you can, in fact, hide the implementation of a template in the `.cpp` file, using a technique called explicit instantiation. I will discuss this technique in more detail in the next chapter on C++ usage.

The static polymorphism example given in the previous section demonstrates another potential source of code bloat. This is because the compiler must generate code for each different version of the `PopAnyStack()` function that is used. This is opposed to the virtual method flavor of polymorphism, which only requires the compiler to generate one such method, but then incurs a run-time cost to know which class's `IsEmpty()` and `Pop()` methods to call. Therefore, if code size is more important to you than run-time cost, you may decide to go with an object-oriented solution rather than use templates. Alternatively, if run-time performance is critical for you, then templates may be the way to go.

Another commonly viewed disadvantage of templates is that most compilers can create verbose, long, or confusing messages for errors that occur in template code. It's not uncommon for simple errors in heavily templated code to produce dozens of lines of error output that cause you to scratch your head for a long time. In fact, there are even products on the market to simplify template error messages and make them easier to decipher, such as the STLFilt utility from BD Software. This is a concern not only for you as the developer of an API, but also for your clients because they will also be exposed to these voluble error messages if they use your API incorrectly.

5.4 DATA-DRIVEN APIs

A data-driven program is one that can perform different operations each time it is run by supplying it with different input data. For example, a data-driven program may simply accept the name of a file on disk that contains a list of commands to execute. This has an impact on the design of an API as it means that instead of relying on a collection of objects that provide various method calls, you provide more generic routines that accept named commands and a dictionary of named arguments. This is sometimes also called a message passing API or event-based API. The following function call formats illustrate how this API type differs from standard C and C++ calls:

- `func(obj, a, b, c)` = flat C-style function
- `obj.func(a, b, c)` = object-oriented C++ function
- `send("func", a, b, c)` = data-driven function with parameters
- `send("func", dict(arg1=a, arg2=b, arg2=c))` = data-driven function with a dictionary of named arguments (pseudo code)

To provide a concrete example of what this looks like, let's see how you might redesign our Stack example using a more data-driven model:

```
Class Stack
{
public:
```

```
    Stack();

    Result Command(const std::string &command, const ArgList &args);
};
```

This simple class could then be used to perform multiple operations, such as

```
s = new Stack();
if (s)
{
    s->Command("Push", ArgList().Add("value", 10));
    s->Command("Push", ArgList().Add("value", 3));
    Stack::Result r = s->Command("IsEmpty");
    while (! r.convertToBool())
    {
        s->Command("Pop");
        r = s->Command("IsEmpty");
    }
    delete s;
}
```

This is a more data-driven API because the individual methods have been replaced by a single method, Command(), that supports multiple possible inputs specified as string data. One could easily imagine writing a simple program that could parse the contents of an ASCII text file containing various commands and executing each command in order. The input file could look something like this:

```
# Input file for data-driven Stack API
Push value:10
Push value:3
Pop
Pop
```

A program to consume this data file using the data-driven stack API would simply take the first whitespace-delimited string on each line (ignoring blank lines and lines that begin with # as a convenience). The program could then create an ArgList structure for any further whitespace-delimited strings that follow the initial command. It would then pass those to the Stack::Command() and continue processing the remainder of the file. This program could then perform vastly different stack operations by supplying a different text file, and notably without requiring the program to be recompiled.

5.4.1 Data-Driven Web Services

Not all interfaces are appropriately represented with a data-driven style. However, this style is particularly suited to stateless communication channels, such as client/server applications where the API allows commands to be sent to a server and optionally to return results to the client. It is also useful for passing messages between loosely coupled components.

In particular, Web services can be represented very naturally using a data-driven API. A Web service is normally accessed by sending a URL with a set of query parameters to a given Web service or by sending a message in some structured format such as JSON (JavaScript Object Notation) or XML.

For instance, the Digg Web site supports an API to let users interact with the Digg.com Web service. As a specific example, the Digg API provides the `digg.getInfo` call to return extended information for a specific digg on a story. This is invoked by sending an HTTP GET request in the form:

```
http://services.digg.com/1.0/endpoint?method=digg.getInfo&digg_id=id
```

This maps well to the sort of data-driven APIs presented previously, where an HTTP request like this could be invoked as follows:

```
d = new DiggWebService();
d->Request("digg.getInfo", ArgList().Add("digg_id", id));
```

This correlates very closely to the underlying protocol, although it still provides an abstraction from the details of that protocol. For example, the implementation can still decide whether it's more appropriate to send the request as a GET or POST, or even a JSON or XML description.

5.4.2 Advantages of Data-Driven APIs

I've already pointed out one of the major benefits of data-driven APIs: that the business logic of a program can be abstracted out into a human-editable data file. In this way, the behavior of a program can be modified without the need to recompile the executable.

You may even decide to support a separate design tool to let users author the data file easily. Several commercial packages work this way, such as FMOD, which includes the FMOD Designer program that allows complex authoring of sound effects. The resulting `.fev` files can be loaded by the data-driven FMOD Event API. Also, the Qt UI toolkit includes the Qt Designer application that lets users create user interfaces in a visual and interactive fashion. The resulting `.ui` files can be loaded at run time by Qt's `QUiLoader` class.

Another major benefit of a data-driven API is that it tends to be far more tolerant of future API changes. That's because adding, removing, or changing a command can, in many cases, have no effect on the signatures of the public API methods. Often it will simply change the supported set of strings that can be passed to the command handler. In other words, passing an unsupported or obsolete command to the handler will not produce a compile-time error. Similarly, different versions of a command can be supported based on the number and type of arguments that are provided, essentially mimicking C++'s method overloading.

Taking the example of the data-driven Stack API, which simply provides a `Stack::Command()` method, a newer version of the API might add support for a `Top` command (to return the top-most element without popping it) and could also extend the `Push` command to accept multiple values, each of which are pushed onto the stack in turn. An example program using these new features might look like

```
s = new Stack();
s->Command("Push", ArgList().Add("value1", 10).Add("value2", 3));
Result r = s->Command("Top");
int top = r.ToInt(); // top == 3
```

Note that adding this new functionality involved no change whatsoever to the function signatures in the header file. It merely changed the supported strings, and the list of arguments, that can be passed to the Command() method. Because of this property, it is much easier to create backward compatible API changes when using a data-driven model, even when removing or changing existing commands. Similarly, it is much easier to create binary compatible changes because it is more likely that you will not need to change the signature of any of your public methods.

One further benefit of data-driven APIs is that they support data-driven testing techniques more easily. This is an automated testing technique where, instead of writing lots of individual test programs or routines to exercise an API, you can simply write a single data-driven program that reads a file containing a series of commands to perform and assertions to check. Then writing multiple tests means simply creating multiple input data files. Test development iteration can therefore be faster because no compilation step is required to create a new test. Also, QA engineers who do not possess deep C++ development skills can still write tests for your API.

Remaining with our Stack example, you could create a test program that accepts input data files such as the following:

```
IsEmpty => True  # A newly created stack should be empty
Push value:10
Push value:3
IsEmpty => False # A stack with two elements is non-empty
Pop => 3
IsEmpty => False # A stack with one element is non-empty
Pop => 10
IsEmpty => True  # A stack with zero elements is empty
Pop => NULL      # Popping an empty stack is an error
```

This test program is very similar to the program described earlier to read Stack commands from a data file. The main difference is that I've added support for a "=>" symbol, which lets you check the result returned by the Stack::Command() method. With that small addition, you now have a flexible testing framework that allows you to create any number of data-driven tests for your API.

TIP

Data-driven APIs map well to Web services and other client/server APIs. They also support data-driven testing techniques.

5.4.3 Disadvantages of Data-Driven APIs

As already stated, the data-driven model is not appropriate for all interfaces. It may be useful for data communication interfaces, such as Web services or for client/server message passing. However, it would not be an appropriate choice for a real-time 3D graphics API.

For one reason, the simplicity and stability of the API come with a run-time cost. This is due to the additional overhead of finding the correct internal routine to call given a command name string. Use of an internal hash table or dictionary that maps supported command names to callable functions can speed this process up, but it will never be as fast as calling a function directly.

Furthermore, another downside of data-driven APIs is that your physical header files do not reflect your logical interface. This means that a user cannot simply look at your public header files and know what functionality and semantics are provided by the interface. However, recall in the very first section of this book that I defined an API as a collection of header files—and associated documentation. Therefore, as long as you provide good API documentation to specify the list of supported commands and their expected arguments you can reasonably compensate for this disadvantage.

Finally, data-driven APIs do not benefit from compile-time checking of your interface. This is because you are essentially performing the parsing and type checking of parameters yourself. This therefore places more burden on you to test your code and ensure that you have not broken any important behavior.

5.4.4 Supporting Variant Argument Lists

Up to this point, I have glossed over the use of our `Result` and `ArgList` types in the various examples given previously. These are meant to represent data values that can contain differently typed values. For example, `ArgList` could be used to pass no arguments, a single integer argument, or two arguments where one is a string and the other is a float. Weakly typed languages such as Python explicitly support this concept. However, C++ does not: arrays and containers must contain elements that are all of the same type, and where that type must be known at compile time. You therefore need to introduce the notion of a value-holding object that can store a value of various possible types. This is often called a variant type.

Furthermore, you need to be able to know what type the value is, and you would like to be able to convert the value to another type as required (e.g., if the type is a string, but you want to treat it as an int). Several toolkits support this notion. Three representative examples include Qt's `QVariant`, Boost's `any`, and Second Life's `LLSD`.

- **QVariant**. Provides a holding object for several common Qt types, including `QChar`, `double`, `QString`, `QUrl`, `QTime`, and `QDate`, among others. Methods are provided to check whether the object contains any value, to determine the type of that value, and to convert that value to another type where possible. A `QVariant` can also hold container objects of variants, such as lists, arrays, and maps of `QVariant` objects, for example, a `QVariant` can contain a `QMap<QString, QVariant>`.
- **boost::any**. This class template allows you to store any value type rather than a fixed set of explicitly supported types. You can then extract the original value by casting it back to the desired type. The class also provides a `type()` method so that you can determine the type of the held object. However, there is no explicit support for converting between different value types other than the conversions already supported by your cast operators.
- **LLSD**. Supports various scalar data types, including boolean, integer, real, UUID, string, date, URI, and binary data. A single `LLSD` can also contain an array or a map (dictionary) of scalar `LLSD` values. Methods are provided to check whether the object contains any value, to determine the type of that value, and to convert that value to another type where possible. Additionally, methods are available as part of the `LLSD` interface to access array and map data within the object, for example, `LLSD::has()` and `LLSD::insert()`.

In terms of implementation, there are several standard ways to implement a variant type. Some common approaches are as follows.

1. **Union**. A union structure is used to hold an instance of each supported type so that the structure only uses enough space to hold the largest of these types. An additional type variable is used to specify which of the union's fields is valid. This technique is used by Microsoft's Win32 VARIANT type.
2. **Inheritance**. Each type is represented by a class that derives from a common abstract base class. The abstract base class specifies methods to return the type identifier and optionally to convert the contents to a different type. This is essentially the approach used by QVariant.
3. **void***. This is similar to the union approach, except that a void* pointer is used to hold onto a pointer to the object, or a copy of the object. As with the union technique, an extra variable is needed to represent the type of the variable pointed to by the void* pointer. This is obviously the least type safe solution of the three.

I will present an API for a simple variant type here to illustrate the desired capabilities of such an object. I will model this example API on QVariant as this is a simple design to understand and more orthogonal than the LLSD approach. (LLSD is non-orthogonal because it duplicates array and map functionality found in other container objects. Interestingly, the developers of the Open Metaverse API, based on the Second Life object model, chose to not duplicate this aspect of LLSD for their OSD class.) While I don't show the implementation details here, the source code that accompanies this book provides a full working example using the inheritance method to store the value type.

Here is the interface for a generic Arg class:

```
class Arg
{
public:
    // constructor, destructor, copy constructor, and assignment
    Arg();
    ~Arg();
    Arg(const Arg&);
    Arg &operator = (const Arg &other);

    // constructors to initialize with a value
    explicit Arg(bool value);
    explicit Arg(int value);
    explicit Arg(double value);
    explicit Arg(const std::string &value);

    // set the arg to be empty/undefined/NULL
    void Clear();

    // change the current value
    void Set(bool value);
    void Set(int value);
    void Set(double value);
    void Set(const std::string &value);

    // test the type of the current value
    bool IsEmpty() const;
    bool ContainsBool() const;
```

```
bool ContainsInt() const;
bool ContainsDouble() const;
bool ContainsString() const;

// can the current value be returned as another type?
bool CanConvertToBool() const;
bool CanConvertToInt() const;
bool CanConvertToDouble() const;
bool CanConvertToString() const;

// return the current value as a specific type
bool ToBool() const;
int ToInt() const;
double ToDouble() const;
std::string ToString() const;

private:
    ...
};
```

Using this declaration for an `Arg`, you could now define an `ArgList` as a string-to-Arg map, such as

```
typedef std::map<std::string, Arg> ArgList;
```

This would allow you to create an interface with an optional number of named arguments that can be of type bool, int, double, or string. For example,

```
s = new Stack();
ArgList args;
args["NumberOfElements"] = Arg(2);
s->Command("Pop", args);
```

Alternatively, you could declare `ArgList` as its own class that contains a private `std::map` and supports convenience routines, such as an `Add()` method to insert a new entry in the map and return a reference to the `ArgList`. This lets you use the Named Parameter Idiom (presented in the previous chapter) to offer a more compact syntax, such as the following:

```
s = new Stack();
s->Command("Pop", ArgList().Add("NumberOfElements", 2));
```

With this new class, you can now support methods that accept a single parameter (of type `ArgList`), which can be used to pass any combination of `bool`, `int`, `double`, or `std::string` arguments. As such, future changes to the API behavior (e.g., adding a new argument to the list of arguments supported by the method) can be made without changing the actual signature of the method.

5.4.5 Case Study: FMOD Data-Driven API

In conclusion, I present a simple program using the FMOD data-driven API to give a real-world example of this API style. Note that this is only one example of a data-driven interface and does not illustrate all of the concepts that I've discussed. However, it does illustrate cases where much of the logic is stored in a data file that is loaded at run time. This is the sound.fev file, which is created by the FMOD Designer tool. The program then shows accessing a named parameter of an event in that file and changing that parameter's value.

```cpp
#include "fmod_event.hpp"
int main(int argc, char *argv[])
{
    FMOD::EventSystem    *eventsystem;
    FMOD::Event    *event;
    FMOD::EventParameter *param;
    float    param_val = 0.0f;
    float    param_min, param_max, param_inc;

    // Initialize FMOD
    FMOD::EventSystem_Create(&eventsystem);
    eventsystem->init(64, FMOD_INIT_NORMAL, 0, FMOD_EVENT_INIT_NORMAL);

    // Load a file created with the FMOD Designer tool
    eventsystem->load("sound.fev", 0, 0);
    eventsystem->getEvent("EffectEnvelope", FMOD_EVENT_DEFAULT, &event);

    // Get a named parameter from the loaded data file
    event->getParameter("param", &param);
    param->getRange(&param_min, &param_max);
    param->setValue(param_val);
    event->start();

    // Continually modulate the parameter until Esc pressed
    param_increment = (param_max - param_min) / 100.0f;
    bool increase_param = true;
    while (! UserPressedEscKey())
    {
        if (increase_param)
        {
            param_val += param_increment;
            if (param_val > param_max)
            {
                param_val = param_max;
                increase_param = false;
            }
        }
        else
        {
            param_val -= param_increment;
            if (param_val < param_min)
            {
                param_val = param_min;
                increase_param = true;
```

```
            }
        }
        param->setValue(param_val);

        eventsystem->update();
        NanoSleep(10);
    }

    // Shut down
    eventsystem->release();
    return 0;
}
```

C++ Usage

6

This chapter dives into the question of what qualities make a good API in C++. The generic API qualities covered in Chapter 2 could be applied to any programming language: the concepts of hiding private details, ease of use, loose coupling, and minimal completeness transcend the use of any particular programming language. While I presented C++-specific details for each of these topics, the concepts themselves are not language specific.

However, many specific C++ style decisions can affect the quality of an API, such as the use of namespaces, operators, friends, and const correctness. I will discuss these issues, and more, in this chapter.

Note that I will defer some performance-related C++ topics, such as inlining and const references, until the next chapter on performance.

6.1 NAMESPACES

A namespace is a logical grouping of unique symbols. It provides a way to avoid naming collisions so that two APIs don't try to define symbols with the same name. For example, if two APIs both define a class called `String`, then you cannot use the two APIs in the same program because only one definition can exist at any time. You should always use some form of namespacing in your APIs to ensure that they can interoperate with any other APIs that your clients may decide to use.

There are two popular ways that you can add a namespace to your API. The first is to use a unique prefix for all of your public API symbols. This is a very common approach and has the benefit that it can be used for vanilla C APIs as well. There are many examples of this type of namespacing, including

- The OpenGL API uses "gl" as a prefix for all public symbols, for example, `glBegin()`, `glVertex3f()`, and `GL_BLEND_COLOR` (Shreiner, 2004).
- The Qt API uses the "Q" prefix for all public names, for example, `QWidget`, `QApplication`, and `Q_FLAGS`.
- The libpng library uses the "png" prefix for all identifiers, for example, `png_read_row()`, `png_create_write_struct()`, and `png_set_invalid()`.
- The GNU GTK+ API uses the "gtk" prefix, for example, `gtk_init()`, `gtk_style_new()`, and `GtkArrowType`.
- The Second Life source code uses the "LL" prefix (short for Linden Lab) for various classes, enums, constants, for example, `LLEvent`, `LLUUID`, and `LL_ACK_FLAG`.

- The Netscape Portable Runtime names all exported types with a "PR" prefix, for example, `PR_WaitCondVar()`, `PR_fprintf()`, and `PRFileDesc`.

The second approach is to use the C++ `namespace` keyword. This essentially defines a scope where any names within that scope are given an additional prefix identifier. For example,

```
namespace MyAPI
{
   class String
   {
   public:
      String();
      ...
   };
}
```

The `String` class in this case must now be referenced as `MyAPI::String`. The benefit of this style is that you don't need to meticulously ensure that every class, function, enum, or constant has a consistent prefix: the compiler does it for you. This method is used by the STL, where all container classes, iterators, and algorithms are contained within the "std" namespace. You can also create nested namespaces, forming a namespace tree. For example, Intel's Threading Build Blocks (TBB) API use the "tbb" namespace for all its public symbols and "tbb::strict_ppl" for internal code. The Boost libraries also make use of nested namespaces, inside of the root "boost" namespace, for example, `boost::variant` contains the public symbols for the Boost Variant API and `boost::detail::variant` contains the internal details for that API.

Using the namespace feature can produce verbose symbol names, particularly for symbols contained within several nested namespaces. However, C++ provides a way to make it more convenient to use symbols within a namespace with the `using` keyword:

```
using namespace std;
string str("Look, no std::");
```

or, more preferably (because it limits the extent of symbols imported into the global namespace),

```
using std::string;
string str("Look, no std::");
```

However, you should never use the `using` keyword in the global scope of your public API headers! Doing so would cause all the symbols in the referenced namespace to become visible in the global namespace. This would subvert the entire point of using namespaces in the first place (Stroustrup, 2000). If you wish to reference symbols in another namespace in your header files, then always use the fully qualified name, for example, `std::string`.

TIP

Always provide a namespace for your API symbols via either a consistent naming prefix or the C++ namespace keyword.

6.2 CONSTRUCTORS AND ASSIGNMENT

If you are creating objects that contain state and that may be copied or assigned by client programs (sometimes called value objects), you need to consider the correct design of your constructors and assignment operator. Your compiler will generate default versions of these methods for you if you don't define them yourself. However, if your class has any dynamically allocated objects, then you must explicitly define these methods yourself to ensure that the objects are copied correctly. Specifically, your compiler can generate default versions for the following four special methods.

- **Default constructor**. A constructor is used to initialize an object after it has been allocated by the new call. You can define multiple constructors with different arguments. The default constructor is defined as the constructor that can be called with no arguments (this could be a constructor with no argument or with arguments that all specify default values). Your C++ compiler will automatically generate a default constructor if you do not explicitly define one.
- **Destructor**. The destructor is called in response to a delete call in order to release any resources that the object is holding. There can be only one destructor for a class. If you do not specify a destructor, your C++ compiler will generate one automatically. The compiler will also generate code to automatically call the destructors for all of your member variables, in the reverse order they appear in the class declaration.
- **Copy constructor**. A copy constructor is a special constructor that creates a new object from an existing object. If you do not define a copy constructor, the compiler will generate one for you that performs a shallow copy of the existing object's member variables. So if your object allocates any resources, you most likely need a copy constructor so that you can perform a deep copy. The copy constructor gets called in the following situations:
  - An object is passed to a method by value or returned by value
  - An object is initialized using the syntax, MyClass a = b;
  - An object is placed in a brace-enclosed initializer list
  - An object is thrown or caught in an exception
- **Assignment operator**. The assignment operator is used to assign the value of one object to another object, for example, a = b. It differs from the copy constructor in that the object being assigned to already exists. Some guidelines for implementing the assignment operator include:

  1. Use a const reference for the right-hand operand.
  2. Return *this as a reference to allow operator chaining.
  3. Destroy any existing state before setting the new state.
  4. Check for self-assignment (a = a) by comparing this to the right-hand operator.

As a corollary to these points, if you wish to create objects that should never be copied by your clients (also known as reference objects), then you should declare the copy constructor and assignment operator as private class members or use boost::noncopyable.

Many novice C++ developers get into trouble because they have a class that allocates resources, and hence requires a destructor, but they define neither a copy constructor nor an assignment operator. For example, consider the following simple integer array class, where I show the implementation of the constructor and destructor inline to clarify the behavior.

```
class Array
{
public:
    explicit Array(int size) :
        mSize(size),
        mData(new int[size])
    {
    }
    ~Array()
    {
        delete [] mData;
    };

    int Get(int index) const;
    void Set(int index, int value);
    int GetSize() const;

private:
    int mSize;
    int* mData;
};
```

This class allocates memory, but does not define either a copy constructor or an assignment operator. As a result, the following code will crash when the two variables go out of scope because the destructor of each will try to free the same memory.

```
{
    Array x(100);
    Array y = x;   // y now shares the same mData pointer as x
}
```

When creating a value object, it is therefore essential that you follow the rule of "The Big Three." This term was introduced by Marshall Cline in the early nineties and essentially states that there are three member functions that always go together: the destructor, the copy constructor, and the assignment operator (Cline et al., 1998). If you define one of these, you normally need to define the other two as well (declaring an empty virtual destructor is one exception, as it does not perform any actual deallocation). James Coplien referred to this same concept as the orthodox canonical class form (Coplien, 1991).

TIP

If your class allocates resources, you should follow the rule of The Big Three and define a destructor, copy constructor, and assignment operator.

6.2.1 Controlling Compiler-Generated Functions

In the C++98 standard, you have little control over the compiler's behavior of automatically generating these special functions. For example, as already noted earlier, if you do not declare a copy constructor, the compiler will always generate one for you. However, in the new C++11 specification, you have explicit control over whether the compiler generates, or does not generate, these functions. For instance, the following example specifically tells the compiler to create a private default constructor and a virtual destructor, using the compiler-generated version of these in both cases.

```
class MyClass
{
public:
    virtual ~MyClass() = default;

private:
    MyClass() = default;
};
```

You can also tell the compiler to disable certain functions that would otherwise be generated for you. For example, this can be used as another way to make a class be non-copyable as an alternative to the technique described earlier of declaring a private copy constructor and assignment operator.

```
class NonCopyable
{
public:
    NonCopyable() = default;
    NonCopyable(const NonCopyable&) = delete;
    NonCopyable & operator=(const NonCopyable&) = delete;
};
```

Of course, these are C++11-only features. However, some compilers already provide experimental support for this functionality, such as the GNU C++ 4.4 compiler.

6.2.2 Defining Constructors and Assignment

Because writing constructors and operators can be a tricky business, here's an example that demonstrates the various combinations. It builds on the previous array example and presents a class for storing an array of strings. Because the array is allocated dynamically, you must define a copy constructor and assignment operator, otherwise the memory will be freed twice on destruction if you copy the array. Here's the declaration of the Array class in the header file:

```
#include <string>

class Array
{
public:
    // default constructor
    Array();
    // non-default constructor
    explicit Array(int size);
    // destructor
    ~Array();
    // copy constructor
```

```
    Array(const Array &in_array);
    // assignment operator
    Array &operator = (const Array &in_array);

    std::string Get(int index) const;
    bool Set(int index, const std::string &str);
    int GetSize() const;

private:
    int mSize;
    std::string *mArray;
};
```

and here are sample definitions for the constructors and assignment operator:

```
#include "array.h"
#include <algorithm>

// default constructor
Array::Array() :
    mSize(0),
    mArray(NULL)
{
}

// non-default constructor
Array::Array(int size) :
    mSize(size),
    mArray(new std::string[size])
{
}

// destructor
Array::~Array()
{
    delete [] mArray;
}

// copy constructor
Array::Array(const Array &in_array) :
    mSize(in_array.mSize),
    mArray(new std::string[in_array.mSize])
{
    std::copy(in_array.mArray, in_array.mArray + mSize, mArray);
}

// assignment operator
Array &Array::operator = (const Array &in_array)
{
    if (this != &in_array) // check for self assignment
```

```
    {
        delete [] mArray; // delete current array first

        mSize = in_array.mSize;
        mArray = new std::string[in_array.mSize];
        std::copy(in_array.mArray, in_array.mArray + mSize, mArray);
    }
    return *this;
}
```

Given the aforementioned Array class, the following code demonstrates when the various methods will be called.

```
Array a;        // default constructor
Array a(10);    // non-default constructor
Array b(a);     // copy constructor
Array c = a;    // copy constructor (because c does not exist yet)
b = c;          // assignment operator
```

Note that there are certain cases where your compiler may elide the call to your copy constructor, for example, if it performs some form of Return Value Optimization (Meyers, 1998).

6.2.3 **The Explicit Keyword**

You may have noticed use of the explicit keyword before the declaration of the non-default constructor in the Array example I just presented. Adding explicit is a good general practice for any constructor that accepts a single argument. It is used to prevent a specific constructor from being called implicitly when constructing an object. For example, without the explicit keyword, the following code is valid C++:

```
Array a = 10;
```

This will call the Array single-argument constructor with the integer argument of 10. However, this type of implicit behavior can be confusing, unintuitive, and, in most cases, unintended. As a further example of this kind of undesired implicit conversion, consider the following function signature:

```
void CheckArraySize(const Array &array, int size);
```

Without declaring the single-argument constructor of Array as explicit, you could call this function as

```
CheckArraySize(10, 10);
```

This weakens the type safety of your API because now the compiler will not enforce the type of the first argument to be an explicit Array object. As a result, there's the potential for the user to forget the correct order of arguments and pass them in the wrong order. This is why you should always use the explicit keyword for any single-argument constructors unless you know that you want to support implicit conversion.

You can also declare your copy constructor to be explicit too. This will prevent implicit invocations of the copy constructor, such as passing an object to a function by value or returning an object by value. However, you will still be able to explicitly call the copy constructor using the "Array a = b" or "Array a(b)" syntax.

TIP

Consider using the explicit keyword before the declaration of any constructor with a single argument.

As a side note, the new C++11 specification lets you use the `explicit` keyword in front of conversion operators as well as constructors. Doing so will prevent those conversion functions from being used for implicit conversions.

6.3 CONST CORRECTNESS

Const correctness refers to use of the C++ `const` keyword to declare a variable or method as immutable. It is a compile-time construct that can be used to maintain the correctness of code that shouldn't modify certain variables. In C++, you can define variables as const, to mean that they should not be modified, and you can also define methods as const, to mean that they should not modify any member variables of the class. Using const correctness is simply good programming practice. However, it can also provide documentation on the intent of your methods, and hence make them easier to use.

TIP

Ensure that your API is const correct.

6.3.1 Method Const Correctness

A const method cannot modify any member variables of the class. In essence, all member variables are treated as const variables inside of a const method. This form of const correctness is indicated by appending the `const` keyword after the method's parameter list. There are two principal benefits of declaring a method as const:

1. To advertise the fact that the method will not change the state of the object. As just discussed, this is helpful documentation for users of your API.
2. To allow the method to be used on const versions of an object. A non-const method cannot be called on a const version of an object.

Scott Meyers describes two camps of philosophy about what a const method represents. There's the bitwise constness camp, which believes that a const method should not change any member variables of a class, and then there's the logical constness camp, which says that a const method may change a member variable if that change cannot be detected by the user (Meyers, 2005). Your C++ compiler conforms to the bitwise approach. However, there are times when you really want it to behave in the logical constness manner. A classic example is if you want to cache some property of a class because it takes too long to compute. For example, consider a `HashTable` class that needs to return the number of elements in the hash table very efficiently. As a result, you decide to cache its size and compute this value lazily, on demand. Given the following class declaration:

```
class HashTable
{
public:
    void Insert(const std::string &str);
    int Remove(const std::string &str);
    bool Has(const std::string &str) const;
    int GetSize() const;
    ...
private:
    int mCachedSize;
    bool mSizeIsDirty;
    ...
};
```

you may want to implement the GetSize() const method as follows:

```
int HashTable::GetSize() const
{
    if (mSizeIsDirty)
    {
        mCachedSize = CalculateSize();
        mSizeIsDirty = false;
    }
    return mCachedSize;
}
```

Unfortunately, this is not legal C++, as the GetSize() method does actually modify member variables (mSizeIsDirty and mCachedSize). However, these are not part of the public interface: they are internal state that lets us offer a more efficient API. This is the reason why there is the notion of logical constness. C++ does provide a way around this problem with the mutable keyword. Declaring the mCachedSize and mSizeIsDirty variables as mutable states that they can be modified within a const method. Using mutable is a great way to maintain the logical constness of your API instead of removing the const keyword on a member function that really should be declared const.

```
class HashTable
{
public:
    ...
private:
    mutable int mCachedSize;
    mutable bool mSizeIsDirty;
    ...
};
```

TIP

Declare methods and parameters as const as soon as you can. Trying to retrofit const correctness into an API at a later date can be a time-consuming and frustrating activity.

6.3.2 Parameter Const Correctness

Use of the `const` keyword can also be used to indicate whether you intend for a parameter to be an input or an output parameter, that is, a parameter used to pass some value into a method or a parameter used to receive some result. For example, consider a method such as

```
std::string StringToLower(std::string &str);
```

It's not clear from this function signature whether this method will modify the string that you pass in. Clearly it returns a string result, but perhaps it also changes the parameter string. It certainly could do so if it wanted to. If the purpose of this method is to take the parameter and return a lowercase version without affecting the input string, then the simple addition of const can make this unequivocally clear.

```
std::string StringToLower(const std::string &str);
```

Now the compiler will enforce the fact that the function `StringToLower()` will not modify the string that the user passes in. As a result, it's clear and unambiguous what the intended use of this function is just by looking at the function signature.

Often you'll find that if you have a const method, then any reference or pointer parameters can also be declared const. While this is not a hard and fast rule, it follows logically from the general promise that the const method does not modify any state. For example, in the following function the `root_node` parameter can be declared const because it's not necessary to modify this object in order to compute the result of the const method:

```
bool Node::IsVisible(const Node &root_node) const;
```

> **TIP**
>
> When passing a reference or pointer into a const method, think about whether that parameter can be declared const too.

6.3.3 Return Value Const Correctness

When returning the result of a function, the main reason to declare that result to be const is if it references internal state of the object. For example, if you are returning a result by value, then it makes little sense to specify it as const because the returned object will be a copy and hence changing it will not affect any of your class's internal state.

Alternatively, if you return a pointer or reference to a private data member, then you should declare the result to be const, as otherwise users will be able to modify your internal state without going through your public API. In this case, you must also think about whether the returned pointer or reference will survive longer than your class. If this is possible, you should consider returning a reference-counted pointer, such as a `std::shared_ptr`, as discussed earlier in Chapter 2.

Therefore, the most common decision you will have with respect to return value const correctness is whether to return the result by value or const reference, that is,

```
// return by value
std::string GetName() const
{
    return mName;
}

// return by const reference
const std::string &GetName() const
{
    return mName;
}
```

In general, I recommend that you return the result by value as it is safer. However, you may prefer the const reference method in a few cases where performance is critical. Returning by value is safer because you don't have to worry about clients holding onto references after your object has been destroyed, but also because returning a const reference can break encapsulation.

TIP _____

Prefer to return the result of a function by value rather than const reference.

On the face of it, our const reference `GetName()` method given earlier seems acceptable: the method is declared to be const to indicate that it doesn't modify the state of the object, and the returned reference to the object's internal state is also declared to be const so that clients can't modify it. However, a determined client can always cast away the constness of the reference and then modify the underlying private data member directly, such as in the following example:

```
// get a const reference to an internal string
const std::string &const_name = object.GetName();

// cast away the constness
std::string &name = const_cast<std::string &>(const_name);

// and modify the object's internal data!
name.clear();
```

6.4 TEMPLATES

Templates provide a versatile and powerful ability to generate code at compile time. They are particularly useful for generating lots of code that looks similar but differs only by type. However, if you decide to provide class templates as part of your public API, several issues should be considered to ensure that you provide a well-insulated, efficient, and cross-platform interface. The following sections address several of these factors.

Note that I will not cover all aspects of template programming, only those features that impact good API design. For a more thorough and in-depth treatment of templates, there are several good books on the market (Alexandrescu, 2001; Josuttis, 1999; Vandevoorde and Josuttis, 2002).

6.4.1 **Template Terminology**

Templates are an often poorly understood part of the C++ specification, so let's begin by defining some terms so that we can proceed from a common base. I will use the following template declaration as a reference for the definitions:

```
template <typename T>
class Stack
{
public:
    void Push(T val);
    T Pop();
    bool IsEmpty() const;

private:
    std::vector<T> mStack;
};
```

This class template describes a generic stack class where you can specify the type of the elements in the stack, T.

- **Template Parameters**: These names are listed after the template keyword in a template declaration. For example, T is the single template parameter specified in our Stack example given earlier.
- **Template Arguments**: These entities are substituted for template parameters during specialization. For example, given a specialization Stack<int>, "int" is a template argument.
- **Instantiation**: This is when the compiler generates a regular class, method, or function by substituting each of the template's parameters with a concrete type. This can happen implicitly when you create an object based on a template or explicitly if you want to control when the code generation happens. For example, the following lines of code create two specific stack instances and will normally cause the compiler to generate code for these two different types.

  ```
  Stack<int> myIntStack;
  Stack<std::string> myStringStack;
  ```

- **Implicit Instantiation**: This is when the compiler decides when to generate code for your template instances. Leaving the decision to the compiler means that it must find an appropriate place to insert the code, and it must also make sure that only one instance of the code exists to avoid duplicate symbol link errors. This is a non-trivial problem and can cause extra bloat in your object files or longer compile and link times to solve. Most importantly for API design, implicit instantiation means that you have to include the template definitions in your header files so that the compiler has access to the definitions whenever it needs to generate the instantiation code.
- **Explicit Instantiation**: This is when the programmer determines when the compiler should generate the code for a specific specialization. This can make for much more efficient compilation and link times because the compiler no longer needs to maintain bookkeeping information for all of its implicit instantiations. However, the onus is then placed on the programmer to ensure that a particular specialization is explicitly instantiated once and only once. From an API perspective, explicit instantiation allows us to move the template implementation into the .cpp file, and so hide it from the user.

- **Lazy Instantiation**: This describes the standard implicit instantiation behavior of a C++ compiler wherein it will only generate code for the parts of a template that are actually used. For example, given the previous two instantiations, if you never called IsEmpty() on the myStringStack object, then the compiler would not generate code for the std::string specialization of that method. This means that you can instantiate a template with a type that can be used by some, but not all, methods of a class template. For example, say one method uses the >= operator, but the type you want to instantiate does not define this operator. This is fine as long as you don't call the particular method that attempts to use the >= operator.
- **Specialization**: When a template is instantiated, the resulting class, method, or function is called a specialization. More specifically, this is an instantiated (or generated) specialization. However, the term specialization can also be used when you provide a custom implementation for a function by specifying concrete types for all the template parameters. I gave an example of this earlier in the API Styles chapter, where I presented the following implementation of the Stack::Push() method, specialized for integer types. This is called an explicit specialization.

```
template <>
void Stack<int>::Push(int val)
{
    // integer specific push implementation
}
```

- **Partial Specialization**: This is when you provide a specialization of the template for a subset of all possible cases. That is, you specialize one feature of the template but still allow the user to specify other features. For example, if your template accepts multiple parameters, you could partially specialize it by defining a case where you specify a concrete type for only one of the parameters. In our Stack example with a single template parameter, you could partially specialize this template to specifically handle pointers to any type T. This still lets users create a stack of any type, but it also lets you write specific logic to handle the case where users create a stack of pointers. This partially specialized class declaration might look like:

```
template <typename T>
class Stack<T *>
{
public:
    void Push(T *val);
    T *Pop();
    bool IsEmpty() const;

private:
    std::vector<T *> mStack;
};
```

6.4.2 Implicit Instantiation API Design

If you want to allow your clients to instantiate your class templates with their own types, then you need to use implicit template instantiation. For example, if you provide a smart pointer class template, smart_pointer<T>, you do not know ahead of time what types your clients will want to instantiate it with. As a result, the compiler needs to be able to access the definition of the template when it is used. This essentially means that you must expose the template definition in your header files. This is the biggest disadvantage of the implicit instantiation approach in terms of robust API design. However, even if you can't necessarily hide the implementation details in this situation, you can at least make an effort to isolate them.

Given that you need to include the template definition in your header file, it's easy, and therefore tempting, to simply inline the definitions directly within the class definition. This is a practice that I have already classified as poor design, and that assertion is still true in the case of templates. Instead, I recommend that all template implementation details be contained within a separate implementation header, which is then included by the main public header. Using the example of our Stack class template, you could provide the main public header:

```cpp
// stack.h
#ifndef STACK_H
#define STACK_H

#include <vector>

template <typename T>
class Stack
{
public:
    void Push(T val);
    T Pop();
    bool IsEmpty() const;

private:
    std::vector<T> mStack;
};

// isolate all implementation details within a separate header
#include "stack_priv.h"

#endif
```

Then the implementation header, stack_priv.h, would look as follows:

```cpp
// stack_priv.h
#ifndef STACK_PRIV_H
#define STACK_PRIV_H

template <typename T>
void Stack<T>::Push(T val)
{
    mStack.push_back(val);
}

template <typename T>
```

```
T Stack<T>::Pop()
{
    if (IsEmpty())
        return T();
    T val = mStack.back();
    mStack.pop_back();
    return val;
}

template <typename T>
bool Stack<T>::IsEmpty() const
{
    return mStack.empty();
}

#endif
```

This technique is used by many high-quality template-based APIs, such as various Boost headers. It has the benefit of keeping the main public header uncluttered by implementation details while isolating the necessary exposure of internal details to a separate header that is clearly designated as containing private details. (The same technique can be used to isolate consciously inlined function details from their declarations.)

The technique of including template definitions in header files is referred to as the Inclusion Model (Vandevoorde and Josuttis, 2002). It's worth noting that there is an alternative to this style called the Separation Model. This allows the declaration of a class template in a .h file to be preceded with the export keyword. Then the implementation of the template methods can appear in a .cpp file. From an API design perspective, this is a far more preferable model, as it would allow us to remove all implementation details from public headers. However, this part of the C++ specification is very poorly supported by most compilers. In particular, neither GNU C++ 4.3 nor Microsoft Visual C++ 9.0 compilers support the export keyword. You should therefore avoid this technique in your APIs to maximize the portability of your API.

6.4.3 **Explicit Instantiation API Design**

If you want to provide only a predetermined set of template specializations for your API and disallow your users from creating further ones, then you do in fact have the option of completely hiding your private code. For example, if you have created a 3D vector class template, Vector3D<T>, you may only want to provide specializations of this template for int, short, float, and double, and you may feel that it's not necessary to let your users create further specializations.

In this case, you can put your template definitions into a .cpp file and use explicit template instantiation to instantiate those specializations that you wish to export as part of your API. The template keyword can be used to create an explicit instantiation. For instance, using our Stack template example given previously, you could create explicit instantiations for the type int with the statement:

```
template class Stack<int>;
```

This will cause the compiler to generate the code for the `int` specialization at this point in the code. As a result, it will subsequently no longer attempt to implicitly instantiate this specialization elsewhere in the code. Consequently, using explicit instantiation can also help increase build times.

Let's take a look at how you can organize your code to take advantage of this feature. Our `stack.h` header file looks almost exactly the same as before, just without the `#include "stack_priv.h"` line:

```
// stack.h
#ifndef STACK_H
#define STACK_H

#include <vector>

template <typename T>
class Stack
{
public:
    void Push(T val);
    T Pop();
    bool IsEmpty() const;

private:
    std::vector<T> mStack;
};

#endif
```

Now you can contain all of the implementation details for this template in an associated `.cpp` file:

```
// stack.cpp
#include "stack.h"
#include <string>

template <typename T>
void Stack<T>::Push(T val)
{
    mStack.push_back(val);
}

template <typename T>
T Stack<T>::Pop()
{
    if (IsEmpty())
        return T();
    T val = mStack.back();
    mStack.pop_back();
    return val;
}
```

```
template <typename T>
bool Stack<T>::IsEmpty() const
{
    return mStack.empty();
}


// explicit template instantiations
template class Stack<int>;
template class Stack<double>;
template class Stack<std::string>;
```

The important lines here are the last three, which create explicit instantiations of the `Stack` class template for the types `int`, `double`, and `std::string`. The user will not be able to create further specializations (and the compiler will not be able to create implicit instantiations for the user either) because the implementation details are hidden in our `.cpp` file. However, our implementation details are now hidden successfully in our `.cpp` file.

To indicate to your users which template specializations they can use (i.e., which ones you have explicitly instantiated for them), you could add a few typedefs to the end of your public header, such as

```
typedef Stack<int> IntStack;
typedef Stack<double> DoubleStack;
typedef Stack<std::string> StringStack;
```

It's worth noting that by adopting this template style, not only do you (and your clients) get faster builds due to the removal of the overhead of implicit instantiation, but also, by removing the template definitions from your header, you reduce the #include coupling of your API and reduce the amount of extra code that your clients' programs must compile every time they #include your API headers.

TIP

Prefer explicit template instantiation if you only need a predetermined set of specializations. Doing so lets you hide private details and can reduce build times.

It's also worth noting that most compilers provide an option to turn off implicit instantiation completely, which may be a useful optimization if you only plan to use explicit instantiation in your code. This option is called `-fno-implicit-templates` in the GNU C++ and Intel ICC compilers.

In the new C++11 specification, support has been added for extern templates. That is, you will be able to use the `extern` keyword to prevent the compiler from instantiating a template in the current translation unit. In fact, support for this feature is already in some current compilers, such as the GNU C++ compiler. With the addition of extern templates, you have the ability to force the compiler to instantiate a template at a certain point and to tell it not to instantiate the template at other points. For example,

```
// explicitly instantiate the template here
template class Stack<int>;
```

```
// do not instantiate the template here
extern template class Stack<int>;
```

6.5 OPERATOR OVERLOADING

In addition to overloading functions, C++ allows you to overload many of the operators for your classes, such as +, *=, or []. This can be very useful to make your classes look and behave more like built-in types and also to provide a more compact and intuitive syntax for certain methods. For example, instead of having to use syntax such as

```
add(add(mul(a,b), mul(c,d)), mul(a,c))
```

you could write classes that support the following syntax:

```
a*b + c*d + a*c
```

Of course, you should only use operator overloading in cases where it makes sense, that is, where doing so would be considered natural to the user of your API and not violate the rule of least surprise. This generally means that you should preserve the natural semantics for operators, such as using the + operator to implement an operation analogous to addition or concatenation. You should also avoid overloading the operators &&, ||, & (unary ampersand), and , (comma) as these exhibit behaviors that may surprise your users, such as short-circuited evaluation and undefined evaluation order (Meyers 1998; Sutter and Alexandrescu, 2004).

As covered earlier in this chapter, a C++ compiler will generate a default assignment operator (=) for your class if you don't define one explicitly. However, if you wish to use any other operators with your objects, then you must explicitly define them, otherwise you'll end up with link errors.

6.5.1 Overloadable Operators

Certain operators cannot be overloaded in C++, such as ., .*, ?:, and ::, the preprocessor symbols # and ##, and the sizeof operator. Of the remaining operators that you can overload for your own classes, there are two main categories:

1. **Unary Operators**: These operators act on a single operand. The list of unary operators includes:

Name	Example	Name	Example
Unary minus	−x	Unary plus	+x
Prefix decrement	−−x	Postfix decrement	x−−
Prefix increment	++x	Postfix increment	x++
Dereference	*x	Reference	&x
Logical NOT	!x	Bitwise NOT	~x
Function call	x()		

2. **Binary Operators**: These operators act on two operands. The list of binary operators includes:

Name	Example	Name	Example
Addition	x + y	Subtraction	x − y
Assignment by addition	x += y	Assignment by subtraction	x −= y
Multiplication	x * y	Division	x / y
Assignment by multiplication	x *= y	Assignment by division	x /= y
Equality	x == y	Inequality	x != y
Assignment	x = y	Comma	x, y
Less than	x < y	Greater than	x > y
Less than or equal to	x <= y	Greater than or equal to	x >= y
Modulo	x % y	Bitwise XOR	x^y
Assignment by modulo	x %= y	Assignment by bitwise XOR	x ^= y
Bitwise AND	x & y	Bitwise OR	x	y
Assignment by bitwise AND	x &= y	Assignment by bitwise OR	x |= y
Logical AND	x && y	Logical OR	x || y
Bitwise left shift	x << y	Bitwise right shift	x >> y
Assignment by bitwise left shift	x <<= y	Assignment by bitwise right shift	x >>= y
Class member access	x -> y	Pointer-to-member selection	x->* y
Array subscript	x[y]	C-style cast	(y) x

6.5.2 Free Operators versus Member Operators

Operators can be defined either as members of your class or as free functions. Some operators have to be defined as class members, but others can be defined either way. For example, the following code illustrates the += operator defined as a class member:

```
class Currency
{
public:
    explicit Currency(unsigned int value);
    // method form of operator+=
    Currency &operator +=(const Currency &other);
    unsigned int GetValue() const;
    ...
};
```

The following code shows an equivalent API using a free function version of the operator:

```
class Currency
{
public:
    explicit Currency(unsigned int value);
```

```
    unsigned int GetValue() const;
    ...
};
```

```
// free function form of operator+=
Currency &operator +=(Currency &lhs, const Currency &rhs);
```

This section covers some best practices for whether you should make your operators free functions or methods.

To begin with, the C++ standard requires that the following operators be declared as member methods to ensure that they receive an lvalue (an expression that refers to an object) as their first operand:

- = Assignment
- [] Subscript
- -> Class member access
- ->* Pointer-to-member selection
- () Function call
- (T) Conversion, i.e., C-style cast
- new/delete

The remaining overloadable operators can be defined as either free functions or class methods. From the perspective of good API design, I recommend that you favor the free function version over the class method version of defining an operator. There are two specific reasons for this.

1. **Operator symmetry**. If a binary operator is defined as a class method, it must have an object to be applied to as the left-hand operand. Taking the * operator as an example, this means that your users would be able to write expressions such as "currency * 2" (assuming that you've defined a non-explicit constructor or a specific * operator for the int type) but not "2 * currency" because 2.operator*(currency) does not make sense. This breaks the commutative property of the operator that your users will expect, that is, that x * y should be the same as y * x. Note also that declaring the * operator as a free function lets you benefit from implicit type conversions for both left- and right-hand operands if you do not declare your constructors as explicit.

2. **Reduced coupling**. A free function cannot access the private details of a class. It is therefore less coupled to the class because it can only access the public methods. This is a general API design statement that was covered in Chapter 2: turn a class method that does not need to access private or protected members into a free function to reduce the degree of coupling in your API (Meyers, 2000; Tulach, 2008).

Having stated this general preference toward free function operators, I now present the exception to this rule: If your operator must access private or protected members of your class, then you should define the operator as a method of the class. I make this exception because otherwise you would have to declare the free function operator to be a friend of your class. As discussed later in this chapter, adding friends to your classes is a greater evil. One specific reason I'll mention here is that your clients cannot change the friendship list of your classes, so they could not add new operators in this same way.

TIP

Prefer declaring operators as free functions unless the operator must access protected or private members or the operator is one of =, [], ->, ->*, (), (T), new, or delete.

6.5.3 Adding Operators to a Class

Let's develop the `Currency` class a little further to make the aforementioned points more concrete. The += operator modifies the contents of an object, and because we know that all member variables should be private, you will most likely need to make the += operator be a member method. However, the + operator does not modify the left-hand operand. As such, it shouldn't need access to private members and can be made a free function. You also need to make it a free function to ensure that it benefits from symmetry behavior, as described earlier. In fact, the + operator can be implemented in terms of the += operator, which allows us to reuse code and provide more consistent behavior. It also reduces the number of methods that might need to be overloaded in derived classes.

```
Currency operator +(const Currency &lhs, const Currency &rhs)
{
    return Currency(lhs) += rhs;
}
```

Obviously, the same technique applies to the other arithmetic operators, such as -, -=, *, *=, /, and /=. For example, *= can be implemented as a member function, whereas * can be implemented as a free function that uses the *= operator.

As for the relational operators ==, !=, <, <=, >, and >=, these must also be implemented as free functions to ensure symmetrical behavior. In the case of our `Currency` class, you can implement these using the public `GetValue()` method. However, if these operators should need access to the private state of the object, there is a way to resolve this apparent dilemma. In this case, you can provide public methods that test for the equality and less than conditions such as `IsEqualTo()` and `IsLessThan()`. All relational operators could then be implemented in terms of these two primitive functions (Astrachan, 2000).

```
bool operator ==(const Currency &lhs, const Currency &rhs)
{
    return lhs.IsEqualTo(rhs);
}
bool operator !=(const Currency &lhs, const Currency &rhs)
{
    return ! (lhs == rhs);
}
bool operator <(const Currency &lhs, const Currency &rhs)
{
    return lhs.IsLessThan(rhs);
}
bool operator <=(const Currency &lhs, const Currency &rhs)
{
```

```
    return ! (lhs > rhs);
}
bool operator >(const Currency &lhs, const Currency &rhs)
{
    return rhs < lhs;
}
bool operator >=(const Currency &lhs, const Currency &rhs)
{
    return rhs <= lhs;
}
```

The last operator I will consider here is <<, which I will use for stream output (as opposed to bit shifting). Stream operators have to be declared as free functions because the first parameter is a stream object. Again, you can use the public `GetValue()` method to make this possible. However, if the stream operator did need to access private members of your class, then you could create a public `ToString()` method for the << operator to call as a way to avoid using friends.

Putting all of these recommendations together, here's what the operators of our `Currency` class might look like:

```
#include <iosfwd>

class Currency
{
public:
    explicit Currency(unsigned int value);
    ~Currency();
    Currency(const Currency &obj);
    Currency &operator =(const Currency &rhs);
    Currency &operator +=(const Currency &rhs);
    Currency &operator -=(const Currency &rhs);
    Currency &operator *=(const Currency &rhs);
    Currency &operator /=(const Currency &rhs);
    unsigned int GetReal() const;

private:
    class Impl;
    Impl *mImpl;
};

Currency operator +(const Currency &lhs, const Currency &rhs);
Currency operator -(const Currency &lhs, const Currency &rhs);
Currency operator *(const Currency &lhs, const Currency &rhs);
Currency operator /(const Currency &lhs, const Currency &rhs);
bool operator ==(const Currency &lhs, const Currency &rhs);
bool operator !=(const Currency &lhs, const Currency &rhs);
bool operator <(const Currency &lhs, const Currency &rhs);
bool operator >(const Currency &lhs, const Currency &rhs);
bool operator <=(const Currency &lhs, const Currency &rhs);
```

```
bool operator >=(const Currency &lhs, const Currency &rhs);
std::ostream& operator <<(std::ostream &os, const Currency &obj);
std::istream& operator >>(std::istream &is, Currency &obj);
```

6.5.4 Operator Syntax

Table 6.1 provides (i) a list of operators that you can overload in your classes and (ii) the recommended syntax for declaring each operator so that they have the same semantics as their built-in counterparts. Table 6.1 omits operators that you cannot overload, as well as those stated previously that you should not overload, such as && and ||. Where an operator can be defined as either a free function or a class method, I present both forms, but I list the free function form first as you should generally prefer this form, unless the operator needs access to protected or private members.

Table 6.1 List of operators and syntax for declaring these in your APIs

Operator Name	Syntax	Sample Operator Declarations
Assignment	x = y	`T1& T1::operator =(const T2& y);`
Dereference	*x	`T1& operator *(T1& x);` `T1& T1::operator *() const;`
Reference	&x	`T1* operator &(T1& x);` `T1* T1::operator &();`
Class member access	x->y	`T2* T1::operator ->();`
Pointer-to-member selection	x->*y	`T2 T1::operator->*(T2 T1::*);`
Array subscript	x[n]	`T2& T1::operator [](unsigned int n);` `T2& T1::operator [](const std::string &s);`
Function call	x()	`void T1::operator ()(T2& x);` `T2 T1::operator ()() const;`
C-style cast	(y) x	`T1::operator T2() const;`
Unary plus	+x	`T1 operator +(const T1& x);` `T1 T1::operator +() const;`
Addition	x + y	`T1 operator +(const T1& x, const T2& y);` `T1 T1::operator +(const T2& y) const;`
Assignment by addition	x += y	`T1& operator +=(T1& x, const T2& y);` `T1& T1::operator +=(const T2& y);`
Prefix increment	++x	`T1& operator ++(T1& x);` `T1& T1::operator ++();`
Postfix increment	x++	`T1 operator ++(T1& x, int);` `T1 T1::operator ++(int);`
Unary minus	−x	`T1 operator −(const T1& x);` `T1 T1::operator −() const;`

Continued

Table 6.1 List of operators and syntax for declaring these in your APIs—cont'd

Operator Name	Syntax	Sample Operator Declarations
Subtraction	x − y	`T1 operator -(const T1& x, const T2& y);` `T1 T1::operator −(const T2& y) const;`
Assignment by subtraction	x −= y	`T1& operator −=(T1& x, const T2& y);` `T1& T1::operator −=(const T2& y);`
Prefix decrement	−−x	`T1& operator −−(T1& x);` `T1& T1::operator −−();`
Postfix decrement	x−−	`T1 operator −−(T1& x, int);` `T1 T1::operator −−(int);`
Multiplication	x * y	`T1 operator *(const T1& x, const T2& y);` `T1 T1::operator *(const T2& y) const;`
Assignment by multiplication	x *= y	`T1& operator *=(T1& x, const T2& y);` `T1& T1::operator *=(const T2& y);`
Division	x / y	`T1 operator /(const T1& x, const T2& y);` `T1 T1::operator /(const T2& y) const;`
Assignment of division	x /= y	`T1& operator /=(T1& x, const T2& y);` `T1& T1::operator /=(const T2& y);`
Modulo	x % y	`T1 operator %(const T1& x, const T2& y);` `T1 T1::operator %(const T2& y) const;`
Assignment of modulo	x %= y	`T1& operator %=(T1& x, const T2& y);` `T1& T1::operator %=(const T2& y);`
Equality	x == y	`bool operator ==(const T1& x, const T2& y);` `bool T1::operator ==(const T2& y) const;`
Inequality	x != y	`bool operator !=(const T1& x, const T2& y);` `bool T1::operator !=(const T2& y) const;`
Less than	x < y	`bool operator <(const T1& x, const T2& y);` `bool T1::operator <(const T2& y) const;`
Less than or equal to	x <= y	`bool operator <=(const T1& x, const T2& y);` `bool T1::operator <=(const T2& y) const;`
Greater than	x > y	`bool operator >(const T1& x, const T2& y);` `bool T1::operator >(const T2& y) const;`
Greater than or equal to	x >= y	`bool operator >=(const T1& x, const T2& y);` `bool T1::operator >=(const T2& y) const;`
Logical NOT	!x	`bool operator !(const T1& x);` `bool T1::operator !() const;`

Bitwise left shift (BLS)	x << y	`T1 operator <<(const T1& x, const T2& y);`
		`ostream& operator <<(ostream &, const T1 &x);`
		`T1 T1::operator <<(const T2& y) const;`

Continued

Operator Name	Syntax	Sample Operator Declarations
Table 6.1 List of operators and syntax for declaring these in your APIs—cont'd		
Assignment by BLS	x <<= y	`T1& operator <<=(T1& x, const T2& y);` `T1& T1::operator <<=(const T2& y);`

Bitwise right shift (BRS)	x >> y	`T1 operator >>(const T1& x, const T2& y);`
		`istream& operator >>(istream &, T1 &x);`
		`T1 T1::operator >>(const T2& y) const;`

Assignment by BRS	x >>= y	`T1& operator >>=(T1& x, const T2& y);` `T1& T1::operator >>=(const T2& y);`
Bitwise NOT	~x	`T1 operator ~(const T1& x);` `T1 T1::operator ~() const;`
Bitwise AND	x & y	`T1 operator &(const T1& x, const T2& y);` `T1 T1::operator &(const T2& y) const;`
Assignment by bitwise AND	x &= y	`T1& operator &=(T1& x, const T2& y);` `T1& T1::operator &=(const T2& y);`
Bitwise OR	x | y	`T1 operator |(const T1& x, const T2& y);` `T1 T1::operator |(const T2& y) const;`
Assignment by bitwise OR	x |= y	`T1& operator |=(T1& x, const T2& y);` `T1& T1::operator |=(const T2& y);`
Bitwise XOR	x ^ y	`T1 operator ^(const T1& x, const T2& y);` `T1 T1::operator ^(const T2& y) const;`
Assignment by bitwise XOR	x ^= y	`T1& operator ^=(T1& x, const T2& y);` `T1& T1::operator °=(const T2& y);`
Allocate object	new	`void* T1::operator new(size_t n);`
Allocate array	new []	`void* T1::operator new[](size_t n);`
Deallocate object	delete	`void T1::operator delete(void* x);`
Deallocate array	delete []	`void T1::operator delete[](void* x);`

6.5.5 Conversion Operators

A conversion operator provides a way for you to define how an object can be converted automatically to a different type. A classic example is to define a custom string class that can be passed to functions that accept a const char * pointer, such as the standard C library functions strcmp() or strlen().

```
class MyString
{
public:
    MyString(const char *string);

    // convert MyString to a C-style string
    operator const char *() { return mBuffer; }
```

```
private:
    char *mBuffer;
    int mLength;
};

// MyString objects get automatically converted to const char *
MyString mystr("Haggis");
int same = strcmp(mystr, "Edible");
int len = strlen(mystr);
```

Note that the conversion operator does not specify a return value type. That's because the type is inferred by the compiler based on the operator's name. Also, note that conversion operators take no arguments. In the C++11 standard, it's also possible to prefix a conversion operator with the `explicit` keyword to prevent its use in implicit conversions.

TIP

Add conversion operators to your classes to let them take advantage of automatic type coercion.

6.6 FUNCTION PARAMETERS

The following sections address a couple of C++ best practices relating to the use of function parameters. This includes when you should use pointers instead of references to pass objects into a function and when you should use default arguments.

6.6.1 Pointer versus Reference Parameters

When specifying parameters for your functions you can choose between passing them as value parameters, pointers, or references. For example,

```
bool GetColor(int r, int g, int b);     // pass by value
bool GetColor(int &r, int &g, int &b);  // pass by reference
bool GetColor(int *r, int *g, int *b);  // pass by pointer
```

You pass a parameter as a reference or pointer when you want to receive a handle for the actual object rather than a copy of the object. This is done either for performance reasons (as discussed in Chapter 7) or so that you can modify the client's object. C++ compilers normally implement references using pointers so they are often the same thing under the hood. However, there are several practical differences, such as

- References are used as if they were a value, for example, `object.Function()` instead of `object->Function()`.
- A reference must be initialized to point to an object and does not support changing the referent object after initialization.
- You cannot take the address of a reference as you can with pointers. Using the & operator on a reference returns the address of the referent object.
- You can't create arrays of references.

The question of whether to use a pointer or a reference for a parameter is really a matter of personal taste. However, I will suggest that in general you should prefer the use of references over pointers for any input parameters. This is because the calling syntax for your clients is simpler and you do not need to worry about checking for NULL values (because references cannot be NULL). However, if you need to support passing NULL or if you're writing a plain C API, then you must obviously use a pointer.

In terms of output parameters (parameters that your function may modify), some engineers dislike the fact that the use of references does not indicate to your clients the fact that a parameter may be changed. For example, the reference and pointer versions of the GetColor() function given earlier can be called by clients as follows:

```
object.GetColor(red, green, blue);      // pass by reference
object.GetColor(&red, &green, &blue);   // pass by pointer
```

In both of these cases, the GetColor() function can modify the value of the red, green, and blue variables. However, the pointer version makes this fact explicit due to the required use of the & operator. For this reason, APIs like the Qt framework prefer to represent output parameters using pointers instead of references. If you decide to follow this convention too—which I recommend—then by implication all of your reference parameters should be const references.

TIP

Prefer the use of const references over pointers for input parameters where feasible. For output parameters, consider using pointers over non-const references to indicate explicitly to the client that they may be modified.

6.6.2 **Default Arguments**

Default arguments are a very useful tool to reduce the number of methods in your API and to provide implicit documentation on their use. They can also be used to extend an API call in a backward-compatible fashion so that older client code will still compile, but newer code can optionally provide additional arguments (although it should be noted that this will break binary compatibility, as the mangled symbol name for the method will necessarily change). As an example, consider the following code fragment for a Circle class:

```
class Circle
{
public:
    Circle(double x=0, double y=0, double radius=10.0);
    ...
};
```

In this case, the user is able to construct a new Circle object in a number of different ways, supplying as much detail as needed. For example,

```
Circle c1();
Circle c2(2.3);
Circle c3(2.3, 5.6);
Circle c4(2.3, 5.6, 1.5);
```

However, there are two issues to be aware of with this example. First, it supports combinations of arguments that don't make logical sense, such as supplying an x argument but no y argument. Also, the default values will be compiled into your client's programs. This means that your clients must recompile their code if you release a new version of the API with a different default radius. In essence, you are exposing the behavior of the API when you do not explicitly specify a radius value.

To illustrate why this might be bad, consider the possibility that you later add support for the notion of different default units, letting the user switch between values specified in meters, centimeters, or millimeters. In this case, a constant default radius of 10.0 would be inappropriate for all units.

An alternative approach is to provide multiple overloaded methods instead of using default arguments. For example,

```
class Circle
{
public:
    Circle();
    Circle(double x, double y);
    Circle(double x, double y, double radius);
    ...
};
```

Using this approach, the implementation of the first two constructors can use a default value for the attributes that are not specified. But importantly, these default values are specified in the .cpp file and are not exposed in the .h file. As a result, a later version of the API could change these values without any impact on the public interface.

TIP

Prefer overloaded functions to default arguments when the default value would expose an implementation constant.

Not all instances of default arguments need to be converted to overloaded methods. In particular, if the default argument represents an invalid or empty value, such as defining NULL as the default value for a pointer or "" for a string argument, then this usage is unlikely to change between API versions. However, if you have cases where you are hardcoding specific constant values into your API that might change in future releases, then you should convert these cases to use the overloaded method technique instead.

As a performance note, you should also try to avoid defining default arguments that involve constructing a temporary object because these will be passed into the method by value and can therefore be expensive.

6.7 AVOID #DEFINE FOR CONSTANTS

The #define preprocessor directive is essentially used to substitute one string with another string in your source code. However, its use is generally frowned upon in the C++ community for a number of good reasons (Cline et al., 1998; DeLoura, 2001; Meyers, 2005). Many of these reasons are related to the subtle problems that can happen if you use #define to specify code macros that you wish to insert into multiple places, such as

```
#define SETUP_NOISE(i,b0,b1,r0,r1)\
    t = vec[i] + 0x1000;\
    b0 = (lltrunc(t)) & 0xff;\
    b1 = (b0+1) & 0xff;\
    r0 = t - lltrunc(t);\
    r1 = r0 - 1.f;
```

However, you should never be using #define in this way for your public API headers because of course it leaks implementation details. If you want to use this technique in your .cpp files, and you understand all of the idiosyncrasies of #define, then go ahead, but never do this in your public headers.

That just leaves the use of #define to specify constants for your API, such as

```
#define MORPH_FADEIN_TIME    0.3f
#define MORPH_IN_TIME        1.1f
#define MORPH_FADEOUT_TIME   1.4f
```

You should avoid even this usage of #define (unless you are writing a pure C API of course) because of the following reasons.

1. **No typing**. A #define does not involve any type checking for the constant you are defining. You must therefore make sure that you explicitly specify the type of the constant you are defining to avoid any ambiguities, such as the use of the "f" suffix on single-precision floating-point constants. If you defined a floating-point constant as simply "10," then it may be assumed to be an integer in certain cases and cause undesired math rounding errors.
2. **No scoping**. A #define statement is global and is not limited to a particular scope, such as within a single class. You can use the #undef preprocessor directive to undefine a previous #define, but this makes little sense for declaring a constant that you want your clients to be able to use.
3. **No access control**. You cannot mark a #define as public, protected, or private. It is essentially always public. You therefore cannot use #define to specify a constant that should only be accessed by derived classes of a base class that you define.
4. **No symbols**. In the example given earlier, symbolic names such as MORPH_IN_TIME may be stripped from your code by the preprocessor, and as such the compiler never sees this name and cannot enter it into the symbol table (Meyers, 2005). This can hide valuable information from your clients when they try to debug code using your API because they will simply see the constant value used in the debugger, without any descriptive name.

The preferred alternative to using #define to declare API constants is to declare a const variable. I will discuss some of the best practices of declaring constants in the later chapter on performance, as it's possible to declare const variables in a way that adds bloat to your clients programs. For now, I will simply present a good conversion of the earlier #define example to be

```
class Morph
{
public:
    static const float FadeInTime;
    static const float InTime;
    static const float FadeOutTime;
    ...
};
```

where the actual values of these constants are specified in the associated .cpp file. (If you really want your users to know what the values of these constants are, then you can tell them this information in the API documentation for the Morph class.) Note that this representation does not suffer from any of the problems listed previously: the constants are typed as floats, scoped to the Morph class, marked explicitly as publicly accessible, and will generate entries in the symbol table.

TIP

Use static const data members to represent class constants instead of #define.

A further use of #define is to provide a list of possible values for a given variable. For example,

```
#define LEFT_JUSTIFIED     0
#define RIGHT_JUSTIFIED    1
#define CENTER_JUSTIFIED   2
#define FULL_JUSTIFIED     3
```

This is better expressed using enumerated types via the enum keyword. Using enums gives you better type safety because the compiler will now ensure that you set any enum values with the symbolic name and not directly as an integer (unless you explicitly cast an int to your enum type of course). This also makes it more difficult to pass illegal values, such as –1 or 23 in the example given earlier. You can turn the aforementioned #define lines into an enumerated type as follows:

```
enum JustificationType {
    LEFT_JUSTIFIED,
    RIGHT_JUSTIFIED,
    CENTER_JUSTIFIED,
    FULL_JUSTIFIED
};
```

6.8 AVOID USING FRIENDS

In C++, friendship is a way for your class to grant full access privileges to another class or function. The friend class or function can then access all protected and private members of your class. This can be useful when you need to split up your class into two or more parts but you still need each part to access private members of the other part. It's also useful when you need to use an internal visitor or callback technique. That is, when some other internal class in your implementation code needs to call a private method in your class.

One alternative would be to expose data members and functions that need to be shared, converting them from private to public so that the other class can access them. However, this would mean that you are exposing implementation details to your clients; details that would not otherwise be part of your logical interface. From this point of view, friends are a good thing because they let you open up access to your class to only specific clients. However, friendship can be abused by your users, allowing them to gain full access to your class's internal details.

For example, consider the following class that specifies a single Node as part of a Graph hierarchy. The Graph may need to perform various iterations over all nodes and therefore needs to keep track of whether a node has been visited already (to handle graph cycles). One way to implement this would be to have the Node object hold the state for whether it has been visited already, with accessors for this state. Because this is purely an implementation detail, you don't want to expose this functionality in the public interface. Instead, you declare it as private, but explicitly give the Graph object access to the Node object by declaring it as a friend.

```
class Node
{
public:
    ...
    friend class Graph;

private:
    void ClearVisited();
    void SetVisited();
    bool IsVisited() const;
    ...
};
```

This seems okay on the face of it: you have kept the various *Visited() methods as private and only permitted the Graph class to access our internal details. However, the problem with this is that the friendship offer is based on the name of the other class only. It would therefore be possible for clients to create their own class called Graph, which would then be able to access all protected and private members of Node (Lakos, 1996). The following client program demonstrates how easy it is to perform this kind of access control violation.

```
#include "node.h"

// define your own Graph class
class Graph
{
public:
    void ViolateAccess(Node *node)
    {
        // call a private method in Node
        // because Graph is a friend of Node
        node -> SetVisited();
    }
};
```

```
...
Node node;
Graph local_graph;
local_graph.ViolateAccess(&node);
```

So, by using friends you are leaving a gaping hole in your API that could be used to circumvent your public API boundary and break encapsulation.

In the example just given, a better solution that obviates the need to use friends would be for the Graph object to maintain its own list of nodes that it has already visited, for example, by maintaining a std::set<Node *> container, rather than storing the visited state in the individual nodes themselves. This is also a better conceptual design because the information about whether another class has processed a Node is not inherently an attribute of the Node itself.

TIP

Avoid using friends. They tend to indicate a poor design and can allow users to gain access to all protected and private members of your API.

6.9 EXPORTING SYMBOLS

In addition to language-level access control features (public, private, and protected), there are two related concepts that allow you to expose symbols in your API at the physical file level. These are:

1. External linkage.
2. Exported visibility.

The term external linkage means that a symbol in one translation unit can be accessed from other translation units, whereas exporting refers to a symbol that is visible from a library file such as a DLL. Only external linkage symbols can be exported.

Let's look at external linkage first. This is the first stage that determines whether your clients can access symbols in your shared libraries. Specifically, global (file scope) free functions and variables in your .cpp file will have external linkage unless you take steps to prevent this. For example, consider the following code that might appear in one of your .cpp files:

```
...
const int INTERNAL_CONSTANT = 42;

std::string Filename = "file.txt";

void FreeFunction()
{
    std::cout << "Free function called" << std::endl;
}
...
```

Even though you have contained the use of these functions and variables inside a .cpp file, a resourceful client could easily gain access to these symbols from their own programs (ignoring symbol exporting issues for the moment). They could then call your global functions directly and modify your global state without going through your public API, thus breaking encapsulation. The following program fragment demonstrates how to achieve this:

```
extern void FreeFunction();
extern const int INTERNAL_CONSTANT;
extern std::string Filename;

// call an internal function within your module
FreeFunction();

// access a constant defined within your module
std::cout << "Constant = " << INTERNAL_CONSTANT << std::endl;

// change global state within your module
Filename = "different.txt";
```

There are a couple of solutions to this kind of external linkage leakage problem.

1. **Static declaration**. Prepend the declaration of your functions and variables with the `static` keyword. This specifies that the function or variable should have internal linkage and hence will not be accessible outside of the translation unit it appears in.
2. **Anonymous namespace**. A more idiomatic C++ solution is to enclose your file-scope functions and variables inside an anonymous namespace. This is a better solution because it avoids polluting the global namespace. This can be done as follows:

```
...
namespace {
    const int INTERNAL_CONSTANT = 42;

    std::string Filename = "file.txt";

    void FreeFunction()
    {
        std::cout << "Free function called" << std::endl;
    }
}
...
```

TIP

Use internal linkage to hide file-scope free functions and variables inside your .cpp files. This means using the static keyword or the anonymous namespace.

For symbols that have external linkage, there is the further concept of exporting symbols, which determines whether a symbol is visible from a shared library. Most compilers provide decorations for classes and functions that let you explicitly specify whether a symbol will appear in the exported symbol table for a library file. However, this tends to be compiler-specific behavior. For example:

1. **Microsoft Visual Studio**. Symbols in a DLL are not accessible by default. You must explicitly export functions, classes, and variables in a DLL to allow your clients to access them. You do this using the __declspec decorator before a symbol. For example, you specify __declspec (dllexport) to export a symbol when you are building a DLL. Clients must then specify __declspec(dllimport) in order to access the same symbol in their own programs.

2. **GNU C++ compiler**. Symbols with external linkage in a dynamic library are visible by default. However, you can use the visibility __attribute__ decorator to explicitly hide a symbol. As an alternative to hiding individual symbols, the GNU C++ 4.0 compiler introduced the -fvisibility=hidden flag to force all declarations to hidden visibility by default. Individual symbols can then be explicitly exported using __attribute__ ((visibility("default"))). This is more like the Windows behavior, where all symbols are considered internal unless you explicitly export them. Using the -fvisibility=hidden flag can also cause a dramatic improvement in load time performance of your dynamic library and produce smaller library files.

You can define various preprocessor macros to deal with these compiler differences in a cross-platform way. Here's an example of defining a DLL_PUBLIC macro to export symbols explicitly and a DLL_HIDDEN macro to hide symbols when using the GNU C++ compiler. Note that you must specify an _EXPORTING define when you build the library file on Windows, that is, /D "_EXPORTING". This is an arbitrary define name—you can call it whatever you like (as long as you also update the code that follows).

```
#if defined _WIN32 || defined __CYGWIN__
    #ifdef _EXPORTING // define this when generating DLL
        #ifdef __GNUC__
            #define DLL_PUBLIC __attribute__((dllexport))
        #else
            #define DLL_PUBLIC __declspec(dllexport)
        #endif
    #else
        #ifdef __GNUC__
            #define DLL_PUBLIC __attribute__((dllimport))
        #else
            #define DLL_PUBLIC __declspec(dllimport)
        #endif
    #endif
    #define DLL_HIDDEN
#else
    #if __GNUC__ >= 4
        #define DLL_PUBLIC __attribute__ ((visibility("default")))
        #define DLL_HIDDEN __attribute__ ((visibility("hidden")))
    #else
        #define DLL_PUBLIC
        #define DLL_HIDDEN
    #endif
#endif
```

For example, to export a class or function of your API you can do the following:

```
DLL_PUBLIC void MyFunction();
class DLL_PUBLIC MyClass;
```

Many compilers also allow you to provide a simple ASCII file that defines the list of symbols that should be exported by a dynamic library so that you don't need to decorate your code with macros such as DLL_PUBLIC. Symbols that do not appear in this file will be hidden from client programs. For example, the Windows Visual Studio compiler supports .def files, whereas the GNU compiler supports export map files. See Appendix A for more details on these export files.

TIP

Explicitly export public API symbols to maintain direct control over classes, functions, and variables accessible from your dynamic libraries. For GNU C++, this implies using the -fvisibility=hidden option.

6.10 **CODING CONVENTIONS**

C++ is a very complex language with many powerful features. The use of good coding conventions can partially help manage this complexity by ensuring that all code follows certain style guidelines and avoids common pitfalls. It also contributes toward consistent code, which I identified as one of the important qualities of a good API in Chapter 2.

TIP

Specify coding standards for your API to help enforce consistency, define processes, and document common engineering pitfalls.

Producing a coding standard document can be a lengthy and factious process, not only because of the complexity of the language but also because of the amount of personal taste and style that it aims to stipulate. Different engineers have different preferences for where to place brackets and spaces, what style of comments to adopt, or whether to use lower or upper camelCase for function names. For example, in this book I have consistently formatted source code snippets with pointer or reference symbols next to variable names, not type names, that is,

```
char *a, *b;
```

instead of

```
char* a, *b;
```

I favor the former style because from a language perspective the pointer is actually associated with the variable, not the type (in both of these cases, a and b are both of type pointer to char). However, other software engineers prefer the latter style.

In this book, I do not advocate that you should adopt any particular style for your projects, but I do urge you to adopt some conventions for your API, whatever they are. The important point is to be consistent. Indeed, it's generally accepted among engineers that when editing a source file you should adopt the conventions that are already in force in that file instead of adding your own style into the mix and producing a file with a mixture of inconsistent styles (or you might be more antisocial and reformat the entire file to your own style).

Because a number of large companies have already gone through the process of creating and publishing coding style documents, you could always simply adopt one of these standards to make the decision easier. Doing a Web search for "C++ coding conventions" should return a large number of hits for your consideration. In particular, the Google C++ style guide is a very extensive document used by many other groups (http://google-styleguide.googlecode.com/). There are also some great books that provide even more depth and detail on numerous code constructs that should be used or avoided (Sutter and Alexandrescu, 2004).

Without making specific suggestions, I will enumerate some of the areas that a good coding standard should cover.

- **Naming conventions**. Whether to use `.cc`, `.c++`, or `.cpp`; capitalization of filenames; use of prefixes in filenames; capitalization of classes, functions, variables, differentiating private members, constants, typedefs, enums, macros, namespaces; use of namespaces; etc.
- **Header files**. How to `#include` headers; ordering `#include` statements; using `#define` guards; use of forward declarations; inlining code policy; etc.
- **Comments**. Comment style; templates for commenting files, classes, functions, and so on; documentation requirements; commenting code with to do notes or highlighting known hacks; etc.
- **Formatting**. Line length limit; spaces versus tabs; placement of braces; spacing between statements; how to break long lines; layout of constructor initialization lists; etc.
- **Classes**. Use of constructors; factories; inheritance; multiple inheritance; interfaces; composition, structs versus classes; access control; etc.
- **Best practices**. Use of templates; use of exceptions; use of enums; const correctness; use of pointers for output parameters; use of pimpl; initialization of all member variables; casting; operator overloading rules; virtual destructors; use of globals; etc.
- **Portablity**. Writing architecture-specific code; preprocessor macros for platforms; class member alignment; etc.
- **Process**. Compiling with warnings as errors; unit tests requirements; use of code reviews; use of use cases; SCM style check hooks; compile with extra checks such as `-Wextra` and `-Weffc++`; etc.

Performance

It's not the focus of this book to tell you how to optimize the performance of your implementation or even to tell you whether it's necessary. Your implementation should be as fast as it needs to be: some APIs are performance critical and must be called many times per second, whereas other APIs are used infrequently and their speed is of less concern. However, a focus of this book is to show you how certain API design decisions can impact performance, and therefore how you can optimize the performance of your interface.

Your implementation may not need to be high performance, but your interface should still be as optimal as possible so that it is not actively undermining performance. Requirements change, and you may find yourself needing to optimize your implementation after the first version of your API has been released. In this situation you will wish that you had considered the performance impact of your API beforehand so that you are not forced to break backward compatibility in order to improve performance.

However, the most important point to make here is that you should strive to never warp your API for performance reasons. Good designs normally correspond with good performance (Bloch, 2008; Tulach, 2008). Your API should continue to provide a clean and logical representation of the problem domain even after you have optimized its implementation. There are cases where this is simply not possible. For example, if you are writing an API that must communicate across a Remote Procedure Call barrier, you may hit the case that the overhead for performing many individual API calls is too slow and instead you feel the need to introduce a vectorized API that batches up many calls into a single method. However, instances such as these are exceptional. A lot can be optimized behind the API—that's why you are writing an API after all—so you should endeavor to limit the effect of any performance improvements to your implementation and not cause this work to change your interface.

> **TIP**
>
> Don't warp your API to achieve high performance.

There are several components to API performance, and I will consider each of these in the following sections.

1. **Compile-time speed**. The impact of your API on the time it takes to compile a client program. This can affect the productivity of your users.
2. **Run-time speed**. The time overhead for calling your API methods. This is important if your methods must be called frequently or must scale well with different input sizes.

3. **Run-time memory overhead**. The memory overhead for calling your API methods. This is important if you expect many of your objects to be created and kept in memory. It can also affect CPU cache performance.
4. **Library size**. The size of the object code for your implementation that clients must link into their applications. This affects the total disk and memory footprint of your clients' applications.
5. **Startup time**. The time it takes to load and initialize a dynamic library that implements your API. Various factors can affect this, such as template resolution, binding unresolved symbols, calling static initializers, and library path searching.

In addition to specific API factors that affect these performance metrics, you should of course investigate your compiler's options to see if there are any flags you can turn on or off to give a performance boost. For example, turning off Run-Time Type Information (RTTI) if you don't need to use the `dynamic_cast` operator is one common decision (`-fno-rtti` for the GNU C++ compiler).

One of the most important lessons to learn about performance optimization is that you should never trust your instincts on which parts of your implementation you think will be slow. You should always measure the actual performance profile of your API in real-world situations and then focus your optimization effort on the areas that give you the biggest impact. A corollary to this is that you don't need to start with the most efficient implementation: do it the easy way first and then figure out which parts of your implementation need to be optimized once everything is working.

At Pixar, we would regularly have various teams work on different components of a particular feature for one of our films. For example, the driving system in *Cars* involved work by the R&D team to implement a generic simulation plugin system, work by GUI engineers to provide direct manipulation controls for animators, and work by the production teams on the movie to integrate everything into their pipeline. Then, once all of the software was functional and integrated, we convened "speed team" meetings to assess where the bottlenecks were and assign work to the relevant engineers so that the overall system would meet specific performance criteria.

The important point is to always remember Amdahl's law. This states that the overall performance improvement gained by optimizing a single part of a system is limited by the fraction of time that the improved part is actually used. You may increase the performance of one part of your API by a factor of 10, but if a client's program only spends 1% of its time in that code, then the overall improvement is reduced to only a factor of 0.1 (10 * 0.01).

TIP

To optimize an API, instrument your code and collect performance data for real-world examples. Then target your optimization effort at the actual bottlenecks. Don't guess at where the performance hot spots are.

7.1 PASS INPUT ARGUMENTS BY CONST REFERENCE

In Chapter 6, I recommended that you prefer const references over pointers to pass input parameters, that is, parameters that are not changed by the function. However, you should prefer pointers over non-const references for output parameters so that their mutability is clearly advertised to clients. This section now offers some additional performance reasons to prefer the use of const references to pass input arguments into a function.

By default, function arguments in C++ are passed "by value." This means that the object being passed into the function is copied and then that copy is destroyed when the function returns. As a result, the original object that is passed into the method can never be modified. However, this involves the overhead of calling the object's copy constructor and then destructor. Instead you should pass a const reference to the object. This has the effect of only passing the pointer to the object, but also ensuring that the object is not modified by the method. This can be particularly important for embedded systems where you have a very limited stack size.

```
void SetValue(std::string str);          // pass by value
void SetValue(std::string &str);         // pass by reference
void SetValue(const std::string &str);   // pass by const reference
```

TIP

Always prefer passing a non-mutable object as a const reference rather than passing it by value. This will avoid the memory and performance costs to create and destroy a temporary copy of the object and all of its member and inherited objects.

This rule only applies to objects. It is not necessary for built-in types, such as int, bool, float, double, or char, because these are small enough to fit in a CPU register. In addition, STL iterators and function objects are designed to be passed by value. However, for all other custom types, you should favor references or const references. Let's look at a specific example.

```
class MyObject
{
public:
    // constructor
    MyObject();
    // destructor
    ~MyObject();
    // copy constructor
    MyObject(const MyObject &obj);
    // assignment operator
    MyObject &operator = (const MyObject &obj);

private:
    std::string mName;
};

class MyObjectHolder
{
public:
    MyObjectHolder();
    ~MyObjectHolder();

    MyObject GetObject() const;
    void SetObjectByValue(MyObject obj);
    void SetObjectByConstReference(const MyObject &obj);
```

```
private:
    MyObject mObject;
};
```

If you assume that the SetObjectByValue() and SetObjectByConstReference() methods both simply assign their argument to the mObject member variable, then the sequence of operations that get performed when each of these methods is called is as follows.

- SetObjectByValue(object)
  - std::string constructor
  - MyObject copy constructor
  - MyObject assignment operator
  - MyObject destructor
  - std::string destructor
- SetObjectByConstReference(object)
  - MyObject assignment operator

The situation becomes worse if MyObject is derived from some base class because then the copy constructor and destructor of each base class in the object hierarchy would also have to be called for the pass by value case.

There is another reason to avoid passing arguments by value and that's the "slicing problem" (Meyers, 2005). This is the problem that if a method accepts a base class argument by value and you pass a derived class, then any extra fields of the derived class will be sliced off. This is because the size of the object to be passed by value is determined, at compile time, to be the size of the base class. Passing arguments as const references instead of passing by value avoids the slicing problem.

7.2 MINIMIZE #INCLUDE DEPENDENCIES

The time it takes to compile a large project can depend greatly on the number and depth of #include files. As such, one of the common techniques for decreasing build times is to try to reduce the number of #include statements in header files.

7.2.1 Avoid "Winnebago" Headers

Some APIs provide a single large header file that pulls in all of the classes and global definitions for the interface. This can seem like a convenient affordance for your clients, however, it only serves to increase the compile-time coupling between your clients' code and your API, which means that even the most minimal use of your API must pull in every public symbol.

For example, the standard Win32 header windows.h pulls in well over 200,000 lines of code (under Visual Studio 9.0). Every .cpp file that includes this header effectively adds over 4 MB of extra code that needs to be loaded from around 90 separate files and compiled for every source file. Similarly, the Mac OS X header Cocoa/Cocoa.h expands to over 100,000 lines of code at over 3 MB.

Precompiled headers can help alleviate this burden by preprocessing these large common include files to a more optimal form, such as a .pch or .gch file. However, a more modular and loosely coupled solution would involve providing a collection of smaller individual headers for each component of your API. Clients can then choose to #include only the declarations for the subset of your API that they are using. This can make for longer lists of #include statements in your client's code, but the result is an overall reduction in the amount of your API that their code must pull in.

7.2.2 Forward Declarations

A header file, A, includes another header file, B, in order to pull in the declaration of a class, function, struct, enum, or other entity that is used in header A. The most common situation in an object-oriented program is that header A wants to pull in the declaration of one or more classes from header B. However, in many situations, header A does not actually need to include header B and can instead simply provide a forward declaration for the classes needed. A forward declaration can be used when

1. The size of the class is not required. If you include the class as a member variable or subclass from it, then the compiler will need to know the size of the class.
2. You do not reference any member methods of the class. Doing so would require knowing the method prototype: its argument and return types.
3. You do not reference any member variables of the class; but you already know to never make those public (or protected).

For example, you can use forward declarations if header A only refers to the name of classes from header B via pointers or references.

```
class B; // forward declaration

class A
{
public:
    void SetObject(const B &obj);

private:
    B *mObj;
};
```

However, if you were to change the definition of class A so that that compiler needs to know the actual size of class B, then you must include the actual declaration of class B, that is, you must #include its header. For example, if you store an actual copy of B inside of A.

```
#include <B.h>

class A
{
public:
    void SetObject(const B &obj);

private:
    B mObj;
};
```

Obviously, you will need to #include the full header in any .cpp file that uses the classes in that header, for example, A.cpp must include B.h. A forward declare simply tells the compiler to add the name to its symbol table with a promise that you'll provide full declaration when it actually needs it.

One interesting point is that a forward declaration is sufficient if you pass a variable to a method by value or return it by value (although you should of course prefer a const reference over passing a parameter by value). You might think that the compiler needs to know the size of the class at this point, but in actual fact it is only needed by the code that implements the method and any client code that calls it. So the following example is quite legal:

```
class B;

class A
{
public:
    void SetObject(B obj);
    B GetObject() const;
};
```

TIP

As a rule of thumb, you should only need to #include the header file for a class if you use an object of that class as a data member in your own class or if you inherit from that class.

Note that it is generally safer to only use forward declarations for your own code. By using forward declarations, you are embedding knowledge of how symbols are declared in the header that you are eliding. For example, if you use forward declares for a foreign header and your API is used in environments with different versions of that header, the declaration of a class within that header could be changed to a typedef or the class could be changed to a templated class, which would break your forward declaration. This is one reason why you should specifically never try to forward declare STL objects, for example, always do #include <string>, never attempt to forward declare std::string. (Note, however, that when using streams, you can use the iosfwd include file to forward declare various template classes in iostreams.)

TIP

Only forward declare symbols from your own API.

Finally, it is worth noting that a header file should declare all of its dependencies, either as forward declarations or as explicit #include lines. Otherwise, the inclusion of the header in other files may become order dependent. This is at odds with the statement to minimize the number of #include statements, but it is an important exception for the sake of API robustness and elegance. A good way to test this is to ensure that an empty .cpp file that only includes your public header can compile without error.

TIP

A header file should #include or forward declare all of its dependencies.

7.2.3 **Redundant #include Guards**

Another way to reduce the overhead of parsing too many include files is to add redundant preprocessor guards at the point of inclusion. For example, if you have an include file, `bigfile.h`, that looks like this

```
#ifndef BIGFILE_H
#define BIGFILE_H

// lots and lots of code

#endif
```

then you might include this file from another header by doing the following:

```
#ifndef BIGFILE_H
#include "bigfile.h"
#endif
```

This saves the cost of pointlessly opening and parsing the entire include file if you've already included it. This may seem like a trivial optimization, and indeed it can be for small include hierarchies. However, if you have a large code base with many include files, this optimization can make a significant difference. Back in 1996, John Lakos performed several experiments to demonstrate the degree of performance improvements that this optimization can affect on a large project. The results were striking (Lakos, 1996). However, given that these results are from the mid-1990s, I designed a similar experiment to test this effect on a modern compiler, and the results correlate well with those of Lakos.

For a given number N, I generated N include files that each included the $N - 1$ other include files. Each include file also contained around 100 lines of class declarations. I also generated N.cpp files, where each .cpp file included only 1 header. I then timed how long it took to compile every .cpp file. This experiment therefore chooses a worst-case $O(n^2)$ include structure, although it also includes the time to run the compiler N times. The experiment was performed for a set of include files that used redundant include guards and a set that did not. Table 7.1 shows averaged results of this experiment using the GNU C++ compiler, version 4.2.1, on an Intel Core 2 Duo processor running Mac OS X 10.6 with 2 GB of RAM.

Table 7.1 Compilation time speedup from using redundant include guards for a worst-case include hierarchy containing N include files

N	Without Guards (s)	With Guards (s)	Speedup
2	0.07	0.07	1.00×
4	0.15	0.14	1.07×
8	0.35	0.31	1.13×
16	0.98	0.76	1.29×
32	4.07	2.12	1.92×
64	25.90	6.82	3.80×
128	226.83	24.70	9.18×

This behavior will, of course, vary by compiler and platform, so in the interest of good experimental technique, I repeated the experiment with the Microsoft C++ compiler, version 14.0, on an Intel Core 2 Quad CPU running Windows XP with 3.25 GB of RAM. Results in this case were even more pronounced, with a speedup of around 18 times for the $N = 128$ case.

TIP

Consider adding redundant #include guards to your headers to optimize compile time for your clients.

By comparison, I found that the experiment showed almost no effect under Linux (1.03 × speedup for $N = 128$), where presumably the combination of the GNU compiler and the Linux disk cache produces a more efficient environment. However, users of your API may be using a broad range of platforms so this optimization could have a large impact on many of them. Even a speedup of only 1.29× could make a big difference to the amount of time that they spend waiting for a build to finish. The code to run the experiment is included in the full source code package on the accompanying Web site for this book so you can try it out for your own platforms.

This technique has been used to practical benefit by many large-scale APIs. To give a rather retro example, the Commodore Amiga platform used this technique to improve the performance of the AmigaOS APIs. For instance, here's what the top of the `intuition/screens.h` header file looked like for the Amiga in the early 1990s:

```
#ifndef INTUITION_SCREENS_H
#define INTUITION_SCREENS_H TRUE
/*
** $Filename: intuition/screens.h $
** $Release: 2.04 Includes, V37.4 $
** $Revision: 36.36 $
** $Date: 91/10/07 $
**
** The Screen and NewScreen structures and attributes
**
** (C) Copyright 1985-1999 Amiga, Inc.
**        All Rights Reserved
*/

#ifndef EXEC_TYPES_H
#include <exec/types.h>
#endif

#ifndef GRAPHICS_GFX_H
#include <graphics/gfx.h>
#endif

#ifndef GRAPHICS_CLIP_H
#include <graphics/clip.h>
#endif
```

```
#ifndef GRAPHICS_VIEW_H
#include <graphics/view.h>
#endif

#ifndef GRAPHICS_RASTPORT_H
#include <graphics/rastport.h>
#endif

#ifndef GRAPHICS_LAYERS_H
#include <graphics/layers.h>
#endif

#ifndef UTILITY_TAGITEM_H
#include <utility/tagitem.h>
#endif
```

7.3 DECLARING CONSTANTS

Often you want to define a number of public constants for your API. This is a great technique for avoiding the proliferation of hardcoded values throughout your client's code, such as maximum values or default strings. For example, you might declare several constants in the global scope of your header in this way.

```
const int MAX_NAME_LENGTH = 128;
const float LOG_2E = log2(2.71828183f);
const std::string LOG_FILENAME = "filename.log";
```

The issue to be aware of here is that only very simple constants for built-in types will be inlined by your C++ compiler. By default, any variable that you define in this way will cause your compiler to store space for the variable in every module that includes your header. In the aforementioned case, this will likely happen for both the float and the string constant. If you declare many constants and your API headers are included in many .cpp files, then this can cause bloat in the client's .o object files and the final binary. The solution is to declare the constants as extern.

```
extern const int MAX_NAME_LENGTH;
extern const float LOG_2E;
extern const std::string LOG_FILENAME;
```

Then define the value of each constant in the accompanying .cpp file. In this way, the space for the variables is only allocated once. This also has the additional benefit of hiding actual constant values from the header file: they are implementation details after all.

A better way to do this is if you can declare the constants within a class. Then you can declare them as static const (so they will not count toward the per-object memory size).

```
// myapi.h
class MyAPI
{
```

```
public:
    static const int MAX_NAME_LENGTH;
    static const int MAX_RECORDS;
    static const std::string LOG_FILENAME;
    };
```

You can then define the value for these constants in the associated .cpp file.

```
// myapi.cpp
const int MyAPI::MAX_NAME_LENGTH = 128;
const int MyAPI::MAX_RECORDS = 65525;
const std::string MyAPI::LOG_FILENAME = "filename.log";
```

You may think that this is a trivial optimization and will save an insignificant amount of space. However, at Linden Lab, we decided to clean up all of these instances in the Second Life Viewer source code. The end effect was an appreciable 10% reduction in the size of the generated files.

Another option to avoid the bloat issue in certain cases is to use enums as an alternative to variables or you could also use getter methods to return the constant values, such as

```
// myapi.h
class MyAPI
{
public:
    static int GetMaxNameLength();
    static int GetMaxRecords();
    static std::string GetLogFilename();
};
```

TIP

Declare global scope constants with extern or declare constants in classes as static const. Then define the value of the constant in the .cpp file. This reduces the size of object files for modules that include your headers. Even better, hide these constants behind a function call.

7.3.1 The New constexpr Keyword

The problem with all of the options just listed is that the compiler can no longer evaluate the const expression at compile time because the actual value is hidden in the .cpp file. For example, clients would not be able to do either of the following:

```
char name1[MyAPI::MAX_NAME_LENGTH];    // illegal
char name2[MyAPI::GetMaxNameLength()]; // illegal
```

However, as part of the new C++11 specification, a new feature has been added to allow for more aggressive compile-time optimizations: the constexpr keyword. This can be used to indicate functions or variables that you know to be constant so that the compiler can perform greater optimization. For example, consider the following code:

```
int GetTableSize(int elems) { return elems * 2; }
double myTable[GetTableSize(2)]; // illegal in C++98
```

This is illegal according to the C++98 standard because the compiler has no way of knowing that the value returned by GetTableSize() is a compile-time constant. However, under the new C++ specification you would be able to tell the compiler that this is in fact the case:

```
constexpr int GetTableSize(int elems) { return elems * 2; }
double myTable[GetTableSize(2)]; // legal in C++11
```

The constexpr keyword can also be applied to variables. However, the fact that it can be used to mark the result of a function as a compile-time constant opens up the door to letting us define constants using a function call while still allowing clients to use the constant value at compile time. For example,

```
// myapi.h (C++11 only)
class MyAPI
{
public:
    constexpr int GetMaxNameLength() { return 128; }
    constexpr int GetMaxRecords() { return 65525; }
    constexpr std::string GetLogFilename() { return "filename.log";}
};
```

7.4 INITIALIZATION LISTS

C++ provides constructor initialization lists to let you easily initialize all of the member variables in your class. Using this feature can afford a slight performance increase over simply initializing each member variable in the body of the constructor. For example, instead of writing

```
// avatar.h
class Avatar
{
public:
    Avatar(const std::string &first, const std::string &last)
    {
        mFirstName = first;
        mLastName = last;
    }

private:
    std::string mFirstName;
    std::string mLastName;
};
```

you could write

```
// avatar.h
class Avatar
{
public:
    Avatar(const std::string &first, const std::string &last) :
        mFirstName(first),
        mLastName(last)
```

```
    {
    }

private:
    std::string mFirstName;
    std::string mLastName;
};
```

Because member variables are constructed before the body of the constructor is called, in the first example the default `std::string` constructor will be called to initialize the `mName` member variable, then inside the constructor the assignment operator is called (DeLoura, 2001). However, in the second example, only the copy constructor is invoked. Using an initialization list therefore avoids the cost of calling the default constructor for each member variable that you include in the list.

Of course, in terms of good API design, you should hide as much implementation detail from your header files as possible. So the best approach is to define the constructor in your header file as follows:

```
// avatar.h
class Avatar
{
public:
    Avatar(const std::string &first, const std::string &last);

private:
    std::string mFirstName;
    std::string mLastName;
};
```

Then provide the constructor and initialization list in the associated `.cpp` file:

```
// avatar.cpp
Avatar::Avatar(const std::string &first, const std::string &last) :
    mFirstName(first),
    mLastName(last)
{
}
```

> **TIP**
>
> Use constructor initialization lists to avoid the cost of a constructor call for each data member, but declare these in the `.cpp` file to hide implementation details.

Here are a few things to be aware of when using initialization lists:

1. The order of variables in the initialization list should match the order that the variables are specified in the class.
2. You cannot specify arrays in an initialization list. However, you can specify a `std::vector`, which may be a better choice of data structure anyway.

3. If you are declaring a derived class, the default constructor for any base classes will be called implicitly. You can use the initialization list to call a non-default constructor instead. If specified, a call to a base class constructor must appear before any member variables.

4. If you have declared any of your member variables as references or as const, then you must initialize them via the initialization list (to avoid the default constructor defining their initial, and only, value).

Furthermore, the new C++11 specification includes improvements in object construction that are relevant here. In C++98, constructors cannot call other constructors. However, this constraint has been loosened in the C++11 standard. Specifically, C++11 will let constructors call other constructors in the same class. This lets you avoid copying code between constructors by delegating the implementation of one constructor to another, such as in the following example:

```
class MyClass
{
public:
    MyClass(int answer) : mAnswer(answer) {}
    MyClass() : MyClass(42) {} // legal in C++11

private:
    int mAnswer;
};
```

While the same effect could be achieved by using a single constructor with a default argument, it would bake the default value into your client's code. The new C++11 syntax lets you hide this value because you can (and should) define the initialization list in the `.cpp` file.

7.5 MEMORY OPTIMIZATION

On modern CPUs, memory latency can be one of the largest performance concerns for a large application. That's because while processor speeds have been improving at a rate of roughly 55% per year, access times for DRAM have been improving at around 7% per year (Hennessy and Patterson, 2006). This has resulted in the so-called Processor–Memory Performance Gap, as shown in Figure 7.1.

Because of this trend, memory overhead is now a principal factor in the execution time of most programs. This is further exacerbated by the fact that the cost for a cache miss, that is, the cost to access main memory, has increased from a few CPU cycles 30 years ago to over 400 cycles on modern architectures. The effect of this is that a seemingly elegant and demonstrably correct algorithm can behave poorly in real-world situations due to unanticipated cache behavior (Albrecht, 2009). As a result, cache-miss optimization has become an extremely important element of performance optimization activities in recent years.

While it is not the focus of this book to provide techniques to optimize your implementation details in the presence of caches, there are some API-related efforts that you can undertake to improve data cache efficiency. One key technique is to reduce the size of your objects: the smaller your objects are, the more of them can potentially fit into a cache. There are several ways that you can reduce the size of your objects.

1. Cluster member variables by type. Modern computers access memory a single "word" at a time. Your C++ compiler will therefore align certain data members so that their memory

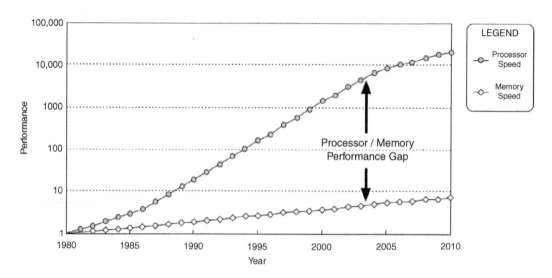

FIGURE 7.1

The widening gap in CPU performance improvements versus memory improvements. Note that the vertical axis is on a logarithmic scale.

Adapted from Hennessy and Patterson (2006). Copyright © Morgan Kaufmann Publishers.

addresses fall on word boundaries. A number of unused padding bytes may be added to a structure in order to make this happen. By clustering all member variables of the same type next to each other, you can minimize the amount of memory lost to these padding bytes. Table 7.2 provides example alignment figures for member variable on the Windows platform.

2. **Use bit fields**. A bit field is a decorator for a member variable that specifies how many bits the variable should occupy, for example, int tinyInt:4. This is particularly useful for packing several bools into a single byte or for squeezing two or more numbers into the space of a single int. The downside is that there is normally a performance penalty for using bit field sizes that are not a multiple of 8, but if memory is your biggest concern then this may be an acceptable cost. When

Table 7.2 Typical alignment of member variables of different types under Windows on x86 CPUs (these sizes may vary by platform and processor)

Type	Size (bytes)	Alignment (bytes)
bool	1	1
char	1	1
short int	2	2
int	4	4
float	4	4
double	8	8
pointer/reference (32 bit)	4	4
pointer/reference (64 bit)	8	8

implementing performance optimizations, you often have to trade speed for size, or vice versa. Remember, when in doubt about the impact of a feature, measure the real-world performance.

3. **Use unions**. A union is a structure where data members share the same memory space. This can be used to allow multiple values that are never used at the same time to share the same area of memory, thus saving space. The size of a union is the size of the largest type in the union. For example,

```
union {
    float floatValue;
    int intValue;
}   FloatOrIntValue;
```

4. **Don't add virtual methods until you need them**. I recommended this as a way to keep an API minimally complete back in Chapter 2, but there are also performance reasons to do this. Once you add one virtual method to a class, that class needs to have a vtable. Only one copy of the vtable needs to be allocated per class type, but a pointer to the vtable is stored in every instance of your object. This adds the size of one pointer to your overall object size (normally 4 bytes for a 32-bit application or 8 bytes for a 64-bit application).

5. **Use explicit size-based types**. The size of various types can differ by platform, compiler, and whether you are building a 32-bit or a 64-bit application. If you want to specify the exact size of a member variable, then you should use a type that specifically enforces this rather than assuming that types such as `bool`, `short`, or `int` will be a specific size. Unfortunately, the way to declare a fixed-size variable varies for different platforms. For example, on UNIX-based systems, the `stdint.h` header file provides types such as `int8_t`, `uint32_t`, and `int64_t` to specify an 8-bit integer, 32-bit unsigned integer, and a 64-bit integer, respectively. However, the Boost library provides platform-independent versions of these types in the `boost/cstdint.hpp` header.

Let's look at an example. The following structure defines a collection of variables to describe a fireworks effect. It contains information about the color and color variance of the firework particles, some flags such as whether the effect is currently active, and a screen location for the effect to begin from. A real fireworks class would have a lot more state, but this is sufficient for illustration purposes.

```
class Fireworks_A
{
    bool mIsActive;
    int mOriginX;
    int mOriginY;
    bool mVaryColor;
    char mRed;
    int mRedVariance;
    char mGreen;
    int mGreenVariance;
    char mBlue;
    int mBlueVariance;
    bool mRepeatCycle;
    int mTotalParticles;
    bool mFadeParticles;
};
```

The variables in this class are ordered roughly in terms of their logical function, without any consideration to how efficiently they are packed in terms of memory. Most member variables are ordered in this way, or sometimes even more randomly by simply adding new variables to the end of the class. For this particular example, the total size for the structure on a 32-bit computer is 48 bytes, that is, `sizeof(Fireworks_A) == 48`.

If you simply cluster the member variables based on their type and sort them based on the size of each type (bools, chars, then ints), then the size of the structure can be reduced to 32 bytes, a 33% reduction.

```
class Fireworks_B
{
    int mRedVariance;
    int mGreenVariance;
    int mBlueVariance;
    int mTotalParticles;
    int mOriginX;
    int mOriginY;
    char mRed;
    char mGreen;
    char mBlue;
    bool mIsActive;
    bool mVaryColor;
    bool mRepeatCycle;
    bool mFadeParticles;
};
```

TIP

Cluster member variables by their type to optimize object size.

You can still squeeze a few more bytes out of the structure, however. By using bit fields you can make each of the bool flags occupy a single bit instead of an entire byte. Doing this lets you get the structure size down to 28 bytes, a 42% reduction.

```
class Fireworks_C
{
    int mRedVariance;
    int mGreenVariance;
    int mBlueVariance;
    int mTotalParticles;
    int mOriginX;
    int mOriginY;
    char mRed;
    char mGreen;
    char mBlue;
    bool mIsActive:1;
    bool mVaryColor:1;
    bool mRepeatCycle:1;
    bool mFadeParticles:1;
};
```

> **TIP**
>
> Consider the use of bit fields to compress an object further, but be aware of their performance impact.

Finally, you can step back and consider the actual size requirements for each variable rather than simply using ints for all integer values. Doing so, you might decide that the RGB variance values only need to be 1 byte, and the screen space coordinates can be 2 bytes each. I'll use the types of char and short, respectively, to simplify what follows, but in reality you could use size-specific types such as int8_t and uint16_t.

```
class Fireworks_D
{
    bool mIsActive:1;
    bool mVaryColor:1;
    bool mRepeatCycle:1;
    bool mFadeParticles:1;
    char mRed;
    char mGreen;
    char mBlue;
    char mRedVariance;
    char mGreenVariance;
    char mBlueVariance;
    int mTotalParticles;
    short mOriginX;
    short mOriginY;
};
```

> **TIP**
>
> Use size-specific types, such as int32_t or uint16_t, to specify the maximum number of required bits for a variable.

This version of our structure occupies only 16 bytes: a reduction of 66% from the original unoptimized size of 48 bytes. That's quite a massive memory savings, just by rearranging the member variables and thinking a little more about how large they need to be. Figure 7.2 shows you exactly where all your memory is going in each of these four configurations.

7.6 DON'T INLINE UNTIL YOU NEED TO

This may seem like strange advice to give in a chapter on performance: don't inline code! However, this is first and foremost a book about APIs, and inlining code in your header files breaks one of the cardinal rules of API design: don't expose implementation details, which is not to say that you should never inline code. Sometimes your performance requirements demand it, but you

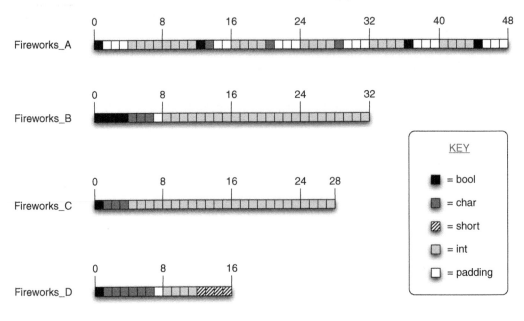

FIGURE 7.2

Memory layout for four different configurations of member variables in a class. Fireworks_A is the original unoptimized version, Fireworks_B employs type clustering, Fireworks_C uses bit fields to compress bool variables, and Fireworks_D uses smaller integer types.

should do so with your eyes wide open and with a full understanding of the implications, such as the following.

1. **Exposing implementation details**. As just covered, the primary reason for avoiding inlining in public API headers is that it causes you to expose the implementation of your API methods directly in the header. I spent an entire section in Chapter 2 detailing why you should not do that.
2. **Code embedded in client applications**. Inlined code in your API headers is compiled directly into your clients' applications. This means that clients must recompile their code whenever you release a new version of the API with any changes to inlined code. They cannot simply drop a new version of your shared library into their installation and expect their application to just work. In other words, inlining breaks binary compatibility.
3. **Code bloat**. Excessive inlining can grow the size of your object files and resulting binary significantly. This is, of course, because each call to an inlined method is replaced by all of the operations of that method. This larger code size can negatively impact performance by causing more disk access and virtual-memory page faults.
4. **Debugging complications**. Many debuggers have problems dealing with inlined code. This is perfectly understandable: it's difficult to put a breakpoint in a function that doesn't actually exist! The common way to circumvent these problems is to turn off inlining for debug code.

As Donald Knuth famously stated: "Premature optimization is the root of all evil" (Knuth, 1974).

Despite these downsides, there still may be cases where you need to put inlined code into your API's public headers. The two main reasons to do this are as follows.

1. **Performance**. Using getter/setter methods to wrap access to member variables can cause a performance impact in your code if those methods are called many times a second. Inlining can recover those performance losses while still allowing you to keep the getter/setter methods (the accompanying source code for this book has a simple program to let you test this for yourself). However, it should be pointed out that marking a function as inline may not necessarily give you performance gains. For one, this is simply a hint to the compiler that can be ignored. Some situations where the request is likely to be ignored are: using loops in the function, calling another inline function, or recursion. Even when the compiler does inline the method, the resulting code could be larger or smaller, and it could be faster or slower, depending on the original size of the method, your CPU's instruction cache, and your virtual memory system (Cline et al., 1998). Inlining tends to work best for small, simple, frequently called functions.
2. **Templates**. You may also be using templates in your header and so are forced to inline the template implementation. Although as covered in the previous chapter on C++ usage, you can sometimes use explicit template instantiation to avoid this.

TIP

Avoid using inlined code in your public headers until you have proven that your code is causing a performance problem and confirmed that inlining will fix that problem.

For those cases where you need to use inlined code, I will discuss the best way to do it. One way to inline code is simply to include the implementation of a method in the class body, such as

```
class Vector
{
public:
    double GetX() const { return mX; }
    double GetY() const { return mY; }
    double GetZ() const { return mZ; }
    void SetX(double x) { mX = x; }
    void SetY(double y) { mY = y; }
    void SetZ(double z) { mZ = z; }

private:
    double mX, mY, mZ;
};
```

This perfectly demonstrates the concern of including implementation details in your header files: a user of your API can look at your header and see exactly how an inlined method is implemented. In this example, the implementation is simple, but it could easily expose much more complexity.

Another way to inline code is by using the C++ `inline` keyword. This approach offers at least one improvement over the syntax I've just shown in that it lets you define the code for a method outside of the class body. Although the code is still in the header, at least you don't obfuscate the class declaration with code.

```cpp
class Vector
{
public:
    double GetX() const;
    double GetY() const;
    double GetZ() const;
    void SetX(double x);
    void SetY(double y);
    void SetZ(double z);

private:
    double mX, mY, mZ;
};

inline void Vector::SetX(double x) { mX = x; }
inline void Vector::SetY(double y) { mY = y; }
inline void Vector::SetZ(double z) { mZ = z; }
inline double Vector::GetX() const { return mX; }
inline double Vector::GetY() const { return mY; }
inline double Vector::GetZ() const { return mZ; }
```

An even better style would be to hide the inline statements in a separate header, where the filename of that header indicates that it contains implementation details. This is the same technique suggested earlier for dealing with templates and is used by several industry-strength APIs, such as Boost headers. Boost uses the convention of a "detail" subdirectory to hold all private details that have to be exposed in header files and then #include those from the public header files. For example,

```cpp
class Vector
{
public:
    double GetX() const;
    double GetY() const;
    double GetZ() const;
    void SetX(double x);
    void SetY(double y);
    void SetZ(double z);

private:
    double mX, mY, mZ;
};

#include "detail/Vector.h"
```

Boost headers also often use the convention of using a "detail" subnamespace to contain all private implementation code, for example, boost::tuples::detail. This is a good practice to further segment necessary private code in public headers.

7.7 **COPY ON WRITE**

One of the best ways to save memory is to not allocate any until you really need to. This is the essential goal of copy-on-write techniques. These work by allowing all clients to share a single resource until one of them needs to modify the resource. Only at that point is a copy made. Hence the name: copy on write. The advantage is that if the resource is never modified then it can be shared for all clients. This is related to the Flyweight design pattern, which describes objects that share as much memory as possible to minimize memory consumption (Gamma et al., 1994).

TIP

Use copy-on-write semantics to reduce the memory cost for many copies of your objects.

   For example, several string objects that store the same text could all share the same memory buffer. Then when one of the strings must modify the text, it creates a copy of the memory buffer so that the modification does not affect the other strings. Figure 7.3 illustrates this concept. Most STL string implementations use copy on write so that passing them by value is fairly inexpensive (Stroustrup, 2000).
   There are several ways to implement copy on write. One popular way is to declare a class template that lets you create pointers to objects managed with copy-on-write semantics in the same way that you would create a shared or weak pointer template. The class normally contains a standard shared pointer, to track the reference count of the underlying object, and provides a private Detach() method for operations that modify the object and hence require detaching from the shared object and creating a new copy. The following implementation uses C++11 shared pointers. This is shown with inline methods within the class declaration for reasons of clarity. In real-world applications, you should of course hide these inline definitions in a separate header as they obscure the

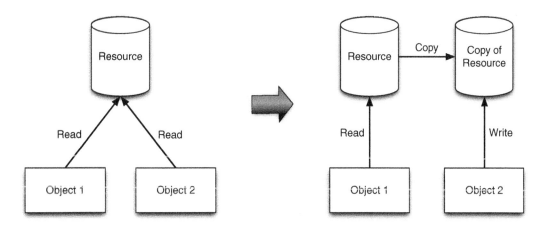

FIGURE 7.3

Illustrating copy on write: both Object1 and Object2 can share the same resource until Object2 wants to change it, at which point a copy must be made so that the changes do not affect Object1's state.

interface declarations. I have hidden the implementation code in this way for the version of the class in the source code package that accompanies this book.

```cpp
#include <memory>

template <class T> class CowPtr
{
public:
    typedef std::shared_ptr<T> RefPtr;

    inline CowPtr() : mPtr(0) {}
    inline ~CowPtr() {}
    inline explicit CowPtr(T *other) : mPtr(other) {}
    inline CowPtr(const CowPtr<T> &other) : mPtr(other.mPtr) {}

    inline T &operator*()
    {
        Detach();
        return *mPtr.get();
    }
    inline const T &operator*() const
    {
        return *mPtr.get();
    }
    inline T *operator->()
    {
        Detach();
        return mPtr.get();
    }
    inline const T *operator->() const
    {
        return mPtr.get();
    }
    inline operator T *()
    {
        Detach();
        return mPtr.get();
    }
    inline operator const T *() const
    {
        return mPtr.get();
    }
    inline T *data()
    {
        Detach();
        return mPtr.get();
    }
    inline const T *data() const
```

```
    {
        return mPtr.get();
    }
    inline const T *constData() const
    {
        return mPtr.get();
    }
    inline bool operator==(const CowPtr<T> &other) const
    {
        return mPtr.get() == other.mPtr.get();
    }
    inline bool operator!=(const CowPtr<T> &other) const
    {
        return mPtr.get() != other.mPtr.get();
    }
    inline bool operator!() const
    {
        return !mPtr.get();
    }
    inline CowPtr<T> & operator=(const CowPtr<T> &other)
    {
        if (other.mPtr != mPtr) {
            mPtr = other.mPtr;
        }
        return *this;
    }
    inline CowPtr &operator=(T *other)
    {
        mPtr = RefPtr(other);
        return *this;
    }

private:
    inline void Detach()
    {
        T* temp = mPtr.get();
        if (temp && ! mPtr.unique()) {
            mPtr = RefPtr(new T(*temp));
        }
    }

    RefPtr mPtr;
};
```

This class can then be used as follows:

```
CowPtr<std::string> string1(new std::string("Share Me"));
CowPtr<std::string> string2(string1);
```

```
CowPtr<std::string> string3(string1);
string3->append("!");
```

In this example, `string2` points to the same object as `string1`, whereas `string3` points to a copy of the object because it needed to modify it. As already mentioned, many implementations of `std::string` will use copy-on-write semantics anyway. I'm simply using this as a convenient example.

There is a loophole that can be exploited in the `CowPtr` implementation I've presented here. It's possible for users to dig into the copy-on-write pointer and access the underlying object in order to hold onto references to its data. They could then modify data directly, thus affecting all `CowPtr` variables sharing that object. For example,

```
CowPtr<std::string> string1(new std::string("Share Me"));
char &char_ref = string1->operator[](1);
CowPtr<std::string> string2(string1);
char_ref = 'p';
```

In this code, the user takes a reference to a character in the underlying `std::string` of `string1`. After `string2` is created, which shares the same memory as `string1`, the user then changes the second character in the shared string directly, causing both `string1` and `string2` to now equal "Spare Me."

The best way to avoid this sort of misuse is simply to not expose `CowPtr` to your clients. In most cases, you don't need your clients to be aware of the fact that you are using a copy-on-write optimization: it's an implementation detail after all. Instead, you could use `CowPtr` to declare member variables in your objects and not change your public API in any way. This is called implicit sharing by the Qt library. For example,

```
// myobject.h
class MyObject
{
public:
    MyObject();

    std::string GetValue() const;
    void SetValue(const std::string &value);

private:
    CowPtr<std::string> mData;
};
```

where the implementation of `MyObject` may look like

```
// myobject.cpp
MyObject::MyObject() : mData(0) {}

std::string MyObject::GetValue() const
{
    return (mData) ? *mData : "";
}
```

```
void MyObject::SetValue(const std::string &value)
{
    mData = new std::string(value);
}
```

In this way, your clients can use your MyObject API without any knowledge that it uses copy on write, but underneath the covers the object is sharing memory whenever possible and enabling more efficient copy and assignment operations.

```
MyObject obj1;
obj1.SetValue("Hello");
MyObject obj2 = obj1;
std::string val = obj2.GetValue();
MyObject obj3 = obj1;
obj3.SetValue("There");
```

In this example, obj1 and obj2 will share the same underlying string object, whereas obj3 will contain its own copy because it modified the string.

7.8 ITERATING OVER ELEMENTS

Iterating over a collection of objects is an extremely common task for client code so it's worth spending some time looking at alternative strategies that offer different strengths and weaknesses. That way you can choose the best solution for your particular API requirements.

7.8.1 Iterators

The STL approach to this problem is to use iterators. These are objects that can traverse over some or all elements in a container class (Josuttis, 1999). An iterator points to a single element in a container, with various operators available, such as operator* to return the current element, operator-> to access the members of the container element directly, and operator++ to step forward to the next element. This design intentionally mimics the interface of plain pointer manipulation in C/C++.

Clients can then use the begin() and end() methods on each container class to return iterators that bound all elements in the container or they can use various STL algorithms that return iterators within the set of all elements, such as std::find(), std::lower_bound(), and std::upper_bound(). The following code segment provides a simple example of using an STL iterator to sum all the values in a std::vector:

```
float sum = 0.0f;
std::vector<float>::const_iterator it;
for (it = values.begin(); it != values.end(); ++it)
{
    sum += *it;
}
```

This is purely an illustrative example. If you really wanted to calculate the sum of all elements in a container, you should prefer the use of the STL algorithm std::accumulate.

In terms of your own API designs, here are some reasons why you may want to adopt an iterator model to allow your clients to iterate over data.

- Iterators are a well-known pattern that most engineers are already familiar with. As such, using an iterator model in your own APIs will minimize the learning curve for users. This addresses the ease-of-use quality introduced in Chapter 2. For example, most engineers will already be aware of any performance issues, such as knowing that they should prefer the preincrement operator for iterators (++it) as opposed to postincrement (it++), to avoid the construction and destruction of temporary variables.
- The iterator abstraction can be applied to simple sequential data structures, such as arrays or lists, as well as more complicated data structures, such as sets and maps, which are often implemented as self-balancing binary search trees such as red-black trees (Josuttis, 1999).
- Iterators can be implemented quite efficiently, even as simply as a pointer in some cases. In fact, std::vector iterators were actually implemented this way in Visual C++ 6 and GNU C++ 3 (although most modern STL implementations now use dedicated iterator classes).
- Iterators can be used to traverse massive data sets that may not even fit entirely into memory. For example, the iterator could be implemented to page in blocks of data from disk as needed and free previously processed blocks. Of course, the client can also stop traversing at any point without having to visit every element in the container.
- Clients can create multiple iterators to traverse the same data and use these iterators simultaneously. In the case where clients wish to insert or delete elements while traversing the container, there are established patterns for doing this while maintaining the integrity of the iterators.

7.8.2 Random Access

An iterator allows clients to traverse linearly through each element in a container. However, you may have cases where you wish to support random access to any element, such as accessing a specific element in an array or vector container. STL container classes that support random accesses provide this in a couple of ways.

1. **The [] operator**. This is meant to simulate the array indexing syntax of C/C++. Normally this operator is implemented without any bounds checking so that it can be made very efficient.
2. **The at() method**. This method is required to check if the supplied index is out of range and throw an exception in this case. As a result, this approach can be slower than the [] operator.

To illustrate these concepts, the iterator source example in the previous section can be recast in terms of the [] operator as follows:

```
float sum = 0.0f;
const size_t len = values.size();
for (size_t it = 0; it < len; ++it)
{
    sum += values[it];
}
```

In terms of performance, these two methods are essentially equivalent. Obviously one approach may prove to be marginally more efficient than the other for a given platform and compiler, but in general they should involve an equivalent degree of overhead.

If you plan to add random access functionality to your API, you should strive to adopt the [] operator and at() method to capitalize on consistency with the STL. However, if your API does not need to provide random access to underlying data, you should prefer using the iterator model over the [] operator approach, simply because an iterator expresses the user's intent more clearly and results in client code that is more obvious and consistent.

7.8.3 **Array References**

As an alternative to iterators, some APIs use an approach where the user passes in an array data structure by reference. The API then fills the array with the requested elements and returns it to the user. The Maya API uses this pattern extensively. Autodesk Maya is a high-end 3D modeling and animation system used extensively in the film and game industry. The package includes a C++ and Python API that provides programmatic access to the underlying 2D and 3D data in a scene.

As an example of this pattern, the `MfnDagNode::getAllPaths()` method is used to return a sequence of node paths in the Maya scene graph. This is achieved by passing in an `MDagPathArray` object by reference, which is then populated with `MDagPath` references. Some reasons for this design, and hence reasons why you may prefer this approach for your own APIs, are as follows.

- The primary purpose of this method is performance. In essence, it is a way to collapse a series of connected nodes of a graph data structure into a sequential array data structure. This provides a data structure that can be very efficiently iterated over, but also locates elements adjacent to each other in memory. The result is a data structure that can take better advantage of CPU caching strategies, as opposed to a tree structure where individual nodes in the tree may be fragmented across the process's address space.
- This technique is particularly efficient if the client keeps the same array around to service multiple calls to `getAllPaths()`. Also, any initial performance overhead to fill the array can be compensated if the array is kept around to support multiple iterations over its elements.
- This technique also offers a specific feature that the iterator model does not: support for noncontiguous elements, that is, a traditional iterator cannot handle different orderings of elements or omit certain elements from a sequence. Whereas using the array reference technique, you can fill the array with any subset of elements in any order.

This concept can be seen in other languages too, such as the `iterator_to_array()` function in PHP, which can be used to convert an iterator into an array for faster traversal in certain cases.

As an alternative to consuming a user-supplied array, you could also return a const container of objects and rely on the compiler's return value optimization to avoid copying data.

> **TIP**
>
> Adopt an iterator model for traversing simple linear data structures. If you have a linked list or tree data structure, then consider using array references if iteration performance is critical.

7.9 **PERFORMANCE ANALYSIS**

As the final section in this chapter on performance, I will take a look at some tools and techniques to help you measure the performance of your system. Most of these are aimed at analyzing the performance of your implementation code and as such are not directly related to how you design your API. However, this is obviously still a very important part of producing an efficient API and therefore worthy of focus.

I will consider several different aspects of performance: time-based performance, memory overhead, and multithreading contention. Also, it should be pointed out that while all of the preceding sections in this chapter dealt with stable features of C++, the following text presents software products that may change over time. Products come, go, change ownership, and change focus. However, I have endeavored to make this list (and the related URLs) as up to date as possible at the time of publication. For a more current list of products, please refer to the accompanying Web site, http://APIBook.com/.

7.9.1 Time-Based Analysis

The most traditional interpretation of performance is how long it takes your code to perform various operations. For example, if you're developing an image processing library, how long does your Sharpen() or RedEyeReduction() method take to run on a given image? The implication here is that you must write some sample or test programs that use your API so that you can then time your API's performance under different real-world scenarios. Assuming that you have written such programs, there are several forms of performance analysis you could consider using:

1. **In-house instrumentation**. The most targeted and efficient profiling you can perform is the kind that you write yourself. Because every piece of software is different, the performance-critical sections of your code will be specific to your API. It is therefore extremely beneficial to have access to a fast timer class that can be inserted into your code at key points to gather accurate timing information. Results can be output to a file and analyzed off line or your clients could integrate a visual display of the timer results into their end-user applications.

   The Second Life Viewer provides this capability via its LLFastTimer class. This works by inserting LLFastTimer() calls into critical sections of the code using an extensible label that identifies the area being analyzed, for example, LLFastTimer(RENDER_WATER). The Second Life Viewer itself then provides a debugging overlay display to view the cumulative result of the timers in real time. See Figure 7.4 for an example of this debugging view.

2. **Binary instrumentation**. This technique involves instrumenting a program or shared library by adding code that records details for each function call. Running the instrumented binary then creates an exact trace of the function calls for that particular session. Processing resulting data can then determine the top call stacks where the program spent most of its time.

   One drawback of this approach is that the extra instrumentation overhead can slow down the program execution significantly, sometimes by as much as 10–100 times, although relative performance should still be preserved. Finally, this technique will obviously not be able to time functions that do not appear as symbols in the binary file, such as inline functions.

3. **Sampling**. This involves use of a separate program that samples your test application continually to determine its program counter. This is a low-overhead statistical technique, meaning that it may not log every single function call made by your application, but with a sufficiently high sample rate it can still be useful in telling you where your application is spending most of its time.

   Sampling can be performed at a system level (e.g., to see if your application spends a lot of time in system calls, e.g., if it is I/O bound) or can be isolated to the functions in your application. In addition to recording time samples, this technique can also refer to sampling processor events, such as cache misses, mispredicted branches, and CPU stalls.

4. **Counter monitoring**. Many commercially available operating systems provide performance counters that report how well various subsystems are performing, such as the processor, memory, network,

FIGURE 7.4

Screenshot of the Second Life Viewer showing its built-in view to display the results of various timers embedded in the code.

disk, and so on. For example, Microsoft provides the Performance Counters API to access counter data on the Windows platform. By monitoring these counters while your application is running you can determine system bottlenecks and also evaluate how inadequate system resources can affect your API's performance.

Given this categorization of performance analyzing techniques, the following list provides a cross section of profiling tools that were on the market at the time of this book's publication.

- **Intel VTune** (http://software.intel.com/en-us/intel-vtune/): This commercial performance analysis suite is available for both Microsoft Windows and Linux platforms. It includes a binary instrumentation feature (called call graph), time- and event-based sampling, and a counter monitor, among various other tools. It comes with extensive and powerful graphical tools to visualize resulting performance data.

- **gprof** (http://www.gnu.org/software/binutils/): gprof is the GNU profiler. It uses binary instrumentation to record the number of calls and time spent within each function. It is integrated with the GNU C++ compiler and is activated via the `-pg` command line option. Running an instrumented binary creates a data file in the current directory that can be analyzed with the gprof program (or the Saturn application on Mac OS X).
- **OProfile** (http://oprofile.sourceforge.net/): This is an open source performance tool for Linux. It is a system-wide sampling profiler that can also leverage hardware performance counters. Profile data can be produced at the function or instruction level, and the software includes support for annotating source trees with profile information.
- **AMD CodeAnalyst** (http://developer.amd.com/cpu/codeanalyst): This freely available profiler from AMD runs on Windows and Linux. It is based on OProfile with specific support for analyzing and visualizing the pipeline stages of AMD processors.
- **Open SpeedShop** (http://www.openspeedshop.org/): This is an open source performance measurement tool for Linux based on SGI's IRIX SpeedShop and currently supported by the Krell Institute. Open SpeedShop uses a sampling technique with support for hardware performance counters. It provides support for parallel and multithreaded programs and also includes a Python scripting API.
- **Sysprof** (http://www.daimi.au.dk/~sandmann/sysprof/): This open source performance profiler for Linux uses a system-wide sampling technique to profile the entire Linux system while your application is running. A simple user interface is provided to browse resulting data.
- **CodeProphet Profiler** (http://www.codeprophet.co.cc/): This freely available tool uses binary instrumentation to collect timing information as your application runs. It supports 32-bit and 64-bit Windows platforms, as well as Windows Mobile installations. A CodeProphet View program is provided to visualize the resulting `.cpg` file.
- **Callgrind** (http://valgrind.org/): This is part of the valgrind instrumentation framework for Linux and Mac OS X. It uses a binary instrumentation technique to collect call graph and instruction data for a given program run. The separate KCachegrind tool can be used to visualize profile data. An optional cache simulator can be used to profile memory access behavior.
- **Apple Shark** (http://developer.apple.com/tools/sharkoptimize.html): Shark is a system-wide sampling profiler written by Apple and provided for free as part of their developer tools. It can also profile hardware and software events, such as cache misses and virtual memory activity. Shark includes an intuitive and easy-to-use interface to browse the hot spots of your Apple applications.
- **DTrace** (http://en.wikipedia.org/wiki/DTrace): This unique and powerful tracing framework can be used to monitor applications in real time. This is done by writing custom tracing programs that can define a list of probes and actions to be performed when a probe fires. Probes include opening a file, starting a process, or executing a specific line of code; actions can analyze the run-time context such as the call stack. Apple added DTrace to Mac OS X 10.5 with an accompanying GUI called Instruments. It is also available as ktrace on FreeBSD.

7.9.2 Memory-Based Analysis

As already stated in this chapter, memory performance can be just as important as time-based performance. Algorithms that allocate and deallocate memory frequently or whose memory allocation profiles do not map well to modern processor caches can end up performing much slower than expected. Also, memory bugs, such as double freeing or accessing unallocated memory, can corrupt data or cause crashes, and memory leaks can build up over time to the point that they consume all available memory and reduce the performance of your clients' applications to a crawl or cause it to crash.

The following tools can be used to profile your API's memory performance and to detect memory bugs.

- **IBM Rational Purify** (http://www.ibm.com/software/awdtools/purify/): This commercial memory debugger uses binary instrumentation to detect memory access errors in C/C++ programs. After a program run, Purify outputs a report file that can be browsed via a graphical interface. It also includes an API that you can access within your programs. Purify is available for Solaris, Linux, AIX, and Windows.
- **Valgrind** (http://valgrind.org/): Valgrind is an open source instrumentation framework for Linux and Mac OS X that began life as a memory profiling tool. However, it has since matured into a more general performance analysis tool. It works by performing binary instrumentation of your executable file and outputs a textual report when your program ends. Several front-end GUIs are available to browse the output file, such as Valkyrie and Alleyoop.
- **TotalView MemoryScape** (http://www.totalviewtech.com/): This commercial memory analysis tool available for UNIX and Mac OS X platforms works without binary instrumentation. It provides a real-time graphical view of your heap memory, including memory usage, allocation bounds violations, and leaks. It handles parallel and multithreaded programs and also incorporates a scripting language to perform batch testing.
- **Parasoft Insure++** (http://www.parasoft.com/): This is a commercial memory debugger available for Windows, Linux, Solaris, AIX, and HP-UX. Insure++ performs instrumentation at the source code level by prepending your compile line with the insure program. You can even set your debugger to stop whenever it detects an error by adding a breakpoint in __Insure_trap_error(). Of course, there is a GUI tool to let you browse the detected memory errors.
- **Coverity** (http://www.coverity.com/): Coverity is a different kind of tool from the others listed. It's a static analysis tool, which means that it checks your source code without actually executing your programs. It records all potential coding errors in a database using a unique ID for each error that is stable across multiple analysis runs. A Web interface is provided to view the results of the static analysis.
- **MALLOC_CHECK_:** The GNU C/C++ compiler supports an alternative memory allocator that is more robust to simple memory errors such as double frees and single-byte buffer overruns. The trade off is that this memory allocator is less efficient so you may not want to use it for production releases, although it can be useful for debugging memory problems. You can turn on this special allocator by setting the MALLOC_CHECK_ environment variable.

7.9.3 Multithreading Analysis

The final aspect of performance covered here is multithreaded performance. Writing efficient multithreaded code is a very difficult task, but luckily there are various tools out there to help you find logical threading errors in your code, such as race conditions or deadlocks, as well as profile the performance of your threaded code to find concurrency bottlenecks.

- **Intel Thread Checker** (http://software.intel.com/en-us/intel-thread-checker/): This is a commercial threading analysis tool available for 32-bit and 64-bit Windows and Linux. It can be used to discover logical threading errors, such as potential deadlocks. You can use it as a command-line tool that outputs a textual report or you can use the accompanying visual GUI that maps potential errors to source code lines.

- **Intel Thread Profiler** (http://software.intel.com/en-us/intel-vtune/): Thread Profiler lets you visualize your threaded application's behavior by displaying a timeline that shows what your threads are doing and how they interact. This lets you determine if you're getting the maximum concurrency from your code. It runs on Windows and Linux. Intel now packages Thread Profiler along with their VTune product.

- **Intel Parallel Studio** (http://software.intel.com/en-us/intel-parallel-studio-home/): Intel's Parallel Studio provides a suite of tools to support parallel applications on multicore systems, including a utility to identify candidate functions for parallelizing, the Intel Threading Building Blocks (TBB) library, an inspector tool to detect threading and memory errors, and a performance analysis tool for parallel applications.

- **RogueWave ThreadSpotter** (http://www.acumem.com/): This tool lets you find performance problems in multithreaded and OpenMP applications on Solaris, Linux, and Windows. It contains all of the functionality of Acumem's single-threaded profiler SlowSpotter (including profilers for memory bandwith/latency and data locality), with the addition of a thread communication and interaction module.

- **Helgrind and DRD** (http://valgrind.org/): Helgrind and DRD are both modules of the open source Valgrind instrumentation framework. They can be used to detect synchronization errors in pthreads-based applications, including misuses of the pthreads API, deadlocks, and race conditions. They can be used on Linux and Mac OS X.

Versioning

8

Up to this point, I have largely considered the design of an API as a discrete task that is finished once the API is fully specified and released to users. Of course, in reality, this is simply the beginning of a continuous and complex process. After an API has been released, that's when the real work begins and when your API development process is put to the test.

Very few, if any, APIs stop development after the 1.0 product is released. There will always be bugs to fix, new features to integrate, workflows to refine, architecture to improve, other platforms to support, and so on.

The primary objective for all releases after the initial release of an API must be to cause zero impact on existing clients, or as close to zero as practically possible. Breaking the interface, or the behavior of the interface, between releases will force your clients to update their code to take advantage of your new API. The more you can minimize the need for this manual intervention on their part, the more likely your users are to upgrade to your new API, or even to keep using your API at all. If your API has a reputation for introducing major incompatible changes with each new release, you are giving your clients incentive to look for an alternative solution. However, an API with a reputation for stability and robustness can be the largest factor in the success of your product.

To this end, this chapter covers the details of API versioning, explaining the different types of backward compatibility and describing how you can actually achieve backward compatibility for your API.

8.1 VERSION NUMBERS

Each release of your API should be accompanied with a unique identifier so that the latest incarnation of the API can be differentiated from previous offerings. The standard way to do this is to use a version number.

8.1.1 Version Number Significance

Many different schemes are used to provide versioning information for a software product. Most of these schemes attempt to impart some degree of the scale of change in a release by using a series of numbers, normally separated by a period (.) symbol (Figure 8.1). Most commonly, either two

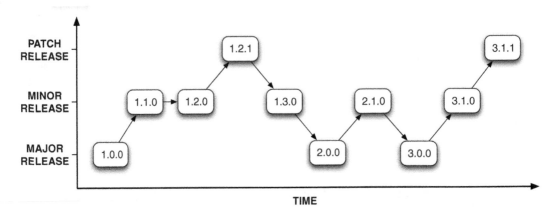

FIGURE 8.1

Illustrating the progression of version numbers using a standard MAJOR.MINOR.PATCH numbering scheme.

or three separate integers are used, for example, "1.2" or "1.2.3." The following list explains the significance of each of these integers.

1. **Major version**. This is the first integer in a version number, for example, **1**.0.0. It is normally set to 1 for the initial release and is increased whenever significant changes are made. In terms of API change, a major version change can signal the backward compatible addition of substantial new features or it can signify that backward compatibility has been broken. In general, a bump of the major version of an API should signal to your users to expect significant API changes.
2. **Minor version**. This is the second integer in a compound version number, for example, 1.**0**.0. This is normally set to 0 after each major release and increased whenever smaller features or significant bug fixes have been added. Changes in the minor version number should not normally involve any incompatible API changes. Users should expect to be able to upgrade to a new minor release without making any changes to their own software. However, some new features may be added to the API, which, if used, would mean that users could not revert to an earlier minor version without changing their code.
3. **Patch version**. The (optional) third integer is the patch number, sometimes also called the revision number, for example, 1.0.**0**. This is normally set to 0 after each minor release and increased whenever important bug or security fixes are released. Changes in patch number should imply no change to the actual API interface, that is, only changes to the behavior of the API. In other words, patch version changes should be backward and forward compatible. That is, users should be able to revert to an earlier patch version and then switch back to a more recent patch version without changing their code (Rooney, 2005).

Some software products employ additional numbers or symbols to further describe a release. For example, an automated build number might be used so that every single build of the software can be differentiated from previous builds. This build number could be derived from the revision number of the last change checked into the revision control system or may be derived from the current date.

Software is often provided to users before the final release in order to get feedback and valuable field testing. In these cases, it is common to add a symbol to the version string to indicate the phase of the development process that the software relates to. For example, "1.0.0a" might refer to an alpha release, "1.0.0b" might refer to a beta release, and "1.0.0rc" might refer to a release candidate. However, you should note that once you start deviating from a purely numeric identification system, doing comparisons of version numbers starts to become more complicated (see Python PEP 0386 at http://www.python.org/dev/peps/pep-0386/ for an example of this complexity).

TIP

It is good practice to include your API's major version number in your library names, particularly if you have made non-backward-compatible changes, for example, `libFoo.so`, `libFoo2.so`, and `libFoo3.so`.

8.1.2 Esoteric Numbering Schemes

I've also decided to list some non-standard or imaginative versioning schemes that have been used by software projects in the past. This section is more for fun than actual practical advice, although each scheme obviously offers advantages for certain situations. For API development, though, I recommend sticking with the widely understood major, minor, patch scheme.

The TeX document processing system, originally designed by Donald Knuth, produces new version numbers by adding additional digits of precision from the value pi, π. The first TeX version number was 3, then came 3.1, then 3.14, and so on. The current version as of 2010 was 3.1415926. Similarly, the version numbers for Knuth's related METAFONT program asymptotically approach the value e, 2.718281.

While this may seem at first to be simply the wry sense of humor of a mathematician, this numbering scheme does actually convey an important quality about the software. Even though Knuth himself recognizes that some areas of TeX could be improved, he has stated that no new fundamental changes should be made to the system and any new versions should only contain bug fixes. As such, use of a versioning scheme that introduces increasingly smaller floating-point digits is actually quite insightful. In fact, Knuth's recognition of the importance of feature stability and backward compatibility, to the extent that he encoded this importance in the versioning scheme for his software, is food for thought for any API designer.

Another interesting versioning scheme is the use of dates as version numbers. This is obviously done explicitly for large end-user software releases such as Microsoft's Visual Studio 2010 and games such as EA's FIFA 10. However, a more subtle system is used by the Ubuntu flavor of the Linux operating system. This uses the year and month of a release as the major and minor version number, respectively. The first Ubuntu release, 4.10, appeared in October 2004 while 9.04 was released during April 2009. Ubuntu releases are also assigned a code name, consisting of an adjective and an animal name with the first same letter, for example, "Breezy Badger" and "Lucid Lynx." With the exception of the first two releases, the first letter of these code names increases alphabetically for each release. These schemes have the benefit of imparting how recent an Ubuntu release is, but they do not convey any notion of the degree of change in a release. This may be fine for a continually evolving operating system, although you should prefer a more traditional number scheme for your API to give your users an indication of the degree of API change to expect in a release.

The Linux kernel currently uses an even/odd numbering scheme to differentiate between stable releases (even) and development releases (odd). For example, Linux 2.4 and 2.6 are stable releases, whereas 2.3 and 2.5 are development releases. This numbering scheme is also used by the Second Life Server releases.

8.1.3 Creating a Version API

Version information for your API should be accessible from code to allow your clients to write programs that are conditional on your API's version number, for example, to call a new method that only exists in recent versions of your API or to work around a bug in the implementation of a known release of your API.

To offer maximum flexibility, users should be able to query your API's version at compile time as well as run time. The compile-time requirement is necessary so that the user can use #if preprocessor directives to conditionally compile against newer classes and methods that would cause undefined reference errors if linking against older versions of your API. The run-time requirement allows clients to choose between different API calls dynamically or to provide logistical logging with your API version number included. These requirements suggest the creation of a version API. I present a simple generic API for this purpose here.

```
// version .h
#include <string>

#define API_MAJOR 1
#define API_MINOR 2
#define API_PATCH 0

class Version
{
public:
    static int GetMajor();
    static int GetMinor();
    static int GetPatch();
    static std::string GetVersion();
    static bool IsAtLeast(int major, int minor, int patch);
    static bool HasFeature(const std::string &name);
};
```

There are a few features of note in this Version class. First, I provide accessors to return the individual major, minor, and patch numbers that comprise the current version. These simply return the values of the respective #define statements, API_MAJOR, API_MINOR, and API_PATCH. While I stated in the C++ usage chapter that you should avoid #define for constants, this is an exception to that rule because you need your users to be able to access this information from the preprocessor.

The GetVersion() method returns the version information as a user-friendly string, such as "1.2.0." This is useful for the client to display in an About dialog or to write to a debug log in their end-user application.

Next I provide a method to let users perform version comparisons. This lets them do checks in their code, such as checking that they are compiling against an API that is greater than or equal to the specified (major, minor, patch) triple. Obviously you could add other version math routines here, but IsAtLeast() provides the most common use case.

TIP

Provide version information for your API.

Finally, I provide a HasFeature() method. Normally when a user wants to compare version numbers, they don't really care about the version number itself but instead are using this designator as a way to determine whether a feature they want to use is present in the API. Instead of making your users aware of which features were introduced in which versions of your API, the HasFeature() method lets them test for the availability of the feature directly. For example, in version 2.0.0 of your API, perhaps you made the API thread safe. You could therefore add a feature tag called "THREAD-SAFE" so that users could do a check such as

```
if (Version::HasFeature("THREADSAFE"))
{
    ...
}
```

While you probably don't need to define any feature tags for your 1.0 release, you should definitely include this method in your Version API so that it is possible for a client to call it in any release of your API. The method can simply return false for 1.0, but for future releases, you can add tags for new features or major bug fixes. These strings can be stored in a std::set lazily (initialized on the first call) so that it's efficient to determine whether a feature tag is defined. The source code that accompanies this book provides an implementation of this concept.

The use of feature tags is particularly useful if you have an open source project where clients may fork your source code or an open specification project where vendors can produce different implementations of your specification. In these cases, there could be multiple versions of your API that offer different feature sets in releases with the same version number. This concept is employed by the OpenGL API, where the same version of the OpenGL API may be implemented by different vendors but with different extensions available. For example, the OpenGL API provides the glGetStringi(GL_EXTENSION, n) call to return the name of the nth extension.

8.2 SOFTWARE BRANCHING STRATEGIES

Before I talk in more depth about API versioning, let's cover some basics about the related topic of software branching strategies. While small projects with one or two engineers can normally get by with a single code line, larger software projects normally involve some form of branching strategy to enable simultaneous development, stabilization, and maintenance of different releases of the software. The next couple of sections cover some things to consider when choosing a branching strategy and policy for your project.

8.2.1 **Branching Strategies**

Every software project needs a "trunk" code line, which is the enduring repository of the project's source code. Branches are made from this trunk code line for individual releases or for development work that must be isolated from the next release. This model supports parallel development where new features can be added to the project while imminent releases can lock down changes and stabilize the existing feature set.

Many different branching schemes can be devised. Each engineering team will normally adapt a strategy to its own individual needs, process, and workflow. However, Figure 8.2 provides

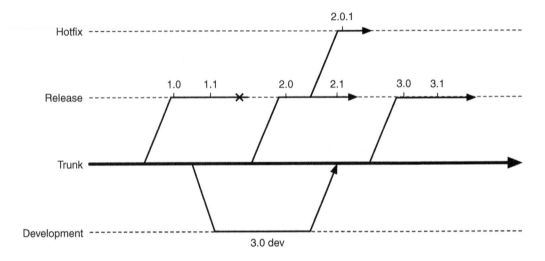

FIGURE 8.2

An example branching diagram for multiple releases of a software product.

one example branching strategy that is frequently seen. In this case, major releases are branched off of trunk, and minor releases occur along those branch lines. If an emergency patch is required while work is happening for the next minor release, then a new branch may be created for that specific "hotfix." Longer-term development work that needs to skip the next release because it won't be ready in time is often done in its own branch and then landed at the appropriate time. Note the resemblance between Figures 8.1 and 8.2. This similarity is of course not accidental.

8.2.2 **Branching Policies**

This basic structure is used by many projects to support parallel development and release management. However, many policy decisions can be used to customize the actual workflow, for example, which branches developers work in, how many development branches are in flight at once, at what point in the process are release branches created, how often changes are merged between branches, whether automatic merges between branches are attempted, and so on.

While different branching policies make sense for different situations, I will comment that in my experience, ongoing development work should happen in the trunk code line, with development branches used where necessary for longer-term work. While QA will necessarily focus on a specific release branch in the run up to a particular release, they should always be focused on trunk, particularly so during periods of development between releases. The trunk is where your project's crown jewels live: this is the code that will live on past individual releases. If no developers or QA engineers are actually working in trunk, and merges are allowed to take place into trunk unattended, the trunk will soon become unstable and buggy.

Your choice of revision control system also has an impact on your branching policy, as different source control management (SCM) products make certain branching strategies easier than others. For example, supporting and merging between branches in Subversion can be a painful endeavor, whereas in distributed SCM systems such as Mercurial or git, branching is designed into the core of the system. For example, using an SCM such as Mercurial, it's possible to consider merging between branches on a daily basis as this is an easy and low-impact operation. The more often you merge between branches, the less code divergence occurs and the easier it will be to eventually land the branch into trunk, if that is the end goal. Release branches will normally just be "end of lifed" when the release is done, as represented by the X symbol after the 1.1 release in Figure 8.2. Another decision factor that relates to your SCM system is whether all your engineers are on-site, in which case a server-based solution such as Perforce is acceptable, or whether you have open source engineers working out of their homes, in which case a distributed solution such as git or Mercurial will be more appropriate.

TIP

Branch only when necessary and branch late. Prefer branching to freezing a code line. Merge between branches early and often. (From the Perforce High-Level Best Practices white paper.)

8.2.3 APIs and Parallel Branches

Once an API has been released, changes to that API should appear (at least externally) to follow a serialized process. That is, you do not release incompatible non-linear versions of your API: the functionality in version N should be a strict superset of the functionality in version N-1. While this may seem obvious, large software projects tend to involve developers working in several parallel branches of the code, and there can be several concurrently supported releases of an API. It is therefore important that teams working in different parallel branches do not introduce incompatible features. There are several policy approaches to deal with this potential problem.

- **Target development branches**. Your project will generally have development branches and release branches. By enforcing that no API changes occur directly in release branches, you minimize the chance that an API change is made in one release but is "lost" in the next release because it was never merged down to trunk. If an API change is needed in a release branch, it should be committed to trunk and then merged up from there. This is generally true of any change in a release branch, but interface changes have a higher cost if they are lost between releases.

- **Merge to trunk often**. Any changes to a public API should either be developed in the common trunk code line or be merged into trunk as early as possible. This also assumes that teams are regularly syncing their development branches to the trunk code, which is good practice anyway. This avoids surprises further down the line when two teams try to merge development branches with conflicting APIs.
- **Review process**. A single API review committee should oversee and vet all changes to public APIs before they are released. It is the job of this committee to ensure that no conflicting or non-backward-compatible changes have been made to APIs. They are the gatekeepers and the last line of defense. This group should be sufficiently empowered to slip release deadlines if necessary to address API problems. I will discuss how to run an API review process later in this chapter.

These solutions attempt to keep one true definition of the API in the trunk code line rather than fracture changes across multiple branches. This may not always be possible, but if you strive for this goal you will make your life easier later.

The problems become more difficult if you have an open source product where users may create forks of your source code and make changes to your APIs that are beyond your control. You obviously cannot do too much about this situation. However, if these changes are to be merged back into your source repository, then you can, and should, apply the same thoughtful review process to community patches as you would to internally developed changes. It can be difficult or awkward to deny changes from open source developers, but you can minimize any hurt feelings by clearly documenting the review process and expectations, offer advice on technical direction early on, and provide constructive feedback on how a patch can be changed to make it more acceptable.

8.2.4 File Formats and Parallel Products

A colleague once described a project that he worked on to me where a decision was made to support two different variants of their product: a Basic version and an Advanced version. Up until that point, there was a single variant of the product and a single file format. The team had a policy of increasing the file format major version number when an incompatible change was introduced into the format, with the last single-variant version being 3.0. The file format was XML based and included a version tag, so it was known which version of the product generated the file. The file format reader would ignore tags that it didn't understand in versions that only differed by minor version number so that it could still read files that were generated from newer but compatible versions of the product. Both the Basic and the Advanced variants could read all files from 3.0 and earlier.

This all seems reasonable so far.

It wasn't long before the Advanced variant introduced new features that required non-backward-compatible additions to the file format so the team decided to increment the major version number to 4.x. However, then there was a need to evolve the entire file format in an incompatible way, that is, to require a major version bump for Basic and Advanced files. To deal with this, the Basic variant format was updated to 5.x and the Advanced variant was bumped to 6.x. The meant that

- 3.x builds couldn't read any of 4.x through 6.x formats, which is fine.
- 4.x builds (old Advanced) couldn't read 5.x files (new Basic) or 6.x files (new Advanced).
- 5.x builds (new Basic) couldn't read 4.x files (old Advanced).

-   6.x builds (new Advanced) could read any existing format, which is also fine.

Then, of course, eventually another major version bump was required, introducing a 7.x (newer Basic) and 8.x (newer Advanced). Things started to get really messy.

With the benefit of hindsight, we talked about how this situation could've been avoided. The key observation is that in this case, the information about which variant had created the file was being conflated with the file format version. One solution would have been to tease apart those two concepts and to write both into the file, that is, a version number, such as "3.2," and a variant name such as "Basic." In this way, the Basic variant could easily know whether it could read a format: it could read any file with an empty or "Basic" variant name. This essentially creates two version number spaces, where the version numbers for the two variants can advance independently of each other. A product first checks the variant name for compatibility and then version number compatibility works in the usual linear fashion.

Learning from this experience, I proffer this advice: when supporting different variants of a product, store the variant's name in any files that should be shared between the variants in addition to the version number of the variant that wrote the file.

TIP

When creating Basic vs Advanced versions of the same APIs, accompany the version number with a "Basic" or "Advanced" string in any generated files. Don't try to use the version number solely to glean whether the file was generated by the Basic or Advanced API.

8.3 LIFE CYCLE OF AN API

This section examines the life of an API and the various phases that it goes through from conception to end of life.

Maintaining an API is not necessarily the same as maintaining a normal software product. This is

FIGURE 8.3

The life cycle of an API. Before the initial release, extensive redesign of the API can be performed. After the initial release, only incremental changes can be tolerated.

because of the extra constraints that are placed on API development to not break existing clients. In a normal end-user software product, if you change the name of a method or class in your code, this doesn't affect the user-visible features of the application. However, if you change the name of a class or method in an API, you may break the code of all your existing clients. An API is a contract, and you must make sure that you uphold your end of the contract.

Figure 8.3 provides an overview of the life span of a typical API. The most important event in this life span is the initial release, marked by the thick vertical bar in Figure 8.3. Before this pivotal point, it's fine to make major changes to the design and interface. However, after the initial release, once your users are able to write code using your API, you have committed to providing backward compatibility and the extent of the changes you can make is greatly limited. Looking at the life span as a whole, there are four general stages of API development (Tulach, 2008).

1. **Prerelease**: Before the initial release, an API can progress through a standard software cycle, including requirements gathering, planning, design, implementation, and testing. Most notably, as already stated, the interface can go through major changes and redesigns during this period. You may actually release these early versions of your API to your users to get their feedback and suggestions. You should use a version number of 0.x for these prerelease versions to make it clear to those users that the API is still under active development and may change radically before 1.0 is delivered.

2. **Maintenance**: An API can still be modified after it has been released, but in order to maintain backward compatibility, any changes must be restricted to adding new methods and classes, as well as fixing bugs in the implementation of existing methods. In other words, during the maintenance phase you should seek to evolve an API, not change it incompatibly. To ensure that changes do not break backward compatibility, it is good practice to conduct regression testing and API reviews before a new version is released.

3. **Completion**: At some point, the project leads will decide that the API has reached maturity and that no further changes should be made to the interface. This may be because the API solves the problems it was designed to solve or may be because team members have moved on to other projects and can no longer support the API. Stability is the most important quality at this point in the life span. As such, only bug fixes will generally be considered. API reviews could still be run at this stage, but if changes are indeed restricted to implementation code and not public headers, then they may not be necessary. Ultimately, the API will reach the point where it is considered to be complete and no further changes will be made.

4. **Deprecation**: Some APIs eventually reach an end-of-life state where they are deprecated and then removed from circulation. Deprecation means that an API should not be used for any new development and that existing clients should migrate away from the API. This can happen if the API no longer serves a useful purpose or if a newer, incompatible API has been developed to take its place.

TIP

After release, you can evolve an API but not change it.

8.4 LEVELS OF COMPATIBILITY

Up to this point I've talked only vaguely about what backward compatibility means. It's now time to get concrete and define our terms more precisely. Accordingly, the next few sections detail what is meant by the specific terms backward compatibility, forward compatibility, functional compatibility, source (or API) compatibility, and binary (or ABI) compatibility.

Often you will provide different levels of compatibility promises for major, minor, and patch releases of your API. For example, you may promise that patch releases will be both backward and forward compatible (Subversion promises this) or you may promise to only break binary compatibility for major releases (KDE promises this for core libraries).

8.4.1 Backward Compatibility

Backward compatibility can be defined simply as an API that provides the same functionality as a previous version of the API. In other words, an API is backward compatible if it can fully take the place of a previous version of the API without requiring the user to make any changes.

This implies that the newer API is a superset of the older API. It can add new functionality, but it cannot incompatibly change functionality that is already defined by the older API. The cardinal rule of API maintenance is to never remove anything from your interface.

There are different types of API backward compatibility, including:

1. Functional compatibility
2. Source compatibility
3. Binary compatibility

I will define each of these in more detail in the following sections.

In addition, there are also data-oriented, backward-compatibility issues, such as

1. Client/server compatibility
2. File format compatibility

For example, if your API involves communication over a network, then you also need to consider the compatibility of the client/server protocol that you use. This means that a client using an older release of the API will still be able to communicate with a newer version of the server. Also, a client using a newer release of the API will still be able to communicate with an older version of the server (Rooney, 2005).

Additionally, if your API stores data in a file or database, then you will need to consider the compatibility of that file format or database schema. For example, more recent versions of the API need to be able to read files generated by older versions of the API.

TIP

Backward compatibility means that client code that uses version N of your API can be upgraded without change to version $N + 1$.

8.4.2 Functional Compatibility

Functional compatibility is concerned with the run-time behavior of an implementation. An API is functionally compatible if it behaves exactly the same as a previous version of the API. However, as Jaroslav Tulach notes, an API will hardly ever be 100% backward compatible in this respect. Even a release that only fixes bugs in implementation code will have changed the behavior of the API, behavior that some clients may actually be depending on.

For example, if your API provides the following function:

```
void SetImage(Image *img);
```

this function may have a bug in version 1.0 of your API, causing it to crash if you pass it a NULL pointer. In version 1.1, you fix this bug so that your code no longer crashes in this case. This has changed the behavior of the API, so it's not strictly functionally compatible. However, it has changed the behavior in a good way: it's fixed a crashing bug. So, while this metric is useful as a basic measure of change in the run-time behavior of an API, that functional change may not necessarily be a bad thing. Most API updates will intentionally break functional compatibility.

As an example of a case where functional compatibility is useful, consider a new version of an API that focused solely on performance. In this case, the behavior of the API is not changed at all. However, the algorithms behind the interface are improved to deliver exactly the same results in less time. In this respect, the new API could be considered 100% functionally compatible.

TIP

Functional compatibility means that version $N + 1$ of your API behaves the same as version N.

8.4.3 Source Compatibility

Source compatibility is a looser definition of backward compatibility. It basically states that users can recompile their programs using a newer version of the API without making any change to their code. This says nothing about the behavior of the resulting program, only that it can be successfully compiled and linked. Source compatibility is also sometimes referred to as API compatibility.

For example, the following two functions are source compatible, even though their function signatures are different:

```
// version 1.0
void SetImage(Image *img);

// version 1.1
void SetImage(Image *img, bool keep_aspect=true);
```

This is because any user code that was written to call the 1.0 version of the function will also compile against version 1.1 (the new argument is optional). In contrast, the following two functions are not source compatible because users will be forced to go through their code to find all instances of the SetImage() method and add the required second parameter.

```
// version 1.0
void SetImage(Image *img);

// version 1.1
void SetImage(Image *img, bool keep_aspect);
```

Any changes that are completely restricted to implementation code, and therefore do not involve changes to public headers, will obviously be 100% source compatible because the interfaces are exactly the same in both cases.

TIP

Source compatibility means that a user who wrote code against version *N* of your API can also compile that code against version *N* + 1 without changing their source.

8.4.4 Binary Compatibility

Binary compatibility implies that clients only need to relink their programs with a newer version of a static library or simply drop a new shared library into the install directory of their end-user application. This is in contrast to source compatibility where users must recompile their programs whenever any new version of your API is released.

This implies that any changes to the API must not impact the representation of any classes, methods, or functions in the library file. The binary representation of all API elements must remain the same, including the type, size, and alignment of structures and the signatures of all functions. This is also often called Application Binary Interface (ABI) compatibility.

Binary compatibility can be very difficult to attain using C++. Most changes made to an interface in C++ will cause changes to its binary representation. For example, here are the mangled names of two different functions (i.e., the symbol names that are used to identify a function in an object or library file):

```
// version 1.0
void SetImage( Image *img )
-> _Z8SetImageP5Image

// version 1.1
void SetImage( Image *img, bool keep_aspect=false )
-> _Z8SetImageP5Imageb
```

These two methods are source compatible, but they are not binary compatible, as evidenced by the different mangled names that each produces. This means that code compiled against version 1.0 cannot simply use version 1.1 libraries because the _Z8SetImageP5Image symbol is no longer defined.

The binary representation of an API can also change if you use different compile flags. It tends to be compiler specific, too. One reason for this is because the C++ standards committee decided not to dictate the specifics of name mangling. As a result, the mangling scheme used by one compiler may differ from another compiler, even on the same platform. (The mangled names presented earlier were produced by GNU C++ 4.3.)

TIP

Binary compatibility means that an application written against version *N* of your API can be upgraded to version *N* + 1 by simply replacing or relinking against the new dynamic library for your API.

Two lists of specific API changes follow, detailing those that will require users to recompile their code and those that should be safe to perform without breaking binary compatibility.

Binary-Incompatible API Changes:

- Removing a class, method, or function.
- Adding, removing, or reordering member variables for a class.
- Adding or removing base classes from a class.
- Changing the type of any member variable.
- Changing the signature of an existing method in any way.
- Adding, removing, or reordering template arguments.
- Changing a non-inlined method to be inlined.
- Changing a non-virtual method to be virtual, and vice versa.
- Changing the order of virtual methods.
- Adding a virtual method to a class with no existing virtual methods.
- Adding new virtual methods (some compilers may preserve binary compatibility if you only add new virtual methods after existing ones).
- Overriding an existing virtual method (this may be possible in some cases, but is best avoided).

Binary-Compatible API Changes:

- Adding new classes, non-virtual methods, or free functions.
- Adding new static variables to a class.
- Removing private static variables (if they are never referenced from an inline method).
- Removing non-virtual private methods (if they are never called from an inline method).
- Changing the implementation of an inline method (however, this requires recompilation to pick up the new implementation).
- Changing an inline method to be non-inline (however, this requires recompilation if the implementation is also changed).
- Changing the default arguments of a method (however, this requires recompilation to actually use the new default argument).
- Adding or removing friend declarations from a class.
- Adding a new enum to a class.
- Appending new enumerations to an existing enum.
- Using unclaimed remaining bits of a bit field.

Restricting any API changes to only those listed in this second list should allow you to maintain binary compatibility between your API releases. Some further tips to help you achieve binary compatibility include the following.

- Instead of adding parameters to an existing method, you can define a new overloaded version of the method. This ensures that the original symbol continues to exist, but provides the newer calling convention, too. Inside of your .cpp file, the older method may be implemented by simply calling the new overloaded method.

```
// version 1.0
void SetImage(Image *img)

// version 1.1
void SetImage(Image *img)
void SetImage(Image *img, bool keep_aspect)
```

(Note that this technique may impact source compatibility if the method is not already overloaded because client code can no longer reference the function pointer &SetImage without an explicit cast.)

- The pimpl idom can be used to help preserve binary compatibility of your interfaces because it moves all of the implementation details—those elements that are most likely to change in the future—into the .cpp file where they do not affect the public .h files.
- Adopting a flat C style API can make it much easier to attain binary compatibility simply because C does not offer you features such as inheritance, optional parameters, overloading, exceptions, and templates. For example, the use of std::string may not be binary compatible between different compilers. To get the best of both worlds, you may decide to develop your API using an object-oriented C++ style and then provide a flat C style wrapping of the C++ API.
- If you do need to make a binary-incompatible change, then you might consider naming the new library differently so that you don't break existing applications. This approach was taken by the libz library. Builds before version 1.1.4 were called ZLIB.DLL on Windows. However, a binary-incompatible compiler setting was used to build later versions of the library, and so the library was renamed to ZLIB1.DLL, where the "1" indicates the API major version number.

8.4.5 Forward Compatibility

An API is forward compatible if client code written using a future version of the API can be compiled without modification using an older version of the API. Forward compatibility therefore means that a user can downgrade to a previous release and still have their code work without modification.

Adding new functionality to an API breaks forward compatibility because client code written to take advantage of these new features will not compile against the older release where those changes are not present.

For example, the following two versions of a function are forward compatible:

```
// version 1.0
void SetImage(Image *img, bool unused=false);

// version 1.1
void SetImage(Image *img, bool keep_aspect);
```

because code written using the 1.1 version of the function, where the second argument is required, can compile successfully in the 1.0 version, where the second argument is optional. However, the following two versions are not forward compatible:

```
// version 1.0
void SetImage(Image *img);

// version 1.1
void SetImage(Image *img, bool keep_aspect=false);
```

This is because code written using the 1.1 version can provide an optional second argument, which, if specified, will not compile against the 1.0 version of the function.

Forward compatibility is obviously a very difficult quality to provide any guarantees about because you can't predict what will happen to the API in the future. You can, however, give this your best effort consideration before the 1.0 version of your API is released. In fact, this is an excellent activity to engage in before your first public release to try to make your API as future proof as possible.

This means that you must give thought to the question of how the API could evolve in the future. What new functionality might your users request? How would performance optimizations affect the API? How might the API be misused? Is there a more general concept that you may want to expose in the future? Are you already aware of functionality that you plan to implement in the future that will impact the API?

Here are some ways that you can make an API forward compatible.

- If you know that you will need to add a parameter to a method in the future, then you can use the technique shown in the first example given earlier, that is, you can add the parameter even before the functionality is implemented and simply document (and name) this parameter as unused.
- You can use an opaque pointer or typedef instead of using a built-in type directly if you anticipate switching to a different built-in type in the future. For example, create a typedef for the float type called Real so that you can change the typedef to double in a future version of the API without causing the API to change.
- The data-driven style of API design, described in the styles chapter, is inherently forward compatible. A method that simply accepts an `ArgList` variant container essentially allows any collection of arguments to be passed to it at run time. The implementation can therefore add support for new named arguments without requiring changes to the function signature.

TIP

Forward compatibility means that client code that uses version *N* of your API can be downgraded without change to version *N* − 1.

8.5 HOW TO MAINTAIN BACKWARD COMPATIBILITY

Now that I have defined the various types of compatibilities, I'll describe some strategies for actually maintaining backward compatibility when releasing newer versions of your APIs.

8.5.1 Adding Functionality

In terms of source compatibility, adding new functionality to an API is generally a safe thing to do. Adding new classes, new methods, or new free functions does not change the interface for preexisting API elements and so will not break existing code.

As an exception to this rule of thumb, adding new pure virtual member functions to an abstract base class is not backward compatible, that is,

```
class ABC
{
public:
    virtual ~ABC();
    virtual void ExistingCall() = 0;
    virtual void NewCall() = 0; // added in new release of API
};
```

This is because all existing clients must now define an implementation for this new method, as otherwise their derived classes will not be concrete and their code will not compile. The workaround for this is simply to provide a default implementation for any new methods that you add to an abstract base class, that is, to make them virtual but not pure virtual. For example,

```
class ABC
{
public:
    virtual ~ABC();
    virtual void ExistingCall() = 0;
    virtual void NewCall(); // added in new release of API
};
```

TIP
_____

Do not add new pure virtual member functions to an abstract base class after the initial release of your API.

In terms of binary (ABI) compatibility, the set of elements that you can add to the API without breaking compatibility is more restricted. For example, adding the first virtual method to a class will cause the size of the class to increase, normally by the size of one pointer, in order to include a pointer to the vtable for that class. Similarly, adding new base classes, adding template parameters, or adding new member variables will break binary compatibility. Some compilers will let you add virtual methods to a class that already has virtual methods without breaking binary compatibility as long as you add the new virtual method after all other virtual methods in the class.

Refer to the list in the Binary Compatibility section for a more detailed breakdown of API changes that will break binary compatibility.

8.5.2 Changing Functionality

Changing functionality without breaking existing clients is a trickier proposition. If you only care about source compatibility, then it's possible to add new parameters to a method as long as you position them after all previous parameters and declare them as optional. This means that users are not forced to update all existing calls to add the extra parameter. I gave an example of this earlier, which I will replicate here for convenience.

```
// version 1.0
void SetImage(Image *img);

// version 1.1
void SetImage(Image *img, bool keep_aspect=true);
```

Also, changing the return type of an existing method, where the method previously had a void return type, is a source compatible change because no existing code should be checking that return value.

```
// version 1.0
void SetImage(Image *img);

// version 1.1
bool SetImage(Image *img);
```

If you wish to add a parameter that does not appear after all of the existing parameters or if you are writing a flat C API where optional parameters are not available, then you can introduce a differently named function and perhaps refactor the implementation of the old method to call the new method. As an example, the Win32 API uses this technique extensively by creating functions that have an "Ex" suffix to represent extended functionality. For example,

```
HWND CreateWindow(                      HWND CreateWindowEx(
    LPCTSTR lpClassName,                    DWORD dwExStyle,
    LPCTSTR lpWindowName,                   LPCTSTR lpClassName,
    DWORD dwStyle,                          LPCTSTR lpWindowName,
    int x,                                  DWORD dwStyle,
    int y,                                  int x,
    int nWidth,                             int y,
    int nHeight,                            int nWidth,
    HWND hWndParent,                        int nHeight,
    HMENU hMenu,                            HWND hWndParent,
    HINSTANCE hInstance,                    HMENU hMenu,
    LPVOID lpParam                          HINSTANCE hInstance,
);                                          LPVOID lpParam
                                        );
```

The Win32 API also provides examples of deprecating older functions and introducing an alternative name for newer functions instead of simply appending "Ex" to the end of the name. For example, the OpenFile() method is deprecated and instead the CreateFile() function should be used for all modern applications.

In terms of template usage, adding new explicit template instantiations to your API can potentially break backward compatibility because your clients may have already added an explicit instantiation for that type. If this is the case, those clients will receive a duplicate explicit instantiation error when trying to compile their code.

In terms of maintaining binary compatibility, any changes you make to an existing function signature will break binary compatibility, such as changing the order, type, number, or constness of parameters, or changing the return type. If you need to change the signature of an existing method and maintain binary compatibility, then you must resort to creating a new method for that purpose, potentially overloading the name of the existing function. This technique was shown earlier in this chapter:

```
// version 1.0
void SetImage(Image *img)

// version 1.1
void SetImage(Image *img)
void SetImage(Image *img, bool keep_aspect)
```

Finally, it will be common to change the behavior of an API without changing the signature of any of its methods. This could be done to fix a bug in the implementation or to change the valid values or error conditions that a method supports. These kinds of changes will be source and binary compatible, but they will break functional compatibility for your API. Often, these will be desired changes that all of your affected clients will find agreeable. However, in cases where the change in behavior may not be desirable to all clients, you can make the new behavior opt-in. For example, if you have added multithreaded locking to your API, you could allow clients to opt-in to this new behavior by calling a `SetLocking()` method to turn on this functionality (Tulach, 2008). Alternatively, you could integrate the ability to turn on/off features with the `HasFeature()` method introduced earlier for the Version class. For example,

```
// version.h
class Version
{
public:
    ...
    static bool HasFeature(const std::string &name);
    static void EnableFeature(const std::string &name, bool);
    static bool IsFeatureEnabled(const std::string &name);
};
```

With this capability, your clients could explicitly enable new functionality while the original behavior is maintained for existing clients, thus preserving functional compatibility. For example,

```
Version::EnableFeature("LOCKING", true);
```

8.5.3 Deprecating Functionality

A deprecated feature is one that clients are actively discouraged from using, normally because it has been superseded by newer, preferred functionality. Because a deprecated feature still exists in the API, users can still call it, although doing so may generate some kind of warning. The expectation is that deprecated functionality may be completely removed from a future version of the API.

Deprecation is a way to start the process of removing a feature while giving your clients time to update their code to use the new approved syntax.

There are various reasons to deprecate functionality, including addressing security flaws, introducing a more powerful feature, simplifying the API, or supporting a refactoring of the API's functionality. For example, the standard C function `tmpnam()` has been deprecated in preference to more secure implementations such as `tmpnam_s()` or `mkstemp()`.

When you deprecate an existing method, you should mark this fact in the documentation for the method, along with a note on any newer functionality that should be used instead. In addition to this documentation task, there are ways to produce warning messages if the function is ever used. Most compilers provide a way to decorate a class, method, or variable as being deprecated and will output a compile-time warning if a program tries to access a symbol decorated in this fashion. In Visual Studio C++, you prefix a method declaration with __declspec(deprecated), whereas in the GNU C++ compiler you use __attribute__ ((deprecated)). The following code defines a DEPRECATED macro that will work for either compiler.

```
// deprecated.h
#ifdef __GNUC__
#define DEPRECATED __attribute__ ((deprecated))
#elif defined(_MSC_VER)
#define DEPRECATED __declspec(deprecated)
#else
#define DEPRECATED
#pragma message("DEPRECATED is not defined for this compiler")
#endif
```

Using this definition, you can mark certain methods as being deprecated in the following way:

```
#include "deprecated.h"
#include <string>

class MyClass
{
public:
   DEPRECATED std::string GetName();
   std::string GetFullName();
};
```

If a user tries to call the `GetName()` method, their compiler will output a warning message indicating that the method is deprecated. For example, the following warning is emitted by the GNU C++ 4.3 compiler:

```
In function 'int main(int, char**)':
warning: 'GetName' is deprecated (declared at myclass.h:21)
```

As an alternative to providing a compile-time warning, you could write code to issue a deprecation warning at run time. One reason to do this is so that you can provide more information in the warning message, such as an indication of an alternative method to use. For example, you could declare a function that you call as the first statement of each function you wish to deprecate, such as

```
void Deprecated(const std::string oldfunc, const std::string newfunc="");
...
```

```
std::string MyClass::GetName()
{
    Deprecated("MyClass::GetName", "MyClass::GetFullName");
    ....
}
```

The implementation of Deprecated() could maintain an std::set with the name of each function for which a warning has already been emitted. This would allow you to output a warning only on the first invocation of the deprecated method to avoid spewage to the terminal if the method gets called a lot. Noel Llopis describes a similar technique in his Game Gem, except that his solution also keeps track of the number of unique call sites and batches up the warnings to output a single report at the end of the program's execution (DeLoura, 2001).

8.5.4 Removing Functionality

Some functionality may eventually be removed from an API, after it has gone through at least one release of being deprecated. Removing a feature will break all existing clients that depend on that feature, which is why it's important to give users a warning of your intention to remove the functionality by marking it as deprecated first.

Removing functionality from an API is a drastic step, but it is sometimes warranted when the methods should never be called any more for security reasons, if that functionality is simply not supported any more, or if it is restricting the ability of the API to evolve.

One way to remove functionality and yet still allow legacy users to access the old functionality is to bump the major version number and declare that the new version is not backward compatible. Then you can completely remove the functionality from the latest version of the API, but still provide old versions of the API for download, with the understanding that they are deprecated and unsupported and should only be used by legacy applications. You may even consider storing the API headers in a different directory and renaming the libraries so that the two APIs do not conflict with each other. This is a big deal, so don't do it often. Once in the lifetime of the API is best. Never is even better.

This technique was used by Nokia's Qt library when it transitioned from version 3.x to 4.x. Qt 4 introduced a number of new features at the cost of source and binary compatibility with Qt 3. Many functions and enums were renamed to be more consistent, some functionality was simply removed from the API, while other features were isolated into a new Qt3Support library. A thorough porting guide was also provided to help clients transition to the new release. This allowed Qt to make a radical step forward and improve the consistency of the API while still providing support for certain Qt 3 features to legacy applications.

8.6 API REVIEWS

Backward compatibility doesn't just happen. It requires dedicated and diligent effort to ensure that no new changes to an API have silently broken existing code. This is best achieved by adding API reviews to your development process. This section presents the argument for performing API reviews, discusses how to implement these successfully, and describes a number of tools that can be used to make the job of reviewing API changes more manageable.

There are two different models for performing API reviews. One is to hold a single prerelease meeting to review all changes since the previous release. The other model is to enforce a precommit change request process where changes to the API must be requested and approved before being checked in. You can of course do both.

8.6.1 The Purpose of API Reviews

You wouldn't release source code to your users without at least compiling it. In the same way, you shouldn't release API changes to your clients without checking that it doesn't break their applications. API reviews are a critical and essential step for anyone who is serious about their API development. In case you need further encouragement, here are a few reasons to enforce explicit checks of your API before you release it to clients.

- **Maintain backward compatibility**. The primary reason to review your API before it is released is to ensure that you have not unknowingly changed the API in a way that breaks backward compatibility. As mentioned earlier, if you have many engineers working on fixing bugs and adding new features, it's quite possible that some will not understand the vital importance of preserving the public interface.
- **Maintain design consistency**. It's crucial that the architecture and design plans that you obsessed about for the version 1.0 release are maintained throughout subsequent releases. There are two issues here. The first is that changes that do not fit into the API design should be caught and recast, as otherwise the original design will become diluted and deformed until you eventually end up with a system that has no cohesion or consistency. The second issue is that change is inevitable; if the structure of the API must change, then this requires revisiting the architecture to update it for new functional requirements and use cases. As a caution, John Lakos points out that if you implement 1 new feature for 10 clients, then every client gets 9 features they didn't ask for and you must implement, test, and support 10 features that you did not originally design for (Lakos, 1996).
- **Change control**. Sometimes a change may simply be too risky. For example, an engineer may try to add a major new feature for a release that is focused on bug fixing and stability. Changes may also be too extensive, poorly tested, appear too late in the release process, violate API principles such as exposing implementation details, or not conform to the coding standards for the API. The maintainers of an API should be able to reject changes that they feel are inappropriate for the current API release.
- **Allow future evolution**. A single change to the source code can often be implemented in several different ways. Some of those ways may be better than others in that they consider future evolution and put in place a more general mechanism that will allow future improvements to be added without breaking the API. The API maintainers should be able to demand that a change be reimplemented in more future-proof fashion. Tulach calls this being "evolution ready" (Tulach, 2008).
- **Revisit solutions**. Once your API has been used in real situations and you've received feedback from your clients on its usability, you may come up with better solutions. API reviews can also be a place where you revisit previous decisions to see if they are still valid and appropriate.

If your API is so successful that it becomes a standard, then other vendors may write alternative implementations. This makes the need for API change control even more critical. For example, the creators of OpenGL recognized this need and so they formed the OpenGL Architecture Review Board (ARB) to govern the standard. The ARB was responsible for changes to the OpenGL API, advancing the standard and defining conformance tests. This ran from 1992 until 2006, at which point control of the API specification was passed to the Khronos Group.

TIP

Introduce an API review process to check all changes before releasing a new version of the API.

8.6.2 Prerelease API Reviews

A prerelease API review is a meeting that you hold just before the API is finally released. It's often a good activity to perform right before or during the alpha release stage. The best process for these reviews for your organization will obviously differ from what works best elsewhere. However, here are some general suggestions to help guide you. First of all, you should identify who the critical attendees are for such a review meeting.

1. **Product owner**. This is the person who has overall responsibility for product planning and for representing the needs of clients. Obviously this person must be technical because your users are technical. In Scrum terminology, the product owner represents the stakeholders and the business.
2. **Technical lead**. The review will generate questions about why a particular change was added and whether it was done in the best way. This requires deep technical knowledge of the code base and strong computer design skills. This person should be intimately familiar with the architectural and design rationale for the API, if they didn't actually develop this themselves.
3. **Documentation lead**. An API is more than code. It's also documentation. Not all issues raised in the review meeting need to be fixed by changing the code. Many will require documentation fixes. Because strong documentation is a critical component of any API, the presence of a person with technical writing skills at the review is very important.

You may decide to add further optional attendees to the review meeting to try and cast a wider net in your effort to assure that the new API release is the best it can be. At Pixar, we performed API reviews for all of the animation systems public APIs delivered to our film production users. In addition to the aforementioned attendees, we would also include representatives from QA, as well as a couple of senior engineers who work day to day in the source code. You will obviously also want someone from project management present to capture all of the notes for the meeting so that nothing gets forgotten.

Depending on the size of your API and the extent of the changes, these meetings can be long and grueling. We would regularly have several 2-hour meetings to cover all of the API changes. You shouldn't rush these meetings or continue them when everyone is getting tired. Assume that they will take several days to complete, and ensure that developers and technical writers have time to implement any required changes coming out of the meeting before the API is released.

In terms of activities that should be performed during an API review, the most important thing is that the meeting should focus on the interface being delivered, not on the specifics of the code. In other words, the primary focus should be on documentation, such as the automatically generated API documentation (see Chapter 9 for specifics on using Doxygen for this purpose). More specifically, you are most interested in the changes in this documentation since the last release. This may involve the use of a tool to report differences between the current API and the previous version. I wrote the API Diff program to perform exactly this function. You can download it for free http://www.apidiff.com/.

For each change, the committee should ask various questions, such as:

- Does this change break backward compatibility?
- Does this change break binary compatibility (if this is a goal)?
- Does this change have sufficient documentation?
- Could this change have been implemented in a more future-proof manner?
- Does this change have negative performance implications?
- Does this change break the architecture model?
- Does this change conform to API coding standards?
- Does this change introduce cyclic dependencies into the code?
- Should the API change include upgrade scripts to help clients update their code or data files?
- Are there existing automated tests for the changed code to verify that functional compatibility has not been impacted?
- Does the change need automated tests and have they been written?
- Is this a change we want to release to clients?
- Does sample code exist that demonstrates the new API?

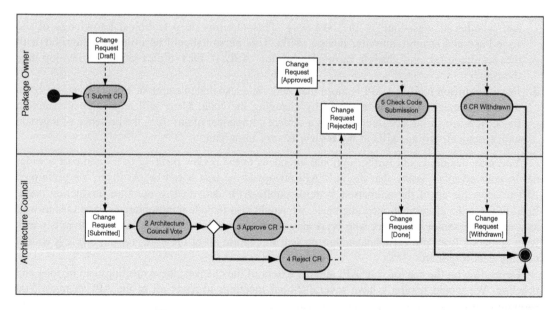

FIGURE 8.4

The public interface change request process for the Symbian platform.

8.6.3 Precommit API Reviews

Of course, you don't have to wait until right before release to catch these problems. The prerelease API review meeting is the last line of defense to ensure that undesirable changes aren't released to users. However, the work of the API review can be decreased greatly if the API owners are constantly vigilant during the development process—watching checkins to the source code and flagging problems early on so that they can be addressed before they reach the API review meeting.

Many organizations or projects will therefore institute precommit API reviews. That is, they will put in place a change request process, where engineers wishing to make a change to the public API must formally request permission for the change from the API review committee. Implementation-only changes that do not affect the public API do not normally need to go through this additional process. This is particularly useful for open source software projects, where patches can be submitted from many engineers with differing backgrounds and skills.

For example, the open-source Symbian mobile device OS imposes a change control process for all Symbian platform public API changes. The stated goal of this process is to ensure that the public API evolves in a controlled manner. The process is started by submitting a change request (CR) with the following information:

- A description of the change and why it's necessary.
- An impact analysis for any clients of the API.
- A porting guide to the new version of the API.
- Updates to backward-compatibility test cases.

This is then reviewed by the architecture council who will either approve or reject the request and provide the rationale for their decision. Once approved, the developer can submit their code, documentation, and test updates. Figure 8.4 provides an overview of this process.

As another example, the Java-based NetBeans project defines an API review process for accepting patches from developers. This is done to supervise the architecture of the NetBeans IDE and related products. Changes to existing APIs, or requests for new APIs, are required to be reviewed before they are accepted into the trunk code line. This process is managed through the NetBeans bug tracking system, where requests for review are marked with the keyword API_REVIEW or API_REVIEW_FAST. The review process will result in a change being either accepted or rejected. In the case of rejection, the developer is normally given direction on improvements to the design, implementation, or documentation that would make the change more acceptable. Of course, similar feedback may still be provided for accepted changes. For details on this process, see http://wiki .netbeans.org/APIReviews.

Precommit reviews are a good way to stay on top of the incoming stream of API changes during the development process. However, it's still useful to schedule a single prerelease API review meeting as well. This can be used to catch any changes that slipped through the cracks, either because an engineer was not aware of the process or didn't realize that it applied to his or her change.

Documentation

In the very first chapter of this book, I defined an API as one or more header files plus supporting documentation. In fact, I claim that an API is incompletely specified unless it includes accompanying documentation. This is because header files do not specify the behavior of the API, only the calling conventions for the various functions and methods. David L. Parnas stated this well (Parnas, 1994):

> Reuse is something that is far easier to say than to do. Doing it requires both good design and very good documentation. Even when we see good design, which is still infrequently, we won't see the components reused without good documentation.

Well-written documentation is therefore a critical element of your API. Accordingly, I am dedicating an entire chapter to this topic. I will start by covering some of the reasons why you should care about documentation and then describe the various types of documentation that you could provide along with several tools that can be used to aid the task of writing documentation.

One of the easiest ways to document your API is to use a tool that automatically extracts comments from your header files and builds API documentation for you. One of the most popular and full-featured of these tools is Doxygen, from Dimitri van Heesch. I will therefore spend some time looking at how you can use Doxygen in your projects and provide some sample templates for documenting various elements of your API.

Documenting your implementation code is good practice too, but that documentation is for your own internal use, whereas the need to document your API header files is more vital because that documentation is for your users.

I feel obliged to admit at this point that most of the source code examples in this book have little or no comments or documentation. This was done simply to keep these examples as minimal and focused as possible, both to make them easier to digest by you, the reader and also so that the book doesn't grow to twice its current size. As a compromise, I have ensured that the source code examples that accompany this book are all well documented, as any API headers that you write should be too.

9.1 REASONS TO WRITE DOCUMENTATION

Hopefully I don't need to convince you that providing your users with details on how to use your API is a good thing. It is certainly true that if you follow the core principles from the qualities chapter then your interfaces should already be consistent, discoverable, and easy to use. However, this is not a replacement for good documentation. Professionally written documentation is an equally important component of delivering high-quality world-class APIs. In fact, good documentation can make the difference between a user adopting your API or looking for an alternative.

9.1.1 Defining Behavior

An API is a functional specification. That is, it should define how to use an interface as well as how the interface should behave. Simply looking at a method in a header file will tell you the number and types of its arguments and the type of its return value, but it says nothing about how that method will behave. To illustrate this point, consider the following definition of a class that represents an RGB color.

```
class RGBColor
{
public:
    RGBColor(float, float, float);
    ~RGBColor();

    float Red() const;
    float Green() const;
    float Blue() const;
    void Set(float, float, float);
};
```

Because this class definition fully specifies the arguments and return types for each method, you can write code that creates instances of this class and call each method. However, there are a number of things that are unknown about the behavior of this class. For example,

- Are the red, green, and blue floating-point values represented by a 0.0 to 1.0 range, as a percentage from 0 to 100%, as a floating-point range from 0.0 to 255.0 (so that the mid-value of 127.5 can be represented accurately), or 0 to 65,535?
- What happens if values outside of this range are passed to the constructor or Set() method? Will it leave them as is, clamp them, take the modulus of the values, or attempt to scale them into the valid range?
- What is the order of the parameters to the constructor and the Set() method? Presumably it's red, green, and then blue, but this hasn't been explicitly documented in the function signatures.

The following updated version of this class provides some documentation, in the form of comments, to help clarify these points. (The triple slash comment style will be explained later in the chapter when I talk more about Doxygen.)

```
/// Represents a single RGB (Red, Green, Blue) color
/// Where (0, 0, 0) represents black and (1, 1, 1) represents white
class RGBColor
{
public:
    /// Create an RGB color from three floats in the range 0..1
    /// Out of range values will be clamped to this range
    RGBColor(float red, float green, float blue);
    ~RGBColor();
```

```
/// Return the red component of the color, in the range 0..1
float Red() const;
/// Return the green component of the color, in the range 0..1
float Green() const;
/// Return the blue component of the color, in the range 0..1
float Blue() const;
/// Set the RGB color with three floats in the range 0..1
/// Out of range values will be clamped to lie between 0..1
void Set(float red, float green, float blue);
};
```

These comments are quite minimal, but nonetheless they do specify the behavior of the API to a sufficient degree for a client to use it. Documentation doesn't have to be long-winded to be thorough. While more details will be appreciated by your users, minimal documentation is better than none at all.

TIP

Good documentation describes how to use your API and how it will behave under different inputs.

It's good practice to write these kinds of comments as you are writing the header file itself. You can always go back and add more content or revise the details once the API is more stable and is approaching release quality. But if you do run out of time and need to get the API out the door quickly, you will at least have some basic level of documentation. Even better, you should explicitly schedule a task to write the documentation for your API before it is released.

You may even consider creating commit hooks (also known as triggers) for your revision control system to reject new public API code that does not include documentation. If that is too draconian a policy, you can still perform the code checks but treat them as advisory feedback rather than roadblocks to checking in new code.

TIP

Write API documentation as you implement each component. Then revise it once the API is complete.

9.1.2 Documenting the Interface's Contract

The term "design by contract" was introduced by Bertrand Meyer as an approach to defining formal specifications for software components (Meyer, 1987). Meyer later trademarked the term in the United States, so many developers now refer to it as contract programming instead. The central notion is that a software component provides a contract, or obligation, for the services that it will provide, and that by using the component a client agrees to the terms of that contract. This concept is founded upon Hoare logic, a formal system developed by Tony Hoare for reasoning about the correctness of programs (Hoare, 1969). The main principles of this model are threefold:

1. **Preconditions**: the client is obligated to meet a function's required preconditions before calling a function. If the preconditions are not met, then the function may not operate correctly.

2. **Postconditions**: the function guarantees that certain conditions will be met after it has finished its work. If a postcondition is not met, then the function did not complete its work correctly.
3. **Class invariant**: constraints that every instance of the class must satisfy. This defines the state that must hold true for the class to operate according to its design.

The best way to specify the details of a contract is in the class and function documentation for your API. In other words, your functions should specify any expected preconditions that must be in force before calling them as well as any resulting postconditions that will be met after they have completed. Also, your class documentation should specify any invariants that will hold true during the observable lifetime of each class, that is, after construction, before destruction, and before and after each public method call. Let's look at a couple of examples to demonstrate this concept more concretely.

A square root function will have the precondition that the input number must be a positive number, or zero. It will have a postcondition that the result of the function squared should equal the input number (within an appropriate tolerance). These conditions can be documented using Doxygen syntax as follows. The next chapter on testing will discuss about how you can enforce these conditions in code.

```
///
/// \brief Calculate the square root of a floating-point number.
/// \pre value >= 0
/// \post fabs((result * result) - value) < 0.001
///
double SquareRoot(double value);
```

To give a more object-oriented example, consider a string container class. This has a class invariant that the length of the string, as returned by the size() method, must always be zero or greater. Also, the pointers returned by c_str() and data() must always be non-NULL. For the class's append() method, the length of the string being changed must grow by the length of the input string. These contract terms are expressed in the following documentation comments. (The term @pre.size() is meant to represent the length of the string before the method is called.)

```
///
/// \brief A container that operates on sequences of characters.
/// \invariant size() >=0 && c_str() != NULL && data() != NULL
/// \invariant empty() implies c_str()[0] == '\0'
///
class String
{
public:
    ...
    ///
    /// \brief Append str to this string object.
    /// \post size() == @pre.size() + str.size()
    ///
    void append(const std::string &str);
    ...
};
```

In terms of inheritance relationships between classes, Ken Pugh notes that the preconditions for derived classes can be weaker, but not stronger, than those in its base classes (Pugh, 2006). That is, a derived class should handle all cases that its base classes handle, but it may decide to handle additional cases by requiring fewer preconditions. In contrast, a derived class should inherit all postconditions from its base classes. That is, a function in a derived class must meet all of its base class postconditions, as well as the further postconditions that it defines itself.

9.1.3 **Communicating Behavioral Changes**

There are many cases where an API change does not involve changes to any class definitions or function signatures. This happens when you change the underlying implementation for a function without affecting its interface. From a code perspective, this change will be invisible to your clients because it doesn't affect the function signatures in your header files. However, the API has indeed changed because its behavior has changed. In other words, the update will be source and binary compatible, but not functionally compatible.

In this case, you can communicate the change by modifying the documentation for the API call. For example, consider the following function that returns a list of children in a hierarchy of nodes:

```
/// Return a list of children in the hierarchy.
///
/// \return A NULL-terminated list of child nodes,
///         or NULL if no children exist.
///
const Node *GetChildren() const;
```

According to the documentation, this function returns a NULL pointer if there are no children in the hierarchy. This behavior forces clients to guard against a NULL return value, such as

```
const Node *children = hierarchy.GetChildren();
if (children)
{
    while (*children != NULL)
    {
        // process node
        children++;
    }
}
```

Now let's say that in a future version of this API you realize that you can make the lives of your clients easier—and improve the stability of their code—if you instead return a valid Node* pointer that points to a NULL value when there are no children. This obviates the need for special NULL checks, so clients could instead write code such as

```
const Node *children = hierarchy.GetChildren();
while (*children != NULL)
{
    // process node
    children++;
}
```

This change did not involve any modification to the function signature for the `GetChildren()` method. However, the change can still be communicated to the client by updating the documentation for the method. For example,

```
/// Return a list of children in the hierarchy.
///
/// \return A non-NULL pointer to a list of child nodes.
///             The list is terminated with a NULL pointer.
///
const Node *GetChildren() const;
```

9.1.4 What to Document

You should document every public element of your API: every class, function, enum, constant, and typedef. If your clients can access it, you should tell them what it is and how they can use it (Bloch, 2008). In particular, you should focus on any important aspects that will help them use your classes and methods productively. This includes describing the behavior of methods, as well as describing their relationship to the rest of the API.

Specifying the units of parameters and return values is another particularly important element of good documentation. When doing so, you should consider whether you need to define the nature, accuracy, and precision of the values, too. A particularly pertinent example is that of a timer class that calls client code every *n* seconds. You may document the units of the timeout to be seconds, but it would still be reasonable for a client to ask:

- Does time refer to real-world (wall clock) time or process time?
- What is the accuracy of the timer?
- Will other API operations affect the accuracy of, or block, the timer?
- Will the timer drift over time or will it always fire relative to the start time?

Defining these additional characteristics will help your users work out whether the class is appropriate for their tasks. For example, an idle task that just needs to perform some trivial work roughly every second doesn't care if it gets woken up after 1.0 seconds or 1.1 seconds. However, an analog clock that increments its second hand on every invocation would soon show the wrong time under the same conditions.

As an aid to working out what you should document for your APIs, the following list provides a checklist of questions to ask yourself when you're producing the documentation for your classes and functions.

- What is the abstraction that a class represents?
- What are the valid inputs, for example, can you pass a NULL pointer?

- What are the valid return types, for example, when does it return true versus false?
- What error conditions does it check for, for example, does it check for file existence?
- Are there any preconditions, postconditions, or side effects?
- Is there any undefined behavior, for example, `sqrt(-1.0)`?
- Does it throw any exceptions?
- Is it thread safe?
- What are the units of any parameters?
- What is the space or time complexity, for example, $O(\log n)$ or $O(n^2)$?
- What is the memory ownership model, for example, is the caller responsible for deleting any returned objects?
- Does a virtual method call any other method in the class, that is, what methods should clients call when they override the method in a derived class?
- Are there any related functions that should be cross-referenced?
- In which version of the API was this feature added?
- Is this method deprecated; if so, what's the alternative?
- Are there any known bugs in this feature?
- Do you wish to share any planned future enhancements?
- Are there any code examples you can provide?
- Does the documentation add extra value or insight, for example, the comment "sets the color" doesn't tell you much you didn't already know for a function called `SetColor()`.

In addition to this list of API behaviors, Diomidis Spinellis presents a short list of qualities that all good code documentation should strive for (Spinellis, 2010). He recommends that documentation should be:

1. Complete
2. Consistent
3. Effortlessly accessible
4. Non-repetitive

TIP

Document every public element of your API.

It's also good practice to have another person review your documentation. As the developer who wrote the code, you are often too close to the problem space and may assume knowledge that the normal user will not have. As Michi Henning puts it, the developer of the API is "mentally contaminated by the implementation" (Henning, 2009). Therefore, have a fellow developer, QA engineer, or technical writer look over your API documentation and be open to the feedback from their fresh perspective.

9.2 TYPES OF DOCUMENTATION

There are various types of documentation that you can provide for your API. Not all of these will be appropriate for your particular project, but it's worth being aware of the various options that your users will expect.

It's also worth noting that many software products provide documentation that can accept contributions from users. This may be via the use of a wiki, where any user can actually create and edit documentation, such as the massive World of Warcraft wiki at http://www.wowwiki .com/, or Web pages that support user comment addendums, such as the PHP manual at http:// www.php.net/manual/. This is obviously a very powerful capability that can build a community around your API and create collective documentation that goes beyond what you could achieve on your own. Even if you don't employ an automated system for user contributions, you should provide a way for them to send feedback to you so that it can be incorporated into the documentation manually.

Much of the documentation that you (or your users) write will apply to specific versions of the API. One trap that is easy to fall into with wiki-based solutions is that the wiki content will eventually refer to a range of versions of the API. It is worth considering how you can create distinct versioned sets of documentation, perhaps creating a completely separate copy of the documentation for each major release. This will allow clients who are using older versions to view the documentation for that specific release, while also letting you keep the latest documentation focused on the current version of the API.

Figure 9.1 shows a screenshot of the Qt Reference Documentation index page. This is included as one example of extensive and well-written documentation that demonstrates all of the various types that I will cover next. It's also worth noting that all of the Qt documentation is versioned along with the API.

9.2.1 Automated API Documentation

The most obvious kind of documentation for an API is the type that is automatically generated from comments in your source code. This allows you to keep the documentation for classes and methods right next to their declaration in the header files. The result is that you're more likely to keep the documentation up to date when you change the API. It's also easy to generate the latest documentation for a new release, and this documentation can have cross-references between related functionality of the API.

TIP

Use an automated documentation tool that extracts API documentation from your header comments.

It's perhaps obvious, but any user documentation comments should appear in your public headers, not `.cpp` files so that they are more readily discoverable by your users. This is particularly important for closed source APIs, where users do not have access to your `.cpp` files.

These source code comments are often maintained by developers. However, the quality of your API documentation can be enhanced greatly if you have professional technical writers perform a pass over the comments for style, grammar, and consistency checks. Also, as a fresh set of eyes, these writers can often provide good feedback and suggest additional information to highlight or improved examples to include. Some technical writers may not feel comfortable changing source code directly, but in those cases they can easily mark up a hardcopy of the documentation and let the developer make the actual code changes.

Home · All Classes · All Functions · Overviews

Qt Reference Documentation

Getting Started	API Reference	Working with Qt
• Installation and First Steps with Qt • Tutorials and Examples • Demonstrations and **New in Qt 4.6**	• Class and Function Documentation • Frameworks and Technologies • How-To's and Best Practices	• Cross-Platform Development with Qt • Unit Testing and Debugging • Deploying Qt Applications
Fundamentals	**User Interface Design**	**Technologies**
• The Qt Object Model • Event System • Threading • Internationalization • Platform Specifics	• Widgets and Layouts • Application Windows • Painting and Printing • Canvas UI with Graphics View • Integrating Web Content	• Input/Output and Resources • Network Programming • SQL Development • XML Processing • Scripting
Community and Resources	**Contributing**	**Licenses**
• Online Resources • Developer Blogs • Support, Training and Services	• Report Bugs and Make Suggestions • Open Repository • Credits	• GNU GPL, GNU LGPL • Commercial Editions • Licenses Used in Qt

Copyright © 2010 Nokia Corporation and/or its subsidiary(-ies)   Trademarks   Qt 4.6.2

FIGURE 9.1

Screenshot of the Qt Reference Documentation Web page, at http://doc.qt.nokia.com/. Copyright © 2010 Nokia Corporation.

A number of tools let you create API documentation from comments in your C++ source code. These can normally generate output in various formats, such as HTML, PDF, and LaTeX. The following list provides links to several of these tools:

- **AutoDuck**: http://helpmaster.info/hlp-developmentaids-autoduck.htm
- **CcDoc**: http://ccdoc.sourceforge.net/
- **CppDoc**: http://www.cppdoc.com/
- **Doc-O-Matic**: http://www.doc-o-matic.com/
- **Doc++**: http://docpp.sourceforge.net/
- **Doxygen**: http://www.doxygen.org/
- **GenHelp**: http://www.frasersoft.net/
- **HeaderDoc**: http://developer.apple.com/darwin/projects/headerdoc/
- **Help Generator**: http://www.helpgenerator.com/
- **KDOC**: http://sirtaj.net/projects/kdoc/

- **ROBODoc**: http://www.xs4all.nl/~rfsber/Robo/robodoc.html
- **TwinText**: http://www.ptlogica.com/

9.2.2 Overview Documentation

In addition to autogenerated API documentation, you should have manually written prose that provides higher-level information about the API. This will normally include an overview of what the API does and why the user should care about it. In a large organization, this task is normally performed by a technical writer. It may even be localized into several different languages. The overview documentation will often cover the following topics:

- A high-level conceptual view of the API: what problem is being solved and how the API works. Diagrams are great if they are appropriate.
- Key concepts, features, and terminology.
- System requirements for using the API.
- How to download, install, and configure the software.
- How to provide feedback or report bugs.
- A statement on the life cycle stage of the API, for example, prerelease, maintenance, stability, or deprecated (see the versioning chapter).

9.2.3 Examples and Tutorials

Examples are really, really important. An API overview is often too high level to allow users to glean how to use your API, and even though you have documentation for every class and method in your API, this doesn't immediately tell the user how to actually use the API to perform a task. Adding even a few small examples can enhance the utility of your documentation greatly. Remember that an API is software for other developers. They just want to know how they can use your interface to get their job done. This can be part of a Getting Started section in your documentation and may include any of the following.

- **Simple and short examples**. These should be minimal and easy to digest snippets of code that demonstrate the API's key functionality. They are not normally code that can be compiled, but instead focus on your API calls without all the boilerplate code that goes around it.
- **Working demos**. These are complete real-world examples that show how the API can be used to perform a more complex and practical task. These should be easy to reuse so that your users have a working starting point for their own projects. You should provide the source code for these with your API.
- **Tutorials and walkthroughs**. A tutorial illustrates the steps that you go through in order to solve a problem rather than simply presenting the end result. This can be a useful way to build up a complex example and to address specific features of the API as you gradually add more calls to the worked example.
- **User contributions**. Your users can be a great source of examples, too. Encourage your users to send you example code that can be added to your collection of demos, perhaps under a specific `contrib` directory so that it is clear that these are not supported by you.

- **FAQs**. A set of answers to frequently asked questions can be a very helpful addition to your documentation set. It lets your users discover quickly and easily if the API suits their needs, how to avoid common pitfalls, or how to solve typical problems.

The act of writing documentation forces you to think from the user's perspective. As such, it can help you identify shortcomings in the API or areas that could be simplified. It's therefore good practice to write the skeleton for high-level documentation and some initial example code early on as a way to force you to think more deeply about the overall design and the use cases of your library.

9.2.4 Release Notes

Each release after the first release should include release notes. These tell your users what has changed since the last release. Release notes are normally terse documents that can include:

- An overview of the release, including a description of what's new or what the focus was for the release, for example, bug fixes only.
- A link to where the release can be found.
- Identification of any source or binary incompatibilities from the previous release.
- A list of bugs fixed in the release.
- A list of features that were deprecated or removed.
- Migration tips for any changes in the API, such as how to use any upgrade scripts provided with the release.
- Any known issues, either introduced in this release or remaining from previous versions.
- Troubleshooting tips to work around known issues.
- Information on how users can send feedback and bug reports.

9.2.5 License Information

You should always specify the license that you are distributing your API under. This lets your clients know what rights you are granting them and what their obligations are. Generally, you will use a license from one of the following two categories.

1. **Proprietary**: For software whose ownership remains with you the publisher and where you prohibit certain uses of the software. Often these software products are closed source and require a licensing fee (although, as a counterexample, the Qt commercial license includes the source code). Proprietary licenses may restrict certain activities such as reverse engineering the software, the number of users or machines, the number of developers, or concurrent use of the software by multiple users.
2. **Free and Open Software**: For software that can be used, studied, and modified without restriction. It can also be copied and redistributed in either modified or unmodified form with no, or minimal, restrictions. The term free refers to the usage rights of the software, not necessarily its price. Software that conforms to this category is referred to as Free and Open Source Software, commonly abbreviated to FOSS or also FLOSS (Free, Libre, Open Source Software).

There are two major bodies that approve FLOSS licenses. The Free Software Foundation (FSF), founded by Richard Stallman in 1985, approves licenses that comply with The Free Software Definition, and the Open Source Initiative (OSI), founded by Bruce Perens and Eric S. Raymond in 1998, approves licenses that comply with their Open Source Definition.

TIP

Specify the license terms for your API prominently.

There are also two principal types of FLOSS licenses.

1. **Copyleft**: Offers the right to distribute modified and unmodified copies of a piece of software and requires that any such derived works must be released under the same terms. There is a further subcategory of weak copyleft, which is often applied to software libraries to allow clients to distribute code that links with that library without requiring that product to be distributed under the library's copyleft license.

2. **Permissive**: Offers the right to distribute modified and unmodified copies of a piece of software and allows the derived work to be distributed under terms that are more restrictive than those in the original license. This means you can provide an open source library, but your clients are not required to make all distributed derivates available as open source.

The following table provides a list of some of the common FLOSS software licenses and a brief overview of their impact on your users. All of these licenses are approved by both the FSF and the OSI. This list is obviously incomplete and meant only as a rough guide. If you have access to a general counsel, you should consult with that person on the best license choice for your product. For more details, refer to http://www.fsf.org/ and http://www.opensource.org/.

License Name	Brief Description
No license	If you do not specify a license, your users have no legal right to use your API unless they ask for your permission directly (as you are the copyright holder).
GNU GPL License	The GNU General Public License (GPL) is a copyleft license, which means that any derived works must also be distributed as GPL. An open source GPL library therefore cannot be used in a proprietary product. The Linux kernel and the GIMP image processing tool are released under the GPL. Nokia's Qt library was originally released under either a commercial or a GPL license.
GNU LGPL License	The GNU Lesser General Public License (LGPL) is a weak copyleft license that allows an open source API to be binary linked to proprietary code. The derived work can be distributed under certain specific conditions, such as providing the source code of the modified or unmodified LGPL library, among others constraints. GTK+ is licensed under the LGPL. Nokia added the LGPL license to Qt as of version 4.5.
BSD License	The BSD license is a simple permissive license that includes a legal disclaimer of liability by a named owner/organization. Normally a modified version of BSD is used, without the "advertising clause." Proprietary code that links against BSD code can be distributed freely. Google released its Chrome browser under the BSD license. The Zend framework and libtiff library also use BSD.

MIT/X11 License	This is a simple permissive license in the same vein as the BSD license. Proprietary code that links against MIT-licensed code can be distributed freely. MIT-licensed software includes Expat, Mono, Ruby on Rails, Lua 5.0 onwards, and the X11 Window System.
Mozilla Public License	This is a weak copyleft license that allows your open source library to be used to build proprietary software. Any code modifications must be redistributed under the MPL license. The Mozilla software products Firefox and Thunderbird are made available under the MPL.
Apache License	This is another permissive license that allows proprietary software to be distributed that is built upon Apache-licensed code. The Apache Web server obviously uses the Apache license. Google also uses it for many of its products, such as Android and the Google Web Toolkit.

This concludes our discussion of the various types of documentation that you might provide for your API. In summary, Figure 9.2 presents another example of the documentation overview of a

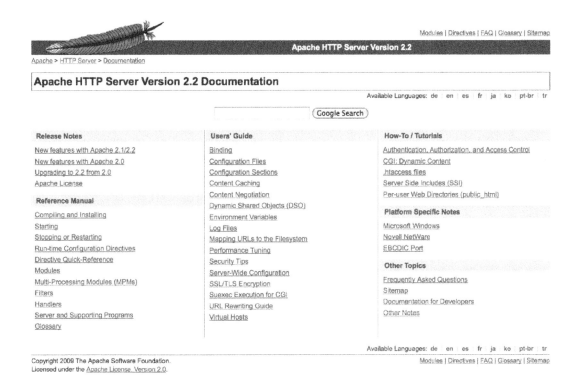

FIGURE 9.2

A screenshot of the documentation Web page for the Apache HTTP Server, http://httpd.apache.org/docs/. Copyright © 2009 The Apache Software Foundation.

well-respected software project: the Apache HTTP Server. Note that this documentation is also localized into several different languages.

9.3 DOCUMENTATION USABILITY

There are several research groups that investigate API documentation usability (Jeong et al., 2009; Robillard, 2009; Stylos and Myers, 2008). This work involves performing usability studies to see how well users can navigate through documentation and perform focused tasks. The desire is to be able to inform API designers about better ways to document their interfaces. The following list presents a summary of some of these findings.

- **Index page**. Provide an overall index page that serves as a jumping off point into the individual documentation elements. This gives users a conceptual map of the entire documentation set. Additionally, each starting point should provide some indication of what it will cover and what class of users it targets (developers, managers, legal, etc.).
- **Consistent look and feel**. API documentation will normally be composed of different elements, some autogenerated, some written by hand, some contributed by users. You should use a consistent and unique style for all these pages so that users are always aware when they are browsing your documentation content or if they have navigated to another Web site.
- **Code examples**. There can often be a lot of documentation for users to read. Consider the massive size of the Microsoft Developer Network library. Providing example code snippets and working demos can help users find and assimilate the information they need to use the API in their own code more quickly.
- **Diagrams**. Clear and concise diagrams that illustrate the high-level concepts can be helpful, particularly for users who just want to scan the documentation quickly. You should use familiar diagram formats where possible, such as UML or entity relationship diagrams.
- **Search**. A good search facility is important to let users find the information they need as fast as possible. All parts of the documentation should be searchable, including the autogenerated API specification as well as any manually written text.
- **Breadcrumbs**. Use navigation aids that let users keep track of their location within the documentation hierarchy and move back up the hierarchy easily. The term "breadcrumbs" is used to describe the common technique of displaying the current location as a series of pages with a separator symbol, for example, "index > overview > concepts." In addition, it can be useful to let users backtrack to various high-level pages easily.
- **Terminology**. Crucial terminology should be defined and used consistently. However, you should avoid specialized or esoteric terminology where it is not necessary as this can serve to confuse and frustrate users.

Related to API usability is the property of ease of learning: a difficult-to-use API will likely also be difficult to learn. To this end, Martin Robillard investigated the question of what makes an API difficult to learn. He found that one of the largest obstacles to learning an API is the supporting documentation and resources. For example, he lists the following hindrances to API learning (Robillard, 2009):

- **Lack of code examples**: Insufficient or inadequate examples are provided.
- **Incomplete content**: Documentation is missing or presented inadequately.
- **Lack of task focus**: No details are offered on how to accomplish specific tasks.
- **No design rationale**: Insufficient or inadequate details provided on the high-level architecture and design rationale.
- **Inaccessible data formats**: Documentation isn't available in the desired format.

In addition to these points, a lot of research has focused on the fact that developers are often reluctant to read API documentation carefully or thoroughly (Zhong et al., 2009). This suggests that providing more documentation can sometimes actually be detrimental because your users may miss the really important points and caveats due to them being buried too deeply. The use of higher-level tutorials and example code can help address this problem. Also, cross-references between related classes and methods can lead the user to discover features that they were not aware of. Some researchers have also suggested using word clouds, or other variable-font techniques, to highlight important or common classes (Stylos et al., 2009).

9.4 USING DOXYGEN

Doxygen is a utility to automatically generate API documentation in various formats based on the comments that you write in your source code. It has support for many languages, including C, C++, Objective-C, Java, Python, Fortran, C#, and PHP, and it can generate output in several formats, including HTML, LaTeX, PDF, XML, RTF, and UNIX man pages, among others.

Doxygen is open source (released under the GNU General Public License), and binaries are provided for several platforms, including Windows, Linux, and Mac. It has been developed since 1997 and is now a mature and powerful system. Due to the fact that it's a very popular tool and is used on many projects, and my goal of providing a practical resource, I've dedicated the rest of this chapter to cover the basics of how you can use Doxygen in your own projects. However, similar guidelines apply to any of the other tools listed earlier in the Automated API documentation section. The Doxygen Web site is http://www.doxygen.org/.

9.4.1 The Configuration File

Doxygen is highly configurable, with over 200 options in recent versions. All of these options can be specified via the Doxygen configuration file. This is an ASCII text file with a simple key = value format. You can generate a default configuration file by running Doxygen with the -g command line argument.

You will then want to edit this configuration file to specify some details about your source code and to change the default behavior in certain cases. Some of the entries I find that I change a lot are as follows:

```
PROJECT_NAME = <name of your project>
FULL_PATH_NAMES = NO
TAB_SIZE = 4
FILE_PATTERNS = *.h *.hpp *.dox
```

```
RECURSIVE = YES
HTML_OUTPUT = apidocs
GENERATE_LATEX = NO
```

With this initial setup performed, you can simply run Doxygen in your source directory, where it will create an `apidocs` subdirectory with your API documentation (assuming that you adopted the `HTML_OUTPUT` setting given earlier). The following sections describe how comments can be added to your code that Doxygen will pick up and add to this generated documentation.

9.4.2 Comment Style and Commands

You must use a special comment style to signal to Doxygen that you wish to add the comment text to the API documentation. There are various comment styles that Doxygen supports, including the following:

```
/**
 * ... text ...
 */

/*!
 * ... text ...
 */

///
/// ... text ...
///

//!
//! ... text ...
//!
```

Which style you adopt is a matter of personal taste: they all behave exactly the same. I will adopt the triple slash style (///) for the rest of this chapter.

Within a comment, there are a number of commands that you can specify to provide specific information to Doxygen. This information will often be formatted specially in the resulting documentation. The following list provides a summary of some of the most useful commands. Refer to the doxygen manual for the complete list.

- `\file` [<filename>]
- `\class` <class name> [<header-file>] [<header-name>]
- `\brief` <short summary>
- `\author` <list of authors>
- `\date` <date description>
- `\param` <parameter name> <description>
- `\param[in]` <input parameter name> <description>
- `\param[out]` <output parameter name> <description>
- `\param[in,out]` <input/output parameter name> <description>

- \return <description of the return result>
- \code <block of code> \endcode
- \verbatim <verbatim text block> \endverbatim
- \exception <exception-object> <description>
- \deprecated <explanation and alternatives>
- \attention <message that needs attention>
- \warning <warning message>
- \since <API version or date when the entity was added>
- \version <version string>
- \bug <description of bug>
- \see <cross-references to other methods or classes>

In addition to these commands, Doxygen supports various formatting commands to change the style of the next word. These include \b (bold), \c (typewriter font), and \e (italics). You can also use \n to force a new line, \\ to enter a backslash character, and \@ to enter the at sign.

9.4.3 **API Comments**

Doxygen allows you to specify overview documentation for your entire API using the \mainpage comment. This lets you provide a high-level description of the API, as well as provide a breakdown of the major classes. This description will appear on the front page of the documentation that Doxygen produces. It is common to store these comments in a separate file, such as overview.dox (this requires updating the FILE_PATTERNS entry of the Doxygen configuration file to include *.dox).

The text in this overview documentation may be long enough to justify breaking into separate sections. In which case, you can use the \section and \subsection commands to introduce this structure. You can even create separate pages to contain more detailed descriptions for certain parts of your API. This can be done with the \page command.

Also, you may find it useful to define groups of behavior for your API so that you can break up the various classes in your API into different categories. For example, you could create groups for classes or files pertaining to file handling, container classes, logging, versioning, and so on. This is done by declaring a group with \defgroup and then using the \ingroup to add any specific element to that group.

Putting these features together, the following comment provides overview documentation for an entire API, which is broken down into three sections and cross-references two additional pages for more detailed descriptions. The pages include a link to show all of the API elements that have been tagged as part of a given group.

```
///
/// \mainpage API Documentation
///
/// \section sec_Contents Contents
///
/// \li \ref sec_Overview
/// \li \ref sec_Detail
/// \li \ref sec_SeeAlso
```

```
///
/// \section sec_Overview Overview
///
/// Your overview text here.
///
/// \section sec_Detail Detailed Description
///
/// Your more detailed description here.
///
/// \section sec_SeeAlso See Also
///
/// \li \ref page_Logging
/// \li \ref page_Versioning
///
///
/// \page page_Logging The Logging System
///
/// Overview of logging functionality
///
/// \link group_Logging View All Logging Classes \endlink
///
///
/// \page page_Versioning API Versioning
///
/// Overview of API Versioning
///
/// \link group_Versioning View All Versioning Classes \endlink
///

/// \defgroup group_Logging Diagnostic logging features
/// See \ref page_Logging for a detailed description.

/// \defgroup group_Versioning Versioning System
/// See \ref page_Versioning for a detailed description.
```

The resulting Doxygen HTML output for this comment (using the default style sheet) is shown in Figure 9.3.

9.4.4 File Comments

You can place a comment at the top of each header file to provide documentation for the entire module. Here's a sample template for these per-file comments.

```
///
/// \file <filename>
///
/// \brief <brief description>
///
```

FIGURE 9.3

The Doxygen HTML output for the \mainpage example.

```
/// \author <list of author names>
/// \date <date description>
/// \since <API version when added>
///
/// <description of module>
///
/// <license and copyright information>
///
```

If this file contains functionality that you want to add to a group that you've defined, then you can also add the \ingroup command to this comment.

9.4.5 Class Comments

Each class in your header can also have a comment to describe the overall purpose of the class. In addition to the sample template given here, you may consider including the \ingroup command if the class belongs to a group you've defined, \deprecated if the class has been deprecated, or \code ... \endcode if you want to provide some example code.

```
///
/// \class <class name> [header-file] [header-name]
///
```

```
/// \brief <brief description>
///
/// <detailed description>
///
/// \author <list of author names>
/// \date <date description>
/// \since <API version when added>
///
```

9.4.6 Method Comments

You can provide documentation for individual methods, detailing the name and a description for each parameter (and optionally if they are in, out, or in/out parameters), as well as a description of the return value. As with the class sample template, you may also consider adding \ingroup or \deprecated, as appropriate.

```
///
/// \brief <brief description>
///
/// <detailed description>
///
/// \param[in] <input parameter name> <description>
/// \param[out] <output parameter name> <description>
/// \return <description of the return value>
/// \since <API version when added>
/// \see <methods to list in the see also section>
/// \note <optional note about the method>
///
```

If you have methods in a class that fall into one or more logical groupings, you can specify this to Doxygen so that it will group the related methods together under a named subsection. This can be used to provide a more appropriate ordering of the class members instead of Doxygen's default behavior. The following code snippet demonstrates the specification of two such member groups:

```
class Test
{
public:
    /// \name <group1-name>
    //@{
    void Method1InGroup1();
    void Method2InGroup1();
    //@}

    /// \name <group2-name>
    //@{
    void Method1InGroup2();
    void Method2InGroup2();
    //@}
};
```

9.4.7 **Enum Comments**

Doxygen also lets you provide comments for enums, including documentation for individual values in the enum. The latter can be done using Doxygen's < comment syntax, which attaches the documentation to the previous element instead of the next element.

```
///
/// \brief <brief description>
///
/// <detailed description>
///
enum MyEnum {
    ENUM_1,  ///< description of enum value ENUM_1
    ENUM_2,  ///< description of enum value ENUM_2
    ENUM_3   ///< description of enum value ENUM_3
}
```

9.4.8 **Sample Header with Documentation**

Putting all of the preceding advice together, here's an entire header file with Doxygen style comments to describe the file, class, and each method. This example is provided in the supporting source code for the book, along with the generated HTML output that Doxygen produced for this file.

```
///
/// \file  version.h
///
/// \brief Access the API's version information.
///
/// \author Martin Reddy
/// \date   2010-07-07
/// \since 1.0
/// \ingroup group_Versioning
///
/// Copyright (c) 2010, Martin Reddy. All rights reserved.
///

#ifndef VERSION_H
#define VERSION_H

#include <string>

///
/// \class Version version.h API/version.h
///
/// \brief Access the version information for the API
///
/// For example, you can get the current version number as
/// a string using \c GetVersion, or you can get the separate
/// major, minor, and patch integer values by calling
```

```
/// \c GetMajor, \c GetMinor, or \c GetPatch, respectively.
///
/// This class also provides some basic version comparison
/// functionality and lets you determine if certain named
/// features are present in your current build.
///
/// \author Martin Reddy
/// \date 2010-07-07
/// \since 1.0
///
class Version
{
public:
    /// \name Version Numbers
    //@{
    ///
    /// \brief Return the API major version number.
    /// \return The major version number as an integer.
    /// \since 1.0
    ///
    static int GetMajor();
    ///
    /// \brief Return the API minor version number.
    /// \return The minor version number as an integer.
    /// \since 1.0
    ///
    static int GetMinor();
    ///
    /// \brief Return the API patch version number.
    /// \return The patch version number as an integer.
    /// \since 1.0
    ///
    static int GetPatch();
    ///
    /// \brief Return the API full version number.
    /// \return The version string, e.g., "1.0.1".
    /// \since 1.0
    ///
    static std::string GetVersion();
    //@}

    /// \name Version Number Math
    //@{
    ///
    /// \brief Compare the current version number against a specific
    ///   version.
    ///
```

```
/// This method lets you check to see if the current version
/// is greater than or equal to the specified version. This may
/// be useful to perform operations that require a minimum
/// version number.
///
/// \param[in] major The major version number to compare against
/// \param[in] minor The minor version number to compare against
/// \param[in] patch The patch version number to compare against
/// \return Returns true if specified version >= current version
/// \since 1.0
///
static bool IsAtLeast(int major, int minor, int patch);
//@}

/// \name Feature Tags
//@{
///
/// \brief Test whether a feature is implemented by this API.
///
/// New features that change the implementation of API methods
/// are specified as "feature tags." This method lets you
/// query the API to find out if a given feature is available.
///
/// \param[in] name The feature tag name, e.g., "LOCKING"
/// \return Returns true if the named feature is available.
/// \since 1.0
///
static bool HasFeature(const std::string &name);
//@}
};

#endif
```

Testing

Every developer, no matter how experienced and meticulous, will introduce bugs into the software they write. This is simply inevitable as an API grows in size and complexity. The purpose of testing is to locate these defects as early as possible so that they can be addressed before they affect your clients.

Modern software development relies heavily on the use of third-party APIs. As your own APIs become more ubiquitous, failures and defects in your code will have the potential to affect a large number of clients and their end-user applications.

As noted earlier, your clients may eventually seek alternative solutions if the code that you deliver is buggy, unpredictable, or crashes regularly. Conscientious testing is therefore a critical part of your API development process because it can be used to increase the reliability and stability of your product. This will ultimately contribute to the success of your API in the marketplace.

> **TIP**
>
> Writing automated tests is the most important thing you can do to ensure that you don't break your users' programs.

This chapter covers various types of automated testing that you can employ, such as unit testing, integration testing, and performance testing. I will also look at how to write good tests, as well as the equally important factor of how to design and implement APIs that are more amenable to testing. Finally, I will complement this discussion by surveying some of the testing tools that you can adopt for your project and look at how you can write tests using a number of popular automated testing frameworks. Along the way, I will discuss process issues such as collaborating with a QA team, using quality metrics, and how to integrate testing into your build process.

10.1 REASONS TO WRITE TESTS

It is a common fallacy that engineers don't like to write tests. From my experience, every good developer understands the need for testing and most have encountered cases where testing has caught a bug in their code. At the end of the day, software engineers are craftspeople who take pride in their work and will probably find it demoralizing to be expected to produce low-quality results. However, if management for a project does not explicitly incorporate the need for testing into the schedule, then engineers are not given the resources and support they need to develop these tests. In general, a software project can pick among being date driven, quality driven, or feature driven. You can pick two of these, but not all three. For example, in the case of the waterfall development process, feature creep and unforeseen problems can easily eliminate any time at the end of a project that was reserved for testing. Consequently, an engineer who attempts to spend time writing automated tests can appear to be less productive within a date- or feature-driven process. Instead, if engineers are empowered to focus on quality, I believe that they will relish the opportunity to write tests for their code.

I experienced this firsthand at Pixar, where we decided to introduce a new policy that engineers had to write unit tests for their code, and furthermore, that all non-GUI code had to achieve 100% code coverage. That is, every line of non-GUI code had to be exercised from test code. Rather than incite a mass rebellion, we found that developers thought this was a good use of their time. The key enabling factor was that we added time to the end of each iteration where all developers could focus on writing tests for their code. Even after 2 years of following this policy, there was universal agreement that the benefits of writing tests outweighed the costs and that maintaining a 100% coverage target was still appropriate.

In case you still need some incentive, here are some reasons why you should employ testing for your own projects.

- **Increased confidence**. Having an extensive suite of automated tests can give you the confidence to make changes to the behavior of an API with the knowledge that you are not breaking functionality. Said differently, testing can reduce your fear of implementing a change. It's quite common to find legacy systems where engineers are uneasy changing certain parts of the code because those parts are so complex and opaque that changes to its behavior could have unforeseen consequences (Feathers, 2004). Furthermore, the code in question may have been written by an engineer who is no longer with the organization, meaning that there is no one who knows "where the bodies are buried" in the code.
- **Ensuring backward compatibility**. It's important to know that you have not introduced changes in a new version of the API that breaks backward compatibility for code written against an older version of the API or for data files generated by that older API. Automated tests can be used to capture the workflows and behavior from earlier versions so that these are always exercised in the latest version of the library.
- **Saving costs**. It is a well-known fact that fixing defects later in the development cycle is more expensive than fixing them earlier. This is because the defect becomes more deeply embedded in the code and exorcising it may also involve updating many data files. For example, Steve McConnell gives evidence that fixing a bug after release can be 10–25 times more expensive than during development (McConnell, 2004). Developing a suite of automated tests lets you discover defects earlier so that they can be fixed earlier, and hence more economically overall.
- **Codify use cases**. Use cases for an API represent supported workflows that your users should be able to accomplish. Developing tests for these use cases before you implement your API can let you know when you have achieved the required functionality. These same tests can then be used on an ongoing basis to catch any regressions in these high-level workflows.
- **Compliance assurance**. Software for use in certain safety- or security-critical applications may have to pass regulatory tests, such as Federal Aviation Administration certification. Also, some organizations may verify that your software conforms to their standards before allowing it to be branded as such. For example, the Open Geospatial Consortium (OGC) has a compliance testing program for software that is to be branded as "Certified OGC Compliant." Automated tests can be used to ensure that you continue to conform to these regulatory and standards requirements.

These points can be summarized by stating that automated testing can help you determine whether you are building the right thing (referred to as validation) and if you are building it right (called verification).

It is worth noting that there can be a downside to writing many tests. As the size of your test suite grows, the maintenance for these tests also grows commensurately. This can result in situations where a good code change that takes a couple of minutes to make might also break hundreds of tests and require many hours of effort to also update the test suite. This is a bad situation to get into because it disincentivizes an engineer from making a good fix due only to the overhead of updating the tests. I will discuss ways to avoid this situation in the following sections. However, it's worth noting that if the fix in question changes the public API, then the extra barrier may be a good thing as it forces the engineer to consider the potential impact on backward compatibility for existing clients.

THE COST OF UNTESTED CODE

There are many examples of catastrophic software failures that have happened over the years. Numerous Web sites maintain catalogs of these bugs, such as the Software Failures List at `http://www.sereferences.com/software-failure-list.php`. In many of these cases, more thorough testing would have averted disaster. For example, in May 1996, a software bug caused the bank accounts of 823 customers of a major U.S. bank to be credited with $924,844,208.32 each. The American Bankers Association described this as the largest error in U.S. banking history. It happened because the bank added new message codes to its ATM transaction software but failed to test them on all ATM protocols.

As an example of the need for backward-compatibility testing, the Tokyo stock exchange halted trading for most of a day during November 2005 due to a software glitch after a systems upgrade.

Failing to meet client requirements can have a large impact on your business. For example, in November 2007, a regional government in the United States brought a multimillion dollar lawsuit against a software services vendor because the criminal justice information software they delivered "minimized quality" and did not meet requirements.

Finally, as an example of the importance of compliance testing, in January 2009, regulators banned a large U.S. health insurance company from selling Medicare programs because of computer errors that posed "a serious threat to the health and safety of Medicare beneficiaries."

10.2 TYPES OF API TESTING

Testing an API is very different from testing an end-user application. However, there are still various techniques that are applicable to both. For example, a common general categorization of software testing activities is:

1. **White box testing**: Tests are developed with knowledge of the source code and are normally written using a programming language.
2. **Black box testing**: Tests are developed based on product specifications and without any knowledge of the underlying implementation. These tests are often performed by manually exercising an end-user application, although they could also be applied to writing code that tests an API based solely on the API specification.
3. **Gray box testing**: A combination of white box and black box testing, where black box testing is performed with knowledge of the implementation details of the software.

These terms can be applied equally to API testing and end-user application testing. However, APIs are not end-user applications: they can only be used by writing code that calls functions defined within a library file. As a result, several types of traditional software testing techniques are not applicable to API testing.

For example, the term system testing refers to testing performed on a complete integrated system. This is normally assumed to be an actual application that can be run by a user. While it is conceivable to consider a large API as a complete integrated system, I will not take that view here. I will instead subscribe to the view that an API is a building block or component that is used to build entire systems. As such, I will not consider system testing to be part of the tasks involved in testing an API.

Furthermore, the area of automated GUI testing is generally not appropriate for APIs, that is, the task of writing automated scripts that run an end-user application and simulate user interactions, such as clicking on buttons or typing text. The exception to this would be if you are actually writing a GUI toolkit that creates these button and text entry widgets. However, in this case, you (and your clients) would be well served by creating a custom testing tool that can navigate and interact with your widget hierarchy for the purposes of automated testing. For example, Froglogic provides an automated GUI testing tool for Qt applications called Squish.

In general, manual testing techniques are not applicable to API tests because there is no user interface to manipulate. Therefore, our focus here will be on tests that are written in code and that can be automated. Automated tests are ones that are executed programmatically on a regular basis, such as during the build process for your API. If tests are not automated, then there is more chance that they won't be run at all, which would defeat the point of writing them.

Consequently, the primary functional test strategies that I'll concentrate on here are unit testing and integration testing. Unit testing verifies that the software does what the programmer expects, while integration testing satisfies the client that the software addresses their needs. You can also write tests to verify the non-functional requirements of your API. Performance testing is one such example of non-functional testing, and I will cover this topic in detail later in this chapter too. However, there are many other types of non-functional testing techniques. The following list provides a selection of some of the most common ones.

- **Performance testing**: Verifies that the functionality of your API meets minimum speed or memory usage requirements.
- **Load testing**: Puts demand, or stress, on a system and measures its ability to handle this load. This often refers to testing with many simultaneous users or performing many API requests per second. This is sometimes also called stress testing.
- **Scalability testing**: Ensures that the system can handle large and complex production data inputs instead of only simple test data sets. This is sometimes also called capacity or volume testing.
- **Soak testing**: Attempts to run software continuously over an extended period to satisfy clients that it is robust and can handle sustained use (e.g., that there are no major memory leaks, counter overflows, or timer-related bugs).
- **Security testing**: Ensures that any security requirements of your code are met, such as the confidentiality, authentication, authorization, integrity, and availability of sensitive information.
- **Concurrency testing**: Verifies the multithreaded behavior of your code to ensure that it behaves correctly and does not deadlock.

> **TIP**
>
> API testing should involve a combination of unit and integration testing. Non-functional techniques can also be applied as appropriate, such as performance, concurrency, and security testing.

10.2.1 Unit Testing

A unit test is used to verify a single minimal unit of source code, such as an individual method or class. The purpose of unit testing is to isolate the smallest testable parts of an API and verify that they function correctly in isolation.

These kinds of tests tend to run very fast and often take the form of a sequence of assertions that return either true or false, where any false result will fail the test. Very often these tests are colocated with the code that they test (such as in a `tests` subdirectory), and they can be compiled and run at the same point that the code itself is compiled. Unit tests tend to be written by developers using knowledge of the implementation; therefore, unit testing is a white box testing technique.

> **TIP**
>
> Unit testing is a white box technique used to verify the behavior of functions and classes in isolation.

To give a concrete example of a unit test, let's consider a function you want to test that converts a string to a double:

```
bool StringToDouble(const std::string &str, double *result);
```

This function accepts a string parameter and returns a boolean to indicate whether the conversion was successful. If successful, the double value is written to the `result` pointer parameter. Given this function, the following unit test performs a series of checks to ensure that it works as expected.

```
void Test_StringToDouble()
{
    double value;

    Assert(StringToDouble("1", &value), "+ve test");
    AssertEqual(value, 1.0, "'1' == 1.0");

    Assert(StringToDouble("-1", &value), "-ve test");
    AssertEqual(value, -1.0, "'-1' == -1.0");

    Assert(StringToDouble("0.0", &value), "zero");
    AssertEqual(value, 0.0, "'0.0' == 0.0");

    Assert(StringToDouble("-0", &value), "minus zero");
    AssertEqual(value, -0.0, "'-0' == -0.0");
    AssertEqual(value, 0.0, "'-0' == 0.0");

    Assert(StringToDouble("3.14159265", &value), "pi");
    AssertEqual(value, 3.14159265, "pi value");
```

```
Assert(StringToDouble("2e10", &value), "large scientific");
AssertEqual(value, 2e10, "");

Assert(StringToDouble("+4.3e-10", &value), "small scientific");
AssertEqual(value, 4.3e-10, "");

AssertFalse(StringToDouble("", &value), "empty");
AssertFalse(StringToDouble(" ", &value), "whitespace");
AssertFalse(StringToDouble("+-1", &value), "+-");
AssertFalse(StringToDouble("1.1.0", &value), "multiple points");
AssertFalse(StringToDouble("text", &value), "not a number");

std::cout << "SUCCESS!" << std::endl;
}
```

Note the use of various helper functions to test the result of each operation: `Assert()`, `AssertFalse()`, and `AssertEqual()`. These are common functions in unit test frameworks that follow the JUnit style, although sometimes other similar function names or capitalizations are used. If any of these JUnit-style assertions fail, then the entire test will fail, normally with a descriptive error message that pinpoints the failure.

JUNIT

JUnit is a unit testing framework that was originally developed for the Java programming language by Kent Beck and Erich Gamma. It is designed around two key design patterns: Command and Composite.

Each test case is a command object that defines one or more `test*()` methods, such as `testMyObject()`, as well as optional `setUp()` and `tearDown()` methods. Multiple test cases can be collated within a test suite. That is, the test suite is a composite of test cases that automatically calls all of the `test*()` methods.

JUnit also provides a number of methods to support assertion-based testing, such as `assertEquals()`, `assertNull()`, `assertTrue()`, and `assertSame()`. If any of these is passed an expression that evaluates to false, then the test case will be marked as failed.

Since the initial popularity of JUnit, the framework has been ported to many other languages and has become known by the more general moniker of xUnit. For example, there is PyUnit for Python, CUnit for C, and CppUnit for C++, among many other implementations.

The example just given is intentionally simple. However, in real software the method or object under test often depends on other objects in the system or on external resources such as files on disk, records in a database, or software on a remote server. This leads to two different views of unit testing.

1. **Fixture setup**. The classic approach to unit testing is to initialize a consistent environment, or fixture, before each unit test is run. For example, to ensure that dependent objects and singletons are initialized, to copy a specific set of files to a known location, or to load a database with a prepared set of initial data. This is often done in a `setUp()` function associated with each test to differentiate test setup steps from the actual test operations. A related `tearDown()` function is often used to clean up the environment once the test finishes. One of the benefits of this approach is that the same fixture can often be reused for many tests.

2. **Stub/mock objects**. In this approach, the code under test is isolated from the rest of the system by creating stub or mock objects that stand in for any dependencies outside of the unit (Mackinnon et al., 2001). For example, if a unit test needs to communicate with a database, a stub database object can be created that accepts the subset of queries that the unit will generate and then return canned data in response, without making any actual connection to the database. The result is a completely isolated test that will not be affected by database problems, network issues, or file system permissions. The downside, however, is that the creation of these stub objects can be tedious and often they cannot be reused by other unit tests. However, mock objects tend to be more flexible and can be customized for individual tests. I'll discuss each of these options in more detail later in the chapter.

> **TIP**
>
> If your code depends on an unreliable resource, such as a database, file system, or network, consider using stub or mock objects to produce more robust unit tests.

10.2.2 Integration Testing

In contrast to unit testing, integration testing is concerned with the interaction of several components cooperating together. Ideally, the individual components have already been unit tested.

Integration tests are still necessary even if you have a high degree of unit test coverage because testing individual units of code in isolation does not guarantee that they can be used together easily and efficiently or that they meet your functional requirements and use cases. For example, the interface of one component may be incompatible with another component or information required by another component may not be exposed appropriately for another component to use. The goal of integration testing is therefore to ensure that all of the components of your API work together well, are consistent, and enable the user to perform the tasks they need.

Integration tests are normally developed against the specification of the API, such as any automatically generated API documentation, and should therefore not require understanding of the internal implementation details. That is, they are written from the perspective of your clients. As such, integration testing is a black box testing technique.

> **TIP**
>
> Integration testing is a black box technique to verify the interaction of several components together.

You can often use the same tools to implement integration tests that you use to write unit tests. However, integration tests usually involve more complex ways to verify that a sequence of operations was successful. For example, a test may generate an output file that must be compared against a "golden" or "baseline" version that is stored with the test in your revision control system. This requires an efficient workflow to update the baseline version in cases where the failure is expected, such as the conscious addition of new elements in the data file or changing the behavior of a function to fix a bug.

A good integration testing framework will therefore include dedicated comparison functions (or diff commands) for each file type that the API can produce. For example, an API may have an ASCII configuration file, where an integration test failure should only be triggered if the value or number of settings changes, but not if the order of the settings in the file changes or if different whitespace

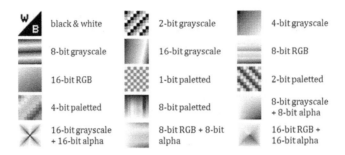

FIGURE 10.1

A subset of Willem van Schaik's PNG image test suite, called PngSuite. See http://www.schaik.com/ for details.

characters are used to separate settings. As another example, an API may produce an image as its result. You therefore need a way to compare the output image against a baseline version of that image. For example, the R&D team at PDI/Dreamworks developed a perceptual image difference utility to verify that the rendered images for their film assets are visibly the same after a change to their animation system. This perceptually based comparison allows for minor imperceptible differences in the actual pixel values to avoid unnecessary failures (Yee and Newman, 2004).

This last example brings up the point that integration testing may also be data driven. That is, a single test program can be called many times with different input data. For example, a C++ parser may be verified with a single integration test that reads a `.cpp` source file and outputs its derivation or abstract syntax tree. That test can then be called many times with different C++ source programs and its output compared against a correct baseline version in each case. Similarly, the libpng library has a `pngtest.c` program that reads an image and then writes it out again. This test is then run in a data-driven fashion using Willem van Schaik's suite of representative PNG images called PngSuite. Figure 10.1 shows a few of the images in PngSuite. This integration test ensures that new changes to libpng do not break its ability to read and write various combinations of the PNG file format, including basic chunk handling, compression, interlacing, alpha transparency, filtering, gamma, and image comments, among other attributes.

Integration testing of APIs can be performed by developers, but in larger organizations it can also be a task that your QA team performs. In fact, a QA engineer will probably refer to this activity as API testing, which is a term that often implies ownership by QA. I've avoided using the specific term API testing here simply because this entire chapter is about testing APIs.

Given that integration tests have a different focus than unit tests, may be maintained by a different team, and normally must be run after the build has completed successfully, these kinds of tests are therefore usually located in a different directory than unit tests. For example, they may live in a sibling directory to the top-level source directory rather than being stored next to the actual code inside the source directory. This strategy also reflects the black box nature of integration tests as compared to white box unit tests.

10.2.3 Performance Testing

Typically, your users will demand a reasonable level of performance from your API. For instance, if you have written a library that provides real-time collision detection between 3D objects for a game engine, your implementation must run fast enough during each frame that it doesn't slow down your clients' games. You could therefore write a performance test for your collision detection code where the test will fail if it exceeds a predefined performance threshold.

As a further example, when Apple was developing their Safari Web browser, page rendering speed was of paramount concern. They therefore added performance tests and defined acceptable speed thresholds for each test. They then put a process in place whereby a checkin would be rejected if it caused a performance test to exceed its threshold. Engineers would have to optimize their code (or somebody else's code if their code was already optimal) before it could be checked in.

TIP

Performance testing of your key use cases helps you avoid introducing speed or memory regressions unknowingly.

A related issue is that of stress testing, where you verify that your implementation can scale to the real-world demands of your users, for example, a Web site that can handle many simultaneous users or a particle system that can handle thousands or millions of particles.

These are classified as non-functional tests because they do not test the correctness of a specific feature of your API, but instead are concerned with its operational behavior in the user's environment. That is, they test the non-functional requirements of your API.

The benefit of writing automated performance tests is that you can make sure that new changes do not adversely impact performance. For example, a senior engineer I worked with once refactored a data loading API to use a `std::string` object instead of a `char` buffer to store successive characters read from a data file. When the change was released, users found that the system took over 10 times longer to load their data files. It turns out that the `std::string::append()` method was reallocating the string each time, growing it by a single byte on each call and hence causing massive amounts of memory allocations to happen. This was ultimately fixed by using a `std::vector<char>` because the `append()` method for that container behaved more optimally. A performance test that monitored the time to load large data files could have discovered this regression before it was released to clients.

TIP

If performance is important for your API, consider writing performance tests for your key use cases to avoid unwittingly introducing performance regressions.

However, performance tests tend to be much more difficult to write and maintain than unit or integration tests. One reason for this is that performance test results are real (floating-point) numbers that can vary from run to run. They are not discrete true or false values. It's therefore advisable to specify a tolerance for each test to deal with the variability of each test run. For example, you might specify 10 ms as the threshold for your collision detection algorithm, but allow for a 15% fluctuation before marking the test as failed. Another technique is to only fail the test after several consecutive data points exceed the threshold to factor out anomalous spikes in performance.

Also, it's best to have dedicated hardware for running your performance tests so that other processes running on the machine do not interfere with the test results. Even with a dedicated machine, you may need to investigate turning off certain system background processes so that they don't affect your timings. This reveals another reason why performance tests are difficult to maintain: they are machine specific. This implies that you need to store different threshold values for each class of machine that you run the tests on.

A further complication of performance testing is the problem of information overload. You may end up with hundreds or even thousands of combinations of each performance test on different hardware, each producing multiple data points throughout a single day. As a result, you will want to store all of your performance results in a database. Also, if you don't have automatic measures to highlight tests that have exceeded their performance threshold, then you may never notice regressions. However, with so many tests, you will likely be inundated with false positives and spend most of your time updating baseline values. At this point, you may have more success considering the issue to be a data mining problem. In other words, collect as much data as possible and then have regular database searches that pick the top 5 or 10 most egregious changes in performance and flag those for investigation by a human.

Mozilla offers a fantastic example of extensive performance testing done well. They have implemented a system where performance tests are run for multiple products across a range of hardware. Results can be browsed with an interactive Web site that displays graphs for one or more performance tests at the same time (see Figure 10.2). For example, the Firefox Web browser has various performance tests, such as startup time, shutdown time, page load time, and DHTML performance.

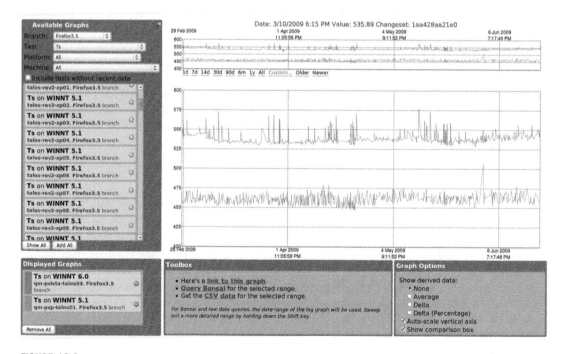

FIGURE 10.2

Mozilla performance test results at http://graphs.mozilla.org/. This example shows startup time results (Ts) for two builds of Firefox 3.5.

The Mozilla graphs Web site will let you pick a version of Firefox, select a test you're interested in, and then see the performance results for that test for a particular machine. You can then add the results for other machines to the graph to compare performance between those setups. (One thing to look out for when reading performance graphs is whether the y axis starts at zero. If results are scaled vertically to fit the screen, then what looks like a large degree of fluctuation could in reality be a tiny overall percentage change.)

10.3 WRITING GOOD TESTS

Now that I've covered the basic types of API testing, I will concentrate on how to write these automated tests. I will cover the qualities that make a good test as well as present standard techniques for writing efficient and thorough tests. I'll also discuss how testing can be shared with a QA team effectively.

10.3.1 Qualities of a Good Test

Before I discuss the details of writing an automated test, I'll present a few high-level attributes of a good test. These are general qualities that you should always bear in mind when building out your test suite. The overall message, however, is that you should treat test code with the same exacting standards that you use in your main API code. If you develop tests that exhibit the following qualities then you should end up with an easy-to-maintain and robust test suite that provides you with a valuable safety net for your API development.

- **Fast**. Your suite of tests should run very quickly so that you get rapid feedback on test failures. Unit tests should always be very fast: in the order of fractions of a second per test. Integration tests that perform actual user workflows, or data-driven integration tests that are run on many input files, may take longer to execute. However, there are several ways to deal with this, such as favoring the creation of many unit tests but a few targeted integration tests. Also, you can have different categories of tests: "fast" (or "checkin" or "continuous") tests run during every build cycle, whereas "slow" (or "complete" or "acceptance") tests run only occasionally, such as before a release.
- **Stable**. Tests should be repeatable, independent, and consistent: every time you run a specific version of a test you should get the same result. If a test starts failing erroneously or erratically then your faith in the validity of that test's results will be diminished. You may even be tempted to turn the test off temporarily, which of course defeats the purpose of having the test. Using mock objects, where all dependencies of a unit test are simulated, is one way to produce tests that are independent and stable to environmental conditions. It's also the only practical way to test date- or time-dependent code.
- **Portable**. If your API is implemented on multiple platforms, your tests should work across the same range of platforms. One of the most common areas of difference for test code running on different platforms is floating point comparisons. Rounding errors, architecture differences, and compiler differences can cause mathematical operations to produce slightly different results on different platforms. Floating point comparisons should therefore allow for a small error, or epsilon, rather than being compared exactly. It's important to note that this epsilon should be relative

to the magnitude of the numbers involved and the precision of the floating-point type used. For instance, single-precision floats can represent only six to seven digits of precision. Therefore, an epsilon of 0.000001 may be appropriate when comparing numbers such as 1.234567, but an epsilon of 0.1 would be more appropriate when comparing numbers such as 123456.7.

- **High coding standards**. Test code should follow the same coding standards as the rest of your API: you should not slip standards just because the code will not be run directly by your users. Tests should be well documented so that it's clear what is being tested and what a failure would imply. If you enforce code reviews for your API code, you should do the same for test code. Similarly, you should not abandon your good engineering instincts simply because you are writing a test. If there is a case for factoring out common test code into a reusable test library, then you should do this. As the size of your test suite grows, you could end up with hundreds or thousands of tests. The need for robust and maintainable test code is therefore just as imperative as for your main API code.

- **Reproducible failure**. If a test fails, it should be easy to reproduce the failure. This means logging as much information as possible about the failure, pinpointing the actual point of failure as accurately as possible, and making it easy for a developer to run the failing test in a debugger. Some systems employ randomized testing (called ad hoc testing) where the test space is so large that random samples are chosen. In these cases, you should ensure that it is easy to reproduce the specific conditions that caused the failure because simply rerunning the test will pick another random sample and may pass.

10.3.2 **What to Test**

Finally, we get to the part about actually writing tests. The way you write a unit test is different from the way you write an integration test. This is because unit tests can have knowledge about the internal structure of the code, such as loops and conditions. However, in both cases the aim is to exercise the capabilities of the API methodically. To this end, there is a range of standard QA techniques that you can employ to test your API. A few of the most pertinent ones are listed here.

- **Condition testing**. When writing unit tests, you should use your knowledge of the code under test to exercise all combinations of any if/else, for, while, and switch expressions within the unit. This ensures that all possible paths through the code have been tested. (I will discuss the details of statement coverage versus decision coverage later in the chapter when I look at code coverage tools.)

- **Equivalence classes**. An equivalence class is a set of test inputs that all have the same expected behavior. The technique of equivalence class partitioning therefore attempts to find test inputs that exercise difference classes of behavior. For example, consider a square root function that is documented to accept values in the range 0 to 65535. In this case there are three equivalence classes: negative numbers, the valid range of numbers, and numbers greater than 65535. You should therefore test this function with values from each of these three equivalence classes, for example, −10, 100, 100000.

- **Boundary conditions**. Most errors occur around the boundary of expected values. How many times have you inadvertently written code with an "off-by-one" error? Boundary condition analysis focuses test cases around these boundary values. For example, if you are testing a routine that inserts an element into a linked list of length n, you should test inserting at position 0, 1, $n-1$, and n.

- **Parameter testing**. A test for a given API call should vary all parameters to the function to verify the full range of functionality. For example, the `stdio.h` function `fopen()` accepts a second argument to specify the file mode. This can take the values "r," "w," and "a," in addition to optional "+" and "b" characters in each case. A thorough test for this function should therefore test all 12 combinations of the mode parameter to verify the full breadth of behavior.

- **Return value assertion**. This form of testing ensures that a function returns correct results for different combinations of its input parameters. These results could be the return value of the function, but they could additionally include output parameters that are passed as pointers or references. For instance, a simple integer multiplication function,

```
int Multiply(int x, int y)
```

could be tested by supplying a range of (x, y) inputs and checking the results against a table of known correct values.

- **Getter/setter pairs**. The use of getter/setter methods is extremely common in C++ APIs, and of course I've advocated that you should always prefer the use of these functions over directly exposing member variables in a class. You should therefore test that calling the getter before calling the setter returns an appropriate default result, and that calling the getter after the setter will return the appropriate value, for example,

```
AssertEqual(obj.GetValue(), 0, "test default");
obj.SetValue(42);
AssertEqual(obj.GetValue(), 42, "test set then get");
```

- **Operation order**. Varying the sequence of operations to perform the same test (where this is possible) can help uncover any order of execution assumptions and non-orthogonal behavior, that is, if API calls have undocumented side effects that are being relied upon to achieve certain workflows.

- **Regression testing**. Backward compatibility with earlier versions of the API should be maintained whenever possible. It is therefore extremely valuable to have tests that verify this goal. For example, a test could try reading data files that were generated by older versions of the API to ensure that the latest version can still ingest them correctly. It's important that these data files are never updated to newer formats when the API is modified. That is, you will end up with live data files, which are up to date for the current version, and legacy data files, which verify the backward compatibility of the API.

- **Negative testing**. This testing technique constructs or forces error conditions to see how the code reacts to unexpected situations. For example, if an API call attempts to read a file on disk, a negative test might try deleting that file, or making it unreadable, to see how the API reacts when it is unable to read the contents of the file. Another example of negative testing is supplying invalid data for an API call. For example, a credit card payment system that accepts credit card numbers should be tested with invalid credit card numbers (negative testing) as well as valid numbers (positive testing).

- **Buffer overruns**. A buffer overrun, or overflow, is when memory is written past the end of an allocated buffer. This causes unallocated memory to be modified, often resulting in data corruption and ultimately a crash. Data corruption errors can be difficult to track down because the crash may occur some time after the actual buffer overrun event. It is therefore good practice to check that an API does not write to memory beyond the size of a buffer. This buffer could be an internal private member of a class or it could be a parameter that you pass into an API call. For example, the `string.h` function `strncpy()` copies at most *n* characters from one string to another. This could be tested by supplying source strings that are equal to and longer than *n* characters and then verifying that no more than *n* characters (including the null terminator, \0) are written to the destination buffer.

- **Memory ownership.** Memory errors are a common cause of crashes in C++ programs. Any API calls that return dynamically allocated memory should document whether the API owns the memory or if the client is responsible for freeing it. These specifications should be tested to ensure that they are correct. For example, if the client is responsible for freeing the memory, a test could request the dynamic object twice and assert that the two pointers are different. A further test could free the memory and then rerequest the object from the API multiple times to ensure that no memory corruption or crashes occur.

- **NULL input.** Another common source of crashes in C++ is passing a NULL pointer to a function that then immediately attempts to dereference the pointer without checking for NULL. You should therefore test all functions that accept a pointer parameter to ensure that they behave gracefully when passed a NULL pointer.

10.3.3 Focusing the Testing Effort

In all likelihood, it will be infeasible to test every possible code path in your API. You will therefore be faced with a decision over which subset of the overall functionality to test. To help you focus your testing effort, the following list enumerates seven ways to determine the biggest bang for your testing buck.

1. Focus on tests that exercise primary use cases or workflows of the API.
2. Focus on tests that cover multiple features or offer the widest code coverage.
3. Focus on the code that is the most complex and hence the highest risk.
4. Focus on parts of the design that are poorly defined.
5. Focus on features with the highest performance or security concerns.
6. Focus on testing problems that would cause the worst impact on clients.
7. Focus early testing efforts on features that can be completed early in the development cycle.

10.3.4 Working with QA

If you are fortunate enough to have a good QA team to support your testing efforts, then they can share responsibility for writing automated tests. For example, it's standard practice for developers to write and own unit tests and for QA to write and own integration tests.

Different software development models produce different interactions with QA. For example, a traditional waterfall method, where testing is performed as a final step before release, means that QA is often treated as a distinct group whose goal of quality is often impacted negatively by delays during the development process. In contrast, more agile development processes, such as Scrum, favor embedding QA as part of the development process and including testing responsibilities within each short sprint or iteration.

In either case, the benefit of working with QA engineers is that they become your first users. As such, they can help ensure that the functional and business requirements of your API are met.

As noted earlier, API testing generally requires writing code because an API is software used to build end-user applications. This implies that your QA engineers must be able to write code in order to work on integration testing effectively. Related to this, Microsoft has traditionally used two broad terms to categorize QA engineers:

1. **A Software Test Engineer (STE)** has limited programming experience and may not even need a strong computer science background. An STE essentially performs manual black box testing.
2. **A Software Design Engineer in Test (SDET)** is able to write code and so is capable of performing white box testing, writing tools, and producing automated tests.

In terms of API testing, you will therefore want a QA engineer who is an SDET rather than an STE. However, even most SDETs will not be able to program in C++, although most will be able to write code in a scripting language. Providing script bindings for your API can therefore offer greater opportunity for your QA team to contribute automated integration tests (see Chapter 11 for details on adding scripting support). Another technique is to write programs that enable data-driven testing. The earlier reference to `pngtest.c` is an example of this: a single program written by a developer that can be used by QA engineers to produce a slew of data-driven integration tests.

10.4 WRITING TESTABLE CODE

Testing an API shouldn't be something that you leave until the end of the process. There are decisions that you make while you are designing and implementing an API that can improve your ability to write robust and extensive automated tests. In other words, you should consider how a class will be tested early on during its development. The following sections will cover various techniques for writing software that is more amenable to automated unit and integration testing.

10.4.1 Test-Driven Development

Test-Driven Development (TDD), or Test-First Programming, involves writing automated tests to verify desired functionality before the code that implements this functionality is written. These tests will of course fail initially. The goal is then to quickly write minimal code to make these tests pass. Then finally the code is refactored to optimize or clean up the implementation as necessary (Beck, 2002).

An important aspect of TDD is that changes are made incrementally, in small steps. You write a short test, then write enough code to make that test pass, and then repeat. After every small change, you recompile your code and rerun the tests. Working in these small steps means that if a test starts to fail, then in all probability this will be caused by the code you wrote since the last test run. Let's take a look at an example to demonstrate this. I'll start with a small test to verify the behavior of a `MovieRating` class (Astels, 2003).

```
void TestNoRatings()
{
    MovieRating *nemo = new MovieRating("Finding Nemo");
    AssertEqual(nemo->GetRatingCount(), 0, "no ratings");
}
```

Given this initial test code, you now write the simplest possible code to make the test pass. Here's an example that satisfies this objective. (I will inline the implementation for the API methods in these examples to make it clearer how the code under test evolves.)

```
class MovieRating
{
public:
    MovieRating(const std::string &name) {}
    int GetRatingCount() const { return 0; }
};
```

This API clearly doesn't do a lot, but it does allow the test to pass. So now you can move on and add some more test code.

```
void TestAverageRating
{
    MovieRating *nemo = new MovieRating("Finding Nemo");
    nemo->AddRating(4.0f);
    nemo->AddRating(5.0f);
    AssertEqual(nemo->GetAverageRating(), 4.5f, "nemo avg rating");
}
```

Now it's time to write the minimal code to make this test pass.

```
class MovieRating
{
public:
    MovieRating(const std::string &name) {}
    int GetRatingCount() const { return 0; }
    void AddRating(float r) {}
    float GetAverageRating() const { return 4.5f; }
};
```

Writing another test will force us to make the implementation more general.

```
void TestAverageRatingAndCount
{
    MovieRating *cars = new MovieRating("Cars");
    cars->AddRating(3.0f);
    cars->AddRating(4.0f);
    cars->AddRating(5.0f);
    AssertEqual(cars->GetRatingCount(), 3, "three ratings");
    AssertEqual(cars->GetAverageRating(), 4.0f, "cars avg rating");
}
```

Now you should extend the implementation to return the number of ratings added and the average of those ratings. The minimal way to do this would be to record the current sum of all ratings and the number of ratings added. For example,

```
class MovieRating
{
```

```
public:
    MovieRating(const std::string &name) :
        mNumRatings(0),
        mRatingsSum(0.0f)
    {
    }
    int GetRatingCount() const
    {
        return mNumRatings;
    }
    void AddRating(float r)
    {
        mRatingsSum += r;
        mNumRatings++;
    }
    float GetAverageRating() const
    {
        return (mRatingsSum / mNumRatings);
    }

private:

    int mNumRatings;
    float mRatingsSum;
};
```

Obviously you can continue this strategy by adding further tests to verify that calling `GetAverage-Rating()` with zero ratings does not crash and to check that adding out-of-range rating values is treated appropriately, but I think you get the general principle.

One of the main benefits of test-driven development is that it forces you to think about your API before you start writing any code. You also have to think about how the API will be used, that is, you put yourself in the shoes of your clients. Another effect of TDD is that you only implement what your tests need. In other words, your tests determine the code you need to write (Astels, 2003). This can help you avoid premature optimization and keeps you focused on the overall behavior.

TIP

Test-Driven Development means that you write unit tests first and then write the code to make the tests pass. This keeps you focused on the key use cases for your API.

TDD does not have to be confined to the initial development of your API. It can also be helpful during maintenance mode. For example, when a bug is discovered in your API, you should first write a test for the correct behavior. This test will of course fail at first. You can then work on implementing the fix for the bug. You will know when the bug is fixed because your test will change to a pass state. Once the bug is fixed, you then have the added benefit of an ongoing regression test that will ensure that the same bug is not introduced again in the future.

10.4.2 Stub and Mock Objects

One popular technique to make your unit tests more stable and resilient to failures is to create test objects that can stand in for real objects in the system. This lets you substitute an unpredictable resource with a lightweight controllable replacement for the purpose of testing. Examples of unpredictable resources include the file system, external databases, and networks. The stand-in object can also be used to test error conditions that are difficult to simulate in the real system, as well as events that are triggered at a certain time or that are based on a random number generator.

These stand-in objects will obviously present the same interface as the real objects they simulate. However, there are a number of different ways to implement these objects. The following list presents some of the options and introduces the generally accepted terminology for each case.

- **Fake object**: An object that has functional behavior but uses a simpler implementation to aid testing, for example, an in-memory file system that simulates interactions with the local disk.
- **Stub object**: An object that returns prepared or canned responses. For example, a `ReadFileAsString()` stub might simply return a hardcoded string as the file contents rather than reading the contents of the named file on disk.
- **Mock object**: An instrumented object that has a preprogrammed behavior and that performs verification on the calling sequence of its methods. For example, a mock object (or simply a mock) can specify that a `GetValue()` function will return 10 the first two times it's called and then 20 after that. It can also verify that the function was called, say, only three times or at least five times or that the functions in the class were called in a given order.

Because the difference between a stub and a mock is often poorly understood, let's demonstrate this with an example. I'll use the example of the children's card game War. This is a simple game where a deck of cards is divided equally between two players. Each player reveals their top card and the player with the highest card takes both cards. If the cards have equal value, each player lays three cards face down and the fourth face up. The highest value card wins all of the cards on the table. A player wins the game by collecting all cards.

I'll model this game with three classes:

1. **Card**: represents a single card, with the ability to compare its value against another card.
2. **Deck**: holds a deck of cards with functions to shuffle and deal cards.
3. **WarGame**: manages the game logic, with functions to play out the entire game and to return the winner of the game.

During actual game play, the `Deck` object will return a random card. However, for the purposes of testing, you could create a stub deck that returns cards in a predefined order. Assuming that the `WarGame` object accepts the deck to use as a parameter to its constructor, you can easily test the logic of `WarGame` by passing it a `StubDeck` that defines a specific and repeatable sequence of cards.

This `StubDeck` would inherit from the real `Deck` class, which means that you must design `Deck` to be a base class, that is, make the destructor virtual as well as any methods that need to be overridden for testing purposes. Here's an example declaration for the `Deck` class.

```
class Deck
{
public:
  Deck();
```

```
    virtual ~Deck();
    virtual void Shuffle();
    virtual int RemainingCards();
    virtual Card DealCard();
};
```

Our StubDeck class can therefore inherit from Deck and override the Shuffle() method to do nothing because you don't want to randomize the card order. Then the constructor of StubDeck could create a specific order of cards. However, this means that the stub class is hardcoded to a single card order. A more general solution would be to extend the class with an AddCard() method. Then you can write multiple tests using StubDeck and simply call AddCard() a number of times to prepare it with a specific order of cards before passing it to WarGame. One way to do this would be to add a protected AddCard() method to the base Deck class (because it modifies private state) and then expose this as public in the StubDeck class. Then you can write

```
#include "wargame.h"

void TestWarGame()
{
    StubDeck deck;
    deck.AddCard("9C");
    deck.AddCard("2H");
    deck.AddCard("JS");
    ...
    WarGame game(deck);
    game.Play();

    AssertEqual(game.GetWinner(), WarGame::PLAYER_ONE);
}
```

So, that's what a stub object would look like (in fact, this could even be considered a fake object too, as it offers complete functionality without the element of randomness). Let's now take a look at what testing with a mock object looks like.

One of the main differences between mock and stub objects is that mocks insist on behavior verification. That is, a mock object is instrumented to record all function calls for an object and it will verify behavior such as the number of times a function was called, the parameters that were passed to the function, or the order in which several functions were called. Writing code to perform this instrumentation by hand can be tedious and error prone. It is therefore best to rely upon a mock testing framework to automate this work for you. I'll use the Google Mock framework here (http://code .google.com/p/googlemock/) to illustrate how mocks can be used to test our WarGame class. The first thing you'll want to do is define the mock using the handy macros that Google Mock provides.

```
#include "wargame.h"
#include <gmock/gmock.h>
#include <gtest/gtest.h>

using namespace testing;

class MockDeck : public Deck
{
```

```
public:
    MOCK_METHOD0(Shuffle, void());
    MOCK_METHOD0(RemainingCards, int());
    MOCK_METHOD0(DealCard, Card());
};
```

The MOCK_METHOD0 macro is used to instrument functions with zero arguments, which is the case for all of the methods in the Deck base class. If instead you have a method with one argument, then you would use MOCK_METHOD1, and so on. Now, let's write a unit test that uses this mock. As I'm using Google Mock to create our mock, I'll also use Google Test as the testing framework. This looks like

```
TEST(WarGame, Test1)
{
    MockDeck deck;

    EXPECT_CALL(deck, Shuffle())
        .Times(AtLeast(1));
    EXPECT_CALL(deck, DealCard())
        .Times(52)
        .WillOnce(Return(Card("JS")))
        .WillOnce(Return(Card("2H")))
        .WillOnce(Return(Card("9C")))
        ...
        ;
    WarGame game(deck);
    game.Play();

    ASSERT_EQ(game.GetWinner(), WarGame::PLAYER_ONE);
}
```

The clever bits are those two EXPECT_CALL() lines. The first one states that the Shuffle() method of our mock object should get called at least once, and the second one states that the DealCard() method should get called exactly 52 times, and that the first call will return Card("JS"), the second call will return Card("2H"), and so on. Note that this approach means that you don't need to expose an AddCard() method for your mock object. The mock object will implicitly verify all of the expectations as part of its destructor and will fail the test if any of these are not met.

TIP
_____

Stub and mock objects can both return canned responses, but mock objects also perform call behavior verification.

In terms of how this affects the design of your APIs, one implication is that you may wish to consider a model where access to unpredictable resources is embodied within a base class that you pass into your worker classes, such as in the case given earlier where you pass the Deck object into the WarGame object. This allows you to substitute a stub or mock version in your test code using inheritance. This is essentially the dependency injection pattern, where dependent objects are passed into a class rather than that class being directly responsible for creating and storing those objects.

However, sometimes it is simply not practical to encapsulate and pass in all of the external dependencies for a class. In these cases, you can still use stub or mock objects, but instead of using inheritance to replace functionality, you can inject them physically at link time. In this case, you name the stub/mock class the same as the class you wish to replace. Then your test program links against the test code and not the code with the real implementation. Using our ReadFileAsString() example given earlier, you could create an alternate version of this function that returns canned data and then link the object .o file with this stub into our test program in place of the object file that holds the real implementation. This approach can be very powerful, although it does necessitate that you create your own abstractions for accessing the file system, network, and so on. If your code directly calls fopen() from the standard library, then you can't replace this with a stub at link time unless you also provide stubs for all other standard library functions that your code calls.

10.4.3 Testing Private Code

The emphasis of this book has been the development of well-designed APIs that offer a logical abstraction while hiding implementation details. However, this can also make it difficult to write thorough unit tests. There will be times when you need to write a unit test that accesses private members of a class in order to achieve full code coverage. Given a class called MyClass, this can be done in two different ways:

1. **Member function**: Declaring a public MyClass::SelfTest() method.
2. **Friend function**: Creating a MyClassSelfTest() free function and declaring it as friend function in MyClass.

I detailed several reasons to avoid friend classes in Chapter 6, although in this case the friend function can be made relatively safe if the MyClassSelfTest() function is defined in the same library as the MyClass implementation, thus preventing clients from redefining the function in their own code. Of note, the Google Test framework provides a FRIEND_TEST() macro to support this kind of friend function testing. However, because the two options are functionally equivalent, and given our general preference to avoid friends unless absolutely necessary, I will concentrate on the first of these options: adding a public SelfTest() method to a class to test its internal details, although the discussion can be applied equally to the friend function solution too.

For example, here is a simple bounding box class that includes a self-test method.

```
// bbox.h
class BBox
{
public:
    BBox();
    BBox(const Point &a, const Point &b);

    Point GetMin() const;
    Point GetMax() const;
    bool Contains(const Point &point) const;
    bool Intersects(const BBox &bbox) const;
    double CenterDistance(const BBox &bbox) const;

    void SelfTest();
```

```
private:
    Point CalcMin(const Point &a, const Point &b);
    Point CalcMax(const Point &a, const Point &b);
    Point GetCenter();
    Point mMin, mMax;
};
```

The SelfTest() method can therefore be called directly from a unit test in order to perform extra validation of the various private methods. This is very convenient for testing, although there are some undesirable qualities of this approach. Namely, you have to pollute your public API with a method that your clients should not call and you may add extra bloat to your library by embedding the test code inside the BBox implementation.

In the first case, there are ways that you can discourage clients from using this function. One trivial way to do this would be to simply add a comment that the method is not for public use. Taking this one step further, you could remove the method from any API documentation you produce so that users never see a reference to it (unless they look directly at your headers of course). You can achieve this with the Doxygen tool by surrounding the function declaration with the \cond and \endcond commands.

```
/// \cond TestFunctions
void SelfTest();
/// \endcond
```

As for the concern that the self-test function may add bloat to your code, there are a couple of ways to deal with this, if you feel it's necessary. One way would be to implement the SelfTest() method in your unit test code, not in the main API code, for example, in test_bbox.cpp not bbox.cpp. Just because you declare a method in your .h file doesn't mean that you have to define it. However, this opens up a similar security hole to using friends. That is, your clients could define the SelfTest() method in their own code as a way to modify the internal state of the object. While the interface of this function restricts what they can do, because they cannot pass in any arguments or receive any results, they can still use global variables to circumvent this.

An alternative would be to conditionally compile the test code. For example,

```
// bbox.cpp
...
void SelfTest()
{
#ifdef TEST
    // lots of test code
#else
    std::cout << "Self-test code not compiled in." << std::endl;
#endif
}
```

The downside of this approach is that you have to build two versions of your API: one with the self-test code compiled in (compiled with -DTEST or /DTEST) and one without the self-test code. If the extra build is a problem, you could compile the self-test code into debug versions of your library but remove it from release builds.

TIP

Use a `SelfTest()` member function to test private members of a class.

It's worth noting that if you wish to provide a self-test function for a C API, then this is a much simpler proposition. For example, you could define an external linkage `SelfTest()` function in the .c file, that is, a non-static function decorated with `__declspec(dllexport)` on Windows, but provide no prototype for the function in the .h file. You then declare the function prototype in your test code so that you can call the function as part of your unit test. In this way, the function does not appear in your header file or any API documentation. In fact, the only way a client could discover the call is if they do a dump of all the public symbols in your shared library.

10.4.4 Using Assertions

An assertion is a way to verify assumptions that your code makes. You do this by encoding the assumption in a call to an assert function or macro. If the value of the expression evaluates to true, then all is well and nothing happens. However, if the expression evaluates to false, then the assumption you made in the code is invalid and your program will abort with an appropriate error (McConnell, 2004).

Assertions are essentially a way for you to include extra sanity tests for your program state directly in the code. As such, these are invaluable complementary aids to help testing and debugging.

Although you are free to write your own assertion routines, the C standard library includes an `assert()` macro in the `assert.h` header (also available in C++ as the `cassert` header). The following example uses this macro to show how you could document and enforce the assumption that a pointer you are about to dereference is non-NULL.

```
#include <cassert>
#include <iostream>

MyClass::MyClass() :
    mStrPtr(new std::string("Hello"))
{
}

MyClass::PrintString()
{
    // mStrPtr should have been allocated in the constructor
    assert(mStrPtr != NULL);
    std::cout << *mStrPtr << std::endl;
}
```

It is common practice to turn off all `assert()` calls for production code so that an end-user application doesn't abort needlessly when the user is running it. This is often done by making assert calls do nothing when they are compiled in release mode versus debug mode. (For this reason, you should never put code that must always be executed into an assertion.) Here's an example of a simple assertion definition that is only active in debug builds.

```
#ifdef DEBUG
#include <assert.h>
#else
#define assert(func)
#endif
```

Assertions should be used to document conditions that you as the developer believe should never occur. They are not appropriate for run-time error conditions that might occur legitimately. If you can recover gracefully from an error then you should always prefer that course of action rather than causing the client's program to crash. For example, if you have an API call that accepts a pointer from the client, you should never assume that it is non-NULL. Instead, you should check to see if the pointer is NULL and return gracefully if that's the case, potentially emitting an appropriate error message. You should not use an assertion for this case. However, if your API enforces the condition that one of your private member variables is always non-NULL then it would be a programming error for it to ever be NULL. This is an appropriate situation for an assertion. In summary, use assertions to check for programming errors; use normal error checking to test for user errors and attempt to recover gracefully in that situation.

TIP

Use assertions to document and verify programming errors that should never occur.

Assertions are used commonly in commercial products as a way to diagnose errors. For instance, several years ago it was reported that the Microsoft Office suite is covered by over 250,000 assertions (Hoare, 2003). These are often used in conjunction with other automated testing techniques, such as running a large suite of unit and integration test cases on debug code with the assertions turned on. This test run will fail if any test code hits an assertion that fails, allowing a developer to follow up and investigate the reason for the failure before it leads to a crash in client code.

It's worth noting that the C++11 standard added a new compile-time assertion called static_assert(). This is not part of the C++98 standard, however early support for this new feature is already available in some C++ compilers, such as Visual Studio 2010 and GNU C++ 4.3. Using static_assert(), if the constant expression resolves to false at compile time, then the compiler displays the provided error message and fails; otherwise, the statement has no effect. For example,

```
// compile-time assertion (C++11 only)
static_assert(sizeof(void *) == 4, "This code only works on 32-bit platforms.");
```

10.4.5 Contract Programming

Bertrand Meyer coined and trademarked the term "design by contract" as a way to prescribe obligations between an interface and its clients (Meyer, 1987). For function calls, this means specifying the preconditions that a client must meet before calling the function and the postconditions that the function guarantees on exit. For classes, this means defining the invariants that it maintains before and after a public method call (Hoare, 1969; Pugh, 2006).

The previous chapter showed you how to communicate these conditions and constraints to your users via your API documentation. Here I will illustrate how you can also implement them in code using assertion-style checks. For instance, continuing with the SquareRoot() function introduced earlier, the following code shows how to implement tests for its precondition and postcondition.

```
double SquareRoot(double value)
{
    // assert the function's precondition
    require(value >= 0);

    double result = 0.0;
    ... // calculate the square root

    // assert the function's postcondition
    ensure(fabs((result * result) - value) < 0.001);
    return result;
}
```

The require() and ensure() calls in this example can be implemented in a similar fashion to the assert() macro described in the previous section, that is, they do nothing if the condition evaluates to true, otherwise they abort or throw an exception. Just as in the use of assertions, it's common to disable these calls for release builds to avoid their overhead in a production environment and to avoid aborting your clients' programs. In other words, you could simply define these functions as follows.

```
// check that a precondition has been met
#define require(cond) assert(cond)

// check that a postcondition is valid
#define ensure(cond) assert(cond)
```

Furthermore, you may implement a private method for your classes to test its invariants, that is, that it's in a valid state. You can then call this method from inside of your functions to ensure that the object is in a valid state when the function begins and ends. If you use a consistent name for this method (which you could enforce through the use of an abstract base class), then you could augment your require() and ensure() macros with a check_invariants() macro as follows.

```
#ifdef DEBUG
// turn on contract checks in a debug build
#define require(cond) assert(cond)
#define ensure(cond) assert(cond)
#define check_invariants(obj) assert(obj && obj->IsValid());
#else
// turn off contract checks in a non-debug build
#define require(cond)
#define ensure(cond)
#define check_invariants(obj)
#endif
```

Putting this all together, here is a further example of contract programming for a string append method.

```cpp
void String::append(const std::string &str)
{
    // no preconditions - references are always non-NULL
    // ensure the consistency of this string and the input string
    check_invariants(this);
    check_invariants(&str);

    // perform the actual string append operation
    size_t pre_size = size();

    ...

    // verify the postcondition
    ensure(size() == pre_size + str.size());
    // and ensure that this string is still self consistent
    check_invariants(this);
}
```

It's interesting to note that when Meyer originally conceived contract programming he added explicit support for this technique in his Eiffel language. He also used an assertion model to implement this support, as I have done here. However, in Eiffel, these assertions would get extracted automatically into the documentation for the class. Because C++ does not have this innate capability, you must manually ensure that the assertions in your implementation match the documentation for your interface.

Nevertheless, one of the benefits of employing this kind of contract programming is that errors get flagged much closer to the actual source of the problem. This can make a huge difference when trying to debug a complex program, as very often the source of an error and the point where it causes a problem are far apart. This is of course a general benefit of using assertions.

TIP

Enforce an interface's contract through the systematic use of assertions, such as `require()`, `ensure()`, and `check_invariants()`.

One particularly important piece of advice to remember when employing this programming style is to test against the interface, not the implementation. That is, your precondition and postcondition checks should make sense at the abstraction level of your API. They should not depend on the specifics of your particular implementation, as otherwise you will find that you have to change the contract whenever you change the implementation.

TIP

Perform contract checks against the interface, not the implementation.

10.4.6 **Record and Playback Functionality**

One feature that can be invaluable for testing (and many other tasks) is the ability to record the sequence of calls that are made to an API and then play them back again at will. Record and playback tools are fairly common in the arena of application or GUI testing, where user interactions such as button presses and keystrokes are captured and then played back to repeat the user's actions. However, the same principles can be applied to API testing. This involves instrumenting every function call in your API to be able to log its name, parameters, and return value. Then a playback module can be written that accepts this log, or journal, file and calls each function in sequence, checking that the actual return values match the previously recorded responses.

Ordinarily this functionality will be turned off by default so that the overhead of creating the journal file does not impact the performance of the API. However, it can be switched on in a production environment to capture actual end-user activity. These journal files can then be added to your test suite as data-driven integration tests or can be played back in a debugger to help isolate problems. You can even use them to refine the behavior of your API based on real-world usage information, such as detecting common invalid inputs and adding better error handling for these cases. Your clients could even expose this functionality in their applications to allow their end users to record their actions and play them back themselves, that is, to automate repetitive tasks in the application. This is often called a macro capability in end-user applications.

There are several different ways that you could instrument your API in this fashion. One of the more clean ways to do this is to introduce a Proxy API that essentially forwards straight through to your main API, but which also manages all of the function call logging. In this way, you don't need to pollute your actual API calls with these details and you always have the option of shipping a vanilla API without any logging functionality. This is demonstrated in the following simple example:

```cpp
bool PlaySound(const std::string &filename)
{
    LOG_FUNCTION("PlaySound");
    LOG_PARAMETER(filename);

    bool result = detail::PlaySound(filename);

    LOG_RESULT(result);
    return result;
}
```

Of course, if you already have a wrapper API, such as a script binding or a convenience API, then you can simply reuse that interface layer. This is also a good place to perform your API contract tests, as described in the previous section.

Gerard Meszaros notes that on its face, record and playback techniques may appear to be counter to agile methodologies such as test-first development. However, he points out that it is possible to use record and playback in conjunction with test-first methodologies as long as the journal is stored in a human-readable file format such as XML (Meszaros, 2003). When this is the case, the record and playback infrastructure can be built early on and then tests can be written as data files rather than in code. This has the additional benefit that more junior QA engineers could also contribute data-driven integration tests to the test suite.

Adding robust record and playback functionality to your API can be a significant undertaking, but the costs are normally worth it when you consider the benefits of faster test automation and the ability to let your clients easily capture reproduction cases for bug reports.

10.4.7 Supporting Internationalization

Internationalization (i18n) is the process of enabling a software product to support different languages and regional variations. The related term localization (l10n) refers to the activity of using the underlying internationalization support to provide translations of application text into a specific language and to define the locale settings for a specific region, such as the date format or currency symbol.

Internationalization testing can be used to ensure that a product fully supports a given locale or language. This tends to be an activity limited to end-user application testing, that is, testing that an application's menus and messages appear in the user's preferred language. However, design decisions made during the development of your API can have an impact on how easily your clients can provide localization support in their applications.

For example, you may prefer to return integer error codes rather than error messages in a single language. If you do return error messages, then it would be helpful to define all of the potential error messages in an appropriate header file that your clients can access so that they can be localized appropriately. Also, you should avoid returning dates or formatted numbers as strings, as these are interpreted differently across locales. For example, "100,000.00" is a valid number in the United States and the United Kingdom, but in France the same number would be formatted as "100 000,00" or "100.000,00."

Several libraries provide internationalization and localization functionality. You could use one of these libraries to return localized strings to your clients and let them specify the preferred locale for the strings that your API returns. These libraries are often very easy to use. For example, the GNU gettext library provides a `gettext()` function to look up the translation for a string and return it in the language for the current locale (assuming that a translation has been provided). Often, this `gettext()` function is aliased to _ so that you can write simple code such as

```
std::cout << _("Please enter your username:");
```

Similarly, the Qt library provides excellent internationalization and localization features. All `QObject` subclasses that use the `Q_OBJECT` macro have a `tr()` member function that behaves similarly to GNU's `gettext()` function, for example,

```
button = new QPushButton(tr("Quit"), this);
```

10.5 AUTOMATED TESTING TOOLS

This section takes a look at some of the tools that can be used to support your automated testing efforts. I will divide these into four broad categories:

1. **Test harnesses.** Software libraries and programs that make it easier to maintain, run, and report results for automated tests.
2. **Code coverage.** Tools that instrument your code to track the actual statements or branches that your tests executed.
3. **Bug tracking.** A database-driven application that allows defect reports and feature requests to be submitted, prioritized, assigned, and resolved for your software.

4. Continuous build systems. A system that rebuilds your software and reruns your automated tests whenever a new change is added.

10.5.1 Test Harnesses

There are many unit test frameworks available for C and C++. Most of these follow a similar design to the classic JUnit framework and provide support for features such as assertion-based testing, fixture setup, grouping of fixtures for multiple tests, and mock objects. In addition to being able to define a single test, a good test framework should also provide a way to run an entire suite of tests at once and report the total number of failures.

I will not attempt to describe all available test harnesses here; a Web search on "C++ test frameworks" will turn up many tools for you to investigate if that is your desire. However, I will provide details for a number of the more popular or interesting frameworks.

- **CppUnit** (http://cppunit.sourceforge.net/): A port of JUnit to C++ originally created by Michael Feathers. This framework supports various helper macros to simplify the declaration of tests, capturing exceptions, and a range of output formats, including an XML format and a compiler-like output to ease integration with an IDE. CppUnit also provides a number of different test runners, including Qt- and MFC-based GUI runners. Version 1 of CppUnit has reached a stable state and future development is being directed toward CppUnit 2. Michael Feathers has also created an extremely lightweight alternative version of CppUnit called CppUnitLite. Here is a sample test case written using CppUnit, based on an example from the CppUnit cookbook.

```
class ComplexNumberTest : public CppUnit::TestFixture
{
public:
  void setUp()
  {
    m_10_1 = new Complex(10, 1);
    m_1_1 = new Complex(1, 1);
    m_11_2 = new Complex(11, 2);
  }
  void tearDown()
  {
    delete m_10_1;
    delete m_1_1;
    delete m_11_2;
  }
  void testEquality()
  {
    CPPUNIT_ASSERT(*m_10_1 == *m_10_1);
    CPPUNIT_ASSERT(*m_10_1 != *m_11_2);
  }
  void testAddition()
  {
    CPPUNIT_ASSERT(*m_10_1 + *m_1_1 == *m_11_2);
  }
```

```
private:
    Complex *m_10_1;
    Complex *m_1_1;
    Complex *m_11_2;
};
```

- **Boost Test** (http://www.boost.org/): Boost includes a Test library for writing test programs, organizing tests into simple test cases and test suites, and controlling their run-time execution. A core value of this library is portability. As such it uses a conservative subset of C++ features and minimizes dependencies on other APIs. This has allowed the library to be used for porting and testing of other Boost libraries. Boost Test provides an execution monitor that can catch exceptions in test code, as well as a program execution monitor that can check for exceptions and non-zero return codes from an end-user application. The following example, derived from the Boost Test manual, demonstrates how to write a simple unit test using this library.

```
#define BOOST_TEST_MODULE MyTest
#include <boost/test/unit_test.hpp>

int add(int i, int j)
{
    return i+j;
}

BOOST_AUTO_TEST_CASE(my_test)
{
    // #1 continues on error
    BOOST_CHECK(add(2, 2) == 4);

    // #2 throws an exception on error
    BOOST_REQUIRE(add(2, 2) == 4);

    // #3 continues on error
    if (add(2, 2) != 4)
        BOOST_ERROR("Ouch...");

    // #4 throws an exception on error
    if (add(2, 2) != 4)
        BOOST_FAIL("Ouch...");

    // #5 throws an exception on error
    if (add(2, 2) != 4)
        throw "Ouch...";

    // #6 continues on error
    BOOST_CHECK_MESSAGE(add(2,2) == 4, "add() result: " << add(2, 2));

    // #7 continues on error
    BOOST_CHECK_EQUAL(add(2, 2), 4);
}
```

- **Google Test** (http://code.google.com/p/googletest/): The Google C++ Testing Framework provides a JUnit-style unit test framework for C++. It is a cross-platform system that supports automatic test discovery (i.e., you don't have to enumerate all of the tests in your test suite manually)
and a rich set of assertions, including fatal assertions (the ASSERT_* macros), non-fatal assertions
(the EXPECT_* macros), and so-called death tests (checks that a program terminates expectedly).
Google Test also provides various options for running tests and offers textual and XML report
generation. As mentioned earlier, Google also provides a mock object testing framework, Google
Mock, which integrates well with Google Test. The following code demonstrates the creation of a
suite of unit tests using Google Test.

```cpp
#include <gtest/gtest.h>

bool IsPrime(int n);

TEST(IsPrimeTest, NegativeNumbers)
{
    EXPECT_FALSE(IsPrime(-1));
    EXPECT_FALSE(IsPrime(-100));
    EXPECT_FALSE(IsPrime(INT_MIN));
}

TEST(IsPrimeTest, TrivialCases)
{
    EXPECT_FALSE(IsPrime(0));
    EXPECT_FALSE(IsPrime(1));
    EXPECT_TRUE(IsPrime(2));
    EXPECT_TRUE(IsPrime(3));
}

TEST(IsPrimeTest, PositiveNumbers)
{
    EXPECT_FALSE(IsPrime(4));
    EXPECT_TRUE(IsPrime(5));
    EXPECT_FALSE(IsPrime(9));
    EXPECT_TRUE(IsPrime(17));
}

int main(int argc, char** argv)
{
    ::testing::InitGoogleTest(&argc, argv);
    return RUN_ALL_TESTS();
}
```

- **TUT** (http://tut-framework.sourceforge.net/): The Template Unit Test (TUT) Framework is a
small portable C++ unit test framework. Because it consists only of header files, there is no
library to link against or deploy. Tests are organized into named test groups, and the framework
supports automatic discovery of all tests that you define. A number of test reporters are provided,

including basic console output and a CppUnit-style reporter. It's also possible to write your own reporters using TUT's extensible reporter interface. Here is a simple canonical unit test written using the TUT framework.

```cpp
#include <tut/tut.hpp>

namespace
{
    tut::factory tf("basic test");
}

namespace tut
{
    struct basic{};
    typedef test_group<basic> factory;
    typedef factory::object object;

    template<> template<>
    void object::test<1>()
    {
      ensure_equals("2+2", 2+2, 4);
    }

    template<> template<>
    void object::test<2>()
    {
      ensure_equals("2*-2", 2*-2, -4);
    }
}
```

10.5.2 Code Coverage

Code coverage tools let you discover precisely which statements of your code are exercised by your tests, that is, these tools can be used to focus your testing activities on the parts of your code base that are not already covered by tests.

Different degrees of code coverage can be measured. I will define each of these with reference to the following simple code example.

```cpp
void TestFunction(int a, int b)
{
    if (a == 1) a++;          // Line 1
    int c = a * b;            // Line 2
    if (a > 10 && b != 0)     // Line 3
        c *= 2;               // Line 4
    return a * c;             // Line 5
}
```

- **Function coverage.** In this coarsest level of code coverage, only function calls are tracked. In the example code, function coverage will only record whether TestFunction() was called at least once. The flow of control within a function has no effect on function code coverage results.

- **Line coverage**. This form of code coverage tests whether each line of code that contains an executable statement was reached. One limitation of this metric can be seen on Line 1 of our code example. Line coverage will consider Line 1 to be 100% exercised even if the a++ statement is not executed; it only matters if the flow of control hits this line. Obviously, you can get around this limitation by putting the if condition and the a++ statement on separate lines.
- **Statement coverage**. This metric measures whether the flow of control reached every executable statement at least once. The primary limitation of this form of coverage is that it does not consider the different code paths that can result from the expressions in control structures such as if, for, while, or switch statements. For example, in our code sample, statement coverage will tell us if the condition on Line 3 evaluated to true, causing Line 4 to be executed. However, it will not tell us if that condition evaluated to false because there is no executable code associated with that result.
- **Basic block coverage**. A basic block is a sequence of statements that cannot be branched into or out of. That is, if the first statement is executed then all of the remaining statements in the block will also be executed. Essentially, a basic block ends on a branch, function call, throw, or return. This can be thought of as a special case of statement coverage, with the same benefits and limitations.
- **Decision coverage**. This code coverage metric measures whether the overall result of the expression in each control structure evaluated to both true and false. This addresses the major deficiency of statement coverage because you will know if the condition in Line 3 evaluated to false. This is also called branch coverage.
- **Condition coverage**. Condition coverage determines whether each boolean subexpression in a control structure has evaluated to both true and false. In our example here, this means that Line 3 must be hit with a > 10, a <= 10, b != 0, and b == 0. Note that this does not necessarily imply decision coverage, as each of these events could occur in such an order that the overall result of the if statement always evaluates to false.

Various programs let you measure the code coverage of C++ code. Each of these supports different combinations of the metrics I've just listed, normally by instrumenting the code that your compiler generates. Most of these tools are commercial offerings, although there are some free and open source options too.

One feature in particular that can be very useful is the ability to exclude certain lines of code from the analysis, often done by adding special comments around those lines of code. This can be used to turn off coverage for lines that legitimately can never be hit, such as methods in a base class that are always overridden; although in these cases it's important that the coverage tool raises an error if the excluded code is ever hit in the future as this may signal an unexpected change in behavior.

Another issue to bear in mind is that you should normally perform code coverage analysis on a build that has been compiled without optimizations, as compilers can reorder or eliminate individual lines of code during optimization.

The following list provides a brief survey of some of the more prominent code coverage analysis tools.

- **Bullseye Coverage** (http://www.bullseye.com/). This coverage tool, from Bullseye Testing Technology, provides function as well as condition/decision coverage, to give you a range of coverage precision. It offers features such as covering system-level and kernel mode code, merging results from distributed testing, and integration with Microsoft Visual Studio. It also gives you the ability to exclude certain portions of your code from analysis. Bullseye is a mature product that has support for a wide range of platforms and compilers.

- **Rational PureCoverage** (http://www.rational.com/). This code coverage analysis tool is sold as part of the PurifyPlus package from IBM. It can report coverage at executable, library, file, function, block, and line levels. PureCoverage can accumulate coverage over multiple runs and merge data from different programs that share the same source code. It offers both graphical and textual output to let you explore its results.
- **Intel Code-Coverage Tool** (http://www.intel.com/). This tool is included with Intel compilers and runs on instrumentation files produced by those compilers. It provides function and basic block coverage and can restrict analysis to only those modules of interest. It also supports differential coverage, that is, comparing the output of one run against another run. The Code-Coverage Tool runs on Intel processors under Windows or Linux.
- **Gcov** (http://gcc.gnu.org/onlinedocs/gcc/Gcov.html). This test coverage program is part of the open-source GNU GCC compiler collection. It operates on code generated by g++ using the -fprofile-arcs and -ftest-coverage options. Gcov provides function, line, and branch code coverage. It outputs its report in a textual format; however, the accompanying lcov script can be used to output results as an HTML report (see Figure 10.3).

Once you have a code coverage build in place and can refer to regular coverage reports for your API, you can start instituting code coverage targets for your code. For example, you might specify that all code must achieve a particular threshold, such as 75, 90, or 100% coverage. The particular target that you select will depend greatly on the coverage metric that you adopt: attaining 100% function coverage should be relatively easy, whereas 100% condition/decision coverage will be far more difficult. From experience, a high and very respectable degree of code coverage would be 100% function, 90% line, or 75% condition coverage.

It's also worth specifically addressing the issue of code coverage and legacy code. Sometimes your API must depend on a large amount of old code that has no test coverage at all. Recall that Michael Feathers defines legacy code as code without tests (Feathers, 2004). In these cases, it may be impractical to enforce the same code coverage targets for the legacy code that you impose for new code. However, you can at least put some basic tests in place and then enforce that no checkin should lower the current coverage level. This effectively means that any new changes to the legacy code should be accompanied with tests. Because enforcing this requirement on a per

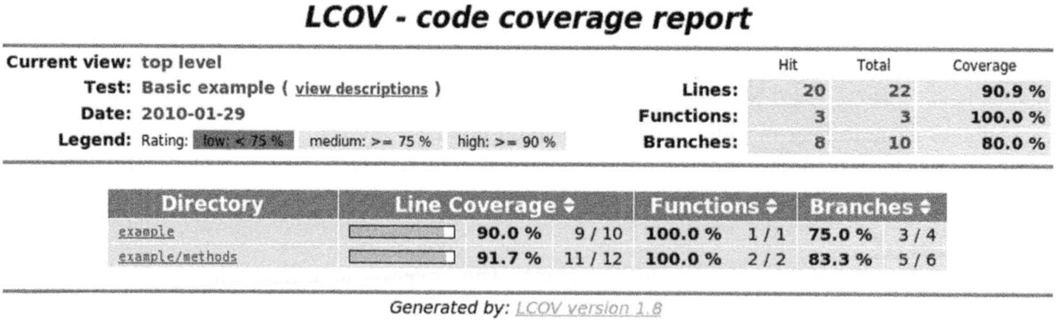

LCOV - code coverage report

Current view: top level			Hit	Total	Coverage
Test: Basic example (view descriptions)		**Lines:**	20	22	**90.9 %**
Date: 2010-01-29		**Functions:**	3	3	**100.0 %**
Legend: Rating: low: < 75 % medium: >= 75 % high: >= 90 %		**Branches:**	8	10	**80.0 %**

Directory	Line Coverage ⬍		Functions ⬍		Branches ⬍	
example	90.0 %	9 / 10	100.0 %	1 / 1	75.0 %	3 / 4
example/methods	91.7 %	11 / 12	100.0 %	2 / 2	83.3 %	5 / 6

Generated by: LCOV version 1.8

FIGURE 10.3

Example HTML gcov code coverage report generated by lcov.

checkin basis can sometimes be difficult (because you have to build the software with the change and run all tests to know whether it should be accepted), another reasonable way to make this work is to record the legacy code coverage for the previous version of the library and ensure that coverage for the new version equals or exceeds this threshold at the time of release. This approach offers a pragmatic way to deal with legacy code and lets you gradually increase the code coverage to acceptable levels over time.

In essence, different modules or libraries in your API may have different code coverage targets. In the past, I have made this clear by updating the code coverage report to display the target for each module and use a color scheme to indicate whether the targets have been met in each case. You can then glance down the report quickly to know if your testing levels are on target.

10.5.3 Bug Tracking

A bug tracking system is an application that lets you keep track of bugs (and often suggestions) for your software project in a database. An efficient bug tracking system that can be mapped well to your development and quality processes is an invaluable tool. Conversely, a poor bug tracking system that is difficult to use and does not fully reveal the state of your software can be an albatross around the neck of your project.

Most bug tracking systems support the triage of incoming bugs, that is, setting the priority (and perhaps severity) of a bug and assigning it to a particular developer. It's also standard practice to be able to define filters for the bugs in the system so that targeted bug lists can be created, such as a list of open crashing bugs or a list of bugs assigned to a particular developer. Related to this, some bug tracking systems will also provide report generation functions, often with the ability to display graphs and pie charts. This can be indispensible for generating quality metrics about your software, which together with code coverage results can be used to direct further testing efforts more efficiently.

It's also worth noting what a bug tracking system is not. For one, it is not a trouble ticket or issue tracking system. These are customer support systems that are used to receive feedback from users, many of which may not be related to software problems. Valid software issues that are discovered by customer support will then be entered into the bug tracking system and assigned to an engineer to work on. Another thing that a bug tracking system is not is a task or project management tool, that is, a system that lets you track tasks and plan work. However, some bug tracking system vendors do provide complementary products that use the underlying infrastructure to provide a project management tool as well.

There are dozens of bug tracking systems on the market and the best one for your project will depend on several factors, such as:

- You may prefer an open source solution so that you have the option to customize it if necessary. For example, many large open source projects use Bugzilla, including Mozilla, Gnome, Apache, and the Linux Kernel. See http://www.bugzilla.org/.
- There are also many commercial packages that provide excellent and flexible bug tracking capabilities that come with support and optionally secure hosting. Atlassian's JIRA is one such popular solution that provides an extremely customizable and robust bug tracking system. Atlassian also provides the related GreenHopper project management system for agile development projects, which lets you manage your user story backlog, task breakdowns, and sprint/iteration planning. See http://www.atlassian.com/.

- Alternatively, you may decide to go with a general project hosting solution that provides revision control features, disk storage quotas, discussion forums, and an integrated bug tracking system. Google Code Hosting is one popular option in this category. See http://code.google.com/hosting/.

10.5.4 Continuous Build System

A continuous build system is an automated process that rebuilds your software as soon as a new change is checked into your revision control system. A continuous build system should be one of the first pieces of technology you put in place for a large project with multiple engineers, independent of any testing needs. It lets you know the current state of the build and identifies build failures as soon as they happen. It is also invaluable for cross-platform development because even the most well-tested change for one platform can break the build for a different platform. There are several continuous build options on the market, including the following.

- **Tinderbox** (https://developer.mozilla.org/en/Tinderbox): An open source solution from the Mozilla team that runs builds and test suites. See Figure 10.4 for an example of the Tinderbox interface.
- **Parabuild** (http://www.viewtier.com/): An enterprise software build and release management system from Viewtier Systems.
- **TeamCity** (http://www.jetbrains.com/teamcity/): A distributed build management and continuous integration server from JetBrains.
- **Electric Cloud** (http://www.electric-cloud.com/): A suite of tools for build/test/deploy automation that supports build parallelization.

However, our focus here is on automated testing. The benefit of a continuous build system for testing is that it provides a mechanism for also running your automated tests on a regular basis and hence to discover test breakages quickly. That is, the result of the automated build can be in one of four states: in progress, pass, build failure, or test failure.

As your test suite grows, so will the time it takes to run all of your tests. It's important that you receive fast turnaround on builds so that if your test run starts taking several hours to complete, then you should investigate some test optimization efforts. One way to do this is to segment your tests into different categories and only run the fast category of tests as part of the continuous build. Another solution is to have multiple automated builds: one that only builds the software and another that builds the software and then runs all tests. This gives engineers the ability to quickly receive feedback about build breakages while still ensuring that a full test suite is run as often as possible.

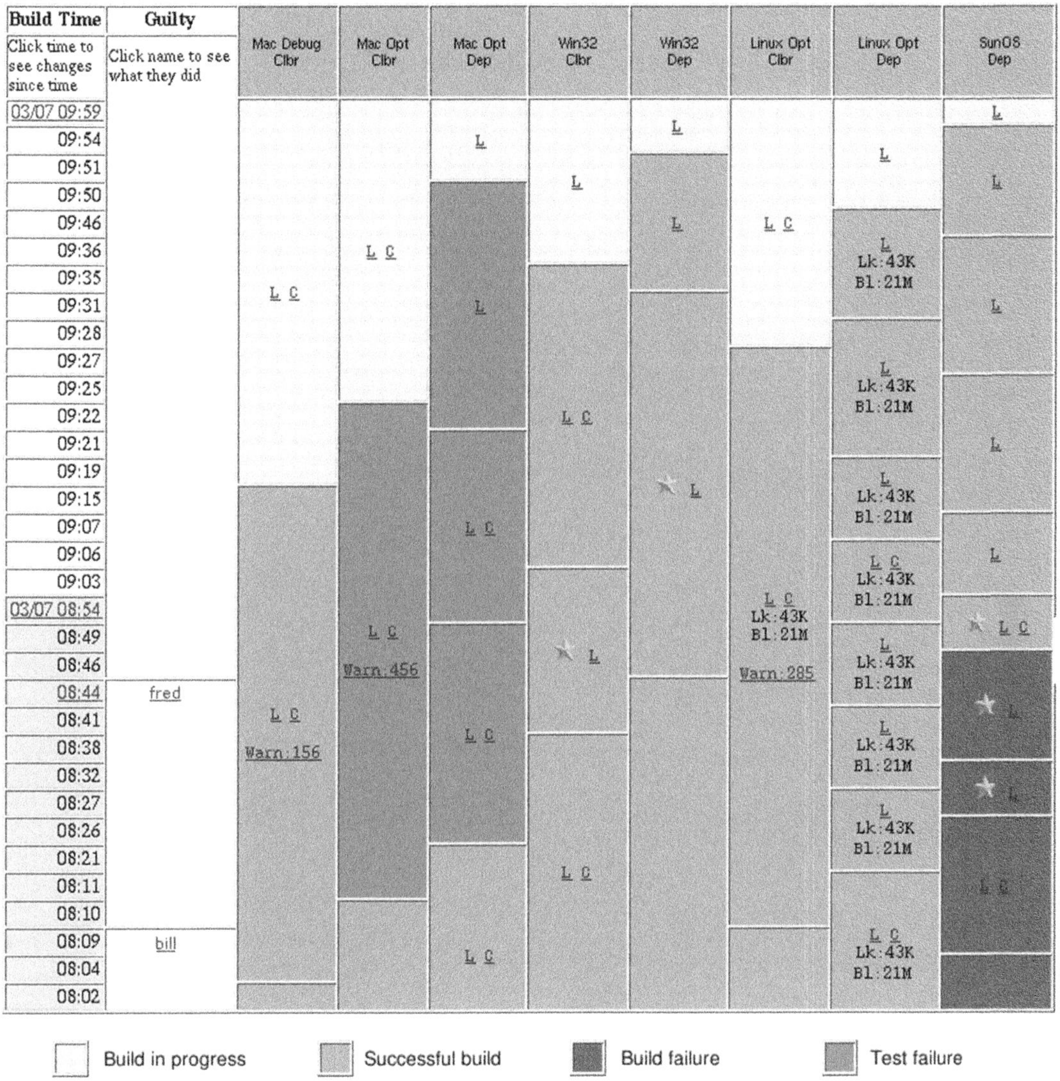

Build Time	Guilty	Mac Debug Clbr	Mac Opt Clbr	Mac Opt Dep	Win32 Clbr	Win32 Dep	Linux Opt Clbr	Linux Opt Dep	SunOS Dep
Click time to see changes since time	Click name to see what they did								
03/07 09:59						L			L
09:54				L					
09:51								L	
09:50				L	L				L
09:46						L	L C		
09:36			L C					L Lk:43K	
09:35		L C						Bl:21M	
09:31				L					L
09:28									
09:27								L	
09:25								Lk:43K	
09:22					L C			Bl:21M	
09:21									L
09:19						★ L		L	
09:15								Lk:43K	
09:07				L C				Bl:21M	
09:06								L C	L
09:03								Lk:43K Bl:21M	
03/07 08:54							L C Lk:43K		
08:49			L C			★ L	Bl:21M	L	★ L C
08:46			Warn:456				Warn:285	Lk:43K Bl:21M	
08:44	fred							L	
08:41		L C		L C				Lk:43K	★ L
08:38		Warn:156						Bl:21M	
08:32									★ L
08:27								L	
08:26								Lk:43K	
08:21					L C			Bl:21M	
08:11									L C
08:10									
08:09	bill			L C				L C Lk:43K	
08:04								Bl:21M	
08:02									

☐ Build in progress   ▨ Successful build   ▨ Build failure   ▨ Test failure

FIGURE 10.4

The Tinderbox continuous build system interface showing eight different builds (columns). The vertical axis is time, with the most recent build at the top. This shows that bill made a checkin and subsequently broke tests for the Mac Opt builds and then fred made a checkin that fixed the build failure for SunOS.

Scripting

11

Up until this chapter, I have focused on general aspects of API design that could be applicable to any C++ project. Having covered the standard API design pipeline, the remaining chapters in this book deal with the more specialized topics of scripting and extensibility. While not all APIs need to be concerned with these topics, they are becoming more popular subjects in modern application development. I therefore felt that a comprehensive book on C++ API design should include coverage of these advanced topics.

Accordingly, this chapter deals with the topic of scripting, that is, allowing your C++ API to be accessed from a scripting language, such as Python, Ruby, Lua, Tcl, or Perl. I will explain why you might want to do this and what some of the issues are that you need to be aware of, and then review some of the main technologies that let you create bindings for these languages.

To make this chapter more practical and instructive, I will take a detailed look at two different script binding technologies and show how these can be used to create bindings for two different scripting languages. Specifically, I will provide an in-depth treatment of how to create Python bindings for your C++ API using Boost Python, followed by a thorough analysis of how to create Ruby bindings using the Simplified Wrapper and Interface Generator (SWIG). I have chosen to focus on Python and Ruby because these are two of the most popular scripting languages in use today; in terms of binding technologies, Boost Python and SWIG are both freely available open source solutions that provide extensive control over the resulting bindings.

11.1 ADDING SCRIPT BINDINGS

11.1.1 Extending versus Embedding

A script binding provides a way to access a C++ API from a scripting language. This normally involves creating wrapper code for the C++ classes and functions that allow them to be imported into the scripting language using its native module loading features, for example, the `import` keyword in Python, `require` in Ruby, or `use` in Perl.

There are two main strategies for integrating C++ with a scripting language:

1. **Extending the language**. In this model, a script binding is provided as a module that supplements the functionality of the scripting language. That is, users who write code with the scripting language can use your module in their own scripts. Your module will look just like any other module for that language. For example, the `expat` and `md5` modules in the Python standard library are implemented in C, not Python.

2. **Embedding within an application**. In this case, an end-user C++ application embeds a scripting language inside of it. Script bindings are then used to let end users write scripts for that specific application that call down into the core functionality of the program. Examples of this include the Autodesk Maya 3D modeling system, which offers Python and Maya Embedded Language (MEL) scripting, and the Adobe Director multimedia authoring platform, which embeds the Lingo scripting language.

Whichever strategy applies to your situation, the procedure to define and build script bindings is the same in each case. The only thing that really changes is who owns the C++ `main()` function.

11.1.2 Advantages of Scripting

The decision to provide access to native code APIs from within a scripting language offers many advantages. These advantages can either apply directly to you, if you provide a supported script binding for your C++ API, or to your clients, who may create their own script bindings on top of your C++-only API. I enumerate a few of these benefits here.

- **Cross-platform**. Scripting languages are interpreted, meaning that they execute plain ASCII source code or platform-independent byte code. They will also normally provide their own modules to interface with platform-specific features, such as the file system. Writing code for a scripting language should therefore work on multiple platforms without modification. This can also be considered a disadvantage for proprietary projects because scripting code will normally have to be distributed in source form.
- **Faster development**. If you make a change to a C++ program, you have to compile and link your code again. For large systems, this can be a time-consuming operation and can fracture engineer productivity as they wait to be able to test their change. In a scripting language, you simply edit the source code and then run it: there is no compile and link stage. This allows you to prototype and test new changes quickly, often resulting in greater engineer efficiency and project velocity.
- **Write less code**. A given problem can normally be solved with less code in a higher-level scripting language versus C++. Scripting languages don't require explicit memory management, they tend to have a much larger standard library available than C++'s STL, and they often take care of complex concepts such as reference counting behind the scenes. For example, the following single line of Ruby code will take a string and return an alphabetized list of all the unique letters in that string. This would take a lot more code to implement in C++.

  ```
  "Hello World".downcase.split("").uniq.sort.join
  => "dehlorw"
  ```

- **Script-based applications**. The traditional view of scripting languages is that you use them for small command-line tasks, but you must write an end-user application in a language such as C++ for maximum efficiency. However, an alternative view is that you can write the core performance-critical routines in C++, create script bindings for them, and then write your application in a scripting language. In Model–View–Controller parlance, the Model and potentially also the View are written in C++, whereas the Controller is implemented using a scripting language. The key insight is that you don't need a super fast compiled language to manage user input that happens at a low frequency.

At Pixar, we actually rewrote our in-house animation toolset this way: as a Python-based main application that calls down into an extensive set of very efficient Model and View C++ APIs. This gave us all the advantages listed here, such as removing the compile-link phase for many application logic changes while still delivering an interactive 3D animation system for our artists.

- **Support for expert users**. Adding a scripting language to an end-user application can allow advanced users to customize the functionality of the application by writing macros to perform repetitive tasks or tasks that are not exposed through the GUI. This can be done without sacrificing the usability of the software for novice users, who will interface with the application solely through the GUI.

- **Extensibility**. In addition to giving expert users access to under-the-covers functionality, a scripting interface can be used to let them add entirely new functionality to the application through plugin interfaces. This means that the developer of the application is no longer responsible for solving every user's problem. Instead, users have the power to solve their own problems. For example, the Firefox Web browser allows new extensions to be created using JavaScript as its embedded scripting language.

- **Scripting for testability**. One extremely valuable side effect of being able to write code in a scripting language is that you can write automated tests using that language. This is an advantage because you can enable your QA team to write automated tests too rather than rely solely on black-box testing. Often (although not exclusively), QA engineers will not write C++ code. However, there are many skilled white-box QA engineers who can write scripting language code. Involving your QA team in writing automated tests can let them contribute at a lower level and provide greater testing coverage.

- **Expressiveness**. The field of linguistics defines the principle of linguistic relativity (also known as the Sapir–Whorf hypothesis) as the idea that people's thoughts and behavior are influenced by their language. When applied to the field of computer science, this can mean that the expressiveness, flexibility, and ease of use of a programming language could impact the kinds of solutions that you can envision. That's because you don't have to be distracted by low-level issues such as memory management or statically typed data representations. This is obviously a more qualitative and subjective point than the previous technical arguments, but it is no less valid or significant.

11.1.3 Language Compatibility Issues

One important issue to be aware of when exposing a C++ API in a scripting language is that the patterns and idioms of C++ will not map directly to those of the scripting language. As such, a direct translation of the C++ API into the scripting language may produce a script module that doesn't feel natural or native in that language. For example,

- **Naming conventions**. C++ functions are often written using either upper or lower camel case, that is, `GetName()` or `getName()`. However, the Python convention (defined in PEP 8) is to use snake case for method names, for example, `get_name()`. Similarly, Ruby specifies that method names should use snake case also.

- **Getters/setters**. In this book, I have advocated that you should never directly expose data members in your classes. Instead, you should always provide getter/setter methods to access those members. However, many script languages allow you to use the syntax for accessing a member variable while still forcing that the access goes through getter/setter methods. In fact, in Ruby, this is the only way that you can access member variables from outside of a class. The result is that instead of C++ style code such as

```
object.SetName("Hello");
std::string name = object.GetName();
```

you can simply write the following, which still involves the use of underlying getter/setter methods:

```
object.name = "Hello"
name = object.name
```

- **Iterators**. Most scripting languages support the general concept of iteratators to navigate through the elements in a sequence. However, the implementation of this concept will not normally harmonize with the STL implementation. For example, C++ has five categories of iterators (forward, bidirectional, random access, input, and output), whereas Python has a single iterator category (forward). Making a C++ object iteratable in a scripting language therefore requires specific attention to adapt it to the semantics of that language, such as adding an __iter__() method in the case of Python.
- **Operators**. You already know that C++ supports several operators, such as `operator+`, `operator+=`, and `operator[]`. Often these can be translated directly into the equivalent syntax of the scripting language, such as exposing C++'s stream `operator<<` as the to_s() method in Ruby (which returns a string representation of the object). However, the target language may support additional operators that are not supported by C++, such as Ruby's power operator (`**`) and its operator to return the quotient and modules of a division (`divmod`).
- **Containers**. STL provides container classes such as `std::vector`, `std::set`, and `std::map`. These are statically typed class templates that can only contain objects of the same type. By comparison, many scripting languages are dynamically typed and support containers with elements of different types. It's much more common to use these flexible types to pass data around in scripting languages. For example, a C++ method that accepts several non-const reference arguments might be better represented in a scripting language by a method that returns a tuple. For example,

```
float width, height;
GetDimensions(&width, &height); // C++

width, height = get_dimensions(); # Python
```

All of this means that creating a good script binding is often a process that requires a degree of manual tuning. Technologies that attempt to create bindings fully automatically will normally produce APIs that don't feel natural in the scripting language. For example, the PyObjC utility provides a bridge for Objective-C objects in Python, but can result in cumbersome constructs in Python, such as methods called `setValue_()`. In contrast, a technology that lets you manually craft the way that functions are exposed in script will let you produce a higher quality result.

11.1.4 **Crossing the Language Barrier**

The language barrier refers to the boundary where C++ meets the scripting language. Script bindings for an object will take care of forwarding method calls in the scripting language down into the relevant C++ code. However, having C++ code call up into the scripting language will not normally happen by default. This is because a C++ API that has not been specifically designed to interoperate with a scripting language will not know that it's running in a script environment.

For example, consider a C++ class with a virtual method that gets overridden in Python. The C++ code has no idea that Python has overridden one of its virtual methods. This makes sense because the C++ vtable is created statically at compile time and cannot adapt to Python's dynamic ability to add methods at run time. Some binding technologies provide extra functionality to make this cross-language polymorphism work. I will discuss how this is done for Boost Python and SWIG later in the chapter.

Another issue to be aware of is whether the C++ code uses an internal event or notification system. If this is the case, some extra mechanism will need to be put in place to forward any C++-triggered events across the language boundary into script code. For example, Qt and Boost offer a signal/slot system where C++ code can register to receive notifications when another C++ object changes state. However, allowing scripts to receive these events will require you to write explicit code that can intercept the C++ events and send them over the boundary to the script object.

Finally, exceptions are another case where C++ code may need to communicate with script code. For example, uncaught C++ exceptions must be caught at the language barrier and then be translated into the native exception type of the script language.

11.2 **SCRIPT-BINDING TECHNOLOGIES**

Various technologies can be used to generate the wrappers that allow a scripting language to call down into your C++ code. Each offers its own specific advantages and disadvantages. Some are language-neutral technologies that support many scripting languages (such as COM or CORBA), some are specific to C/C++ but provide support for creating bindings to many languages (such as SWIG), some provide C++ bindings for a single language (such as Boost Python), whereas others focus on C++ bindings for a specific API (such as the Pivy Python bindings for the Open Inventor C++ toolkit).

I will list several of these technologies here, and then in the remainder of the chapter I will focus on two in more detail. I have chosen to focus on portable yet C++-specific solutions rather than considering the more general and heavyweight interprocess communication models such as COM or CORBA. To provide greater utility, I will look at one binding technology that lets you define the script binding programmatically (Boost Python) and another that uses an interface definition file to generate code for the binding (SWIG).

Any script binding technology is essentially founded upon the Adapter design pattern, that is, it provides a one-to-one mapping of one API to another API while also translating data types into their most appropriate native form and perhaps using more idiomatic naming conventions. Recognizing this fact means that you should also be aware of the standard issues that face API wrapping design patterns such as Proxy and Adapter. Of principal concern is the need to keep the two APIs synchronized over time. As you will see, both Boost Python and SWIG require you to keep redundant files in sync as you evolve the C++ API, such as extra C++ files in the case of Boost and separate interface files in the case of SWIG. This often turns out to be the largest maintenance cost when supporting a scripting API.

11.2.1 Boost Python

Boost Python (also written as boost::python or Boost.Python) is a C++ library that lets C++ APIs interoperate with Python. It is part of the excellent Boost libraries, available from http://www.boost.org/. With Boost Python you can create bindings programmatically in C++ code and then link the bindings against the Python and Boost Python libraries. This produces a dynamic library that can be imported directly into Python.

Boost Python includes support for the following capabilities and features in terms of wrapping C++ APIs:

- C++ references and pointers
- Translation of C++ exceptions to Python
- C++ default arguments and Python keyword arguments
- Manipulating Python objects in C++
- Exporting C++ iterators as Python iterators
- Python documentation strings
- Globally registered type coercions

11.2.2 SWIG

SWIG is an open source utility that can be used to create bindings for C or C++ interfaces in a variety of high-level languages. The supported languages include scripting languages such as Perl, PHP, Python, Tcl, and Ruby, as well as non-scripting languages such as C#, Common Lisp, Java, Lua, Modula-3, OCAML, Octave, and R.

The central design concept of SWIG is the interface file, normally given a .i file extension. This file is used to specify the generic bindings for a given module using C/C++ as the syntax to define the bindings. The general format of a SWIG interface file is as follows:

```
// example.i
%module <module-name>
%{
// declarations needed to compile the generated C++ binding code
%}
// declarations for the classes, functions, etc. to be wrapped
```

The SWIG program can then read this interface file and generate bindings for a specific language. These bindings are then compiled to a shared library that can be loaded by the scripting language. For more information about SWIG, see http://www.swig.org/.

11.2.3. Python-SIP

SIP is a tool that lets you create C and C++ bindings for Python. It was originally created for the PyQt package, which provides Python bindings for Nokia's Qt toolkit. As such, Python-SIP has specific support for the Qt signal/slot mechanism. However, the tool can also be used to create bindings for any C++ API.

SIP works in a very similar fashion to SWIG, although it does not support the range of languages that SWIG does. SIP supports much of the C/C++ syntax for its interface specification files and uses a similar syntax for its commands as SWIG (i.e., tokens that start with a % symbol), although it supports a different set and style of commands to customize the binding. Here is an example of a simple Python-SIP interface specification file.

```
// Define the SIP wrapper for an example library.

// define the Python module name and generation number
%Module example 0

class Example {

// include example.h in the wrapper that SIP generates
%TypeHeaderCode
#include <example.h>
%End

public:
   Example(const char *name);
   char *GetName() const;
};
```

11.2.4 COM Automation

Component Object Model (COM) is a binary interface standard that allows objects to interact with each other via interprocess communication. COM objects specify well-defined interfaces that allow software components to be reused and linked together to build end-user applications. The technology was developed by Microsoft in 1993 and is still used today, predominantly on the Windows platform, although Microsoft now encourages the use of .NET and SOAP.

COM encompasses a large suite of technologies, but the part I will focus on here is COM Automation, also known as OLE Automation or simply Automation. This involves Automation objects (also known as ActiveX objects) being accessed from scripting languages to perform repetitive tasks or to control an application from script. A large number of target languages are supported, such as Visual Basic, JScript, Perl, Python, Ruby, and the range of Microsoft .NET languages.

A COM object is identified by a Universally Unique ID (UUID) and exposes its functionality via interfaces that are also identified by UUIDs. All COM objects support the IUnknown interface methods of AddRef(), Release(), and QueryInterface(). COM Automation objects additionally implement the IDispatch interface, which includes the Invoke() method to trigger a named function in the object.

The object model for the interface being exposed is described using an interface description language (IDL). IDL is a language-neutral description of a software component's interface, normally stored in a file with an .idl extension. This IDL description can then be translated into various forms using the MIDL.EXE compiler on Windows. The generated files include the proxy DLL code for the COM object and a type library that describes the object model. The following sample shows an example of the Microsoft IDL syntax:

```
// Example.idl
import "mydefs.h","unknown.idl";
[
    object, uuid(d1420a03-d0ec-11b1-c04f-008c3ac31d2f),
]
interface ISomething : IUnknown
{
    HRESULT MethodA([in] short Param1, [out] BKFST *pParam2);
    HRESULT MethodB([in, out] BKFST *pParam1);
};


[
    object, uuid(1e1423d1-ba0c-d110-043a-00cf8cc31d2f),
    pointer_default(unique)
]
interface ISomethingElse : IUnknown
{
    HRESULT MethodC([in] long Max,
            [in, max_is(Max)] Param1[],
            [out] long *pSize,
            [out, size_is(, *pSize)] BKFST **ppParam2);
};
```

There is also a framework called Cross-Platform Component Object Model, or XPCOM. This is an open source project developed by Mozilla and used in a number of their applications, including the Firefox browser. XPCOM follows a very similar design to COM, although their components are not compatible or interchangeable.

11.2.5 CORBA

The Common Object Request Broker Architecture (CORBA) is an industry standard to allow software components to communicate with each other independent of their location and vendor. In this regard, it is very similar to COM: both technologies solve the problem of communication between objects from different sources and both make use of a language-neutral IDL format to describe each object's interface.

CORBA is cross-platform with several open source implementations and provides strong support for UNIX platforms. It was defined by the Object Management Group in 1991 (the same group that manages the UML modeling language). CORBA offers a wide range of language bindings, including Python, Perl, Ruby, Smalltalk, JavaScript, Tcl, and the CORBA Scripting Language (IDLscript). It also supports interfaces with multiple inheritance versus COM's single inheritance.

In terms of scripting, CORBA doesn't require a specific automation interface as COM does. All CORBA objects are scriptable by default via the Dynamic Invocation Interface, which lets scripting languages determine the object's interface dynamically. As an example of accessing CORBA objects from a scripting language, here is a simple IDL description and how it maps to the Ruby language.

```
// example.idl
interface myInterface
{
    struct MyStruct { short value; };
};

// example.rb
require 'myInteface'
s = MyInterface::MyStruct.new
s.value = 42
```

11.3 ADDING PYTHON BINDINGS WITH BOOST PYTHON

The rest of this chapter is dedicated to giving you a concrete understanding of how to create script bindings for your C++ API. I begin by showing you how to create Python bindings using the Boost Python libraries.

Python is an open source dynamically typed language designed by Guido van Rossum and first appeared in 1991. Python is strongly typed and features automatic memory management and reference counting. It comes with a large and extensive standard library, including modules such as `os`, `sys`, `re`, `difflib`, `codecs`, `datetime`, `math`, `gzip`, `csv`, `socket`, `json`, and `xml`, among many others. One of the more unusual aspects of Python is the fact that indentation is used to define scope, as opposed to curly braces in C and C++. The original CPython implementation of Python is the most common, but there are other major implementations, such as Jython (written in Java) and Iron Python (targeting the .NET framework). For more details on the Python language, refer to http://www.python.org/.

As already noted, Boost Python is used to define Python bindings programmatically, which can then be compiled to a dynamic library that can be loaded directly by Python. Figure 11.1 illustrates this basic workflow.

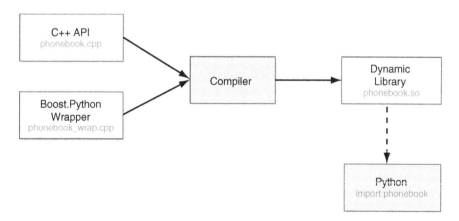

FIGURE 11.1

The workflow for creating Python bindings of a C++ API using Boost Python. White boxes represent files; shaded boxes represent commands.

11.3.1 Building Boost Python

Many Boost packages are implemented solely as headers, using templates and inline functions, so you only need to make sure that you add the Boost directory to your compiler's include search path. However, using Boost Python requires that you build and link against the `boost_python` library, so you need to know how to build Boost.

The recommended way to build Boost libraries is to use the bjam utility, a descendant of the Perforce Jam build system. So first you will need to download bjam. Prebuilt executables are available for most platforms from http://www.boost.org/.

Building the boost libraries on a UNIX variant, such as Linux or Mac, involves the following steps:

```
% cd <boost-root-directory>
% ./bootstrap.sh --prefix=<install-dir>
% ./bjam toolset=<toolset> install
```

The `<toolset>` string is used to define the compiler that you wish to build under, for example, "gcc," "darwin," "msvc," or "intel."

If you have multiple versions of Python installed on your machine, you can specify which version to use via bjam's configuration file, a file called `user-config.bjam` that you should create in your home directory. You can find out more details about configuring bjam in the Boost.Build manual, but essentially you will want to add something like the following entries to your `user-config.bjam` file:

```
using python
    : 2.6                        # version
    : /usr/local/bin/python2.6   # executable Path
    : /usr/local/include/python2.6  # include path
    : /usr/local/lib/python2.6   # lib path
```

On Windows, you can perform similar steps from the command prompt (just run `bootstrap.bat` instead of `boostrap.sh`). However, you can also simply download prebuilt boost libraries from http://www.boostpro.com/. If you use the prebuilt libraries, you will need to make sure that you compile your script bindings using the same version of Python used to compile the BoostPro libraries.

11.3.2 Wrapping a C++ API with Boost Python

Let's start by presenting a simple C++ API, which I will then expose to Python. I'll use the example of a phone book that lets you store phone numbers for multiple contacts. This gives us a manageable, yet non-trival, example to build upon throughout the chapter. Here's the public definition of our phonebook API.

```
// phonebook.h
#include <string>

class Person
{
public:
    Person();
    explicit Person(const std::string &name);
```

```
    void SetName(const std::string &name);
    std::string GetName() const;
    void SetHomeNumber(const std::string &number);
    std::string GetHomeNumber() const;
};

class PhoneBook
{
public:
    int GetSize() const;
    void AddPerson(Person *p);
    void RemovePerson(const std::string &name);
    Person *FindPerson(const std::string &name);
};
```

Note that this will let us demonstrate a number of capabilities, such as wrapping multiple classes, the use of STL containers, and multiple constructors. I will also take the opportunity to demonstrate the creation of Python properties in addition to the direct mapping of C++ member functions to Python methods.

The `Person` class is essentially just a data container: it only contains getter/setter methods that access underlying data members. These are good candidates for translating to Python properties. A property in Python behaves like a normal object but uses getter/setter methods to manage access to that object (as well as a deleter method for destroying the object). This makes for more intuitive access to class members that you want to behave like a simple data member while also letting you provide logic that controls getting and setting the value.

Now that I have presented our C++ API, let's look at how you can specify Python bindings for it using boost::python. You will normally create a separate `.cpp` file to specify the bindings for a given module, where it's conventional to use the same base filename as the module with a `_wrap` suffix appended, that is, I will use `phonebook_wrap.cpp` for our example. This wrap file is where you specify the classes that you want to expose and the methods that you want to be available on those classes. The following file presents the boost::python code necessary to wrap our `phonebook.h` API.

```cpp
// phonebook_wrap.cpp
#include "phonebook.h"
#include <boost/python.hpp>

using namespace boost::python;

BOOST_PYTHON_MODULE(phonebook)
{
    class_<Person>("Person")
        .add_property("name", &Person::GetName, &Person::SetName)
        .add_property("home_number", &Person::GetHomeNumber,
                &Person::SetHomeNumber)
        ;
    class_<PhoneBook>("PhoneBook")
        .def("size", &PhoneBook::GetSize)
        .def("add_person", &PhoneBook::AddPerson)
```

```
        .def("remove_person", &PhoneBook::RemovePerson)
        .def("find_person", &PhoneBook::FindPerson,
            return_value_policy<reference_existing_object>())
        ;
    }
```

Note that for the `Person` class, I defined two properties, called `name` and `home_number`, and I provided the C++ getter/setter functions to control access to those properties (if I only provided a getter method then the property would be read only). For the `PhoneBook` class, I defined standard methods, called `size()`, `add_person()`, `remove_person()`, and `find_person()`, respectively. I also had to specify explicitly how I want the pointer return value of `find_person()` to behave.

You can then compile the code for `phonebook.cpp` and `phonebook_wrap.cpp` to a dynamic library. This will involve compiling against the headers for Python and boost::python as well as linking against the libraries for both. The result should be a `phonebook.so` library on Mac and Linux or `phonebook.dll` on Windows. (Note: Python doesn't recognize the `.dylib` extension on the Mac.) For example, on Linux:

```
g++ -c phonebook.cpp
g++ -c phonebook_wrap.cpp -I<boost_includes> -I<python_include>
g++ -shared -o phonebook.so phonebook.o phonebook_wrap.o -lboost_python -lpython
```

TIP

Make sure that you compile your script bindings with the same version of Python that your Boost Python library was built against.

At this point, you can directly load the dynamic library into Python using its `import` keyword. Here is some sample Python code that loads our C++ library and demonstrates the creation of `Person` and `Phonebook` objects. Note the property syntax for accessing the `Person` object, for example, `p.name`, versus the method call syntax for the `PhoneBook` members, for example, `book.add_person()`.

```python
#!/usr/bin/python

import phonebook

# create the phonebook
book = phonebook.PhoneBook()

# add one contact
p = phonebook.Person()
p.name = 'Martin'
p.home_number = '(123) 456-7890'
book.add_person(p)

# add another contact
p = phonebook.Person()
```

```
p.name = 'Genevieve'
p.home_number = '(123) 456-7890'
book.add_person(p)

# display number of contacts added (2)
print "No. of contacts =", book.size()
```

11.3.3 Constructors

In our `phonebook_wrap.cpp` file, I didn't specify constructors for the `Person` or `PhoneBook` classes explicitly. In this case, Boost Python will expose the default constructor for each class, which is why I was able to write:

```
book = phonebook.PhoneBook()
```

However, note that in the C++ API, the `Person` class has two constructors, a default constructor and a second constructor that accepts a string parameter:

```
class Person
{
public:
    Person();
    explicit Person(const std::string &name);
    ....
};
```

You can tell Boost Python to expose both of these constructors by updating the wrapping code for `Person` to specify a single constructor in the class definition and then list further constructors using the `.def()` syntax.

```
class_<Person>("Person", init<>())
    .def(init<std::string>())
    .add_property("name", &Person::GetName, &Person::SetName)
    .add_property("home_number", &Person::GetHomeNumber,
            &Person::SetHomeNumber)
    ;
```

Now you can create `Person` objects from Python using either constructor.

```
#!/usr/bin/python

import phonebook

p = phonebook.Person()
p = phonebook.Person('Martin')
```

11.3.4 Extending the Python API

It's also possible to add new methods to the Python API that don't exist in the C++ API. This is used most commonly to define some of the standard Python object methods, such as __str__() to return a human-readable version of the object or __eq__() to test for equality.

In the following example, I have updated the `phonebook_wrap.cpp` file to include a static free function that prints out the values of a `Person` object. I then use this function to define the `Person.__str__()` method in Python.

```cpp
// phonebook_wrap.cpp
#include "phonebook.h"
#include <boost/python.hpp>
#include <sstream>
#include <iostream>

using namespace boost::python;

static std::string PrintPerson(const Person &p)
{
    std::ostringstream stream;
    stream << p.GetName() << ": " << p.GetHomeNumber();
    return stream.str();
}

BOOST_PYTHON_MODULE(phonebook)
{
    class_<Person>("Person", init<>())
        .def(init<std::string>())
        .add_property("name", &Person::GetName, &Person::SetName)
        .add_property("home_number", &Person::GetHomeNumber,
                &Person::SetHomeNumber)
        .def("__str__", &PrintPerson)
        ;
    ....
}
```

This demonstrates the general ability to add new methods to a class. However, in this particular case, Boost Python provides an alternative way to specify the __str__() function in a more idiomatic fashion. You could define `operator<<` for `Person` and tell Boost to use this operator for the __str__() method. For example,

```cpp
#include "phonebook.h"
#include <boost/python.hpp>
#include <iostream>

using namespace boost::python;

std::ostream &operator<<(std::ostream &os, const Person &p)
{
    os << p.GetName() << ": " << p.GetHomeNumber();
    return os;
}
```

```
BOOST_PYTHON_MODULE(phonebook)
{
   class_<Person>("Person", init<>())
      .def(init<std::string>())
      .add_property("name", &Person::GetName, &Person::SetName)
      .add_property("home_number", &Person::GetHomeNumber,
            &Person::SetHomeNumber)
      .def(self_ns::str(self))
      ;
}
```

With this definition for `Person.__str__()` you can now write code like the following (entered at the interactive Python interpreter prompt, >>>):

```
>>> import phonebook
>>> p = phonebook.Person('Martin')
>>> print p
Martin:
>>> p.home_number = '(123) 456-7890'
>>> print p
Martin: (123) 456-7890
```

While I am talking about extending the Python API, I will note that the dynamic nature of Python means that you can actually add new methods to a class at run time. This is not a Boost Python feature, but a core capability of the Python language itself. For example, you could define the `__str__()` method at the Python level, as follows:

```
#!/usr/bin/python

import phonebook

def person_str(self):
   return "Name: %s\nHome: %s" % (self.name, self.home_number)

# override the __str__ method for the Person class
phonebook.Person.__str__ = person_str
p = phonebook.Person()
p.name = 'Martin'
p.home_number = '(123) 456-7890'
print p
```

This will output the following text to the shell.

```
Name: Martin
Home: (123) 456-7890
```

11.3.5 Inheritance in C++

Both C++ and Python support multiple inheritance, and Boost Python makes it easy to expose all of the base classes of any C++ class. I'll show how this is done by turning the `Person` class into a base class (i.e., provide a virtual destructor) and adding a derived class called `PersonWithCell`, which adds the ability to specify a cell phone number. This is not a particularly good design choice, but it serves our purposes for this example.

```cpp
// phonebook.h
#include <string>

class Person
{
public:
    Person();
    explicit Person(const std::string &name);
    virtual ~Person();

    void SetName(const std::string &name);
    std::string GetName() const;
    void SetHomeNumber(const std::string &number);
    std::string GetHomeNumber() const;
};

class PersonWithCell : public Person
{
public:
    PersonWithCell();
    explicit PersonWithCell(const std::string &name);

    void SetCellNumber(const std::string &number);
    std::string GetCellNumber() const;
};
```

You can then represent this inheritance hierarchy in Python by updating the wrap file as follows:

```cpp
BOOST_PYTHON_MODULE(phonebook)
{
    class_<Person>("Person", init<>())
        .def(init<std::string>())
        .add_property("name", &Person::GetName, &Person::SetName)
        .add_property("home_number", &Person::GetHomeNumber,
                &Person::SetHomeNumber)
        ;
    class_<PersonWithCell, bases<Person> >("PersonWithCell")
        .def(init<std::string>())
        .add_property("cell_number", &PersonWithCell::GetCellNumber,
                &PersonWithCell::SetCellNumber)
        ;
    ...
}
```

Now you can create `PersonWithCell` objects from Python as follows:

```
#!/usr/bin/python

import phonebook
book = phonebook.PhoneBook()

p = phonebook.Person()
p.name = 'Martin'
p.home_number = '(123) 456-7890'
book.add_person(p)

p = phonebook.PersonWithCell()
p.name = 'Genevieve'
p.home_number = '(123) 456-7890'
p.cell_number = '(123) 097-2134'
book.add_person(p)
```

11.3.6 Cross-Language Polymorphism

You can create classes in Python that derive from C++ classes that you've exposed with Boost Python. For example, the following Python program shows how you could create the `PersonWithCell` class directly in Python and still be able to add instances of this class to `PhoneBook`.

```
#!/usr/bin/python

import phonebook

book = phonebook.PhoneBook()

class PyPersonWithCell(phonebook.Person):
    def get_cell_number(self):
        return self.cell
    def set_cell_number(self, n):
        self.cell = n
    cell_number = property(get_cell_number, set_cell_number)

p = PyPersonWithCell()
p.name = 'Martin'
p.home_number = '(123) 456-7890'
p.cell_number = '(123) 097-2134'
book.add_person(p)
```

Of course, the `cell_number` property on `PyPersonWithCell` will only be callable from Python. C++ will have no idea that a new method has been dynamically added to an inherited class.

It's also important to note that even C++ virtual functions that are overridden in Python will not be callable from C++ by default. However, Boost Python does provide a way to do this if cross-language polymorphism is important for your API. This is done by defining a wrapper class that multiply inherits from the C++ class being bound as well as Boost Python's wrapper class template. This wrapper class can then check to see if an override has been defined in Python for a given virtual function and then call that method if it is defined. For example, given a C++ class called `Base` with a virtual method, you can create the wrapper class as follows:

```
class Base
{
public:
    virtual ~Base();
    virtual int f();
};

class BaseWrap : Base, wrapper<Base>
{
public:
    int f()
    {
        // check for an override in Python
        if (override f = this->get_override("f"))
          return f();

        // or call the C++ implementation
        return Base::f();
    }
    int default_f()
    {
        return this->Base::f();
    }
};
```

Then you can expose the `Base` class as follows:

```
class_<BaseWrap, boost::non-copyable>("Base")
    .def("f", &Base::f, &BaseWrap::default_f)
    ;
```

11.3.7 **Supporting Iterators**

Boost Python also lets you create Python iterators based on STL iterator interfaces that you define in your C++ API. This lets you create objects in Python that behave more "Pythonically" in terms of iterating through the elements in a container. For example, you can add `begin()` and `end()` methods to the `PhoneBook` class that provide access to STL iterators for traversing through all of the contacts in the phone book.

```
class PhoneBook
{
public:
    int GetSize() const;
    void AddPerson(Person *p);
    void RemovePerson(const std::string &name);
    Person *FindPerson(const std::string &name);
```

```
    typedef std::vector<Person *> PersonList;
    PersonList::iterator begin();
    PersonList::iterator end();
};
```

With these additional methods, you can extend the wrapping for the PhoneBook class to specify the __iter__() method, which is the Python way for an object to return an iterator.

```
BOOST_PYTHON_MODULE(phonebook)
{
    ...
    class_<PhoneBook>("PhoneBook")
        .def("size", &PhoneBook::GetSize)
        .def("add_person", &PhoneBook::AddPerson)
        .def("remove_person", &PhoneBook::RemovePerson)
        .def("find_person", &PhoneBook::FindPerson,
          return_value_policy<reference_existing_object>())
        .def("__iter__", range(&PhoneBook::begin, &PhoneBook::end));
        ;
}
```

Now, you can write Python code that iterates through all of the contacts in a PhoneBook object as follows:

```
#!/usr/bin/python

import phonebook

book = phonebook.PhoneBook()
book.add_person(phonebook.Person())
book.add_person(phonebook.Person())

for person in book:
    print person
```

11.3.8 Putting It All Together

Combining all of the features that I've introduced in the preceding sections, here is the final definition of the phonebook.h header and the phonebook_wrap.cpp boost::python wrapper.

```
// phonebook.h
#include <string>
#include <vector>

class Person
{
public:
    Person();
    explicit Person(const std::string &name);
```

```cpp
    virtual ~Person();

    void SetName(const std::string &name);
    std::string GetName() const;
    void SetHomeNumber(const std::string &number);
    std::string GetHomeNumber() const;
};

class PersonWithCell : public Person
{
public:
    PersonWithCell();
    explicit PersonWithCell(const std::string &name);
    void SetCellNumber(const std::string &number);
    std::string GetCellNumber() const;
};

class PhoneBook
{
public:
    int GetSize() const;
    void AddPerson(Person *p);
    void RemovePerson(const std::string &name);
    Person *FindPerson(const std::string &name);
    typedef std::vector<Person *> PersonList;
    PersonList::iterator begin() { return mList.begin(); }
    PersonList::iterator end() { return mList.end(); }
};

// phonebook_wrap.cpp
#include "phonebook.h"
#include <boost/python.hpp>
#include <sstream>
#include <iostream>

using namespace boost::python;

std::ostream &operator<<(std::ostream &os, const Person &p)
{
    os << p.GetName() << ": " << p.GetHomeNumber();
    return os;
}

static std::string PrintPersonWithCell(const PersonWithCell *p)
{
    std::ostringstream stream;
    stream << "Name: " << p->GetName() << ", Home: ";
    stream << p->GetHomeNumber() << ", Cell: ";
    stream << p->GetCellNumber();
```

```
      return stream.str();
}

BOOST_PYTHON_MODULE(phonebook)
{
    class_<Person>("Person", init<>())
        .def(init<std::string>())
        .add_property("name", &Person::GetName, &Person::SetName)
        .add_property("home_number", &Person::GetHomeNumber,
                &Person::SetHomeNumber)
        .def(self_ns::str(self))
        ;
    class_<PersonWithCell,
        bases<Person> >("PersonWithCell")
        .def(init<std::string>())
        .add_property("cell_number", &PersonWithCell::GetCellNumber,
                &PersonWithCell::SetCellNumber)
        .def("__str__", &PrintPersonWithCell)
        ;
    class_<PhoneBook>("PhoneBook")
        .def("size", &PhoneBook::GetSize)
        .def("add_person", &PhoneBook::AddPerson)
        .def("remove_person", &PhoneBook::RemovePerson)
        .def("find_person", &PhoneBook::FindPerson,
          return_value_policy<reference_existing_object>())
        .def("__iter__", range(&PhoneBook::begin, &PhoneBook::end));
        ;
}
```

11.4 ADDING RUBY BINDINGS WITH SWIG

The following sections will look at another example of creating script bindings for C++ APIs. In this case I will use the Simplified Wrapper and Interface Generator and I will use this utility to create bindings for the Ruby language.

Ruby is an open source dynamically typed scripting language that was released by Yukihiro "Matz" Matsumoto in 1995. Ruby was influenced by languages such as Perl and Smalltalk with an emphasis on ease of use. In Ruby, everything is an object, even types that C++ treats separately as built-in primitives such as int, float, and bool. Ruby is an extremely popular scripting language and is often cited as being more popular than Python in Japan, where it was originally developed. For more information on the Ruby language, see http://www.ruby-lang.org/.

SWIG works by reading the binding definition within an interface file and generating C++ code to specify the bindings. This generated code can then be compiled to a dynamic library that can be loaded directly by Ruby. Figure 11.2 illustrates this basic workflow. Note that SWIG supports many scripting languages. I will use it to create Ruby bindings, but it could just as easily be used to create Python bindings, Perl bindings, or bindings for several other languages.

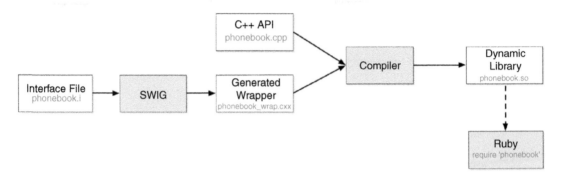

FIGURE 11.2

The workflow for creating Ruby bindings of a C++ API using SWIG. White boxes represent files; shaded boxes represent commands.

11.4.1 Wrapping a C++ API with SWIG

I'll start with the same phone book API from the Python example and then show how to create Ruby bindings for this interface using SWIG. The phone book C++ header looks like

```
// phonebook.h
#include <string>

class Person
{
public:
    Person();
    explicit Person(const std::string &name);

    void SetName(const std::string &name);
    std::string GetName() const;
    void SetHomeNumber(const std::string &number);
    std::string GetHomeNumber() const;
};

class PhoneBook
{
public:
    bool IsEmpty() const;
    int GetSize() const;
    void AddPerson(Person *p);
    void RemovePerson(const std::string &name);
    Person *FindPerson(const std::string &name);
};
```

Let's take a look at a basic SWIG interface file to specify how you want to expose this C++ API to Ruby.

```
// phonebook.i
%module phonebook
%{

// we need the API header to compile the bindings
#include "phonebook.h"

%}

// pull in the built-in SWIG STL wrappings (note the '%')
%include "std_string.i"
%include "std_vector.i"

class Person
{
public:
    Person();
    explicit Person(const std::string &name);

    void SetName(const std::string &name);
    std::string GetName() const;
    void SetHomeNumber(const std::string &number);
    std::string GetHomeNumber() const;
};

class PhoneBook
{
public:
    bool IsEmpty() const;
    int GetSize() const;
    void AddPerson(Person *p);
    void RemovePerson(const std::string &name);
    Person *FindPerson(const std::string &name);
};
```

You can see that the interface file looks very similar to the phonebook.h header file. In fact, SWIG can parse most C++ syntax directly. If your C++ header is very simple, you can even use SWIG's %include directive to simply tell it to read the C++ header file directly. I've chosen not to do this so that you have direct control over what you do and do not expose to Ruby.

Now that you have an initial interface file, you can ask SWIG to read this file and generate Ruby bindings for all the specified C++ classes and methods. This will create a phonebook_wrap.cxx file, which you can compile together with the C++ code to create a dynamic library. For example, the steps on Linux are

```
swig -c++ -ruby phonebook.i # creates phonebook_wrap.cxx
g++ -c phonebook_wrap.cxx -I<ruby-include-path>
g++ -c phonebook.cpp
g++ -shared -o phonebook.so phonebook_wrap.o phonebook.o -L<ruby-lib-path> -lruby
```

11.4.2 Tuning the Ruby API

This first attempt at a Ruby binding is rather rudimentary. There are several issues that you will want to address to make the API feel more natural to Ruby programmers. First off, the naming convention for Ruby methods is to use snake case instead of camel case, that is, add_person() instead of AddPerson(). SWIG supports this by letting you rename symbols in the scripting API using its %rename command. For example, you can add the following lines to the interface file to tell SWIG to rename the methods of the PhoneBook class.

```
%rename("size") PhoneBook::GetSize;
%rename("add_person") PhoneBook::AddPerson;
%rename("remove_person") PhoneBook::RemovePerson;
%rename("find_person") PhoneBook::FindPerson;
```

Recent versions of SWIG actually support an -autorename command line option to perform this function renaming automatically. It is expected that this option will eventually be turned on by default.

Second, Ruby has a concept similar to Python's properties to provide convenient access to data members. In fact, rather elegantly, all instance variables in Ruby are private and must therefore be accessed via getter/setter methods. The %rename syntax can be used to accomplish this ability too. For example,

```
%rename("name") Person::GetName;
%rename("name=") Person::SetName;
%rename("home_number") Person::GetHomeNumber;
%rename("home_number=") Person::SetHomeNumber;
```

Finally, you may have noticed that I added an extra IsEmpty() method to the PhoneBook C++ class. This method simply returns true if no contacts have been added to the phone book. I've added this because it lets me demonstrate how to expose a C++ member function as a Ruby query method. This is a method that returns a boolean return value and by convention it ends with a question mark. I would therefore like the IsEmpty() C++ function to appear as empty? in Ruby. This can be done using either SWIG's %predicate or %rename directives.

```
%rename("empty?") PhoneBook::IsEmpty;
```

With these amendments to our interface file, our Ruby API is starting to feel more native. If you rerun SWIG on the interface file and rebuild the phonebook dynamic library, you can import it directly into Ruby and write code such as

```
#!/usr/bin/ruby

require 'phonebook'

book = Phonebook::PhoneBook.new

p = Phonebook::Person.new
p.name = 'Martin'
p.home_number = '(123) 456-7890'
book.add_person(p)
```

```
p = Phonebook::Person.new
p.name = 'Genevieve'
p.home_number = '(123) 456-7890'
book.add_person(p)

puts "No. of contacts = #{book.size}"
```

Note the use of the p.name getter and p.name= setter, as well as the snake case add_person() method name.

11.4.3 **Constructors**

Our Person class has two constructors: a default constructor that takes no parameters and a non-default constructor that takes a std::string name. Using SWIG, you simply have to include those constructor declarations in the interface file and it will automatically create the relevant constructors in Ruby. That is, given the earlier interface file, you can already do:

```
#!/usr/bin/ruby

require 'phonebook'

p = Phonebook::Person.new
p = Phonebook::Person.new('Genevieve')
```

In general, method overloading is not quite as flexible in Ruby as it is in C++. For example, SWIG will not be able to disambiguate between overloaded functions that map to the same types in Ruby, for example, a constructor that takes a short and another that takes an int or a constructor that takes a pointer to an object and another that takes a reference to the same type. SWIG does provide a way to deal with this by letting you ignore a given overloaded method (using %ignore) or renaming one of the methods (using %rename).

11.4.4 **Extending the Ruby API**

SWIG lets you extend the functionality of your C++ API, for example, to add new methods to a class that will only appear in the Ruby API. This is done using SWIG's %extend directive. I will demonstrate this by adding a to_s() method to the Ruby version of our Person class. This is a standard Ruby method used to return a human-readable representation of an object, equivalent to Python's __str__() method.

```
// phonebook.i
%module phonebook
%{

#include "phonebook.h"
#include <sstream>
#include <iostream>

%}
```

```
...
class Person
{
public:
    Person();
    explicit Person(const std::string &name);

    void SetName(const std::string &name);
    std::string GetName() const;
    void SetHomeNumber(const std::string &number);
    std::string GetHomeNumber() const;

    %extend {
        std::string to_s() {
          std::ostringstream stream;
          stream << self->GetName() << ": ";
          stream << self->GetHomeNumber();
          return stream.str();
        }
    }
};
...
```

Using this new definition for our `Person` binding, you can write the following Ruby code:

```
#!/usr/bin/ruby

require 'phonebook'

p = Phonebook::Person.new
p.name = 'Martin'
p.home_number = '(123) 456-7890'
puts p
```

The `puts p` line will print out the `Person` object using our `to_s()` method. In this case, this results in the following output:

```
Martin: (123) 456-7890
```

11.4.5 Inheritance in C++

As with the constructor case just given, there's nothing special that you have to do to represent inheritance using SWIG. You simply declare the class in the interface file using the standard C++ syntax. For example, you can add the following `PersonWithCell` class to our API:

```
// phonebook.h
#include <string>

class Person
```

```
{
public:
    Person();
    explicit Person(const std::string &name);
    virtual ~Person();

    void SetName(const std::string &name);
    std::string GetName() const;
    void SetHomeNumber(const std::string &number);
    std::string GetHomeNumber() const;
};

class PersonWithCell : public Person
{
public:
    PersonWithCell();
    explicit PersonWithCell(const std::string &name);

    void SetCellNumber(const std::string &number);
    std::string GetCellNumber() const;
};
...
```

Then you can update the SWIG interface file as follows:

```
// phonebook.i
...
%rename("name") Person::GetName;
%rename("name=") Person::SetName;
%rename("home_number") Person::GetHomeNumber;
%rename("home_number=") Person::SetHomeNumber;

class Person
{
public:
    Person();
    explicit Person(const std::string &name);
    virtual ~Person();

    void SetName(const std::string &name);
    std::string GetName() const;
    void SetHomeNumber(const std::string &number);
    std::string GetHomeNumber() const;
    ...
};

%rename("cell_number") PersonWithCell::GetCellNumber;
%rename("cell_number=") PersonWithCell::SetCellNumber;
```

```
class PersonWithCell : public Person
{
public:
   PersonWithCell();
   explicit PersonWithCell(const std::string &name);

   void SetCellNumber(const std::string &number);
   std::string GetCellNumber() const;
};
...
```

You can then access this derived C++ class from Ruby as follows:

```
#!/usr/bin/ruby

require 'phonebook'

p = Phonebook::Person.new
p.name = 'Martin'
p.home_number = '(123) 456-7890'

p = Phonebook::PersonWithCell.new
p.name = 'Genevieve'
p.home_number = '(123) 456-7890'
p.cell_number = '(123) 097-2134'
```

Ruby supports only single inheritance, with support for additional mixin classes. C++ of course supports multiple inheritance. Therefore, by default, SWIG will only consider the first base class listed in the derived class: member functions in any other base classes will not be inherited. However, recent versions of SWIG support an optional -minherit command line option that will attempt to simulate multiple inheritance using Ruby mixins (although in this case a class no longer has a true base class in Ruby).

11.4.6 Cross-Language Polymorphism

By default, if you override a virtual function in Ruby you will not be able to call the Ruby method from C++. However, SWIG gives you a way to enable this kind of cross-language polymorphism via its "directors" feature. When you enable directors for a class, SWIG generates a new wrapper class that derives from the C++ class as well as SWIG's director class. The director class stores a pointer to the underlying Ruby object and works out whether a function call should be directed to an overridden Ruby method or the default C++ implementation. This is analogous to the way that Boost Python supports cross-language polymorphism. However, SWIG creates the wrapper class for you behind the scenes: all you have to do is specify which classes you want to create directors for and then enable the directors feature in your %module directive. For example, the following update to our interface file will turn on cross-language polymorphism for all our classes:

```
%module(directors="1") phonebook
%{
```

```
#include "phonebook.h"
#include <sstream>
#include <iostream>

%}

%feature("director");
...
```

11.4.7 **Putting It All Together**

I have evolved our simple example through several iterations in order to add each incremental enhancement. So I will finish off this section by presenting the entire C++ header and SWIG interface file for your reference. First of all, here is the C++ API:

```
// phonebook.h
#include <string>

class Person
{
public:
    Person();
    explicit Person(const std::string &name);
    virtual ~Person();

    void SetName(const std::string &name);
    std::string GetName() const;
    void SetHomeNumber(const std::string &number);
    std::string GetHomeNumber() const;
};

class PersonWithCell : public Person
{
public:
    PersonWithCell();
    explicit PersonWithCell(const std::string &name);

    void SetCellNumber(const std::string &number);
    std::string GetCellNumber() const;
};

class PhoneBook
{
public:
    bool IsEmpty() const;
    int GetSize() const;
    void AddPerson(Person *p);
    void RemovePerson(const std::string &name);
```

```
      Person *FindPerson(const std::string &name);
   };
```

and here is the final SWIG interface (.i) file:

```
   %module(directors="1") phonebook
   %{

   #include "phonebook.h"
   #include <sstream>
   #include <iostream>

   %}

   %feature("director");
   %include "std_string.i"
   %include "std_vector.i"
   %rename("name") Person::GetName;
   %rename("name=") Person::SetName;
   %rename("home_number") Person::GetHomeNumber;
   %rename("home_number=") Person::SetHomeNumber;

   class Person
   {
   public:
      Person();
      explicit Person(const std::string &name);
      virtual ~Person();

      void SetName(const std::string &name);
      std::string GetName() const;
      void SetHomeNumber(const std::string &number);
      std::string GetHomeNumber() const;

      %extend {
         std::string to_s() {
           std::ostringstream stream;
           stream << self->GetName() << ": ";
           stream << self->GetHomeNumber();
           return stream.str();
         }
      }
   };

   %rename("cell_number") PersonWithCell::GetCellNumber;
   %rename("cell_number=") PersonWithCell::SetCellNumber;
```

```
class PersonWithCell : public Person
{
public:
   PersonWithCell();
   explicit PersonWithCell(const std::string &name);

   void SetCellNumber(const std::string &number);
   std::string GetCellNumber() const;
};

%rename("empty?") PhoneBook::IsEmpty;
%rename("size") PhoneBook::GetSize;
%rename("add_person") PhoneBook::AddPerson;
%rename("remove_person") PhoneBook::RemovePerson;
%rename("find_person") PhoneBook::FindPerson;

class PhoneBook
{
public:
   bool IsEmpty() const;
   int GetSize() const;
   void AddPerson(Person *p);
   void RemovePerson(const std::string &name);
   Person *FindPerson(const std::string &name);
};
```

Extensibility

This final chapter discusses the topic of API extensibility. By this, I mean the ability of your clients to modify the behavior of your interface without requiring you to evolve the API for their specific needs. This can be a critical factor in your ability to maintain a clean and focused interface while also delivering a flexible system that lets your users solve problems that you had never anticipated. This concept is expressed by the Open/Closed Principle, which was discussed in Chapter 4, that an API should be open for extension but closed for modification (Meyer, 1997).

To offer a real-world example, the Marionette animation system at Pixar supported key-frame animation with a range of possible interpolation schemes between animation keys, such as Bézier, Catmull-Rom, linear, and step interpolation. However, during development of *The Incredibles* and *Cars* it became necessary to allow our production users to devise and iterate on more sophisticated interpolation routines. Instead of continually updating the core animation system every time our users needed to change their custom interpolation algorithm, I devised a plugin system that allowed production users to create dynamic libraries that could be discovered at run time and would then be added to the set of built-in interpolation routines. This proved to be a very effective way to resolve production-specific needs while still maintaining a generic filmmaking system.

This chapter is dedicated to various techniques that allow you to achieve the same level of flexibility in your own APIs. I will spend most of the chapter detailing how to create industrial-strength, cross-platform plugin architectures for your C and C++ APIs, but I will also cover other extensibility techniques using inheritance and templates.

12.1 EXTENDING VIA PLUGINS

In the most common scenario, a plugin is a dynamic library that is discovered and loaded at run time as opposed to a dynamic library that an application is linked against at build time. Plugins can therefore be written by your users, using a well-defined plugin API that you provide. This allows them to extend the functionality of your API in designated ways. Figure 12.1 illustrates this concept, where the white boxes represent artifacts that your users produce.

It should be noted, however, that static library plugins are also possible, such as for embedded systems where all plugins are statically linked into the application at compile time. This is useful to ensure that a plugin can be found at run time and that it has been built under the same environment as the main executable. However, I will focus on the dynamic library model in this chapter, as this poses the most design challenges and gives users the ability to add new plugins to the system at run time.

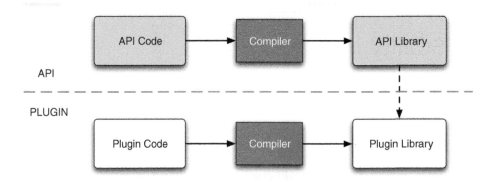

FIGURE 12.1

A plugin library is a dynamic library that can be compiled separately from a Core API and explicitly loaded by the API on demand.

12.1.1 Plugin Model Overview

Many examples of commercial software packages allow their core functionality to be extended through the use of C/C++ plugins. For example, the Apache Web server supports C-based "modules," Adobe Photoshop supports a range of plugin types to manipulate images, and Web browsers such as Firefly, Chrome, and Opera support the Netscape Plugin API (NPAPI) for the creation of browser plugins such as the Adobe Flash or PDF Reader plugins. The Qt toolkit can also be extended via the QPluginLoader class. (A server-based plugin API such as Apache's module interface is sometimes referred to as a Server API, or SAPI.)

Some of the benefits of adopting a plugin model in your API are as follows.

- **Greater versatility**. Your API can be used to solve a greater range of problems, without requiring you to implement solutions for all of those problems.
- **Community catalyst**. By giving your users the ability to solve their own problems within the framework of your API, you can spark a community of user-contributed additions to your base design.
- **Smaller updates**. Functionality that exists as a plugin can be updated easily independently of the application by simply dropping in a new version of the plugin. This can often be a much smaller update than distributing a new version of the entire application.
- **Future proofing**. Your API may reach a level of stability where you feel that no further updates are necessary. However, further evolution of the functionality of your API can continue through the development of plugins, allowing the API to maintain its usefulness and relevance for a greater period of time. For example, the NPAPI has changed little in recent years, but it is still a popular method to write plugins for many Web browsers.
- **Isolating risk**. Plugins can be beneficial for in-house development too by letting engineers change functionality without destabilizing the core of your system.

As was just hinted, a plugin system doesn't have to be used only by your clients. You can develop parts of your Core API implementation as plugins too. In fact, this is actually a good practice because it ensures that you fully exercise your plugin architecture and that you live in the same world as your users ("eat your own dog food"). For example, the GNU Image Manipulation Program (GIMP) ships many of its built-in image processing functions as plugins using its GIMP Plugin API.

NETSCAPE PLUGINS

The Netscape Plugin API (NPAPI) provides a cross-platform plugin API to embed custom functionality inside of various Web browsers. The interface grew out of work from Adobe Systems to integrate a PDF viewer into early versions of the Netscape browser. This plain C plugin API is still used today to embed native code extensions inside of Web browsers, such as Mozilla Firefox, Apple Safari, and Google Chrome. For example, Shockwave Flash, Apple QuickTime, and Microsoft Silverlight are implemented as browser plugins (try typing "about:plugins" into Firefox to see a list of installed plugins).

The NPAPI gives native code the following capabilities inside a Web browser:

- Register new MIME types.
- Draw into a region of the browser window.
- Receive mouse and keyboard events.
- Send and receive data over HTTP.
- Add hyperlinks or hot spots that link to new URLs.
- Communicate with the Document Object Model.

While I was at SRI International in the 1990s, we developed a Web-based 3D terrain visualization system called TerraVision (Leclerc and Lau, 1994). This started life as a desktop application that required a four-processor SGI Onyx RealityEngine[2]. However, as commodity graphics hardware advanced, we were eventually able to make it run as a plugin inside of Netscape Navigator and Microsoft Explorer on a standard PC.

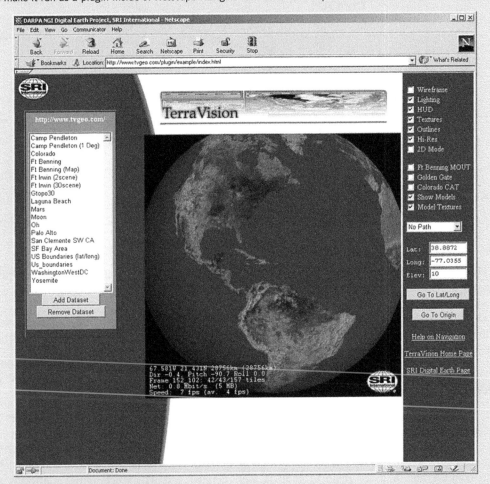

Because TerraVision was a complex multithreaded application, to make this work in a non-thread-safe browser environment we had to run it in a separate process. That is, our Netscape plugin would create a new process for TerraVision to run in and pass it a window handle to draw into. All communication between the plugin and the TerraVision processes happened via pipe I/O.

12.1.2 Plugin System Design Issues

There are many different ways to design a plugin system. The best solution for your current project may not be the best choice for your next project. I will therefore start by trying to tease out some of the high-level issues that you should be aware of when devising a plugin system.

At the same time, there are also a number of general concepts applicable to all plugin systems. For example, when supporting dynamic library plugins, you will always need a mechanism to load a dynamic library and access symbols in that file. In general, when creating any plugin system, there are two major features that you must design (see Figure 12.2).

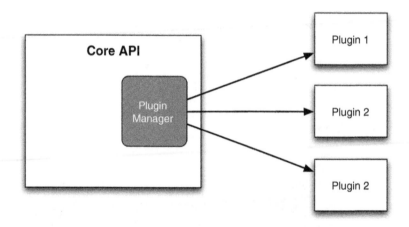

FIGURE 12.2

The Plugin Manager lives in the Core API. It discovers and loads plugins that have been built against the Plugin API.

1. **The Plugin API**: This is the API that your users must compile and link against in order to create a plugin. I differentiate this from your Core API, which is the larger code base into which you are adding the plugin system.
2. **The Plugin Manager**: This is an object (often a singleton) in the Core API code that manages the life cycle of all plugins, that is, loading, registration, and unloading. This object can also be called the Plugin Registry.

With these general concepts in hand, let's take a look at some of the design decisions that will affect the precise plugin architecture that you should build for your API.

- **C versus C++.** As discussed earlier in the versioning chapter, the C++ specification does not define a specific ABI. Therefore, different compilers, and even different versions of the same compiler, can produce code that is binary incompatible. The implication for a plugin system is that plugins developed by clients using a compiler with a different ABI may not be loadable. In contrast, the ABI for plain C code is well defined and will work across platforms and compilers.

- **Versioning**. You will want some way to know whether a plugin was built with an incompatible version of your API. Because determining what constitutes an incompatible API can be difficult to surmise automatically, it is often left to the plugin writer to specify. For example, Firefox's Extensions API lets you specify a minimum and maximum version range that the extension is known to work with (with a system to easily update an extension's max version for occasions when an incompatible API is released). It's also useful to know which version of the API a plugin was compiled against. This could be embedded in the plugin automatically or again it could be left to the plugin writer to specify. For example, Google's Android API lets you specify an `android:targetSdkVersion` in addition to `android:minSdkVersion` and `android:maxSdkVersion`.

- **Internal versus external metadata**. Metadata, such as a human-readable name and version information, can either be defined within the plugin code itself or can also be specified in a simple external file format. The benefit of using an external metadata file is that you don't actually have to load all plugins in order to know the set of all available objects. For example, you may want to present a list of all plugins to the user and then only load the plugins they chose to use. The downside, however, is that you cannot simply drop a new plugin into a directory and have it be loaded automatically. You must also include a per-plugin metadata file, or update a global metadata file for all plugins, depending on the particular approach you adopt.

- **Generic versus specialized Plugin Manager**. One approach to implementing the Plugin Manager is to make it very low level and generic, that is, it simply loads plugins and accesses symbols in those plugins. However, doing so can mean that the Plugin Manager does not know about the existence of concrete types in your API. As a result, it will probably have to return objects as `void*` pointers and you must cast those to concrete types before using them. Alternatively, a Plugin Manager that can, at a minimum, forward declare the types for any objects in a plugin can produce a more type safe solution, although as a result it cannot be implemented independently of your API. A middle ground is to introduce a dynamic run-time typing system into your API, where the Plugin Manager can return references in terms of a generic type that can be registered later by your API.

- **Security**. You must decide how much you will trust user plugins. Plugins are arbitrarily compiled code that you allow to run in your process. A plugin could therefore potentially do anything, from accessing data that it should not, to deleting files on the end-user's hard drive, to crashing the entire application. If you need to protect against such malicious plugins, then you may consider creating a socket-based solution, where plugins run in a separate process and communicate with the Core API through an IPC channel. Alternatively, you could implement bindings for a language that supports sandboxing of user scripts, such as JavaScript or .NET/Mono, and require all plugins to be written in that scripting language.

- **Static versus dynamic libraries**. As already mentioned, it is possible to define plugins as static libraries, meaning that they must be compiled into the application program. The more common solution for consumer applications is to use dynamic libraries so that users can write their own plugins and extend the application at run time. A constraint for writing static plugins is that you must ensure that no two plugins define the same symbols, that is, the initialization function for each plugin must be named uniquely, such as `<PluginName>_PluginInit()`. In the case of dynamic library plugins, you can use the same initialization function name for every plugin, such as `PluginInit()`.

12.1.3 Implementing Plugins in C++

I've identified that supporting C++ plugins can be difficult due to cross-platform and cross-compiler ABI problems. However, because this is a book about C++ API design, let's take a few more moments to present some solutions that let you use C++ plugins more robustly.

First off, if you are happy requiring that plugin developers use the same version of the same compiler that you use for building your API, then you should have nothing to worry about.

If that's not the case, one solution is to use a binding technology for your plugins, for example, an IPC solution such as COM on Windows, or creating script bindings for your API and letting users write extensions using a cross-platform scripting language such as Python or Ruby (as covered in the previous chapter).

If you absolutely need to use C++ plugins for maximum performance or you feel that creating a COM or script binding is too heavyweight for your needs, there are still ways that you can use C++ more safely in plugins. The following list offers several best practices, many of which are implemented by the open source DynObj library available on http://www.codeproject.com/.

- **Use abstract base classes**. Implementing virtual methods of an abstract base class can insulate a plugin from ABI problems because a virtual method call is usually represented as an index into a class's vtable. Theoretically, the vtable format can differ between compilers, but in practice this tends not to happen. (Note, however, that different compilers may order overloaded virtual methods differently so it's best to avoid these.) All of the methods in the interface need to be pure virtual, although inlined methods can be used safely too as the code will get embedded directly into the plugin.
- **Use C linkage for free functions**. All global functions in your Plugin API should use C linkage to avoid C++ ABI issues, that is, they should be declared with `extern "C"`. Similarly, function callbacks that a plugin passes to the Core API should also use C linkage for maximum portability.
- **Avoid STL and exceptions**. Different implementations of STL classes such as `std::string` and `std::vector` may not be ABI compatible. It is therefore best to avoid these containers in any function calls between the Core API and Plugin API. Similarly, because the ABI for exceptions tends to be unstable across compilers, these should be avoided in your Plugin API.
- **Don't mix allocators**. It's possible for plugins to be linked against a different memory allocator than your API. For example, on Windows it's common for debug builds to use a different allocator than release builds. The implication for the design of our plugin system is that either the plugin must allocate and free all of its objects or the plugin should pass control to the Core API to create and destroy all objects. However, your Core API should never free objects that were allocated by a plugin, and vice versa.

Putting all of this information together, I will now develop a flexible and robust cross-platform C++ plugin system. The plugin system will allow new C++ classes to be registered with the Core API by providing one or more factory methods. I will continue our extensible factory example from Chapter 3 and augment it to allow new IRenderer classes to be registered from plugins, where these plugins are loaded dynamically at run time rather than being compiled into the Core API. Furthermore, the plugin architecture will support different approaches to storing plugin metadata, either within an accompanying external file or within the plugins themselves.

12.1.4 **The Plugin API**

The Plugin API is the interface that you provide to your users to create plugins. I'll call it pluginapi.h in our example here. This header file will contain functionality that allows plugins to communicate with the Core API.

When the Core API loads a plugin, it needs to know which functions to call or symbols to access in order to let the plugin do its work. This means that you should define specifically named entry points in the plugin that your users must provide. There are several different ways that you can do this. For example, when writing a GIMP plugin, you must define a variable called PLUG_IN_INFO that lists the various callbacks defined in the plugin.

```
#include <libgimp/gimp.h>

GimpPlugInInfo PLUG_IN_INFO =
{
    NULL, /* called when GIMP starts */
    NULL, /* called when GIMP exits */
    query, /* procedure registration and arguments definition */
    run, /* perform the plugin's operation */
};
```

Netscape Plugins use a similar, although slightly more flexible, technique. In this case, plugin writers define an NP_GetEntryPoints() function and fill in the appropriate fields of the NPPluginFuncs structure that the browser passes in during plugin registration. The NPPluginFuncs structure includes size and version fields to handle future expansion.

Another solution is to have specifically named functions that the Core API can call, if they are exported by the plugin. I will adopt this approach for our example because it is simple and scalable; for example, it doesn't rely on a fixed size array or structure.

The two most basic callbacks that a plugin should provide are an initialization function and a cleanup function. As noted earlier, these functions should be declared with C linkage to avoid name mangling differences between compilers. If you want to develop a cross-platform plugin system, you will also have to deal with correctly using __declspec(dllexport) and __declspec(dllimport) decorators on Windows. Instead of requiring our plugin developers to know all of these details, I will provide some macros to simplify everything. (As stated earlier, you should avoid preprocessor macros for declaring things such as API constants; however, they are perfectly valid to affect compile-time configuration like this.)

Also, I've decided that our plugin should be allowed to register new IRenderer derived classes so I'll provide a Plugin API call to let plugins do just this. Here's a first draft of our Plugin API:

```
// pluginapi.h
#include "defines.h"
#include "renderer.h"

#define CORE_FUNC   extern "C" CORE_API
#define PLUGIN_FUNC   extern "C" PLUGIN_API

#define PLUGIN_INIT() PLUGIN_FUNC int PluginInit()
#define PLUGIN_FREE() PLUGIN_FUNC int PluginFree()
```

```
typedef IRenderer *(*RendererInitFunc)();
typedef void (*RendererFreeFunc)(IRenderer *);

CORE_FUNC void RegisterRenderer(const char *type,
                                RendererInitFunc init_cb,
                                RendererFreeFunc free_cb);
```

This header provides macros to define the initialization and cleanup functions for a plugin: PLUGIN_INIT() and PLUGIN_FREE(), respectively. I also provide the PLUGIN_FUNC macro to let plugins export functions for the Core API to call, as well as the CORE_FUNC macro that exports Core API functions for plugins to call. Finally I provide a function, RegisterRenderer(), which allows plugins to register new IRenderer classes with the Core API. Note that a plugin must provide both an init function and a free function for their new IRenderer classes to ensure that allocations and frees happen within the plugin (to address the point that you should not mix memory allocators).

You may also note use of the CORE_API and PLUGIN_API defines. These let us specify the correct DLL export/import decorators under Windows. CORE_API is used to decorate functions that are part of the Core API, and PLUGIN_API is used for functions that will be defined in plugins. The definition of these macros is contained in the defines.h header and looks like:

```
// defines.h
#ifdef _WIN32
#ifdef BUILDING_CORE
#define CORE_API __declspec(dllexport)
#define PLUGIN_API __declspec(dllimport)
#else
#define CORE_API __declspec(dllimport)
#define PLUGIN_API __declspec(dllexport)
#endif
#else
#define CORE_API
#define PLUGIN_API
#endif
```

Note that you must build your Core API with the BUILDING_CORE define set for these macros to work correctly, for example, add /DBUILDING_CORE to the compile line on Windows. This define is not needed when compiling plugins.

Finally, for completeness, here are the contents of the renderer.h file, which is also included by pluginapi.h.

```
// renderer.h

class IRenderer
{
public:
    virtual ~IRenderer() {}
    virtual bool LoadScene(const char *filename) = 0;
    virtual void SetViewportSize(int w, int h) = 0;
    virtual void SetCameraPosition(double x, double y, double z) = 0;
```

```
    virtual void SetLookAt(double x, double y, double z) = 0;
    virtual void Render() = 0;
};
```

This is essentially the same definition presented in Chapter 3, except that I have changed the `LoadScene()` method to accept a `const char *` parameter instead of a `std::string` (to address our concerns about binary compatibility of STL classes between compilers).

12.1.5 **An Example Plugin**

Now that I have developed a rudimentary Plugin API, let's examine what a plugin built against this API might look like. The basic parts that you need to include are:

1. The new `IRenderer` class.
2. Callbacks to create and destroy this class.
3. A Plugin initialization routine that registers our create/destroy callbacks with the Core API.

Here is the code for such a plugin. This plugin defines and registers a new renderer called "opengl." This is defined in a new `OpenGLRenderer` class that derives from our `IRenderer` abstract base class.

```cpp
// plugin1.cpp
#include "pluginapi.h"
#include <iostream>

class OpenGLRenderer : public IRenderer
{
public:
    ~OpenGLRenderer() {}
    bool LoadScene(const char *filename) { return true; }
    void SetViewportSize(int w, int h) {}
    void SetCameraPosition(double x, double y, double z) {}
    void SetLookAt(double x, double y, double z) {}
    void Render() { std::cout << "OpenGL Render" << std::endl; }
};

PLUGIN_FUNC IRenderer *CreateRenderer()
{
    return new OpenGLRenderer();
}

PLUGIN_FUNC void DestroyRenderer(IRenderer *r)
{
    delete r;
}

PLUGIN_INIT()
{
    RegisterRenderer("opengl", CreateRenderer, DestroyRenderer);
    return 0;
}
```

In this example, I have defined a PLUGIN_INIT() function, which will get run whenever the plugin is loaded. This registers our OpenGLRenderer factory function, CreateRenderer(), and the associated destruction function, DestroyRenderer(). These are both defined using PLUGIN_FUNC to ensure that they are exported correctly with C linkage.

The RegisterRenderer() function essentially just calls the RendererFactory::RegisterRenderer() method presented in Chapter 3 (with the addition of also being able to pass a destruction callback as well as the CreateCallback). There are a couple of reasons why I added an explicit registration function to the Plugin API rather than letting plugins register themselves directly with the RendererFactory. One reason is simply to give us a layer of abstraction so that you could change RendererFactory in the future without breaking existing plugins. Another reason is to avoid plugins calling methods that use STL strings: note that RegisterRenderer uses a const char * to specify the renderer name.

12.1.6 The Plugin Manager

Now that you have a Plugin API and you can build plugins against this API, you need to be able to load and register those plugins into the Core API. This is the role of the Plugin Manager. Specifically, the Plugin Manager needs to handle the following tasks.

- Load metadata for all plugins. These metadata can either be stored in a separate file (such as an XML file) or be embedded within the plugins themselves. In the latter case, the Plugin Manager will need to load all available plugins to collate metadata for all plugins. These metadata let you present the user with a list of available plugins for them to choose between.
- Load a dynamic library into memory, provide access to the symbols in that library, and unload the library if necessary. This involves using dlopen(), dlclose(), and dlsym() on UNIX platforms (including Mac OS X) and LoadLibrary(), FreeLibrary(), and GetProcAddress() on Windows. I provide details about these calls in Appendix A.
- Call the plugin's initialization routine when the plugin is loaded, and call the cleanup routine when the plugin is unloaded. These functions are defined by PLUGIN_INIT() and PLUGIN_FREE() within the plugin.

Because the Plugin Manager provides a single point of access to all of the plugins in the system, it is often implemented as a singleton. In terms of design, the Plugin Manager can be thought of as a collection of Plugin Instances, where each Plugin Instance represents a single plugin and offers functionality to load and unload that plugin. Here is an example implementation for a Plugin Manager:

```
// pluginmanager.cpp
#include "defines.h"
#include <string>
#include <vector>

class CORE_API PluginInstance
{
public:
    explicit PluginInstance(const std::string &name);
    ~PluginInstance();
```

```
   bool Load();
   bool Unload();
   bool IsLoaded() const;
   std::string GetFileName() const;
   std::string GetDisplayName() const;

private:
   PluginInstance(const PluginInstance &);
   const PluginInstance &operator =(const PluginInstance &);
   class Impl;
   Impl *mImpl;
};

class CORE_API PluginManager
{
public:
   static PluginManager &GetInstance();
   bool LoadAll();
   bool Load(const std::string &name);
   bool UnloadAll();
   bool Unload(const std::string &name);
   std::vector<PluginInstance *> GetAllPlugins();

private:
   PluginManager();
   ~PluginManager();
   PluginManager(const PluginManager &);
   const PluginManager &operator =(const PluginManager &);
   std::vector<PluginInstance *> mPlugins;
};
```

This design decouples the ability to access metadata for all plugins from the need to load those plugins. That is, if metadata such as the plugin's display name are stored in an external file, you can call PluginManager::GetAllPlugins() without loading the actual plugins. However, if metadata are stored in the plugins, then GetAllPlugins() can simply call LoadAll() first. The following example presents a sample external metadata file based on an XML syntax:

```
<?xml version="1.0" encoding='UTF-8'?>
<plugins>
   <plugin filename="oglplugin">
      <name>OpenGL Renderer</name>
   </plugin>
   <plugin filename="dxplugin">
      <name>DirectX Renderer</name>
   </plugin>
   <plugin filename="mesaplugin">
      <name>Mesa Renderer</name>
   </plugin>
</plugins>
```

Irrespective of the approach to store plugin metadata within an external file or embedded within each plugin, the following code outputs the display name for all available plugins:

```
std::vector<PluginInstance *> plugins =
    PluginManager::GetInstance().GetAllPlugins();

std::vector<PluginInstance *>::iterator it;
for (it = plugins.begin(); it != plugins.end(); ++it)
{
    PluginInstance *pi = *it;
    std::cout << "Plugin: " << pi->GetDisplayName() << std::endl;
}
```

A related issue is that of plugin discovery. The aforementioned API does not restrict the ability for the implementation of `PluginManager::Load()` to search multiple directories to discover all plugins. The name passed to this `Load()` method can be a base plugin name without any path or file extension, for example, "glplugin." The `Load()` method can then search various directories and look for files with extensions that may be platform specific, for example, `libglplugin.dylib` on Mac OS X or `glplugin.dll` on Windows. Of course, you can always introduce your own plugin filename extension. For example, Adobe Illustrator uses the `.aip` extension for its plugins, and Microsoft Excel uses the `.xll` extension.

The following Core API initialization code registers a single built-in renderer and then loads all plugins, allowing additional renderers to be added to the system at run time:

```
class MesaRenderer : public IRenderer
{
public:
    bool LoadScene(const char *filename) { return true; }
    void SetViewportSize(int w, int h) {}
    void SetCameraPosition(double x, double y, double z) {}
    void SetLookAt(double x, double y, double z) {}
    void Render() { std::cout << "Mesa Render" << std::endl; }
    static IRenderer *Create() { return new MesaRenderer(); }
};
...
// create a built-in software renderer
RendererFactory::RegisterRenderer("mesa", MesaRenderer::Create);

// discover and load all plugins
PluginManager::GetInstance().LoadAll();
```

12.1.7 Plugin Versioning

As a final note, I will expand on the topic of plugin versioning. As with API versioning, you will want to make sure that the release of your first plugin system includes a versioning system. You could either co-opt the version number of your Core API or introduce a specific Plugin API version number. I suggest the latter because the Plugin API is actually a separate interface from the Core API and the two may change at a different rate. For example, Google's Android API uses the notion of

Table 12.1 Android API level for each version of the Android platform	
Platform Version	**API Level**
Android 2.1	7
Android 2.0.1	6
Android 2.0	5
Android 1.6	4
Android 1.5	3
Android 1.1	2
Android 1.0	1

API Level (Table 12.1). This is a single integer that increases monotonically with each new version of the Android API.

One of the most important pieces of information you will want to access is the Plugin API version that a given plugin was built against. This can let you determine if a plugin is incompatible with the current release and therefore should not be registered, for example, if the plugin was built with a later version of the API or an incompatible older API. Given the importance of this information, it is advisable to embed this information automatically in every plugin. This ensures that the correct version is always compiled into the plugin every time that it is rebuilt successfully. Given the Plugin API already proposed, you could include this information in the PLUGIN_INIT() macro because users must call this in order for the plugin to do anything. For example,

```
// pluginapi.h
...
#define PLUGIN_API_VERSION 1

#define PLUGIN_INIT() \
    const int PluginVersion = PLUGIN_API_VERSION; \
    PLUGIN_FUNC int PluginInit()
...
```

In addition, users can optionally specify a minimum and maximum version of the API that the plugin will work with. The minimum version number will be more commonly specified. For example, if the plugin uses a new feature that was added to the API in a specific release, that release should be specified as the minimum version. Specifying a maximum version number is only useful after a new version of the API has been released and the plugin writer finds that it breaks their plugin. Normally, the maximum version will be unset because plugin writers should assume that future API releases will be backward compatible.

This min/max version number could either be specified in an external metadata format, such as

```
<?xml version="1.0" encoding='UTF-8'?>
<plugins>
    <plugin filename="plugin1">
        <name>OpenGL Renderer</name>
```

```
        <minversion>2</minversion>
    </plugin>
    ...
</plugins>
```

Alternatively, you can extend the Plugin API with additional calls to let plugins specify this information in code.

```
...
#define PLUGIN_MIN_VERSION(version) \
    PLUGIN_API int PluginMinVersion = version

#define PLUGIN_MAX_VERSION(version) \
    PLUGIN_API int PluginMaxVersion = version
...
```

12.2 EXTENDING VIA INHERITANCE

The focus of this chapter thus far has been supporting API extensibility at run time via plugins. However, there are other ways that your clients can extend the functionality of your API for their own purposes. The primary object-oriented mechanism for extending a class is inheritance. This can be used to let your users define new classes that build upon and modify the functionality of existing classes in your API.

12.2.1 Adding Functionality

Jonathan Wood has a video on Microsoft's Visual C++ Developer Center where he demonstrates extending MFC's CString class via inheritance in order to create a CPathString class that adds some path manipulation functions to the basic string class. The resulting class looks something like

```
class CPathString : public CString
{
public:
    CPathString();
    ~CPathString();
    CString GetFileName();
    CString GetFileExtension();
    CString GetFileBase();
    CString GetFilePath();
};
```

This is a simple example of extending an existing class where only new methods are added to the base class.

An important point to reiterate here is that this can only be done safely if the base class was designed to be inherited from. The primary indicator for this is whether the class has a virtual destructor. In the CPathString example, MFC's CString class does not have a virtual destructor. This means that there are cases when the destructor for CPathString will not be called, such as

```
CString *str = new CPathString();
delete str;
```

In this particular case, this is not an issue because all of the new CPathString methods are stateless, that is, they do not allocate any memory that must be freed by the CPathString destructor. However, this does highlight the issue that if you expect your users to inherit from any of your classes, you should declare the destructor for those classes to be virtual.

TIP

Declaring a virtual destructor for a class is a signal to your users that you have designed it to be inherited from.

12.2.2 Modifying Functionality

In addition to adding new member functions to a class, we know that C++ allows you to define functions in a derived class that override existing functions in a base class if they have been marked as virtual in the base class. [Note that C++ lets you redefine, i.e., hide, a non-virtual base class method in a derived class, but you should never do this (Meyers, 2005).] This can provide even more avenues for your users to customize the behavior of a class, if you give them the hooks to do so.

For example, all UI widgets in the Qt library provide the following virtual methods:

```
virtual QSize minimumSizeHint() const;
virtual QSize sizeHint() const;
```

This allows users of the Qt library to create derived classes of these widgets and change their appearance. To illustrate this, the following class inherits from the standard Qt button widget and overrides the sizeHint() method to specify the preferred size of the button. The result of this can be seen in Figure 12.3.

FIGURE 12.3

A standard Qt QPushButton widget (left), and a derived class of QPushButton that overrides the sizeHint() virtual method (right).

```
class MySquareButton : public QPushButton
{
public:
    QSize sizeHint() const
```

```
    {
        return QSize(100, 100);
    }
};
```

This code works because `sizeHint()` is a known method of every widget and is called by the layout classes to determine the widget's preferred size. That is, the creators of the Qt library explicitly designed this point of customization into the toolkit and allowed users to modify it in their own derived classes by deliberately declaring the method to be virtual. APIs that allow users to selectively override or specialize their default behavior in this way are called "frameworks," which is why Qt is often referred to as an application or UI framework. This is also an example of the Template Method design pattern, where a generic algorithm allows one or more of its steps to be overridden to support different behaviors.

It's important to note that simply changing the size of the widget by calling the `resize()` method in the `MySquareButton` constructor is not the same thing. The effect of this would be to forcibly set the size of the button. However, the point of `sizeHint()` is to provide an indication of the preferred size to the UI layout engine, that is, to other classes in the API, so that it can override this size when necessary to satisfy other widget size constraints.

This could be implemented without a virtual `sizeHint()` method. For example, non-virtual `setSizeHint()` and `getSizeHint()` methods could be added to the widget base class. However, this would require the base class to store the hint information as a data member in the object, and hence increase the size of every object that inherits from it. In contrast, the use of the `sizeHint()` virtual method supports the ability for a class to simply calculate the preferred size on each invocation, without the need to store the size within the object instance.

In the chapter on performance, I cautioned you to only add virtual methods to a class when you need them. That advice is still valid. In the aforementioned example, designers of the Qt API added these virtual methods to their API carefully and consciously to produce a flexible way for their users to extend the base functionality of their classes.

12.2.3 Inheritance and the STL

Programmers who are new to C++ and the Standard Template Library often try to subclass STL containers, such as

```
#include <string>

class MyString : public std::string
{
public
    ...
};
```

However, as already noted, you should only attempt to derive from a class that defines a virtual destructor. STL container classes do not provide virtual destructors; in fact, they have no virtual methods for you to override at all. This is a clear indication that these classes were not meant to be inherited from. Attempting to do so could introduce subtle and difficult-to-debug resource leaks into your code, and your clients' code. The general rule is therefore that you should never inherit from STL container classes.

As an alternative, you could use composition to add functionality to an STL container in a safe manner. That is, use an `std::string` as a private data member and provide accessor methods that thinly wrap the underlying `std::string` methods. Then you can add your own methods to this class. For example,

```
class MyString
{
public:
    MyString() : mStr("") {}
    explicit MyString(const char *str) : mStr(str) {}

    bool empty() const { return mStr.empty(); }
    void clear() { mStr.clear(); }
    void push_back(char c) { mStr.push_back(c); }
    ...
private:
    std::string mStr;
};
```

However, the STL does provide a few classes that were designed for inheritance. One of the most obvious of these is `std::exception`. This is the base class for all STL exceptions, including `bad_alloc`, `bad_cast`, `bad_exception`, `bad_typeid`, `lock_error`, `logic_error`, and `runtime_error`. You can define your own exceptions that derive from `std::exception` quite simply:

```
class DivByZeroException : public std::exception
{
public:
    const char *what() const
    {
        return "Division by zero attempted";
    }
};
```

Another part of the STL that supports extension through inheritance is the iostream library. This is actually a very powerful, well-designed, and extensible API that provides various stream abstractions. A stream can be thought of simply as a sequence of bytes waiting to be processed, such as the standard `cin` input stream and `cout` output stream. You can write custom stream classes by deriving either from a particular stream class or from the `streambuf` base class. For example, you could create custom stream classes to send and receive HTTP data to/from a Web server.

There is also the Boost Iostreams library, which makes it easier to work with STL streams and stream buffers and also provides a framework for defining filters on streams and buffers. The library comes with a collection of handy filters, including regular expression filtering and data compression schemes such as zlib, gzip, and bzip2.

12.2.4 Inheritance and Enums

There are times when your users may want to extend an enum that you define in one of your base classes, for example, to add further enumerators for new features that they have added in their derived classes. This can be done quite easily in C++ as follows.

```
class Base
{
public:
    enum SHAPE {
        CIRCLE,
        SQUARE,
        TRIANGLE,
        SHAPE_END = TRIANGLE
    };
};

class Derived : public Base
{
public:
    enum SHAPE {
        OVAL = SHAPE_END + 1,
        RECTANGLE,
        HEXAGON
    };
};
```

Here is an example that demonstrates the use of this extended enum:

```
std::cout << "CIRCLE="   << Derived::CIRCLE   << std::endl;
std::cout << "SQUARE="   << Derived::SQUARE   << std::endl;
std::cout << "TRIANGLE=" << Derived::TRIANGLE << std::endl;
std::cout << "OVAL="     << Derived::OVAL     << std::endl;
std::cout << "RECTANGLE=" << Derived::RECTANGLE << std::endl;
std::cout << "HEXAGON="  << Derived::HEXAGON  << std::endl;
```

The important part that makes this work in a robust way is the fact that the Base class defined SHAPE_END so that the Derived class could add new values after the last value defined by Base::SHAPE. This is therefore a good practice for you to adopt when defining enums in classes that you expect to be subclassed by your clients. Without this, your clients could pick an arbitrarily large integer to start numbering their enumerators, for example, OVAL=100, although this is a less elegant solution.

TIP

For enums in a base class, add an enumerator for the last value in the enum, such as <enum-name>_END.

12.2.5 The Visitor Pattern

Various generic design patterns were presented back in Chapter 3. However, I deferred discussion of the Visitor design pattern until now as it is specifically targeted at API extensibility. The core goal of the Visitor pattern is to allow clients to traverse all objects in a data structure and perform a given operation on each of those objects. This pattern is essentially a way to simulate the addition of new virtual methods to an existing class. It therefore provides a useful pattern for your clients to extend the functionality of your API. For example, a Visitor pattern could be used to let clients provide a set of methods that operate on every node in a scene graph hierarchy or to traverse the derivation tree of a programming language parser and output a human-readable form of the program.

Let's develop a visitor example to illustrate how this pattern works. I'll use the example of a scene graph hierarchy that describes a 3D scene, such as that used by Open Inventor, OpenSceneGraph, or the Virtual Reality Modeling Language. To keep the example simple, our scene graph will contain only three different node types: Shape, Transform, and Light. Figure 12.4 shows an example hierarchy using these node types.

I'll begin by defining our abstract visitor interface. Clients can create concrete subclasses of this interface in order to add custom operations to the scene graph. It essentially declares a Visit() method for each node type in the scene graph.

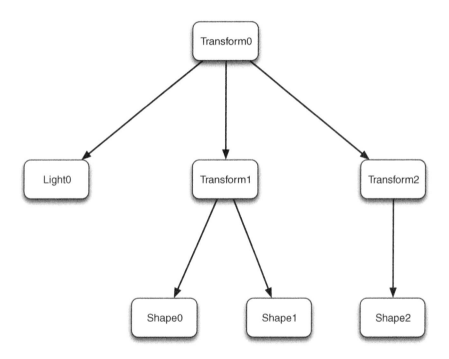

FIGURE 12.4

Example scene graph hierarchy showing nodes of different types.

```
// nodevisitor.h
class ShapeNode;
class TransformNode;
class LightNode;

class INodeVisitor
{
public:
    virtual ~INodeVisitor() {}
```

```
   virtual void Visit(ShapeNode &node) = 0;
   virtual void Visit(TransformNode &node) = 0;
   virtual void Visit(LightNode &node) = 0;
};
```

Now let's take a look at our scene graph API. This provides the declarations for each of our node types, as well as a skeleton SceneGraph class. Each node type derives from a base node type, called BaseNode.

```
// scenegraph.h
#include <string>

class INodeVisitor;

class BaseNode
{
public:
   explicit BaseNode(const std::string &name);
   virtual ~BaseNode() {}
   virtual void Accept(INodeVisitor &visitor) = 0;

private:
   std::string mName;
};

class ShapeNode : public BaseNode
{
public:
   explicit ShapeNode(const std::string &name);
   void Accept(INodeVisitor &visitor);
   int GetPolygonCount() const;
};

class TransformNode : public BaseNode
{
public:
   explicit TransformNode(const std::string &name);
   void Accept(INodeVisitor &visitor);
};

class LightNode : public BaseNode
{
public:
   explicit LightNode(const std::string &name);
   void Accept(INodeVisitor &visitor);
};

class SceneGraph
```

```
{
public:
    SceneGraph();
    ~SceneGraph();
    void Traverse(INodeVisitor &visitor);

private:
    SceneGraph(const SceneGraph &);
    const SceneGraph &operator =(const SceneGraph &);
    class Impl;
    Impl *mImpl;
};
```

Note that each of the node types declares an `Accept()` method, taking a visitor object as its parameter. This method is used to call the appropriate `Visit()` method in the visitor class. This can be thought of as a way to have a single virtual method in each node that can then call any user-supplied virtual method. See Figure 12.5 for a UML diagram that shows this Visitor pattern.

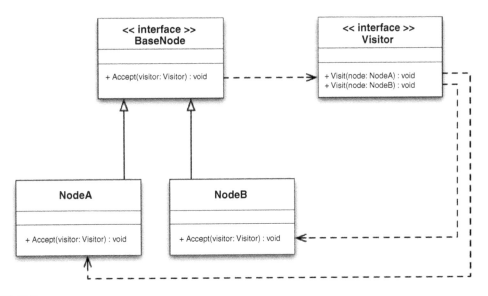

FIGURE 12.5

UML diagram of the Visitor design pattern.

```
// scenegraph.cpp
void ShapeNode::Accept(INodeVisitor &visitor)
{
    visitor.Visit(*this);
}
```

```
void TransformNode::Accept(INodeVisitor &visitor)
{
    visitor.Visit(*this);
}

void LightNode::Accept(INodeVisitor &visitor)
{
    visitor.Visit(*this);
}
```

Building upon this infrastructure, the `SceneGraph::Traverse()` method can be implemented by navigating the scene graph hierarchy and then calling the `Accept()` method for every node in the graph. Your clients can then define custom visitor classes to perform arbitrary operations on the scene graph. This is done without exposing any details about how the scene graph is implemented. For example, the following code demonstrates how a client could write a visitor to count the number of each node type in the scene graph and also sum the polygon count for all shape nodes in the scene graph:

```
class MyVisitor : public INodeVisitor
{
public:
    int mNumShapes;
    int mNumPolygons;
    int mNumTransforms;
    int mNumLights;

    MyVisitor() :
        mNumShapes(0),
        mNumPolygons(0),
        mNumTransforms(0),
        mNumLights(0)
    {
    }
    void Visit(ShapeNode &node)
    {
        mNumPolygons += node.GetPolygonCount();
        ++mNumShapes;
    }
    void Visit(TransformNode &node)
    {
        ++mNumTransforms;
    }
    void Visit(LightNode &node)
    {
        ++mNumLights;
    }
};
...
```

```
MyVisitor visitor;
scenegraph.Traverse(visitor);
std::cout << "Shapes: " << visitor.mNumShapes << std::endl;
std::cout << "Polygons: " << visitor.mNumPolygons << std::endl;
std::cout << "Transforms:" << visitor.mNumTransforms << std::endl;
std::cout << "Lights: " << visitor.mNumLights << std::endl;
```

This example demonstrates many of the benefits of the Visitor pattern, with the most relevant benefit to the topic of extensibility being that clients can effectively plug their own methods into your class hierarchy. However, other benefits include the colocation of all code that performs a single coherent operation. For example, all of the code that implements the node counting functionality in this example is contained with the single MyVisitor class rather than being distributed across all of the individual node classes. A further benefit is that the state required to count the various nodes and the number of polygons (mNumShapes, mNumPolygons, mNumTransforms, and mNumLights) is isolated in the MyVisitor class rather than being stored directly in, and hence increasing the size of, the SceneGraph object.

However, there are some significant downsides to the Visitor pattern too. The flexibility of being able to add new methods to a related set of classes comes at the cost of making it more difficult to add new related classes. Note, in visitor.h, that the visitor interface must know about every class that can be visited, that is, all of our node types. Therefore, adding a new node type to our scene graph will require the visitor interface to also be updated. As a result, the Visitor pattern is used most appropriately in cases where the class hierarchy is stable (Alexandrescu, 2001).

To address this problem, let's consider adding a new node type, called CameraNode, to our scene graph. The naive way to do this would be to add another Visit() pure virtual method to the INodeVisitor interface that accepts a CameraNode reference. However, we know that adding a pure virtual method to an interface is a bad thing to do in terms of API backward compatibility because it will break all existing client code. Instead, there are a couple of alternative ways to solve this problem.

1. Thinking ahead, you could release the first version of INodeVisitor with a Visit() pure virtual method for BaseNode. This will effectively become a catch-all method that will be called if a node type is encountered for which there is not an explicit Visit() method (BaseNode::Accept() will also have to be modified so that it is no longer a pure virtual method). The inelegant consequence of this is that users must use a sequence of dynamic_cast calls inside of this catch-all method to work out which node type has been passed in. Adopting this solution would change the visitor interface as follows:

```
// nodevisitor.h
class ShapeNode;
class TransformNode;
class LightNode;
class BaseNode;

class INodeVisitor
{
public:
```

```
        virtual void Visit(ShapeNode &node) = 0;
        virtual void Visit(TransformNode &node) = 0;
        virtual void Visit(LightNode &node) = 0;
        virtual void Visit(BaseNode &node) = 0; // catch-all
    };
```

2. A better solution is to add a new `Visit()` virtual method for the new node type instead of a pure virtual method. That is, you provide an empty implementation for the new method so that existing code will continue to compile, while still allowing users to implement a type-safe `Visit()` method for the new node type where appropriate. This would change the `INodeVisitor` interface as follows:

```
    // nodevisitor.h
    class ShapeNode;
    class TransformNode;
    class LightNode;
    class CameraNode;

    class INodeVisitor
    {
    public:
        virtual void Visit(ShapeNode &node) = 0;
        virtual void Visit(TransformNode &node) = 0;
        virtual void Visit(LightNode &node) = 0;
        virtual void Visit(CameraNode &node);
    };
```

12.2.6 Prohibiting Subclassing

As a final note on extending via inheritance, I will address the situation where you want to prohibit users from inheriting derived classes from the classes you provide to them. In Java, you can declare a class to be final to prevent others from inheriting from it, but C++ does not have a similar concept.

As already noted, if you declare a class with a non-virtual destructor, this should be a signal to a good programmer that they should think twice about inheriting from the class. However, if you want a physical mechanism to prevent users from subclassing one of your classes, the easiest way to do this is to make all of its constructors private. Any attempt to derive from this class will produce a compile error because the derived class's constructor cannot call your class's constructor. You can then provide a factory method to let users create instances of the object.

```
    class NonBase
    {
    public:
        static NonBase* Create() { return new NonBase (); }

    private:
        NonBase();
    };
```

```
class Derived : public NonBase {};
Derived d; // compile error!
```

The downside of this approach is that instances of NonBase cannot be created on the stack. Your clients must instead always allocate instances of NonBase using the NonBase::Create() static function. If this is undesirable, there is another solution. You can instead rely on virtual inheritance to ensure that no concrete class can inherit from NonBase, as follows (Cline et al., 1998).

```
class NonBase;

class NonBaseFinal
{
private:
   NonBaseFinal() {}
   friend class NonBase;
};

class NonBase :virtual public NonBaseFinal
{
public:
   ...
};

class Derived : public NonBase {};
Derived d; // compile error!
```

12.3 EXTENDING VIA TEMPLATES

C++ is often referred to as a multiparadigm language because it supports different styles of programming, such as procedural, object oriented, and generic. Inheritance is the primary way to extend classes using object-oriented concepts. However, when programming with templates, the default way to extend an interface is to specialize a template with concrete types.

For example, the STL provides various container classes, such as std::vector and std::set. You can use these container classes to create data structures that contain arbitrary data types, such as std::vector<MyCustomClass *>, which the creators of the STL had no way of knowing about when they designed the library.

Similarly, C++11 provides the ability to create reference-counted pointers that can hold any pointer type without having to resort to using void*. This provides a powerful and generic facility that can be customized by clients to create type-safe shared pointers to any object, such as std::shared_ptr<MyCustomClass>.

Templates therefore offer an excellent way for you to write extensible code that can be applied to many different types, including types that your clients define in their own code. The next couple of sections present the concept of policy-based templates to help you maximize the flexibility of your class templates, and I will also investigate a curiously common template pattern that provides static polymorphism as an alternative to the dynamic polymorphism of object-oriented programming.

12.3.1 Policy-Based Templates

Andrei Alexandrescu popularized the use of policy-based templates in his book (Alexandrescu, 2001). The term refers to the approach of building complex behaviors out of smaller classes, called policy classes, where each of these define the interface for a single aspect of the overall component. This concept is implemented using class templates that accept several template parameters (often template template parameters), instantiated with classes that conform to the interface for each policy. By plugging in different policy classes, you can produce an exponentially large number of concrete classes.

For example, Alexandrescu presents the following design for a smart pointer class template that accepts several policy classes to customize its behavior (Alexandrescu, 2001):

```
template
<
    typename T,
    template <class> class OwnershipPolicy = RefCounted,
    class ConversionPolicy = DisallowConversion,
    template <class> class CheckingPolicy = AssertCheck,
    template <class> class StoragePolicy = DefaultSPStorage
>
class SmartPtr;
```

The type that `SmartPtr` points toward is represented by the template parameter `T`. The remaining parameters specify various policies, or behaviors, for the smart pointer. These can be instantiated with classes that conform to a defined interface for each parameter and provide alternative implementations for the smart pointer. Here's an overview of each parameter's purpose.

- **OwnershipPolicy**: Specifies the ownership model for the smart pointer. Predefined policy classes include `RefCounted`, `DeepCopy`, and `NoCopy`.
- **ConversionPolicy**: Determines whether implicit conversion to the type of the object being pointed to is allowed. The two available classes are `AllowConversion` and `DisallowConversion`.
- **CheckingPolicy**: Specifies the error checking strategy. The predefined policy classes for this parameter include `AssertCheck`, `RejectNull`, and `NoCheck`.
- **StoragePolicy**: Defines how the object being pointed to is stored and accessed, including `DefaultSPStorage`, `ArrayStorage`, and `HeapStorage`.

Policy-based design recognizes the fact that there is a multiplicity of solutions for every problem in computer science. Use of these generic components means that clients have a choice between literally thousands of solutions simply by supplying different combinations of policy classes at compile time.

The first step in creating your own policy-based templates is to decompose a class into orthogonal parts. Anything that can be done in multiple ways is a candidate for factoring out as a policy. Policies that depend on each other are also candidates for further decomposition or redesign. There is of course nothing new here. The essence of good software engineering is being able to recognize the more general and flexible abstraction that a specific problem can be implemented in terms of.

Taken to the extreme, a host class (as policy-based templates are often called) becomes a shell that simply assembles a collection of policies to produce aggregate behavior. However,

Alexandrescu does state that you should try to keep the number of policy classes small for any given host class, noting that it becomes awkward to work with more than four to six template parameters. This correlates well with the cognitive limit of our working memory, which is believed to be seven plus or minus two (Miller, 1956).

It is also very useful to provide typedefs for specific combinations of policy classes that you use for a given task. For example, if your API passes around smart pointers that use non-default policies, it would be tedious to have to specify all those parameters all the time, and changing those policies in the future would require your clients to update all of their code accordingly. Instead, you can introduce a typedef for the specific pointer type, such as

```
typedef SmartPtr <Shape,
                  RefCounted,
                  AllowConversion,
                  NoChecked> ShapePtr;
```

12.3.2 The Curiously Recurring Template Pattern

In this final section on extensibility via templates, I present an interesting C++ idiom that was first observed by James Coplien in early template code (Coplien, 1995) and which may prove useful in your own API designs. The Curiously Recurring Template Pattern (CRTP) involves a template class that inherits from a base class using itself as a template parameter. Said differently (to perhaps make that last sentence more clear), it's when a base class is templated on the type of its derived class. This provides the fascinating quality that the base class can access the namespace of its derived class. The general form of this pattern is as follows:

```
template <typename T> class Base;
class Derived : public Base<Derived>;
```

The CRTP is essentially just a way to provide compile-time polymorphism. That is, it allows you to inherit an interface from a base class, but to avoid the overhead of virtual method calls at run time. In this way, it can be thought of as a "mixin" class, that is, an interface class with implemented methods.

As a practical example of this pattern, the CRTP can be used to track statistics for each specialization of a template. For example, you can use it to track a count of all existing objects of a given type or the total amount of memory occupied by all existing objects of a given type. I will demonstrate the latter.

The following class provides the base class declaration for our memory tracker interface:

```
// curious.h
template <typename TrackedType>
class MemoryTracker {
public:
    // return memory used by existing objects:
    static size_t BytesUsed();

protected:
    MemoryTracker();
    MemoryTracker (MemoryTracker<TrackedType> const&);
    virtual ~MemoryTracker();
```

```
private:
   size_t ObjectSize();
   static size_t mBytes; // byte count of existing objects
};
```

```
#include "curious_priv.h"
```

For completeness, I also provide the associated definitions for this base class:

```
template <typename TrackedType>
size_t MemoryTracker<TrackedType>::BytesUsed() {
   return MemoryTracker<TrackedType>::mBytes;
}

template <typename TrackedType>
MemoryTracker<TrackedType>::MemoryTracker() {
   MemoryTracker<TrackedType>::mBytes += ObjectSize();
}

template <typename TrackedType>
MemoryTracker<TrackedType>::MemoryTracker (MemoryTracker<TrackedType>
const&) {
   MemoryTracker<TrackedType>::mBytes += ObjectSize();
}

template <typename TrackedType>
MemoryTracker<TrackedType>::~MemoryTracker() {
   MemoryTracker<TrackedType>::mBytes -= ObjectSize();
}

template <typename TrackedType>
inline size_t MemoryTracker<TrackedType>::ObjectSize() {
   // [*] access details of the derived class
   return sizeof(*static_cast<TrackedType *>(this));
}

// initialize counter with zero
template <typename TrackedType>
size_t MemoryTracker<TrackedType>::mBytes = 0;
```

The clever part here is the line directly after the comment marked [*]. Here, the base class is accessing details of the derived class, in this case the size of the derived class. However, in a different example, it could just as easily call a method in the derived class.

Using the CRTP, now you can keep track of all memory currently consumed by a certain class derived from this MemoryTracker class. This can even be used to track memory usage of individual template specializations, as the following example shows. All of these derived classes will essentially inherit the BytesUsed() method from our base class described earlier, but, significantly, the method will be bound at compile time, not run time.

```
template <typename T>
class MyClass1 : public MemoryTracker<MyClass1<T> > {
public:
    int mValue; // sizeof(MyClass1) == sizeof(int)
};

class MyClass2 : public MemoryTracker<MyClass2> {
public:
    int mValue; // sizeof(MyClass2) == sizeof(int)
};
...
MyClass1<char> c1, c2;
MyClass1<wchar_t> w1;
MyClass2 i1, i2, i3;
std::cout << MyClass1<char>::BytesUsed() << std::endl;
std::cout << w1.BytesUsed() << std::endl;
std::cout << MyClass2::BytesUsed() << std::endl;
```

This code will print out the values 8, 4, and 12, assuming a 32-bit system where `sizeof(MyClass1) ==` `sizeof(MyClass2) ==` 4 bytes. That is, there are two instances of `MyClass1<char>` (8 bytes), one instance of `MyClass1<wchar_t>` (4 bytes), and three instances of `MyClass2` (12 bytes).

Libraries

A library lets you package the compiled code and data that implement your API so that your clients can embed these into their own applications. Libraries are the instruments of modularization. This appendix covers the different types of libraries that you can use and how you can create them on various platforms. It also covers physical aspects of API design, namely exposing the public symbols of your API in the symbol export table of its library file.

The characteristics, usage, and supporting tools for libraries are inherently platform specific. How you work with a Dynamic Link Library (DLL) on Windows is different from how you work with a Dynamic Shared Object (DSO) on UNIX. I have therefore decided to organize the bulk of the content in this appendix by platform, specifically Windows, Linux, and Mac OS X. This also has the benefit of not distracting you with platform-specific details that you do not care about for your current project.

A.1 STATIC VERSUS DYNAMIC LIBRARIES

There are two main forms of libraries you can create. The decision on which one you employ can have a significant impact on your clients' end-user applications in terms of tangible factors such as load time, executable size, and robustness to different versions of your API. These two basic types are static libraries and shared libraries. I will describe each in detail over the following sections.

A.1.1 Static Libraries

A static library contains object code that is linked with an end-user application and then becomes part of that executable. Figure A.1 illustrates this concept. A static library is sometimes called an archive because it is essentially just a package of compiled object files. These libraries normally have a file extension of `.a` on UNIX and Mac OS X machines or `.lib` on Windows, for example, `libjpeg.a` or `jpeg.lib`.

Some implications of distributing your API's implementation as a static library are:

- A static library is only needed to link an application. It is not needed to run that application because the library code is essentially embedded inside the application. As a result, your clients can distribute their applications without any additional run-time dependencies.
- If your clients wish to link your library into multiple executables, each one will embed a copy of your code. If your library is 10 MB in size and your client wishes to link this into five separate

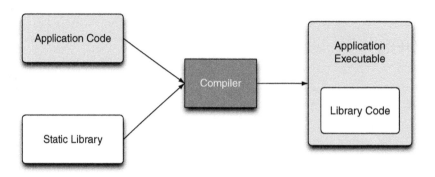

FIGURE A.1

Linking a static library into an application causes the library code to be embedded in the resulting executable.

programs, then you could be adding up to 50 MB to the total size of their product. Note that only the object files in the static library that are actually used are copied to the application. So in reality the total size of each application could be less than this worst case.

- Your clients can distribute their applications without any concerns that it will find an incompatible library version on the end-user's machine or a completely different library with the same name from another vendor.
- However, if your clients want to be able to hot patch their application, that is, they want to update the version of your library used by their application, they must replace the entire executable to achieve this. If this is done as an Internet-based update, the end user may have to download a much larger update and hence wait longer for the update to complete.

A.1.2 Dynamic Libraries

Dynamic libraries are files linked against at compile time to resolve undefined references and then distributed with the end-user application so that the application can load the library code at run time (see Figure A.2). This normally requires use of a dynamic linker on the end user's machine to determine and load all dynamic library dependencies at run time, perform the necessary symbol relocations, and then pass control to the application. For example, the Linux dynamic linker is called `ld.so` and on the Mac it is called `dyld`. Often, the dynamic linker supports a number of environment variables to modify or debug its behavior. For example, refer to `'man dyld'` on the Mac.

Dynamic libraries are sometimes called shared libraries because they can be shared by multiple programs. On UNIX machines they can be called Dynamic Shared Objects, and on Windows they are referred to as Dynamic Link Libraries. They have a `.so` file extension on UNIX platforms, `.dll` on Windows, and `.dylib` on Mac OS X, for example, `libjpeg.so` or `jpeg.dll`.

Some implications of using dynamic libraries to distribute your API include the following.

- Your clients must distribute your dynamic library with their application (as well as any dynamic libraries that your library depends on) so that it can be discovered when the application is run.

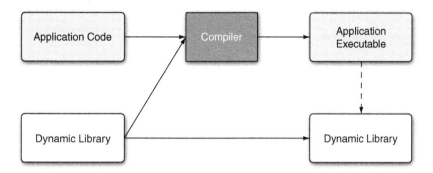

FIGURE A.2

A dynamic library is used to link an application and is then distributed with that application so that the library can be loaded at run time.

- Your clients' applications will not run if the dynamic library cannot be found, for example, if the library is deleted or moved to a directory that is not in the dynamic library search path. Furthermore, the application may not run if the dynamic library is upgraded to a newer version or overwritten with an older version.
- Using dynamic libraries can often be more efficient than static libraries in terms of disk space if more than one application needs to use the library. This is because the library code is stored in a single shared file and not duplicated inside each executable. Note that this is not a hard and fast rule, however. As noted earlier, the executable only needs to include the object code from the static library that is actually used. So if each application uses only a small fraction of the total static library, the disk space efficiency can still rival that of a single complete dynamic library.
- Dynamic libraries may also be more efficient in terms of memory. Most modern operating systems will attempt to only load the dynamic library code into memory once and share it across all applications that depend upon it. This may also lead to better cache utilization. By comparison, every application that is linked against a static library will load duplicate copies of the library code into memory.
- If your clients wish to hot patch their application with a new (binary compatible) version of your shared library, they can simply drop in the replacement library file and all of their applications will use this new library without having to recompile or relink.

> **TIP**
>
> You should prefer to distribute your library as a dynamic library to give your users greater flexibility. If your library is sufficiently small and stable, you may also decide to provide a static library version.

It's also important to understand the behavior of dynamic libraries that depend on other dynamic libraries. If your library depends on other dynamic libraries, then you must also ship those libraries with your SDK, unless you can reasonably expect the end-user's platform to have those libraries

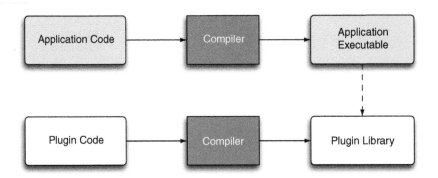

FIGURE A.3

A plugin library is a dynamic library that can be compiled separately from the application and explicitly loaded by the application on demand.

preinstalled. This is a transitive property: you must also ship all of the dependencies of your dependencies. Essentially, the entire chain of dynamic libraries must be available to the application at run time for it to be able to run. Of course, if your dynamic library links against a static library then you don't need to provide that static library to your clients because the code from the static library will be added directly to your dynamic library.

A.1.3 Dynamic Libraries as Plugins

Dynamic libraries are normally linked against an application and then distributed with that application so that the operating system can load the library when the application is launched. However, it is also possible for an application to load a dynamic library on demand without the application having been compiled and linked against that library.

This can be used to create plugin interfaces, where the application can load additional code at run time that extends the basic capabilities of the program. For example, most Web browsers support plugins to handle specific content types, such as displaying Adobe Flash animations or viewing Apple QuickTime movies. This use of dynamic libraries is illustrated in Figure A.3.

In terms of API development, this gives you the capability to create extensible APIs that allow your clients to drop in new functionality that your API will then load and execute. The Netscape Plugin API is an example of this: it is the API that you develop against in order to create a plugin (i.e., dynamic library) that browsers such as Firefox, Safari, Opera, and Chrome can then load and run. I discussed the use of plugins to create extensible APIs in Chapter 12.

A.2 LIBRARIES ON WINDOWS

On Windows, static libraries are represented with .lib files, whereas dynamic libraries have .dll file extensions. Additionally, you must accompany each .dll file with an import library, or .lib file. The import library is used to resolve references to symbols exported in the DLL. For example, the

Win32 User Interface API is implemented in `user32.dll`, with an accompanying `user32.lib`. Note that while they share the same `.lib` file extension, a static library and an import library are actually different file types. If you plan to distribute both static and dynamic library versions of your API, then you will need to avoid a filename collision by either naming the static library differently or placing each in a separate directory. For example,

static:	`foo_static.lib`		**static:**	`static/foo.lib`
dynamic:	`foo.dll`	or	**dynamic:**	`dynamic/foo.dll`
import:	`foo.lib`		**import:**	`dynamic/foo.lib`

On Windows, several other file formats are actually implemented as DLLs. These include:

- ActiveX Controls files (`.ocx`)
- Device Driver files (`.drv`)
- Control Panel files (`.cpl`)

A.2.1 Importing and Exporting Functions

As discussed in Chapter 6, if you want a function to be callable from a DLL on Windows, you must explicitly mark its declaration with the following keyword:

```
__declspec(dllexport)
```

For example,

```
__declspec(dllexport) void MyFunction();
class __declspec(dllexport) MyClass;
```

Conversely, if you want to use an exported DLL function in an application then you must prefix the function prototype with the following keyword:

```
__declspec(dllimport)
```

Consequently, it's common to employ preprocessor macros to use the export declaration when building an API but the import decoration when using the same API in an application. It's also important to note that because these `__declspec` decorations may cause compile errors on non-Windows compilers, you should only use them when compiling under Windows. The following preprocessor code provides a simple demonstration of this. (See Section 6.9 in Chapter 6 for a more complete cross-platform example.)

```
// On Windows, compile with /D "_EXPORTING" to build the DLL
#ifdef _WIN32
#ifdef _EXPORTING
#define DECLSPEC __declspec(dllexport)
#else
#define DECLSPEC __declspec(dllimport)
#endif
#else
```

```
#define DECLSPEC
#endif
```

You can then declare all of the symbols you want to export from your DLL as follows:

```
DECLSPEC void MyFunction();
class DECLSPEC MyClass;
```

As an alternative to modifying your source code with these __declspec declarations, you can create a module definition .def file to specify the symbols to export. A minimal DEF file contains a LIBRARY statement to specify the name of the DLL the file is associated with, and an EXPORTS statement followed by a list of symbol names to export.

```
// MyLIB.def
LIBRARY "MyLIB"
EXPORTS
    MyFunction1
    MyFunction2
```

The DEF file syntax also supports more powerful manipulations of your symbols, such as renaming symbols or using an ordinal number as the export name to help minimize the size of the DLL. The ordinal number represents the position of a symbol's address pointer in the DLL's export table. Using ordinal numbers for your DLL symbols can produce slightly faster and smaller libraries. However, from an API stability perspective this can be risky because seemingly innocuous changes to the DEF file can then change the exported symbols for your API. Therefore, I recommend using full symbol names rather than ordinal values when specifying your DLL exports.

A.2.2 The DLL Entry Point

DLLs can provide an optional entry point function to initialize data structures when a thread or process loads the DLL or to clean up memory when the DLL is unloaded. This is managed by a function called DllMain() that you define and export within the DLL. If the entry point function returns FALSE, this is assumed to be a fatal error and the application will fail to start. The following code provides a DLL entry point template.

```
BOOL APIENTRY DllMain(HANDLE dllHandle,
                      DWORD reason,
                      LPVOID lpReserved)
{
    switch (reason)
    {
    case DLL_PROCESS_ATTACHED:
        // A process is loading the DLL
        break;
    case DLL_PROCESS_DETACH:
        // A process unloads the DLL
        break;
```

```
     case DLL_THREAD_ATTACHED:
        // A process is creating a new thread
        break;
     case DLL_THREAD_DETACH:
        // A thread exits normally
        break;
     }
     return TRUE;
  }
```

A.2.3 Creating Libraries on Windows

The following steps describe how to create a static library on Windows. These steps are for Microsoft Visual Studio 2008 (9.0), although the steps are similar for other versions of Visual Studio.

1. Select the menu File > New > Project
2. Select the Visual C++ > Win32 option and the Win32 Project icon

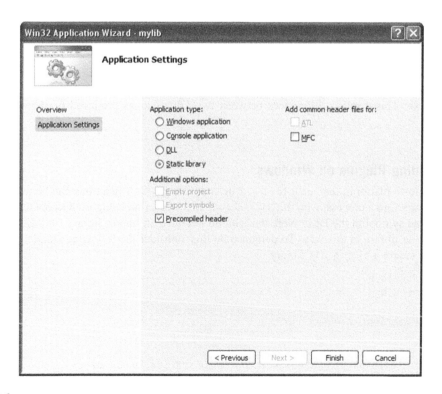

FIGURE A.4

Creating a new static library or DLL in Visual Studio 2008.

3. The Win32 Application Wizard should appear
4. Select the Static library option under Application type (see Figure A.4)

You can then add new or existing source files to your project under the Source Files folder in the left-hand pane. Then, when you perform a build for your project, the result will be a static library .lib file.

The steps to create a DLL are very similar. The only difference is during Step 4, where you will select the **DLL** option instead of Static library. Then, when you build your project, Visual Studio will generate a .dll file and an associated .lib import file.

A.2.4 Useful Windows Utilities

A number of programs can help you manage DLLs on Windows and investigate DLL problems. Many of these are command-line tools that you can run from the MS-DOS prompt. A few of these DLL utilities are:

- **tasklist.exe**: This program can be used to find out which dynamic libraries a running Windows EXE file depends on, for example,

  ```
  tasklist /m /fi "IMAGENAME eq APPNAME.EXE"
  ```
- **depends.exe**: The dependency walker utility will recursively scan an executable to discover all of its dependent DLLs. It will check for missing DLLs, invalid DLLs, and circular dependencies, among other error conditions.
- **dlister.exe**: This utility provides a log of all the DLLs installed on your computer. This can be output as a text file or a database file.
- **dcomp.exe**: This displays differences between two DLL listings produced by the dlister.exe program.

A.2.5 Loading Plugins on Windows

On the Windows platform, the LoadLibrary() or LoadLibraryEx() functions can be used to load a dynamic library into a process, with the GetProcAddress() function being used to obtain the address of an exported symbol in the DLL. Note that you do not need an import library .lib file in order to load a dynamic library in this way. To demonstrate this, consider the following simple plugin interface used to create a plugin.dll library.

```
#ifndef PLUGIN_H
#define PLUGIN_H

#include <string>

extern "C"
__declspec(dllexport) void DoSomething(const std::string &name);

#endif
```

Then the following code snippet illustrates how to load this DLL on demand and call the DoSomething() method from that library.

```
// open the dynamic library
HINSTANCE handle = LoadLibrary("plugin.dll");
if (! handle)
{
    std::cout << "Cannot load plugin!" << std::endl;
    exit(1);
}

// get the DoSomething() function from the plugin
FARPROC fptr = GetProcAddress(handle, "DoSomething");
if (fptr == (FARPROC)NULL)
{
    std::cout << "Cannot find function in plugin: " << error;
    std::cout << std::endl;
    FreeLibrary (handle);
    exit(1);
}

// cast fptr and call the DoSomething() function
typedef void (*StringFuncType)(const std::string &);
StringFuncType strfunc = (StringFuncType) fptr;
(*strfunc)("Hello There!");

// close the shared library
FreeLibrary (handle);
```

A.3 LIBRARIES ON LINUX

The following sections provide an overview of creating and managing static and shared libraries on Linux. The emphasis here is to surface the important issues and techniques. However, for a deeper treatment, I recommend reading Ulrich Drepper's excellent article "How to Write Shared Libraries," available online at http://people.redhat.com/drepper/dsohowto.pdf.

A.3.1 Creating Static Libraries on Linux

On Linux, a static library is simply an archive of object (.o) files. You can use the Linux ar command to compile a number of object files into a static library. For example, the following commands demonstrate how to compile three .cpp files to .o files using the GNU C++ compiler and then creating a static library from those object files.

```
g++ -c file1.cpp
g++ -c file2.cpp
g++ -c file3.cpp
ar -crs libmyapi.a file1.o file2.o file3.o
```

The -c option to g++ tells the compiler to produce a .o file from the input .cpp file. The options to ar are -c creates an archive, -r inserts the supplied .o files into that archive, and -s creates an index for the archive (equivalent to the older convention of running ranlib on the resulting archive).

Your users can then link against your library using the -l option to ld or g++. This specifies the name of the library to link against. The -L linker option can also be used to specify the directory where your library can be found. For example,

```
g++ usercode.cpp -o userapp -L. -lmyapi
```

In this example, the end-user application userapp is created by compiling usercode.cpp and linking against the libmyapi.a static library in the same directory.

The order of archives on this command line is significant. For each archive that the linker finds on the command line, it looks to see if that archive defines any symbols that were referenced from any object files specified earlier on the command line. If it does define any needed symbols, the object files with those symbols are copied into the executable. It is therefore best practice to specify libraries at the end of the command line (Mitchell et al., 2001).

While I am discussing the creation of static libraries, it is worth noting proper usage of the -static compiler option. This flag is used for the creation of executables, not libraries. It is therefore applicable to users of your API, but not to the building of your API itself. This flag instructs the compiler to prefer linking the static versions of all dependent libraries into the executable so that it depends on no dynamic libraries at run time.

A.3.2 Creating Dynamic Libraries on Linux

Creating a dynamic library on Linux is a very similar process to creating a static library. Using the GNU C++ compiler, you can simply use the -shared linker option to generate a .so file instead of an executable.

On platforms where it is not the default behavior, you should also specify either the -fpic or the -fPIC command line option to instruct the compiler to emit position-independent code (PIC). This is needed because the code in a shared library may be loaded into a different memory location for different executables. It's therefore important to generate PIC code for shared libraries so that user code does not depend on the absolute memory address of symbols. The following example illustrates how to compile three source files into a dynamic library.

```
g++ -c -fPIC file1.c
g++ -c -fPIC file2.c
g++ -c -fPIC file3.c
g++ -shared -o libmyapi.so -fPIC file1.o file2.o file3.o
```

Users can then link your dynamic library into their code using the same compile line shown earlier for the static library case, that is,

```
g++ usercode.cpp -o userapp -L. -lmyapi
```

If you have both a static library and a dynamic library with the same base name in the same directory, that is, libmyapi.a and libmyapi.so, the compiler will use the dynamic library (unless you use the -static library option to require only static libraries to be used). To favor use of a static library over a dynamic library with the same base name, you could place the static library in a different directory and ensure that this directory appears earlier in the library search path (using the -L linker option).

Note that in a dynamic library, all code is essentially flattened into a single object file. This is in contrast to static libraries that are represented as a collection of object files that can be copied individually into an executable as needed (i.e., object files in a static archive that are not needed are not copied into the executable image). As a result, loading a dynamic library will involve loading all the code defined in that .so file (Mitchell et al., 2001).

By default, all symbols in a DSO are exported publicly (unless you specify the -fvisibility= hidden compiler option). However, the GNU C++ compiler supports the concept of export maps to define explicitly the set of symbols in a dynamic library that will be visible to client programs. This is a simple ASCII format where symbols can be listed individually or using glob-style expressions. For example, the following map file, export.map, specifies that only the DoSomething() function should be exported and that all other symbols should be hidden.

```
{
   global: DoSomething;
   local: *
};
```

This map file can then be passed to the compiler when building a dynamic library using the --version-script linker option, as in the following example:

```
g++ -shared -o libmyapi.so -fPIC file1.o file2.o file3.o \
   -Wl,--version-script=export.map
```

A.3.3 Shared Library Entry Points

It's possible to define functions that will be called automatically when your shared library is loaded or unloaded. This can be used to perform library initialization and cleanup operations without requiring your users to call explicit functions to perform this.

One way to do this is using static constructors and destructors. This will work for any compiler and any platform, although you should remember that the order of initialization of static constructors is not defined across translation unit boundaries, that is, you should never depend on static variables in other .cpp files being initialized. Bearing this caveat in mind, you could create a shared library entry point in one of your .cpp files as follows:

```
class APIInitMgr
{
public:
   APIInitMgr()
   {
      std::cout << "APIInitMgr Initialized." << std::endl;
   }
   ~APIInitMgr()
   {
      std::cout << "APIInitMgr Destroyed." << std::endl;
   }
};

static APIInitMgr sInitMgr;
```

There is an alternate, more elegant, approach. However, it is specific to the GNU compiler. This involves using the constructor and destructor __attribute__ decorations for functions. For example, the following code shows you how to define library initialization and cleanup routines and hide these within one of your .cpp files.

```
static void __attribute__ ((constructor)) APIInitialize()
{
    std::cout << "API Initialized." << std::endl;
}

static void __attribute__ ((destructor)) APICleanup()
{
    std::cout << "API Cleaned Up." << std::endl;
}
```

If you use this approach, you should be aware that your shared library must not be compiled with the GNU GCC arguments -nostartfiles or -nostdlib.

A.3.4 Useful Linux Utilities

Several standard Linux utilities can help you work with static and shared libraries. Of particular note is the GNU libtool shell script. This command provides a consistent and portable interface for creating libraries on different UNIX platforms. The libtool script can be used in various ways, but in its simplest form you can just give libtool a list of object files, specify either the -static or the -dynamic option, and it will then create a static or dynamic library, respectively. For example,

```
libtool -static -o libmyapi.a file1.o file2.o file3.o
```

The libtool script can be very useful if you want your source code to compile easily on a range of UNIX platforms without worrying about the idiosyncrasies of creating libraries on each platform.

Another useful command for working with libraries is nm, which can be used to display symbol names in an object file or library. This is useful to find out if a library defines or uses a given symbol. For example, the following command line will output all of the global (external) symbols in a library:

```
nm -g libmyapi.a
```

This will produce output like the following:

```
00000000 T _DoSomething
00000118 S _DoSomething.eh
    U __ZNSo1sEPFRSoS_E
    U __ZNSt8ios_base4InitC1Ev
    U __ZNSt8ios_base4InitD1Ev
    U __ZSt4cout
...
```

The character in the second column specifies the symbol type, where "T" refers to a text section symbol that is defined in this library and "U" refers to a symbol that is referenced by the library but is not defined by it. An uppercase letter represents an external symbol, whereas a lowercase character represents an internal symbol. The string in the third column provides the mangled symbol name. This can be unmangled using the c++filt command, for example,

```
c++filt __ZNSt8ios_base4InitD1Ev
std::ios_base::Init::~Init()
```

Another useful command is ldd. This can be used to display the list of dynamic libraries that an executable depends on. Because this will display the full path that will be used for each library, you can see which version of a dynamic library will be loaded and whether any dynamic libraries cannot be found by the operating system. For example, the following output is produced on Linux for a simple executable.

```
% ldd userapp
    linux-gate.so.1 => (0xb774a000)
    libstdc++.so.6 => /usr/lib/libstdc++.so.6 (0xb7645000)
    libm.so.6 => /lib/tls/i686/cmov/libm.so.6 (0xb761f000)
    libgcc_s.so.1 => /lib/libgcc_s.so.1 (0xb7600000)
    libc.so.6 => /lib/tls/i686/cmov/libc.so.6 (0xb74bb000)
    /lib/ld-linux.so.2 (0xb774b000)
```

An executable that has been linked with the -static option will not depend on any dynamic libraries. Running ldd on such an executable results in the following output on Linux:

```
% ldd userapp
    not a dynamic executable
```

Finally, if you have a static library it's possible to convert it to a dynamic library if it was compiled with position-independent code (e.g., -fPIC). Recall that a static archive (.a) is just a packaging of object files (.o). You can therefore extract the individual object files using the ar command and then relink them as a dynamic library. For example,

```
ar -x libmyapi.a
g++ -shared -o libmyapi.so *.o
```

A.3.5 Loading Plugins on Linux

On Linux platforms, you can use the dlopen() function call to load a .so file into the current process. Then you can use the dlsym() function to access symbols within that library. This lets you create plugin interfaces, as described earlier. For example, consider the following very simple plugin interface:

```
#ifndef PLUGIN_H
#define PLUGIN_H

#include <string>

extern "C"
void DoSomething(const std::string &name);

#endif
```

You can build a dynamic library for this API, such as `libplugin.so`. Then the following code demonstrates how to load this library and call the `DoSomething()` function within that `.so` file:

```cpp
typedef void(*FuncPtrT)(const std::string &);
const char *error;

// open the dynamic library
void *handle = dlopen("libplugin.so", RTLD_LOCAL | RTLD_LAZY);
if (! handle)
{
    std::cout << "Cannot load plugin!" << std::endl;
    exit(1);
}
dlerror();

// get the DoSomething() function from the plugin
FuncPtrT fptr = (FuncPtrT) dlsym(handle, "DoSomething");
if ((error = dlerror()))
{
    std::cout << "Cannot find function in plugin: " << error;
    std::cout << std::endl;
    dlclose(handle);
    exit(1);
}

// call the DoSomething() function
(*fptr)("Hello There!");

// close the shared library
dlclose(handle);
```

A.3.6 Finding Dynamic Libraries at Run Time

When you run an executable that depends on a dynamic library, the system will search for this library in a number of standard locations, normally /lib and /usr/lib. If the .so file cannot be found in any of these locations the executable will fail to launch. Recall that the ldd command can be used to tell you if the system cannot find any dependent dynamic library. This is obviously a concern for creating executable programs that depend on your API. Three main options are available to your clients to ensure that any executable they build using your API can find your library at run time.

1. The client of your API ensures that your library is installed in one of the standard library directories on the end user's machine, for example, /usr/lib. This will require the end user to perform an installation process and to have root privileges in order to copy files into a system directory.

2. The LD_LIBRARY_PATH environment variable can be set to augment the default library search path with a colon-separated list of directories. Your clients could therefore distribute a shell script to

run their application where that script sets the `LD_LIBRARY_PATH` variable to an appropriate directory where your dynamic library can be found.

3. Your clients can use the rpath (run path) linker option to burn the preferred path to search for dynamic libraries into their executable. For example, the following compile line will produce an executable that will cause the system to search in `/usr/local/lib` for any dynamic libraries:

```
g++ usercode.cpp -o userapp -L. -lmyapi -Wl,-rpath,/usr/local/lib
```

A.4 LIBRARIES ON MAC OS X

The Mac OS X operating system is built on a version of BSD UNIX called Darwin. As such, many of the details presented earlier for Linux apply equally well to the Mac. However, there are a few differences that are worth highlighting between Darwin and other UNIX platforms such as Linux.

A.4.1 Creating Static Libraries on Mac OS X

Static libraries can be created on Mac OS X in the same way as for Linux, that is, using `ar` or `libtool`. However, there are some different behaviors when linking a static library into an application.

In particular, Apple discourages use of the `-static` compiler option to generate executables with all library dependencies linked statically. This is because Apple wants to ensure that applications always pull in the latest system libraries that they distribute. In fact, the gcc man page states that `-static` "will not work on Mac OS X unless all libraries (including `libgcc.a`) have also been compiled with `-static`. Since neither a static version of `libSystem.dylib` nor `crt0.o` is provided, this option is not useful to most people."

Essentially, the `-static` option on the Mac is reserved for building the kernel, or for the very brave.

Related to this situation, by default the Mac linker will scan through all paths in the library search path looking for a dynamic library. If it fails, it will then scan the paths again looking for a static library. This means that you cannot use the trick of favoring a static library by placing it in a directory that appears earlier in the library search path. However, there is a linker option called `-search-paths-first` that will cause the linker to look in each search path for a dynamic library and then, if not found, to look for a static library in the same directory. This option makes the Mac linker behavior more like the Linux linker in this respect. Note, however, that there is no way to favor linking against a static library over a dynamic library on the Mac when both are located in the same directory.

A.4.2 Creating Dynamic Libraries on Mac OS X

Dynamic libraries can be created on Mac OS X in a very similar way to the Linux instructions given earlier. There is one important difference in that you should use the `-dynamiclib` option to g++ to create dynamic libraries on the Mac instead of `-shared`.

```
g++ -c -fPIC file1.c
g++ -c -fPIC file2.c
g++ -c -fPIC file3.c
```

```
g++ -dynamiclib -o libmyapi.so -fPIC file1.o file2.o file3.o \
   -headerpad_max_install_names
```

Also, note the use of the `-headerpad_max_install_names` option. This flag is highly recommended when building dynamic libraries on the Mac for reasons I will explain in a moment.

It should also be noted that the `ldd` command is not available on Mac OS X. Instead, you can use the `otool` command to list the collection of dynamic libraries that an executable depends on, that is,

```
otool -L userapp
```

A.4.3 Frameworks on Mac OS X

Mac OS X also introduces the concept of frameworks as a way to distribute all the files necessary to compile and link against an API in a single package. A framework is simply a directory with a `.framework` extension that can contain various resources such as dynamic libraries, header files, and reference documentation. It is essentially a bundle, in the `NSBundle` sense. This bundling of all necessary development files in a single package can make it easier to install and uninstall a library. Also, a framework can contain multiple versions of a library in the same bundle to make it easier to maintain backward compatibility for older applications.

The following directory listing gives an example layout for a framework bundle, where the `->` symbol represents a symbol link.

```
MyAPI.framework/
   Headers -> Versions/Current/Headers
   MyAPI -> Versions/Current/MyAPI
   Versions/
      A/
       Headers/
           MyHeader.h
       MyAPI
      B/
       Headers/
           MyHeader.h
       MyAPI
      Current -> B
```

Most of Apple's APIs are distributed as frameworks, including Cocoa, Foundation, and Core Services. They can be found under the `/Developer/SDKs` directory, assuming that you have installed the Mac OS X development environment. You may therefore wish to distribute your API as a framework on the Mac to make it appear more like a native Mac library.

You can build your API as a framework using Apple's XCode development environment. This can be done by selecting the **File** > **New Project** menu and then selecting Framework in the left-hand panel (see Figure A.5). By default, you can choose to have your project setup to use either Carbon or Cocoa frameworks. If you don't need either of these (i.e., you are writing a pure C++ library), you can simply remove these frameworks after XCode has created the project for you.

FIGURE A.5

Creating a Framework project using Apple's XCode IDE.

Clients can link against your framework by supplying the -framework option to g++ or ld. They can also specify the -F option to specify the directory to find your framework bundle.

A.4.4 Finding Dynamic Libraries at Run Time

The same Linux principles for finding dynamic libraries at run time apply to applications run under Mac OS X, with a couple of small differences. The first is that the environment variable used to augment the library search path is called DYLD_LIBRARY_PATH (although LD_LIBRARY_PATH is now also supported by more recent versions of Mac OS X).

Also, Mac OS X does not support the Linux -rpath linker option. Instead, it provides the notion of install names. An install name is a path that is burned into a Mach-O binary to specify the path to search for dependent dynamic libraries. This path can be specified relative to the executable program by starting the install name with the special string @executable_path.

You can specify an install name when you build your dynamic library, but your clients may also change this path using the install_name_tool utility. However, they cannot specify a path that is longer than the original path in the .dylib. This is why it is always advisable to build your dynamic libraries with the -headerpad_max_install_names option on the Mac: to give your clients the flexibility to change the library's install name to whatever they wish.

The following commands demonstrate how a client could change the install name for your library and change the install name for their executable:

```
install_name_tool -id @executable_path/../Libs/libmyapi.dylib \
    libmyapi.dylib

install_name_tool -change libmyapi.dylib \
    @executable_path/../Libs/libmyapi.dylib \
    UserApp.app/Contents/MacOS/executable
```

Bibliography

[1] T. Albrecht, Pitfalls of Object Oriented Programming, in: Proceedings of Game Connect: Asia Pacific (GCAP) 2009, Melbourne, Australia, 2009.

[2] T. Alexander (Ed.), Massively Multiplayer Game Development, Charles River Media, 2003. ISBN 1584502436.

[3] A. Alexandrescu, Modern C++ Design: Generic Programming and Design Patterns Applied, Addison-Wesley Professional, 2001. ISBN 0201704315.

[4] K. Arnold, Programmers Are People, Too, ACM Queue 3 (5) (2005) July 6, 2005.

[5] D. Astels, Test-Driven Development: A Practical Guide, second ed., Prentice Hall, 2003. ISBN 0131016490.

[6] O.L. Astrachan, A Computer Science Tapestry: Exploring Computer Science with C++, second ed., McGraw-Hill, 2000. ISBN 0072465360.

[7] L. Bass, P. Clements, R. Kazman, Software Architecture in Practice, second ed., Addison-Wesley Professional, 2003. ISBN 0321154959.

[8] K. Beck, Test Driven Development: By Example, Addison-Wesley Professional, 2002. ISBN 0321146530.

[9] K. Beck, Implementation Patterns, Addison-Wesley Professional, 2007. ISBN 0321413091.

[10] J. Blanchette, The Little Manual of API Design, Trolltech (2008) June 19, 2008. http://www.chaos.troll.no/~shausman/api-design/api-design.pdf.

[11] J. Bloch, How to Design a Good API and Why it Matters, JavaPolis 2005, December 12–16, 2005, Antwerp, Belgium.

[12] J. Bloch, Effective Java, second ed., Prentice Hall, 2008. ISBN 0321356683.

[13] G. Booch, R.A. Maksimchuk, M.W. Engle, B.J. Young, J. Conallen, K.A. Houston, Object Oriented Analysis and Design with Applications, third ed., Addison-Wesley Professional, 2007. ISBN 020189551X.

[14] G. Booch, J. Rumbaugh, I. Jacobson, Unified Modeling Language User Guide, second ed., Addison-Wesley Professional, 2005. ISBN 0321267974.

[15] P. Bourque, R. Dupuis, A. Abran, J.W. Moore, L. Tripp (Eds.), The Guide to the Software Engineering Body of Knowledge, IEEE Press, 2004. 2004 Version. ISBN 0769523307.

[16] F. Brooks, The Mythical Man-Month: Essays on Software Engineering, second ed., Addison-Wesley Professional, 1995. ISBN 0201835959.

[17] M.P. Cline, G. Lomow, M. Girou, C++ FAQs, second ed., Addison-Wesley Professional, 1998. ISBN 0201309831.

[18] A. Cockburn, Writing Effective Use Cases, Addison-Wesley Professional, 2000. ISBN 0201702258.

[19] M. Cohn, User Stories Applied: For Agile Software Development, Addison-Wesley Professional, 2004. ISBN 0321205685.

[20] J.O. Coplien, Advanced C++ Programming Styles and Idioms, Addison-Wesley Professional, 1991. ISBN 0201548550.

[21] J.O. Coplien, Curiously Recurring Template Patterns, C++ Report 7 (2) (1995) 24–27. ISBN 10406042.

[22] W. Cunningham, The WyCash Portfolio Management System, OOPSLA '92 Experience Report, March 26, Vancouver, Canada, 1992, pp. 29–30.

[23] M. DeLoura (Ed.), Game Programming Gems 2, Charles River Media, 2001. ISBN 1584500549.

[24] S.C. Dewhurst, C++ Gotchas: Avoiding Common Problems in Coding and Design, Addison-Wesley Professional, 2002. ISBN 0321125185.

[25] E. Evans, Domain-Driven Design: Tackling Complexity in the Heart of Software, Addison-Wesley Professional, 2003. ISBN 0321125215.

[26] R. Faber, Architects as Service Providers, IEEE Software 27 (2) (2010) 33–40. March/April 2010.

[27] M.C. Feathers, Working Effectively with Legacy Code, Prentice Hall, 2004. ISBN 0131177052.

[28] B. Foote, J. Yoder, Big Ball of Mud, Fourth Conference on Pattern Languages of Programs (PLoP '97), September 1997, Monticello, Illinois. http://www.laputan.org/mud/.

[29] M. Fowler, K. Beck, J. Brant, W. Opdyke, D. Roberts, Refactoring: Improving the Design of Existing Code, Addison-Wesley Professional, 1999. ISBN 0201485672.

[30] T.L. Friedman, The World Is Flat 3.0: A Brief History of the Twenty-First Century, Picador, 2007. ISBN 0312425074.

[31] E. Gamma, R. Helm, R. Johnson, J.M. Vlissides, Design Patterns: Elements of Reusable Object-Oriented Software, Addison-Wesley Professional, 1994. ISBN 0201633612.

[32] E. Gamma, R. Helm, R. Johnson, L. O'Brien, Design Patterns 15 Years Later: An Interview with Erich Gamma, Richard Helm, and Ralph Johnson, InformIT (2009) October 22. http://www.informit.com/articles/article.aspx?p=1404056.

[33] M.R. Headington, Removing Implementation Details from C++ Class Declarations, in: Proceedings of the 26th ACM SIGCSE Symposium on Computer Science Education, Nashville, Tennessee, 1995, pp. 24–28.

[34] J.L. Hennessy, D.A. Patterson, Computer Architecture: A Quantitative Approach, fourth ed., Morgan Kaufmann, 2006. ISBN 0123704901.

[35] M. Henning, API Design Matters, Commun. ACM 52 (5) (2009) 46–56.

[36] C.A.R. Hoare, An Axiomatic Basis for Computer Programming, Commun. ACM 12 (10) (1969) 576–580, 583. October 1969.

[37] C.A.R. Hoare, Assertions: A Personal Perspective, IEEE Ann. Hist. Comput 25 (2) (2003) 14–25. April/June 2003.

[38] C. Hofmeister, R. Nord, D. Soni, Applied Software Architecture, Addison-Wesley Professional, 2009. ISBN 0321643348.

[39] A. Hunt, D. Thomas, The Pragmatic Programmer: From Journeyman to Master, Addison-Wesley Professional, 1999. ISBN 020161622.

[40] ISO/IEC 14882:1998, Programming Languages—C++, International Organization for Standardization, Geneva, Switzerland (Revised by ISO/IEC 14882:2003), 1998.

[41] ISO/IEC 14882:2003, Programming Languages—C++, International Organization for Standardization, Geneva, Switzerland, 2003.

[42] ISO/IEC TR 19768:2007, Information Technology—Programming Languages—Technical Report on C++ Library Extensions, International Organization for Standardization, Geneva, Switzerland, 2007.

[43] I. Jacobson, Object-Oriented Software Engineering: A Use Case Driven Approach, Addison-Wesley Professional, 1992. ISBN 0201544350.

[44] S. Jeong, Y. Xie, J. Beaton, B. Myers, J. Stylos, R. Ehret, et al., Improving Documentation for eSOA APIs through User Studies, Second International Symposium on End User Development (IS-EUD'2009), March 2–4, 2009, Springer-Verlag, Siegen, Germany, 2009, pp. 86–105.

[45] N.M. Josuttis, The C++ Standard Library: A Tutorial and Reference, Addison-Wesley Professional, 1999. ISBN 0201379260.

[46] D. Knuth, Structured Programming with Go to Statements, ACM Comput. Surv. 6 (4) (1974) 268. December 1974.

[47] T.D. Korson, V.K. Vaishnavi, An Empirical Study of the Effects of Modularity on Program Modifiability, In papers presented at the 1st workshop on empirical studies of programmers, Washington, DC, 1986, pp. 168–186.

[48] J. Lakos, Large-Scale C++ Software Design, Addison-Wesley Professional, 1996. ISBN 0201633620.

[49] Y.G. Leclerc, S.Q. Lau, TerraVision: A Terrain Visualization System, Technical Note 540, Artificial Intelligence Center, SRI International, Menlo Park, CA, 1994. April 1994.

[50] K.J. Lieberherr, I. Holland, Assuring Good Style for Object-Oriented Programs, IEEE Software 6 (5) (1989) 38–48. September 1989.

[51] B. Liskov, Data abstraction and hierarchy, OOPSLA '87, keynote address, October 4–8, Orlando, Florida, 1987, pp. 17–34.

[52] S. McConnell, Code Complete: A Practical Handbook of Software Construction, second ed., Microsoft Press, 2004. ISBN 0735619670.

[53] T. Mackinnon, S. Freeman, P. Craig, Endo-Testing: Unit Testing with Mock Objects, in: Extreme Programming Examined, Addison Wesley Longman, 2001, pp. 287–301 (Chapter 17).

[54] R.C. Martin, Design Principles and Design Patterns, Object Mentor article, 2000. http://www.objectmentor .com/resources/articles/Principles_and_Patterns.pdf.

[55] R.C. Martin, Agile Software Development: Principles, Patterns, and Practices, Prentice Hall, 2002. ISBN 0135974445.

[56] N. Medvidovic, R.N. Taylor, A Classification and Comparison Framework for Software Architecture Description Languages, IEEE Transaction on Software Engineering 26 (1) (2000) 70–93.

[57] S.J. Mellor, M.J. Balcer, Executable UML: A Foundation for Model-Driven Architecture, Addison-Wesley Professional, 2002. ISBN 0201748045.

[58] G. Meszaros, Agile Regression Testing using Record & Playback, in: Proceedings of OOPSLA '03, October 26–30, Anaheim, CA, 2003, pp. 353–360.

[59] B. Meyer, Programming as Contracting, Report TR-EI-12/CO. Interactive Software Engineering, Goleta, CA, 1987.

[60] B. Meyer, Object-Oriented Software Construction, second ed., Prentice Hall, 1997. ISBN 0136291554.

[61] S. Meyers, More Effective C++: 35 New Ways to Improve Your Programs and Designs, Addison-Wesley Professional, 1998. ISBN 020163371X.

[62] S. Meyers, How Non-Member Functions Improve Encapsulation, Dr. Dobb's Journal (2000) February 1, 2000, http://www.drdobbs.com/.

[63] S. Meyers, The Most Important Design Guideline? IEEE Software 21 (4) (2004) July/August 2004.

[64] S. Meyers, Effective C++: 55 Specific Ways to Improve Your Programs and Designs, third ed., Addison-Wesley Professional, 2005. ISBN 0321334876.

[65] S. Meyers, A. Alexandrescu, C++ and the Perils of Double-Checked Locking, Dr. Dobb's Journal (2004) July 2004, http://www.drdobbs.com/.

[66] G.A. Miller, The Magical Number Seven, Plus or Minus Two: Some Limits on Our Capacity for Processing Information. Psychol Rev 63 (2) (1956) 81–97.

[67] M.L. Mitchell, A. Samuel, J. Oldham, Advanced Linux Programming, Sams, 2001. ISBN 0735710430.

[68] J.M. Neighbors, Software Construction Using Components, Ph.D. Dissertation. Technical Report UCI-ICS-TR-160, Department of Information and Computer Science, University of California, Irvine, 1980.

[69] D.L. Parnas, On the Criteria to be Used in Decomposing Systems into Modules. Commun. ACM 15 (12) (1972) 1053–1058. December 1972.

[70] D.L. Parnas, Designing Software for Ease of Extension and Contraction. IEEE Transactions on Software Engineering 5 (2) (1979) 128–138. March 1979.

[71] D.L. Parnas, Software Aging, in: Proceedings of the 16th International Conference on Software Engineering, Sorrento, Italy, 1994, pp. 279–287.

[72] B.C. Pierce, Types and Programming Languages, The MIT Press, 2002. ISBN 0262162091.

[73] K. Pugh, Interface Oriented Design, Pragmatic Bookshelf, 2006. ISBN 0976694050.

[74] J.B. Rainsberger, Use Your Singletons Wisely, IBM Developer Works, July 1 2001, http://www.ibm.com/ developerworks/webservices/library/co-single.html.

[75] E.S. Raymond, The Art of UNIX Programming, Addison-Wesley Professional, 2003. ISBN 0131429019.

[76] M.P. Robillard, What Makes APIs Hard to Learn? Answers from Developers. IEEE Software 26 (6) (2009) 27–34. November 2009.

[77] G. Rooney, Preserving Backward Compatibility, O'Reilly OnLamp.com, 2005. http://onlamp.com/pub/a/onlamp/2005/02/17/backwardscompatibility.html.

[78] S. Shlaer, S.J. Mellor, Object-Oriented Systems Analysis: Modeling the World in Data, Prentice Hall, 1988. ISBN 013629023X.

[79] D. Shreiner (Ed.), OpenGL Reference Manual: The Official Reference Document to OpenGL, Version 1.4., fourth ed., Addison-Wesley Professional, 2004. ISBN 032117383X.

[80] A. Snyder, Encapsulation and Inheritance in Object-Oriented Programming Languages, in: Proceedings of OOPSLA '86, 1986, pp. 38–45. Printed as SIGPLAN Notices, 21(11).

[81] D. Spinellis, Code Documentation, IEEE Software 27 (4) (2010) 18–19. July/August 2010.

[82] W. Stevens, G. Myers, L. Constantine, Structured Design. IBM Systems Journal 13 (2) (1974) 115–139.

[83] B. Stroustrup, The C++ Programming Language: Special Edition, third ed., Addison-Wesley Professional, 2000. ISBN 0201700735.

[84] J. Stylos, A. Faulring, Z. Yang, B.A. Myers, Improving API Documentation Using API Usage Information, in: Proceedings of IEEE Symposium on Visual Languages and Human-Centric Computing (VL/HCC), Corvallis, Oregon, 2009. pp. 119–126. September 20–24.

[85] J. Stylos, B. Graf, D. Busse, C. Ziegler, R. Ehret, J. Karstens, A Case Study of API Redesign for Improved Usability, in: IEEE Symposium on Visual Languages and Human-Centric Computing (VL/HCC), Herrsching am Ammersee, Germany, 2008, pp. 189–192. September 15–19.

[86] J. Stylos, B. Myers, The Implications of Method Placement on API Learnability, in: Proceedings of the 16th ACM SIGSOFT Symposium on Foundations of Software Engineering (FSE), Atlanta, GA, 2008, pp. 105–112. November 9–14.

[87] H. Sutter, Exceptional C++: 47 Engineering Puzzles, Programming Problems, and Solutions, Addison-Wesley Professional, 1999. ISBN 0201615622.

[88] H. Sutter, Virtuality, C/C++ Users Journal 19(9) (2001), September 2001.

[89] H. Sutter, A. Alexandrescu, C++ Coding Standards: 101 Rules, Guidelines, and Best Practices, Addison-Wesley Professional, 2004. ISBN 0321113586.

[90] J. Tulach, Practical API Design: Confessions of a Java Framework Architect, Apress, 2008. ISBN 1430209739.

[91] D. Vandevoorde, N.M. Josuttis, C++ Templates: The Complete Guide, Addison-Wesley Professional, 2002. ISBN 0201734842.

[92] K.W. Wiegers, Software Requirements, second ed., Microsoft Press, 2003. ISBN 0735618798.

[93] M. Wolf, Why Globalization Works, Yale University Press, 2004. ISBN 0300102526.

[94] H.Y. Yee, A. Newman, A Perceptual Metric for Production Testing, ACM SIGGRAPH 2004 Sketches. August 8–12, Los Angeles, CA, 2004.

[95] H. Zhong, L. Zhang, T. Xie, H. Mei, Inferring resource specifications from natural language API documentation, in: Proceedings of 24th IEEE Conference on Automated Software Engineering (ASE), Auckland, New Zealand, 2009, pp. 307–318. November 16–20.

Index

Note: Page numbers followed by *b* indicate boxes, *f* indicate figures and *t* indicate tables.

Related Titles from Morgan Kaufmann

Programming Language Pragmatics, Third Edition
By Michael Scott
ISBN: 9780123745149

Programming Massively Parallel Processors
By David B. Kirk and Wen-mei W. Hwu
ISBN: 9780123814722

The Art of Multiprocessor Programming
By Maurice Herlihy and Nir Shavit
ISBN: 9780123705914

Why Programs Fail, Second Edition
A Guide to Systematic Debugging
By Andreas Zeller
ISBN: 9780123745156

Semantic Web for the Working Ontologist, Second Edition
Effective Modeling in RDFS and OWL
By Dean Allemang and Jim Hendler
ISBN: 9780123859655

Learning Processing
A Beginner's Guide to Programming Images, Animation, and Interaction
By Daniel Shiffman
ISBN: 9780123736024

mkp.com